The New Internationalists

The New Internationalists

Activist Volunteers in the European
Refugee Crisis

Sue Clayton

Goldsmiths
Press

Copyright © 2020 Goldsmiths Press
First published in 2020 by Goldsmiths Press
Goldsmiths, University of London, New Cross
London SE14 6NW

Printed and bound by Versa Press
Distribution by the MIT Press
Cambridge, Massachusetts, and London, England

Copyright © 2020 Sue Clayton

A CIP record for this book is available from the British Library

ISBN (pbk) 9781912685660
ISBN (ebk) 9781912685677

www.gold.ac.uk/goldsmiths-press

Cover image credits:

1. A German volunteer demonstrates in support of refugees in the 2020 coronavirus crisis. (Image credit: Christian Mang).

2. Survivors being rescued in the Mediterranean by the MSF ship *Bourbon Argos* in 2016. (Image Credit: Sara Creta).

3. Guests recover on board the volunteer ship *Sea-Watch 2* the Greek coast in 2016. (Image credit: Judith Buethe)

4. Berliners oppose restrictions imposed on refugee rights in the 2020 coronavirus pandemic. (Image credit: Christian Mang).

5. Painting of Carola Rackete, *Sea-Watch 3* captain who rescued 53 migrants then faced jail. (Image credit: Paola Formica)

6. Greek riot police guard the closed Greek-North Macedonian border at Idomeni in 2016. (Image credit: Treasa O'Brien)

Contents

WAY-STATIONS

THE NORTHERN FRONTIER

BRINGING IT HOME

Foreword

Gulwali Passarlay

Thirteen years ago, I made the dangerous journey from Afghanistan to Europe as an unaccompanied 12-year-old, and now have status here in the UK. Many of the people supporting me in my hardship and showing compassion were volunteers. I was touched by the kindness and support of volunteers with providing basic necessities of life, like food, water and shelter in Athens, Rome and Paris, and particularly in Calais. I was so grateful to all the wonderful people out there who supported and helped me in my most desperate situations and give huge thanks to all volunteers and friends for continuing their efforts and dedications.

Now I myself have spent the last ten years so volunteering and giving back to the community. I have founded an organisation, called My Bright Kite, that aims to improve the wellbeing and inclusion of young refugees who arrive here – because making the journey is only half the story; young people then have to find a place for themselves and ways they can fit in and belong. I have written an account of my own journey, *The Lightless Sky*, and have been asked to events across the UK to share my experiences. People are mostly kind and generous and often want to know how they can help refugees. I encourage people to write to their MPs, go on protests for social justice and get active and engaged with their local City of Sanctuary group or refugee support network, or I suggest they volunteer in the UK with refugee charities or in refugee camps in Calais and Greece. I am humbled by how they have then gone on to travel to refugee camps across the world to support the efforts and work of independents and NGOs. It is amazing to see ordinary people doing extraordinary work, when EU governments have been failing refugees, and to see the massive volunteer movement that has come to the rescue of literally millions of refugees who entered Europe in 2015 and since. I have every hope that this book will inspire people in the same way, and give the knowledge and the inspiration that they need.

As we see across Europe, things seem to have changed in the last few years and the environment has become so much less welcoming. With governments not always helping, or being hostile to refugees, and NGOs not always up to the job, the role of volunteers has become essential – and is now a whole new movement. It has been alarming to see humanitarian workers treated as criminals in Italy and Greece, as well as the Stansted 15, peaceful protesters, having been criminalised for supporting asylum seekers in the UK. We all need to go on speaking out and be advocates for human rights for refugees and those who support them.

Gulwali Passarlay, BA (Hons) MPA, author of *The Lightless Sky*

Foreword

Lord Alf Dubs

As a member of the UK Parliament I have been actively involved with the plight of unaccompanied child refugees in Europe, and of children separated from family members in Europe seeking reunification. As I worked to introduce the so-called "Dubs Amendment" into UK law, I visited many places where refugees are suffering terribly, including the Moria camp on the Greek island of Lesvos, where thousands of refugees are surviving in extremely cramped and unsanitary conditions. The Moria camp was built to accommodate around 2,000 people but it is estimated that there are as many as 20,000 living there now. Beyond the camp are makeshift shelters where refugees, including children, live rough among the rubbish, rain and mud outside its gates. In France, I've seen many lone children fending for themselves in the outskirts of Calais, many of whom have been trafficked. They are hungry and destitute and at risk of violence, including at the hands of the police, who carry tear-gas.

Some of these children have the right to legal routes to safety in the UK; my amendment to the Brexit EU Withdrawal Bill, which asked the government to uphold the right of unaccompanied children stranded in Europe to apply for legal family reunion with relatives in the UK after Brexit, was defeated in the Commons. However, the UK Government has on more than one occasion reiterated its commitment to assisting these children, and the campaign to hold them to that commitment carries on. Other unaccompanied children stranded in Europe – so-called "Dubs" children (those with no family at all) – also have a legal right to safe passage to the UK after my amendment to the 2016 Immigration Act was passed, enshrining that right.

The struggle to make changes and to hold governments to account all across Europe is an arduous one. We can all feel defeated at times in the face of indifference, or open hostility, from so many quarters. But it has been the volunteer movement, which sprang up locally all over Europe in 2015 and then set up dynamic international networks, that goes on inspiring me. As long as the volunteers are working, I will be working with them. Their passion and commitment inspire me to keep up the pressure in Westminster. My campaign has received a lot of publicity, but there are thousands of volunteers whose work goes unnoticed, who are making huge differences to the lives of refugees every day. For many of them, visiting the camps in Greece or Calais has reinforced their commitment to the cause of refugees and they have returned more determined than ever to support people who are suffering so much there, particularly children. Groups like People2People, Help Refugees, Worldwide Tribe, Indigo Volunteers, Safe Passage, One Happy Family, Starfish Foundation, Refugee Community Kitchen, Calais Action, Care4Calais, Kesha Niya, Quartiers Solidaires, Plateforme Citoyenne, Help Refugees and literally hundreds more, working alone or joining with NGOs like Médecins Sans Frontières and sea-rescue missions like Open Arms and Sea-Watch, conduct rescues, supply food and shelter, offer support and solidarity and provide long-term help at peoples' final destinations.

Often governments and the media would have us think the "crisis" of arrivals is over – but this is not the case. More and more refugees arrive daily in Greece and there are thousands stranded in Europe in camps, at borders and living rough, supported in large part by volunteers from the UK, Ireland, France, Spain, Italy, Germany, Serbia, Greece and elsewhere. The volunteer project is not just to offer "aid" but to speak up for people's rights, and to support them in becoming accepted and self-sufficient, and in finding a place that can feel like home.

I believe that all government ministers should now be fully aware of the terrible conditions in the Moria camp and across the Greek islands, where it is thought 36,000 refugees are currently surviving. No country alone can solve this global crisis, but we all have a part to play. It is vital that we – politicians, governments, NGOs and the grassroots volunteer sector from across Europe – work together to find solutions. We know that there are 3 or 4 million refugees in Turkey, 1 million in Syria and 1 million in Jordan. Each country in Europe – perhaps with the exception of Germany and Sweden – can do more to help refugees than they are currently doing. Indeed, when German Chancellor Angela Merkel in 2015–2016 asked other EU countries to play their part and take some responsibility, many refused. The so-called Visegrád countries – the Czech Republic, Hungary, Poland and Slovakia – as well as Croatia and Serbia, have been particularly hostile.

Unfortunately, refugees are being exploited for political gain and in many cases they are being used as pawns in a political game. Right-wing extremists are pushing governments to build walls and fences, close borders, separate families and drive people who deserve legal protection into the hands of criminals and traffickers.

That is why I am particularly pleased and honoured to contribute a Foreword to this book. What these volunteers have done is change the way the world sees refugees and counter right-wing hostility towards them with humanity.

This book is full of examples of ordinary, not-always-"political" people who first got involved by donating a few simple items, or driving with friends across the Channel to drop them off. What they then saw and heard, it is clear from the testimonies in this book, has changed them forever, and given them a sharper and more critical understanding of the global refugee crisis and the inadequacies of our responses to it. To every single one of you who has collected, donated, sewed tents, sailed boats, kept guard, taught kids, dried tears, chopped food, put up shelters and kept your dignity and compassion while channelling your righteous calls for fairness and change, thank you. Your stories are what keep us all involved, and help us to continue together.

Lord Alf Dubs, House of Lords, March 2020

Preface

Sue Clayton

This collected work is about the "refugee crisis" in Europe in the years from the summer of 2015 to early 2020. Conflicts in Syria and crises in Afghanistan, Iraq, Sudan, Eritrea and elsewhere brought almost 2 million asylum seekers on perilous journeys to a Europe which, far from offering them safety and security, in large part proved unwilling or unable to accommodate them. With the notable exception of Angela Merkel's Germany, the official line of most other European states ranged from indifference to open hostility. The new arrivals, having in many cases already faced war and violence, abuse by traffickers and near-drowning at sea, were met on arrival by closed borders, police aggression, the abuse of many of their human rights and a lack of the most basic food or shelter. Commentators have said that, especially for young people, the trauma many faced by their official treatment in Europe was worse than what they had faced in their home countries.

My own experiences of working with and filming refugees in the Calais "Jungle" and other parts of Europe have brought me into contact with hundreds of volunteers of a completely new order. Thus, I have come to understand first-hand that set against the generalised hostility has been a powerful new force, the flowering of what I call here the "activist volunteer" movement: a grassroots mobilisation of people of every age, skill and background, who as individuals or in small groups responded to a humanitarian crisis that neither governments nor the larger aid agencies seemed willing or able to address. Some were local citizens responding to people arriving at their coasts, ports, border-points and railway stations. Others travelled to the "Hotspots" from elsewhere in Europe and beyond. Yet more collected goods and raised funds to supply the camps, provided welcome and settlement support at final destinations, and campaigned for legal and civil rights. And many refugees themselves committed to support those arriving after them, to ease their way.

Between them, this mobilisation of over half-a-million people across Europe sourced hundreds of thousands of tents, trainers and waterproofs, baby clothes, sanitary towels and sleeping bags. They built huts and put up tents; they cooked thousands of meals a day and sourced clean water. They cut hair, charged phones and cleaned toilets. They gave legal and medical advice and support. They set up crèches, language classes, therapy, music, theatre and arts. When EU and member state rescue missions withdrew from the Mediterranean, they scoured the sea for shipwrecks, then faced arrest for saving lives. They were abused and tear-gassed by police in the makeshift camps. They listened to a million stories, and laughed and wept with each person who told them. They drank endless cups of tea with the new arrivals in cold, leaky tents, and when people got to some kind of permanent settlement they found them cots and pillowcases, played football with them, fasted and broke bread and prayed together. They battled the state for help and for refugee rights. They railed against governments for not providing all this aid, and they railed against themselves and each other for making mistakes, for not doing enough, not doing more. They brought corpses out of the sea so that families could have closure; they helped bury the dead and mourn with those grieving, and repatriated bodies back home. What they did, and continue to do, was and is in every way truly extraordinary, and demands to be documented.

As well as what they did, they bore unique witness to a crisis that is one of Europe's most shameful episodes, and their testimonies hold vital knowledge that the world needs to hear. They continue to fight and campaign, and to feed and ferry people, even as states have begun to criminalise their actions. They do these things overwhelmingly not out of a grandiose idea of white-saviourism or do-good cliché, but because they believe that all of our humanity depends on how we treat those who need our help, especially when our own countries and governments may have contributed to the disasters in theirs. They seek to accept and support the new arrivals – and to do that, they argue that we must all dismantle the pernicious borders in our own minds, the "us and them", the ideological walls that separate us as much as do the concrete walls, checkpoints and fences that have come to haunt this new Europe. This book is for them and for our new arrivals, in solidarity.

There is a further dedication to Anna Campbell, a Calais volunteer who in 2018 died fighting with the Kurdish Women's Protection Units in Syria, at the end of this book.

Acknowledgements

Sue Clayton

There are five people without whom this book could not have been achieved in this form. Anna-Louise Milne discussed the premise with me at length, and rightly argued for situating the testimonies within the framework of current geopolitics and political movements. John Borton brought his encyclopaedic knowledge of this field and related issues in NGO debates to bear on the research, provided many invaluable contacts and was an excellent adviser. Tess Berry-Hart and Caroline Gregory brought their grounded experience as activists all over Europe, providing contacts and bringing their own critique as well as writing and taking on administrative work. Natalie Galvau worked tirelessly on administration and graphic design. Thank you, and I hope the book meets your expectations.

More thanks go to those who provided research input and contacts and helped source images: Sumita Shah, Marco Branda, Jean-Noel Fessy, Nidžara Ahmetašević, Simona Bonardi, Pru Waldorf, Johan Leman, Brendan Woodhouse, Caoimhe Butterly, Angelo Lo Maglio, Alessandra Rizzo, Jack Sapoch, Robin Vandervoordt, Alex Cooper and Isabel Rey-Sastre. Translations were done or facilitated by Maria Hagan, Marco Branda, Roberta Lentini, Esther-Jo Steiner, Isabel Rey-Sastre, Katerina Georgiadis and Cecilie Thorsen.

Eighteen writers contributed to the Flashpoint sections: an attempt to build a new history based around volunteers' evidence and understanding of the times and places in the refugee "crisis". I had to persuade people who were stylistically very diverse to write in a quite rigorous format, as I believed it was crucial to present this new history in a way that is consistent, authoritative and truly revelatory. I thank them for their patience, and I hope they will agree that the sum of the Flashpoints achieves that.

Finally, over 170 grassroots individuals and groups responded to my call for personal testimonies, and many more supplied images. Many of the testimonies clearly cost the authors a lot to commit to paper, and made for powerful and humbling reading. They all inform the commentary and have helped shape this important shared narrative. Those who were happy for their names to be used are listed in the Appendix at the end of the book. I could not quote from all of them in the print version of this book – but there will be an e-version of this book where all of the testimonies can be read in full.

Finally thanks to Goldsmiths Press and the MIT Press for their support and enthusiasm for this project, and to Goldsmiths colleagues for their interest and ideas. And to those who supported me through my own volunteer journey and in writing this book: Katie Willis, Penny and Gonzo Walford, Jeremy Gully, Behroze Gandhy, Jim Moody, Linda Clayton, Adam Goff, Toufique Hossain and Daniel Trilling.

And to Yemane and his friends for their extraordinary resilience, and for showing the way.

Contributors

Nidžara Ahmetašević Nidžara is a journalist and scholar in transitional justice, media, human rights and migration. Her work has been published widely in the international press. In 2015 she joined the Are You Syrious? information team, and from 2016 to 2018 she co-ordinated 30 volunteers globally to produce the Daily Digest. She collaborates on many other projects, particularly in Bosnia and Herzegovina, Serbia, Croatia and Greece.

Tess Berry-Hart Tess is a UK playwright, novelist and refugee rights activist, who works on both verbatim and fictional artistic projects involving human rights in art and theatre. She volunteered in Calais, Lesvos and Athens, and helped establish the Citizens of the World Choir for refugees and friends and refugee aid charity Calais Action. As well as writing for the book, Tess was a principal researcher and administrator on the project.

Simona Bonardi Simona has been collecting testimonies since 2015 around the humanitarian crisis of new arrivals in Europe, travelling to Italy, Switzerland, France, Greece, North Macedonia and Turkey. Based in Zurich, she now collaborates with organisations and networks of citizens to help individuals in need.

John Borton John has worked for almost 40 years in the humanitarian sector in a variety of research, evaluation and capacity development roles. His current positions are: Senior Research Associate, Humanitarian Policy Group, Overseas Development Institute, London; Honorary Lecturer, Humanitarian and Conflict Response Institute, University of Manchester; and Trustee and volunteer convenor at Herts Welcomes Refugees.

Charlotte Burck Charlotte is an honorary consultant systemic psychotherapist at London's Tavistock Clinic and set up the Refugee Resilience

Collective with Gillian Hughes in March 2016, working with refugees and supporting volunteers.

Sue Clayton   Sue is a UK writer and film director. She has written and directed fiction features, shorts, campaign films and documentaries internationally, commissioned by Film 4, BBC, ITV and many others. She has worked with refugees, particularly unaccompanied minors, for over 15 years. Her award-winning 2012 film *Hamedullah: The Road Home* follows a young refugee in the UK who was deported back to Afghanistan. Her 2017 film *Calais Children: A Case to Answer* was used as evidence in the UK High Court to challenge the UK Government's failure to process the claims of unaccompanied minors stranded when the Calais Jungle closed. As an activist she has screened the film around 300 times worldwide. In 2019 she directed *The Stansted 15: On Trial* about the criminalisation of peaceful human rights protesters. Sue is co-author of *Unaccompanied Young Migrants: Identity, Care and Justice* (2018) and Professor of Film and Television at Goldsmiths, University of London, where she teaches Social Activist Film. She also consults for Channel 4 News and ITV News on refugee stories.

Justine Corrie   Justine works in the UK and France as a Core Process psychotherapist and group facilitator. She was active in Calais between 2015 and 2017, offering psychological support and trauma care for volunteers.

Sara Creta   Sara is a visual journalist and research fellow at Dublin City University. She has worked with humanitarian and human rights organisations and communities in Sudan, Ethiopia, Bangladesh, Libya, Chad, Cameroon, Morocco, Gaza and on Mediterranean rescue missions.

Dan Dowling   Dan is a freelance business consultant and General Secretary of the Refugee Aid Network UK (RAN), which was formed in 2015 to fundraise and provide food and medical aid across Europe and beyond.

Natalie Galvau   Natalie has a BA in Design from Goldsmiths, University of London Her research centres on humanitarian design and she has taken an active role in several refugee support initiatives. She worked on the image administration and design for this book.

Caroline Gregory   Caroline is a writer and journalist who since 2015 has led refugee aid initiatives mainly in France and Greece. She collaborated with Oxford University on a book and exhibition, "Lande: The Calais Jungle and Beyond". She was a principal researcher on this book.

Maddie Harris   Maddie has been working to support refugees and displaced people across Europe since September 2015. She was first an independent volunteer in Dunkerque and in Thessaloniki, Greece, then set up a grassroots human rights organisation, the Humans for Rights Network, in 2016. She is also co-creator of the Refugee Solidarity Summit.

Gillian Hughes   Gillian is a clinical psychologist and systemic psycho-therapist who manages the clinical services at Freedom from Torture (London) and set up the Refugee Resilience Collective with Charlotte Burck in March 2016.

Anna-Louise Milne   Anna-Louise works between cultural history, multilingualism and urban sociology for the University of London Institute in Paris. She is involved in a collective-writing venture with people living in forced displacement called the Numimeserian Collection. She is a member of Quartiers Solidaires in Paris, which fights for refugee and migrant rights and provides daily food distributions.

Treasa O'Brien   Treasa is an activist based in Ireland working intersectionally on issues of women's rights, queer rights, migrants and refugees, class and climate change. She is a filmmaker, writer and educator.

Mirko Orlando   Mirko is a photographer, writer and illustrator working in Turin, Italy for national and international magazines, focusing on ethnic minorities, poverty and marginalisation. He is the author of the photobook *Il Volto (e la voce) della Strada* and *Paradiso Italia*, a graphic journalism project on the Italian immigration system.

Niki Papadogiannakis   Niki researches migration situations in Belgium and Lebanon, and was involved in supervising SB OverSeas' project in Brussels, Belgium. In 2018, she was a volunteer interpreter for asylum seekers in Athens, Greece.

Maria Pisani   Maria is based in Malta and has been working with asylum seekers and refugees since 2004. She is an academic, researcher and activist. She is the co-founder of the Integra Foundation, an NGO in Malta.

Kester Ratcliff   Kester spent a total of six months between 2015 and 2017 with refugees in Greece, Lesvos, Chios and Athens, first driving with Médecins Sans Frontières and then mostly in legal aid organisations, including documenting around 150 refugee cases.

Jack Sapoch   Jack has been a volunteer for the humanitarian NGO No Name Kitchen since 2018. He was originally based in Velika Kladuša, Bosnia and Herzegovina, where he co-ordinated the collection of testimonies from individuals affected by border violence in the region.

Sumita Shah   Sumita has been working to support refugees, displaced people and volunteers since 2015. She was an independent volunteer in Athens, and now has wider oversight of the situation in Greece. She is founder of the Athens Volunteers Information and Co-ordination Group.

Pru Waldorf   Pru is a social justice activist and refugee rights advocate, volunteering and running projects in the UK and Greece since 2015. She is a founder member of Calais Action and of WeAreOne:collective and a co-creator of the Refugee Solidarity Summit. She is also concerned with grassroots network-building and the wellbeing and support of activists and volunteers.

Elle Wilkins   Elle has been a caseworker in the Public Law team at Duncan Lewis since 2018. She specialises in protection claims, particularly for Afghan and Nigerian claimants. She spent a month volunteering on Lesvos with a legal charity in 2019 and has been monitoring developments since.

Map of major migration routes to and across Europe, 2015

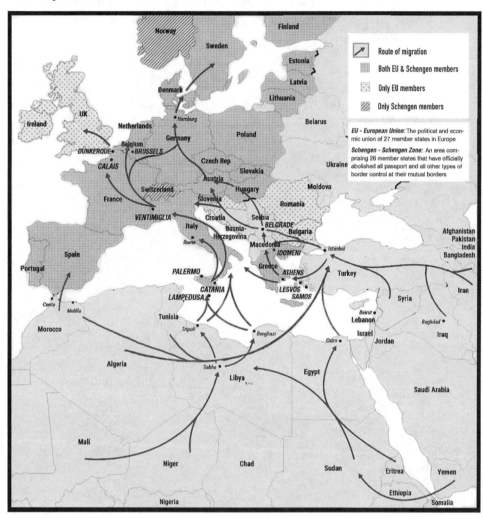

Source: Jack Sapoch, No Name Kitchen.

1

Filling the Gap: Refugee Arrivals 2015–2020 and Europe's Crisis of Humanitarianism

Sue Clayton

This collection brings together the voices of nearly 200 activists, volunteers, journalists and academics across ten countries, documenting an unprecedented situation that many of us never expected to witness in Europe. In the absence of adequate state and NGO support, it fell to several hundred thousand unpaid volunteers to respond to the largest movement of people in Europe since the Second World War. Using direct first-hand testimonies from grassroots volunteers, journalistic accounts from the flashpoints of the crisis and some critical framing, my aim is to construct here a unique picture – one never fully shown by media and governments – of a humanitarian emergency that has had devastating consequences for nearly 2 million lives, and whose effects are felt still, even though states and media would have us believe the "crisis" is over.

While there have been increasing numbers of studies and portraits of refugees themselves in this crisis (Jones, 2016; Kingsley, 2016; Trilling, 2019), there is as yet no full account of the actions and the observations of the grassroots volunteers. When researching and writing this book, I was aware that each of the topics – increased police violence against volunteers at Calais; why the EU tried to halt sea-rescues in the Mediterranean; what caused the arrests of peaceful volunteers in remote La Roya; what made Balkan states close their borders; why most volunteers are women – could easily have generated a chapter or a book in its own right. But even with its inevitable shorthand and omissions, a broad overview such as this is badly needed for two reasons.

First, I seek to bring into the open the extraordinary and untypical nature of what the volunteers did on the ground. From a position of little or no initial funding or organisation they provided logistical operations and support that saved lives and improved the conditions for almost 2 million people – for, just as this was the largest movement of people in Europe since the Second World War, it was equally the largest civic mobilisation in response. The first-hand testimonies here offer important insights into the precarity of the refugees' situation – and by association that of many of the volunteers, who increasingly in the last two years have been attacked and criminalised for performing a humanitarian role. Also, as Burck, Corrie and Hughes discuss in Chapter 7, both refugees and volunteers have also shown, alongside vulnerabilities, extraordinary resilience. Grassroots volunteers have gone from filling emergency stop-gap roles to forming a variety of permanent networks to support the health, social care, housing and educational needs of refugees, and have also in increasing numbers advocated for them through legal challenges, marches, protests and through their own media campaigns – hence my coining of the term "activist volunteer". Both I and authors Borton (Chapter 2) and Milne (Chapter 9) consider ways in which this mobilisation is a departure from previous aid or charitable initiatives, and can be seen to be a new kind of social intervention, with innovative new forms of organisation and effect. We also explore its relation to other historical precedents and to contemporary movements like pro-democracy, climate change and anti-deportation campaigns.

A further reason for producing this account is to reflect on the current culture and politics of Europe, and what its treatment of refugees and volunteers tells us about how humanitarianism and human rights are currently being understood and practised here. In my view, the sets of roles played by volunteers have re-drawn the map of civic responsibility and citizenship. While European governments argued over refugee quotas and border closures, and balked at sanctioning refugee camps in our affluent West, local and international grassroots activists were engaged in dragging bodies, alive or dead and decomposed, from the sea as Greek soldiers openly fired on boats still arriving, and in providing food and shelter for thousands trapped at closed borders in the Balkans in sub-zero temperatures. They faced prison for driving people to hospital or offering them food. Many in Calais were to end up tear-gassed by the French riot police (CRS), whose funding came in part from the UK Government (Clayton, 2017). Many still continue the practice of compiling daily reports of police violence and abuses of the most basic human rights. This kind of activity is clearly not on a par with more traditionally received notions of aid or charity as espoused by Oxfam, Live Aid, Comic Relief and many other organisations – traditions of giving which have been criticised for offering a panacea for Western guilt, without necessarily bringing about real change in geopolitical power relations (Ahmed and Smith, 2018). By contrast, this recent mobilisation was – or became – a passionate defence of human rights and humanitarian values that many of us never expected to have to defend in a Europe we thought we knew; it was strange enough to meet a starving and injured Eritrean child on Europe's city streets, but stranger beyond belief to be threatened with arrest for giving food to that child, or to be charged with human trafficking for taking that child to get medical help.

Thus, this collection is not only an account of the "refugee crisis" from these engaged participants' point of view. It also aims to reverse the gaze that the Western world turned on refugees, to investigate instead our own responsibilities in a Europe that has chosen to close its borders by historic deals with Turkey and Libya, and chosen to defend those borders in militaristic ways, creating in many states a hostile environment for those refugees and undocumented migrants who remain here. When she was Home Secretary, Theresa May argued that the UK's declared "hostile environment policy" was introduced because "it is what people want" (iNews, 2019). I argue here that the mass mobilisation of ordinary people – old and young, women and men, skilled and unskilled, declaredly political and unpolitical, local and cosmopolitan – speaks of a dissatisfaction with that policy, and offers a cogent critique of the direction in which both the EU and its member states are trying to take us. This mobilisation, together with the popular outcry against the so-called Windrush deportations (The Week, 2019) and against US President Trump's Mexican border detention policies, all speak of a critical resistance that makes every gesture to support a refugee not only an act of aid or humanitarianism, but one of protest against the overt hostility and shocking breaches of international conventions which have come to blight the developed world.

Below I will give a brief summary of the global conditions that brought higher-than-usual numbers to Europe from 2015–2016, which are further elaborated in Chapter 2. Before I do so, it is perhaps worth countering some myths about who was coming to European shores and why. Of the 70.8 million displaced people in the world today, over 80% remain within 100 kilometres of their home country (UNHCR, 2019a). Thus, the states receiving the highest numbers of refugees - Turkey and Pakistan - have hosted over 5 million people in the last decade. In such a global context, the arrival of almost 2 million to the European Union, a wealthy economic zone with a population of over 600 million, was not perhaps so disproportionate, and belies the idea popular with politicians and some sections of the media that all the displaced people in the world are heading for Europe. For even those who have the resources to travel further, often choose to stay near to their home countries for reasons of language, cultural familiarity or the hope of being able to later return home as easily as possible. Of those who undertake longer journeys, many are motivated by joining family members who may already have settled in other countries. Many from Afghanistan and Iraq who seek asylum in Europe served alongside British and European forces, for which they and their families were later persecuted. Others come from countries that were previously British or other European territories (Eritrea, Niger, Sudan) and gravitate to the "parent country", where the language and culture may feel familiar. And – perhaps surprisingly to our Western notions of intentionality and agency – some refugees end up in Europe as it were by default; one of the people described in a testimony, Lilliana, says that she, like many others, had hoped Libya would a place of opportunity and employment, but had not anticipated the harsh treatment refugees receive there, saying "she would rather die quickly at sea than slowly in Libya".

In the first months of 2015, almost half the rising numbers crossing to Europe were Syrians fleeing the bombing of their country. A further fifth were from Afghanistan, and the rest were mainly displaced Iraqi Kurds, Christian Eritreans escaping persecution and others in flight from Sudan, Ethiopia and West African states. They crossed the Mediterranean from Turkey to the nearby Greek islands of Lesvos, Chios and Samos; and from the North African coast to Lampedusa and the Sicilian ports of Palermo and Catania. By the end of 2015 more than 1 million were to make these fraught journeys, and at least 6,000 would die at sea. 800,000 alone arrived on the Greek islands, which were entirely unequipped to deal with them. In the Central Mediterranean, the Italian rescue operation "Mare Nostrum", based off the Italian coast, was replaced in 2016 by the EU force Frontex, whose declared mission was to focus on "security" by repelling boats in distress, rather than rescue – and whose practices are proven to have caused significantly more migrant deaths at sea (*The Guardian*, 2019). European leaders held high-profile summits in 2015–2016 which were quick to label the new arrivals as both economic migrants and a "security threat" (UNHCR, 2019b). Individual European states responded in diverse ways, from Germany's much-publicised offer to accommodate substantial numbers of Syrians, to Hungary and Serbia closing their borders and refusing to co-operate with proposed settlement targets for EU member states (BBC News, 2015).

The UK Government, with its self-declared "hostile environment" immigration policy, put out negative rhetoric as Prime Minister David Cameron described the new arrivals to Europe as a "swarm", and the UK admitted proportionately far fewer people under refugee protocols than other EU states. In the years from 2016 to 2019, the number of new arrivals fell steeply as a result of a Eur. 6-billion deal brokered by the EU with Turkey, whereby the Turkish Government would accept returned asylum seekers from Greece and other EU states, and step up its coastal surveillance, in return for substantial payments (EC Europa EU, 2018). There was widespread concern that Turkey's poor human rights record, as well as its historical enmity with Kurdish populations, made this neither a satisfactory nor a sustainable outcome. Worse, in 2017 the EU renegotiated with Libya an agreement that Italy would train the Libyan Coastguard and "migrants picked up in Libyan coastal waters – and not international waters – can be legally returned to Libya" (Human Rights Watch, 2019; Al Jazeera, 2019). It was astonishing to many that the EU should make such an agreement with a country internationally condemned for its unspeakable record of trafficking, kidnapping, extortion and torture of refugees who pass through eastern Africa to the Mediterranean. Since the numbers have slowed, both governmental and media attention has waned considerably. Yet 50,000 people remain stranded in Greece (Rescue.org, 2019), up to 8,000 in Bosnia and Herzegovina (France24, 2019) and thousands more are held at closed borders such as in Ventimiglia, Calais and Dunkerque – to say nothing of those who remain even less visible, trapped in Libya's vicious unregulated "camps". The total deaths by drowning since 2015 now stand at nearly 35,000 – over 22,000 more than when the picture of Alan Kurdi was supposed to have changed hearts and minds.

What is the status of these new arrivals? Based on nationality criteria, and on reports produced by legal bodies and NGOs, certainly those from Syria and Eritrea had strong claims on arrival for refugee protection. And given, for instance, the questionable country guidance used by the UK Home Office for making decisions on Afghanistan and Eritrea (RightToRemain, 2018) there are arguably many other human rights factors that would qualify these arrivals, especially groups like unaccompanied children, for protection. There is no denying that the situation has been fraught with legal and political complexities, such as national differences over implementing the EU's Dublin Regulation, and German Chancellor Angela Merkel's proposed refugee quota system. And many arrivals had ambivalent status, being trafficked for labour or escaping conditions of poverty or the effects of climate change, which would not be considered grounds for asylum but may again qualify under human rights grounds.

However, whether or not all are ultimately granted status, they nonetheless have the right under international protocols (Free Movement, 2019) to at least make an asylum or humanitarian protection claim in Europe – just as those from Central and Latin America have such rights in the United States of America. And I would argue that while doing so, they have a right to be treated with dignity and humanity. In my view,

the concerning fact has not only been that European states were unprepared to process such applications, but that they were in most cases
actively unwilling to do so, as evidenced by how few countries signed up
to the quotas proposed by Merkel in 2016 (*The New York Times*, 2017).
The argument widely used by these states for creating aggressive and
hostile environments was that treating people in a humanitarian way
would result in more arrivals, and encourage traffickers. This has been
proven to be a false assumption; the Human Trafficking Foundation
report of 2017 chaired by Baroness Butler-Sloss concludes that the so-
called "pull factor" is not so compelling as right-wing governments and
media would have us believe (Anti-Slavery Commissioner, 2017). There
has also been a clear racist element in arguments for making life difficult for new migrants – as evidenced by routine discrimination against
African migrants who are almost always branded "illegal" and "economic" (UNHCR, 2019b). And while many governments were openly
hostile, what surprised many of us more was that established NGOs and
international aid organisations seemed unable to rise to the challenges
presented. As Borton argues in Chapter 2 of this book, such organisations
were used to functioning in developing countries and while they had at
least some protocols in place to set up camps in Europe, they were not
able persuade European states to sanction permanent settlements.

It is against this background that hundreds of thousands of European
citizens chose to reject the messages of their governments and the mainstream news, and with extraordinary speed formed grassroots networks
and began to help. Some of these were communities on the doorstep
of the emerging catastrophes – local people and groups on the Greek
islands of Lesvos, Samos and Chios; in Sicily; on the more remote Italian
island of Lampedusa; and on Malta. As numbers grew unmanageable
for local communities, complex and sometimes strained relationships
grew between local support and newly-arriving international volunteers.
Thousands more supporters, remote from these landing sites, contributed
by fundraising and transporting supplies. And of course migrants and
refugees themselves, either within the framework of their own social and
cultural groupings or in concert with these new initiatives, contributed –
many choosing to stay on at places of landing or border camps for months

and years after they could have moved onto their planned destinations – the accounts of some of whom are included here.

Who were the European volunteers? It is estimated that in the UK alone, over 80,000 people either set off for the ports and way-stations of Europe, or began their own fundraising for these missions and made plans to welcome those who were due to arrive here and settle. As the testimonies in this book show, they came from a variety of backgrounds and starting-points. In the UK, for instance, volunteers became active through established faith groups like the Quakers and Catholic, Muslim and Jewish faith communities, via existing networks like JCORE (the Jewish Council for Racial Equality). Others came from active organisations like STAR (Student Action for Refugees) and the Cities of Sanctuary network, which was already engaged in supporting arrivals. There were also more overtly political networks like Stand Up to Racism and No Borders. Some groups that became involved were aligned to professions, and had pre-existing experience in their fields, such as Doctors Without Borders and Social Workers Without Borders. From these beginnings and through social media, spontaneous groups formed all over the UK. A Brighton directory, for example (Brighton and Hove, 2019), quotes 17 groups active in 2019, including direct-campaign groups like Calais Action Brighton, Help Refugees and Sanctuary-on-Sea, broader campaign and policy groups like Brighton Migrant Solidarity and the Aegean Solidarity Network, groups to support young people like the Hummingbird Project, cultural and arts groups like Refugee Radio and Bestfoot Music and legal and rights advisory groups such as the Black and Minority Ethnic Community Partnership and Voices in Exile. This range illustrates a typical cross-section of work being done – welcoming those refugees who had arrived, supporting their rights, fundraising and campaigning for those still stranded around Europe and generally raising public awareness of broader policy issues. Typical activities would include advice clinics and social welcome events for those newly arrived, one-to-one help for new arrivals with language and administrative issues, public talks and meetings, demonstrations against government policy, socials with food, music and arts performances to raise awareness and fundraise, collecting money and goods to send to camps and "Hotspots" in France, Greece and the Balkans and organising short-term and long-term group visits to these destinations to deliver the aid and volunteer for tasks at border-points and in the camps.

As Milne discusses in Chapter 9 of this book, there are many progressive and leftist traditions that offer precedents for this type of "political" or "activist" humanitarianism. Again with reference to the UK, we have witnessed in the past British women and men volunteer to fight against Franco's Fascist regime in the Spanish Civil War (Hopkins, 1998; *The Guardian*, 2011) and, in the 1980s, to live and work in Nicaragua to express solidarity with the Sandinista movement against US-backed *Contra* forces (Jones, 1986). While it may seem to be overstating the dangers faced by present-day volunteers to compare them with such movements, the testimonies in this book attest to physical danger and extremely traumatic situations faced by volunteers in Europe. There have many solidarity movements in UK and Europe, such as those supporting Angola and Chile in their respective liberation campaigns (Wilkinson, 1992), the anti-Apartheid struggle in South Africa and many spontaneous public actions (Greenham Common, Stop the City, Extinction Rebellion). But none has presented the unique features we have seen come together in the recent refugee crisis – emergency physical aid needed for vast numbers, not delivered by the state, and often delivered in situations of danger and precarity. It has been a common theme among the testimonies that many who wanted to protest European policy, and organise politically, felt unable to do so because the demands of delivering direct aid were more pressing: go on a demonstration or help provide 1,000 emergency tents for people stranded in minus degrees? Another reason to write this book was to reflect not just on what has been achieved, but how such priorities can be managed in the future.

I have emphasised above that providing aid, in this activist sense, can be seen to come from various leftist traditions of solidarity for oppressed groups – certainly in the UK this was our experience, and Milne in Chapter 9 discusses similar precedents in other European countries. However, it remains true that a very large proportion of those that became involved did so initially neither because of their organised faith nor their professional or political affiliations, but more because of a strength of personal feeling, amplified in local communities, as people responded to the terrible news headlines of 2015 and 2016 by saying that "something had to be done". There is no denying that many individuals and groups started out naively. As I have mentioned, there have been various critiques of styles of aid that remain rooted in old-world colonial notions of "us and them", where the most well-meaning actions of charity simply reproduce a dependent donor–recipient relationship rather than pay attention to more fundamental changes of perspective that may be needed to solve long-term issues. Some of our contributors talk of beginning by seeing their involvement as a kind of interesting adventure, or a one-off act to assuage their conscience – what has become known in aid discourses as "Voluntourism" (Vastri, 2012). However, such attitudes tend to dissipate quickly on the ground when, for instance, volunteers in the Calais Jungle are hit by tear-gas or are brutally treated by police, or when they learn that refugees are complex real people who can and should exert their own agency. In several of our testimonies, volunteers confess to have begun with simplistic "white saviour" ideas, only to ruefully report that one wide-eyed weekend in Lesvos or Idomeni became several years of giving up their homes, families and careers to form whole new organisations or simply labour away in any place where the need was great.

Volunteers, of course, have as many characteristics as refugees – neither group can be over-defined, whitewashed or sanctified in the name of making a political argument. But I will end this introduction by risking two generalisations, which have been borne out by my years of action and research. First, while I would not call the grassroots volunteer activists' actions a political movement, I would certainly call it a mobilisation, and I would also argue that it has had a transformative effect on the consciousness of those involved, in the same way that initiatives such as national liberation movements and the women's movement have been characterised by the sense of a fundamental shift in consciousness. I have not met a single volunteer, local or international, who has not undergone some level of transformation while doing this work, not only in their politics but in their understanding of the world, of the geopolitical crisis facing us and the dangers of walling off Europe. They understand how the refugee becomes a symbol of the other, the threat, the danger, and how associating with refugees can bring aggression, scorn and rejection on the volunteers themselves, causing them to re-evaluate what they find important in comradeship and citizenship. Second, this increased awareness can come at a high cost. Many of those working longer-term, particularly in the camps, have experienced post-traumatic stress disorder (PTSD) and what is called vicarious trauma, triggered by repeated listening to, and identifying with, the trauma that refugees have faced. Corrie's survey, discussed in Chapter 7, found that over 80% of volunteers experienced high levels of stress, flashbacks, sleeplessness and feelings of inadequacy and failure to be able to "make things better". Borton talks about the "fragility" of this sector, and Burck, Corrie and Hughes in Chapter 7 consider how models of resilience evidenced in refugee communities might teach volunteers by example how to acclimatise to these dangers, and suggest more resilient working practices. I also hope that the testimonies here, however painful some of them are to read, will remind grassroots volunteers how valued and significant their work is, offer insights to be shared and suggest how this mobilisation is sustainable into the future.

This book consists of five analytical perspectives, 16 factual summaries of key times and places in this story which I call "Flashpoints", and curated extracts taken from over 170 testimonies I invited from volunteers across Europe and beyond (these will all later be published in full in the e-book). The book does not claim to be a comprehensive account of all the historical events of the last four years, if such a thing were possible. However, the Flashpoints provide key reference by which to read volunteers' personal accounts. Together, the book's elements form a kind of topological history, almost mimicking the network of the EU's designated "Hotspots" but additionally referencing local histories, prior movements of people and contexts of culture and law to bring something that I believe is much richer than a simple account of events. The testimonies also have unique value as they give first-hand evidence of many events and situations that either were not recorded, or were misrepresented, by institutions and the press. (An example would be frequent reporting that camp riots had been caused by inter-ethnic fighting between refugees, where in fact most disturbances were observed by volunteers to be over poor conditions or police attacks.) The testimonies also are in part self-reflexive and allow us to reflect on the role of the volunteer, and the new frontiers of a very active humanitarianism that are here expressed. Often the academic chapters, Flashpoints and testimonies refer to the same events and situations, but what is crucial is how each time they are presented we gain further nuance and context, to give a more fully-dimensional understanding of what went on.

I will end with some points of definition. I have called this collection *The New Internationalists*, but this should not suggest that I focus only on those volunteers who left their home countries to work as volunteers elsewhere. I have observed from this research and my own experiences of volunteering over very many years that the vast majority of volunteers – whether they are providing aid in their own home or town, are running campaigns and fundraising online or are off in the camps – develop a more international outlook in terms of their political responses to this crisis. I have chosen the phrase "activist volunteers" to reflect this and to make a differentiation from more traditional uses of the term "volunteer". Many of the younger and politically active volunteers would also describe themselves as "grassroots", which further suggests democratic and open forms of organisation.

Definitions become more complex when it comes to those around the terms migrants/undocumented migrants/refugees/asylum seekers/ displaced people/"*sans-papiers*". As I have indicated in this chapter, there are many new and diverse reasons why people are on the move. Not all of these fit the guidelines of the UN Refugee Convention, but some fall under the aegis of other legal frameworks, whether they be related to child protection, the UN's Article 8 "right to family life", anti-trafficking legislation or particular national or international agreements for the protection of certain nationalities or ethnicities. As several contributors to this book make clear, one of the greatest causes for concern in the recent crisis has been Europe's slowness in processing applications, or reluctance to process them at all – so in very many cases it is still not clear who of the new arrivals do qualify, and on what grounds. Also, it is perfectly possible for a person to be a refugee and a migrant, and trafficked – so these terms can sometimes be more obfuscating than helpful. Thus, I have allowed each contributor to assign their own terms in the context of what they write. As well as the above, others used are, for instance, "the new arrivals" and "people on the move". I would like to think that new descriptors, allowing new possibilities of identity, might emerge from this process.

And last, a note on images. Most of the pictures in this collection were selected from hundreds sent to me by volunteers themselves, and so represent a kind of parallel narrative to the testimonies. As a media practitioner myself, I have taken great care in the selection. I have tried to give a sense of the vast numbers of people in this crisis but to avoid reducing refugees to "masses", and so dehumanising them. I have tried, as in the curated testimonies, to emphasise the extreme suffering and hardship that many refugees have faced, but not to be sensationalist or voyeuristic, nor paint them as seemingly passive victims – for, as Burck, Corrie and Hughes discuss in Chapter 7, it is vital to respect their resilience and commitment to survival. I also badly wanted to show the staggering scale of aid that grassroots volunteers provided, in both physical goods and deeds, time and labour and emotional commitment – and that, ironically, has been the most difficult of all to show. This is because volunteers may photograph what they observe while working, but are usually far too busy with the task in hand to fully represent their own actions and contributions. And even for the most justifiable of uses – for instance, to circulate as an aid to fundraising – many would be hesitant to take "promotional" shots for fear of coming across as do-gooders or "saviours", or distracting the narrative from those they support. So this image collection very clearly shows volunteers' representations of the movement of people, and the responses of nation-states and police, but their own presence sometimes remains oblique. Cavernous warehouses stacked with cartons; a now-deserted "legal centre" in a burnt-out lean-to; a grabbed shot of a proud refugee child in new shoes, stored as a personal memory; a lone volunteer on dawn lookout across the sea to Turkey. It is easy enough for the mass media to inundate us with shock images of the "refugee crisis", and spin narratives of righteous anger, pity or fear. It is harder to show this silent army of supporters, juggling a dozen roles at once, meeting daily crises head-on, learning as they went, often unsure of the rules – and many times, without question, in utter disbelief as to what they were witnessing. No surprise, then, that the public is largely unaware of them – all the more reason to study the images here carefully, as an important sub-text to what the volunteers did, and saw, and heard.

References

Ahmed, A. and Smith, J. (eds) (2018) *Humanitarian Action and Ethics*. London: Zed Books.

Al-Jazeera (2019) "Anti-Migration Deal between Italy and Libya Renewed", 2 November. www.aljazeera.com/news/2019/11/deal-curb-migrant-arrivals-italy-libya-renewed-191102122821537.html.

Anti-Slavery Commissioner (2017) "An Independent Inquiry into the Situation of Separated and Unaccompanied Minors in Parts of Europe", July. www.antislaverycommissioner.co.uk/media/1262/nobody-deserves-to-live-this-way.pdf.

Brighton and Hove (2019) "Refugees, Asylum Seekers and Migrants Directory", updated 1 May. https://brighton-and-hove.cityofsanctuary.org/local-resources.

Clayton, S. (2017) *Calais Children: A Case to Answer*. Film, 62 min. Eastwest Pictures UK. www.eastwestpictures.co.uk.

EC Europa EU (2018) "EU Facility for Refugees in Turkey: The Commission Proposes to Mobilise Additional Funds for Syrian Refugees", 14 March. https://ec.europa.eu/commission/presscorner/detail/en/IP_18_1723.

France24 (2019) " 'It's the Jungle': Bosnian Migrant Camp in Crisis", 24 October. www.france24.com/en/20191024-it-s-the-jungle-bosnian-migrant-camp-in-crisis.

Free Movement (2019) "Are Refugees Obliged to Claim Asylum in the First Safe Country they Reach?", 2 January. www.freemovement.org.uk/are-refugees-obliged-to-claim-asylum-in-the-first-safe-country-they-reach/.

The Guardian (2011) "The Secret History of Britain's Spanish War Volunteers", 28 June 2011. www.theguardian.com/commentisfree/2011/jun/28/mi5-spanish-civil-war-britain.

The Guardian (2019) "ICC Submission Calls for Prosecution of EU over Migrant Deaths", 3 June. www.theguardian.com/law/2019/jun/03/icc-submission-calls-for-prosecution-of-eu-over-migrant-deaths.

Hopkins, J. (1998) *Into the Heart of the Fire: The British in the Spanish Civil War.* Stanford, CA: Stanford University Press.

Human Rights Watch (2019) "No Escape from Hell", 21 January. www.hrw.org/report/2019/01/21/no-escape-hell/eu-policies-contribute-abuse-migrants-libya.

iNews (2019) "MPs Question Theresa May on 'Discriminatory' Immigration Policies in One of her Final PMQs", 19 June 2019. https://inews.co.uk/news/politics/mps-grill-theresa-may-on-discriminatory-unjust-and-racist-immigration-policies-in-one-of-her-final-commons-clashes-as-pm-500106.

Jones, J. (ed.) (1986) *Brigadista: Harvest and War in Nicaragua.* New York: Praeger Publishers.

Jones, R. (2016) *Violent Borders: Refugees and the Right to Move.* London: Verso.

Kingsley, P. (2016) *The New Odyssey: The Story of Europe's Refugee Crisis.* London: Guardian Faber Publishing.

The New York Times (2017) "EU Countries Must Accept their Share of Migrants, Court Rules", 6 September. www.nytimes.com/2017/09/06/world/europe/eu-migrants-hungary-slovakia.html.

Rescue.Org (2019) "Refugees in Limbo: Greece". www.rescue.org/country/greece.

RightToRemain (2018) "Recent Country Guidance on Afghanistan", 21 May. https://righttoremain.org.uk/recent-country-guidance-on-afghanistan/.

Trilling, D. (2019) *Lights in the Distance: Exile and Refuge at the Borders of Europe.* London: Pan Macmillan.

UNHCR (2019a) "Global Trends: Forced Displacement in 2017". www.unhcr.org/5b27be547.pdf.

UNHCR (2019b) "Press Coverage of the Refugee and Migrant Crisis in the EU: A Content Analysis of Five European Countries". www.unhcr.org/56bb369c9.html.

The Week (2019) "Who are the Windrush Generation and How Did the Scandal Unfold?", 6 March. www.theweek.co.uk/92944/who-are-the-windrush-generation-and-why-are-they-facing-deportation.

Vastri, W. (2012) *Volunteer Tourism in the Global South: Giving Back in Neoliberal Times.* London: Routledge.

Wilkinson, M.D. (1992) "The Chile Solidarity Campaign and British Government Policy towards Chile, 1973–1990", *European Review of Latin American and Caribbean Studies/Revista Europea de Estudios Latinoamericanos y del Caribe,* 52(June): 57–74.

2

The Background to the Activist Volunteer Response

John Borton

The response by "activist volunteers" to the needs of the large numbers of refugees and undocumented migrants arriving in Europe in 2015 and over the period since was extraordinary in terms of its scale, its widespread basis and what has been achieved. It has also demonstrated that large numbers of European citizens were not prepared to accept the inadequate and often hostile and inhumane actions of their governments seeking to deter refugees and undocumented migrants from entering or remaining on their territory, nor were they willing to accept the existence of camps with squalid conditions that, had they been in Africa or the Middle East, would have warranted humanitarian action by international agencies. Drawing on previous work I was involved in (Borton et al. 2016; HPN, 2016; Borton and Collinson, 2017) and on available media coverage of the role of activists in the crisis, this chapter aims to provide a backdrop to the many testimonies presented in this volume by explaining the context in 2015 and how that context has evolved in the period since. It also provides a broad outline of the response by volunteers and grassroots groups and what was achieved.[1]

Refugee and Undocumented Migrant Arrivals to Europe

Between January 2015 and July 2019, nearly 1.8 million refugees and undocumented migrants arrived in the EU, the peak coming during the nine-month period between July 2015 and March 2016, when over 1 million people arrived (see Figure 2.1).

Who were those arriving in Europe? According to UNHCR data, during the peak year of 2015, 49% of those arriving were from Syria, 21% from Afghanistan and 8% from Iraq – all countries experiencing civil conflict, population displacement and insecurity.

The overwhelming majority (97% of the total) arrived by sea, crossing the Mediterranean through three main routes – the Eastern Mediterranean route (principally Turkey to the Greek islands), which largely accounted for the highest numbers in 2015 and early 2016; the Central Mediterranean route (principally from Libya to Italy); and the Western Mediterranean route (from Tunisia and Morocco to Spain).

Following the March 2016 EU–Turkey agreement (discussed later in this chapter), the principal route shifted from the Eastern Mediterranean to the much riskier Central Mediterranean route and, as it did so, the national composition of those arriving changed and became more complex. By 2017 the top three nationalities arriving in the EU were Nigerian (10%), Syrian (10%) and Guinean (7%). During the first seven months of 2019 the top three nationalities were Afghan (14%), Moroccan (13%) and Syrian (13%).

The sea crossings, especially the much longer Central Mediterranean route, were and continue to be extremely perilous as they were invariably made in vessels that were unsuitable for open-water crossings or were dangerously overcrowded and at constant risk of taking on water or capsizing. Though Italian and then EU naval vessels were deployed in search-and-rescue (SAR) missions during the period from 2013 to early 2017, the policy then pursued by the Italian Government, and later also by the EU, was to encourage, equip and fund a "coastguard" operated by the Tripoli-based Libyan Government of National Accord (GNA) to prevent and/or capture and return migrant boats to Libyan soil. Though recognised by the UN, the GNA has a terrible human rights record and most of those returned to Libya were held in appalling conditions, forced to work, abused and sometimes sold as slaves (Human Rights Watch, 2019; United Nations, 2017). Over the period from January 2015 to July 2019, no fewer than 15,475 people died attempting the sea crossings (Missing Migrants, 2019).

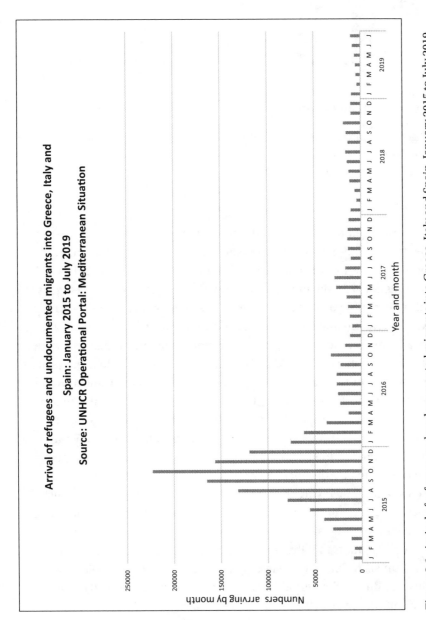

Figure 2.1 Arrival of refugees and undocumented migrants into Greece, Italy and Spain, January 2015 to July 2019. Source: UNHCR Operational Portal: Mediterranean Situation.

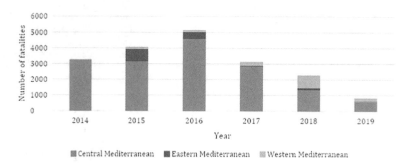

Figure 2.2 Annual refugee and undocumented migrant deaths in the Mediterranean by route.
Source: Missing Migrants Project.

In November 2015, countries to the north of Greece began restricting the passage of refugees and undocumented migrants only to those from Syria, Iraq and Afghanistan. In March 2016, FYR Macedonia, Croatia and Slovenia closed their borders to all refugees, stranding some 54,000 in Greece. In the same month the EU–Turkey agreement, intended to stop the flow from Turkey to Greece, came into effect: the number arriving in the 12 months following the deal were just 2.6% of those who had arrived in the 12 months before the deal. From then until mid-2017, the perilous Central Mediterranean route from Libya to Lampedusa and Sicily became the principal route for new arrivals to Europe. But in July 2017, as a result of Italian and EU support to the Libyan Coast Guard and efforts to reduce the operation of NGO and volunteer-operated SAR vessels, the number of arrivals on this route also dropped sharply. The 2018 Italian elections resulted in a coalition involving the right-wing League and the anti-establishment Five Star Movement which introduced a range of anti-immigrant policies and a refusal to let rescue vessels land refugee and undocumented migrants in Italy. The Western Mediterranean route (Morocco and Tunisia to Spain) was a less significant route, with 124,000 crossing this way during the period 2015–2018 and an average of 2,400 arriving each month during 2019.

Where did the Refugees and Undocumented Migrants Go and How Were They Treated?

Over the peak months of 2015 and early 2016, the normal national and EU procedures for registering and fingerprinting refugees and undocumented migrants arriving in Greece were overwhelmed. Those arriving in the Aegean islands were allowed to travel by ferry to the Greek mainland, and then onwards by bus, train and on foot through (what is now) North Macedonia and then on to Germany and other northern European countries. Under the sheer pressure of numbers, normal procedures were waived, or the rules changed to allow the refugees to move onward to their preferred destination. Their ability to travel northwards was abruptly brought to an end in the spring of 2016 by a combination of the EU–Turkey deal, border closures to the north of Greece and by the Greek authorities preventing refugees crossing to the mainland. In effect the Aegean islands became "holding grounds", or what some have termed "island prisons" (Witte, 2018).

At the best of times the provision of accommodation and support for arriving refugees and undocumented migrants is sadly a low priority for most governments. With the unprecedented numbers arriving in 2015, conditions in many reception facilities were, and often still are, overcrowded and insanitary. So poor were detention and living conditions in Greece as early as 2011 that the European Court of Human Rights found them to be in breach of Article 3 of the European Convention on Human Rights prohibiting "inhuman or degrading treatment". At the end of 2018 the nominal accommodation capacity at the five EU-termed "Hotspots" on Lesvos, Chios, Samos, Leros and Kos was 6,438, while nearly double that number (11,683) were being forced to live there under geographical restriction (Greek Council of Refugees, 2019). With an upturn in the number of arrivals on the islands in the summer of 2019, so the overcrowding worsened. By February 2020, the number of refugees on the five islands had increased to 42,000 and tensions were running high, not only between the camp residents and the Greek islanders but also between the islanders and the plans of the recently elected centre-right government to move some refugees to the mainland and construct new "closed" detention camps to hold and process newly arrived asylum seekers. At the end of February, riots erupted on Lesvos and Chios as islanders, angry at delays in moving refugees to the mainland and relieving pressure on their islands, sought to prevent the start of construction of the new closed camps and fought running battles with riot police (Associated Press in Lesvos, 2020). For some European governments, the provision of inadequate facilities was also a deliberate policy choice as part of their wider strategies intended to deter potential asylum seekers. As early as 2012, Theresa May, then UK Home Secretary (later to become prime minister), declared the aim of planned immigration legislation "to create here in Britain a really hostile environment for illegal migration" (Kirkup and Winnett, 2012).

For those who were able to choose where they headed in 2015, their decisions were influenced by a wide range of factors, such as the location of relatives and the promise of family reunification, familiarity with a particular language, the economic situation and the likelihood of finding work in different countries, or the availability and accuracy of information about different countries. Though the Common European Asylum System (CEAS) sets minimum standards within the EU for the treatment of asylum applicants and the processing of their claims, it is important to note that EU member states make their own national decisions about asylum applications. This leads to wide variations in asylum "recognition rates". In 2016, for instance, an Afghan adult had only a 1.7% chance of being recognised as a refugee in Bulgaria compared to a 97% chance in Italy and a 60% chance in Germany. Where refugees and undocumented migrants were aware of such differences, this may also have contributed to their decisions about which countries to head for.

A key problem for those travelling north intending to submit an asylum claim in, say, Germany, Sweden or the UK was that their rights and legal status were ambiguous in the period in which they submitted their asylum claim. While international refugee law provides a clear normative and legal framework for identifying and protecting those who have applied for asylum and those who have been granted refugee status, there is no regime of specific rights or institutions governing "irregular migrants". Though entitled to fundamental protections under international human rights law, in practice they do not usually have access to these protections. In 2015, and still today, the decision by refugees and undocumented migrants to attempt to travel "irregularly" across the EU to submit an asylum claim in another country carries with it the significant risk of ambiguous rights and lack of legal protections.

Germany

By a huge margin Germany was the destination for many of those arriving in 2015 and early 2016, receiving just over 1.2 million applications for asylum in those two years (see Figure 2.3). (However, of this number more than 250,000 applications were rejected and many of those rejected will have since been deported.)

With its large economy and high employment rates Germany was always going to be seen as a desirable destination for those arriving. In August 2015, German Government officials acknowledged the reality

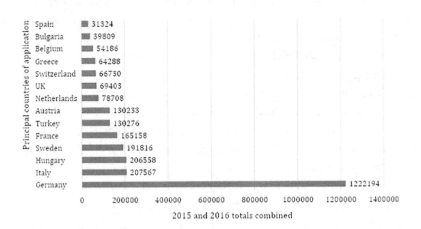

Figure 2.3 Asylum applications by country, 2015 and 2016 combined.

Source: ECRE (2017).

that asylum applicants from Syria would not be returned to Greece under the provisions of the Dublin Regulation.[2] Angela Merkel's assertion a few days later that "Wir schaffen das" ("we can manage this") publicly signalled that Germany was the European country most open to Syrians – and the flow towards Germany increased dramatically (Delcker, 2016). The following five months witnessed an extraordinary *Willkommenskultur* (welcoming culture) as an estimated 8 million people (10% of the population) helped refugees in some way during 2015 (Brunner and Rietzschel, 2016). The German Federal Office for Migration and Refugees (BAMF) was responsible for managing the reception and registration of the refugees, in which it was supported by Regional Refugee Councils and nationally established organisations such as Flüchtlinge Willkommen and PRO ASYL.

But it was volunteers, referred to as *Flüchtlingshilfe* (refugee helpers), from local church groups, sports and football clubs and spontaneously formed groups such as the "Migration Hub Network" and "Give Something Back to Berlin" who did much of the practical work. Volunteers set up "welcome groups" greeting arriving refugees with water and food at the main railway stations, provided clothing, furniture and household goods to families that arrived with nothing, ran German-language courses and children's play groups and provided legal advice and bureaucratic support. The head of one volunteer group in Bavaria estimated that, in late 2015, there were approximately 6,000 local groups comprising 30–40 volunteers each. But just four months after the start of the *Willkommenskultur* it all began to change – at least on the part of the German Government. Following a spate of sex attacks in Cologne on New Year's Eve 2015 that were blamed on "migrants", the political tide began to turn against refugees. The ISIS-inspired terrorist attacks in Nice in July 2016, in Paris in November 2016 and in Berlin in December 2016 only strengthened this shift in a generalised suspicion and mistrust of refugees and asylum applicants in Germany. Faced with a significant decline in her popularity ratings, at the end of January 2016 Angela Merkel announced a new "asylum package" with the aim of limiting and ultimately reducing the number of refugees in Germany. Chartered deportation flights carrying rejected Afghan asylum seekers to Kabul began in December

2016. However, in 2016 the number of those providing some sort of support to refugees was still 7 million; though 1 million below the 2015 figure, this nevertheless represented 9% of the population.

Hungary

Under the leadership of Viktor Orban, Hungary has been the most xenophobic and hostile EU country towards refugees and undocumented migrants. In February 2015, the government launched a campaign demonising refugees and migrants, portraying the issue as one of the main challenges facing Hungary. In September 2015, a 110-mile razor-wire barrier was completed along Hungary's border with Serbia, and the border was closed to asylum seekers. Special legislation was introduced in border districts (later extended across the whole country) making it a criminal offence to be an undocumented migrant. Between July and September 2016, over 19,000 refugees and undocumented migrants were prevented from entering Hungary or were escorted back to the Serbian border. Many were physically abused by "personnel in uniform" (AIDA, 2017). Since then asylum applications may only be made in transit zones at the border, where the applicants have to remain for the entire asylum procedure without any legal basis for their detention or judicial remedies (AIDA, 2018). The levels of violence directed at those on the border and those apprehended inside Hungary have been regularly reported on by agencies and international bodies (MSF, 2017). As barriers were put up and admission criteria changed in the autumn of 2015 and the winter of 2015/2016, so the refugees and undocumented migrants diverted to alternative routes north, or remained backed up at particular crossings in the hope that they might open. Hungary's construction of the fence along its border with Serbia in September 2015 diverted tens of thousands of refugees through Croatia and Slovenia towards Austria and Germany. So fluid was the situation in the second half of 2015 that national authorities and aid agencies found it hard to keep up with the rapidly changing situation. As crowds built up at new or blocked crossing points, it was often volunteers who were the first to distribute water and food and other support. In the period before legislation was introduced making being an undocumented migrant an offence, Migration Aid (A Segítök – literally "We Help") was also formed from Facebook groups and began distributing supplies to refugees arriving at Budapest's Keleti Station. Migration Aid groups were also formed at other points around the country, and during July and August 2015, 500 volunteers distributed 140,000 bottles of water, 50,000 sandwiches, 73,000 packages of toothbrushes, toothpaste and soap, 8,000 pairs of shoes, 6,000 sleeping bags, 390 tents and nearly 30 tonnes of clothes (Migration Aid, 2016). Also, in August 2015, a musician and his wife in Zagreb, Croatia were moved by TV news film of refugees crossing into Croatia from Hungary at Roszke. Together with a group of friends they drove to Roszke and distributed food and other items. Returning to Zagreb they organised a fundraising concert, "Are You Syrious?" – a name that was later adopted for their grassroots organisation. Money raised from the concert was used to hire a truck and transport food for 4,000 people to Tovarnik, another entry point to Croatia from Hungary. After this, they established a supply station at Bapska on the border with Serbia, where at that time no other humanitarian agencies were present, even though 7,000 people a day were crossing into Croatia.

The EU Response

The EU response to the dramatic increase in the number of refugees and undocumented migrants entering the European Union was developed over the course of meetings of interior ministers and the European Council during the summer and autumn of 2015. There were three principal elements. First was a burden-sharing proposal to relocate 120,000 asylum seekers from Italy, Greece and Hungary – the so-called "frontline states" – to all other EU countries over a two-year period – though Denmark, Ireland and the United Kingdom were excluded from this scheme as a result of their opt-out provisions. Second, a policy was introduced to focus EU support on selected entry locations, called

"Hotpots", where all arrivals should be processed through these "first reception" facilities. And finally, efforts began to reach an agreement with Turkey to more actively stem the flow of refugees from Turkey to the EU.

However, this relocation policy encountered strong resistance from the Czech Republic, Hungary, Slovakia and Poland, who opposed the mandatory reallocation of refugees between member states. In Hungary the issue of whether the country should accept a mandatory alloca- tion of just 1,294 refugees was even put to a national referendum. By September 2016, after just 4,500 refugees had been relocated through the scheme, European Commission President Jean-Claude Juncker had to admit that "solidarity cannot be forced". The Commission's attempt to achieve solidarity and burden-sharing in the EU's approach to the crisis had failed. As the UN Secretary-General had put it as early as August 2015, this was "a crisis of solidarity, not a crisis of numbers". As far as the "Hotspots" policy went, the EU went on to approve the creation of "Hotspots" at key arrival points in Greece and Italy, where there would be more rigorous systems for screening and fingerprinting of refugees and undocumented migrants. The first of these became operational at Moria camp on Lesvos in October 2015, and soon four more were opened on the Greek islands of Chios, Samos, Leros and Kos and five in Italy on Lampedusa, at Trapani, Pozzallo and Messina in Sicily and at Taranto on the mainland. While the Hotspots certainly made it easier for the author- ities to fingerprint and begin the asylum application process, the pro- vision of accommodation at and near the Hotspots has been woefully inadequate. According to Amnesty International, in December 2018, over 12,500 people were still living in tents and containers unsuitable for winter in the five Greek Hotspots. In addition to serious overcrowding, asylum seekers experienced unsanitary and unhygienic conditions and gender-based violence (Amnesty International, 2018).

As far as the EU–Turkey proposal was concerned, German-led discussions between the EU and Turkey began in October 2015 over ways of reducing the numbers of refugees and migrants from Turkey to Greece. The talks led in March 2016 to a statement known as the "EU– Turkey Joint Action Plan", whereby Turkish authorities would do more to stem the flow of refugees and migrants and would take back refugees and migrants arriving in Greece after 20 March 2016 whose claims for asylum in Greece had been rejected. For each failed asylum seeker returned to Turkey, one Syrian refugee would be accepted into the EU. In return, Turkey would receive up to Eur. 6 billion in payments to a Facility for Refugees by 2018, and the EU would provide for visa-free travel to Europe for Turkish citizens (European Commission, 2016). The statement was strongly criticised by human rights and humanitarian organisations, with the UN High Commissioner for Refugees expressing deep "concern about any arrangement that would involve the blanket return of anyone from one country to another without spelling out the refugee protection safeguards under international law" (Spindler, 2016).

The complete closure of the Macedonian, Croatian and Slovenian borders at the beginning of March 2016 and the implementation of the EU–Turkey Joint Action Plan on 19 March transformed the situation from being that of a refugee population on the move to one that had become trapped and static. Though the majority (some 50,000) were stranded in Greece, thousands more were stranded in pockets to the north in Macedonia, Serbia, Bosnia and Herzegovina, Croatia and Slovenia, and in Sicily and Italy and countries to the north. Some decided to apply for asylum in the country where they were, while others opted to try to keep moving northwards clandestinely on their own or by paying people smugglers – though it is hard to know the numbers as so little information was collected. Information is also scarce on the numbers who stayed put and received official help, and those that remained outside official systems (or were denied) official provision, and as a result were wholly dependent on the support of volunteers and grassroots groups. What is known is that by August 2019, close to 900,000 asylum seekers in the EU were waiting to have their claims processed and were condemned to living in limbo. Of these, 44% of the pending requests were in Germany, with Italy next, at 12%. The rejection rate for asylum requests across the EU stood at 37% in 2016, but by 2019 this had almost doubled to 64%. This implies that nearly two-thirds of those still awaiting asylum will fail and either be returned to their own country or to a neighbouring country outside of the EU – a shocking statistic, and probably not one that will receive coverage in much right-of-centre media.

"Too Little, Too Late": The Response of Humanitarian Agencies

With a small number of honourable exceptions like Médecins Sans Frontières (MSF), Médecins du Monde and some national Red Cross Societies, the overall response by the established humanitarian sector to the material needs (food, water, shelter and health) of refugees and undocumented migrants was shockingly inadequate and unsatisfactory (DeLargy, 2016; MSF, 2015). On Lesvos, despite the dramatic increase in the numbers arriving on the island in May and June 2015, it was not until October that the international response really began to catch up with the scale of need. While some agencies announced a presence on Lesvos in August, in several cases these were simply assessment missions rather than actual operations. Operational UN capacity in Greece was limited to the UNHCR, which was focusing its support on the national authorities. Few international NGOs were formally registered in Greece, and the need to register contributed to the delay in some of the larger humanitarian NGOs getting mobilised. Experienced humanitarian personnel from organisations such as Oxfam, Save the Children and the International Rescue Committee (IRC) arriving on Lesvos and other islands appeared surprised to find that the normal humanitarian co-ordination arrangements were not already in place. It is generally accepted that much of the water and food provided on Lesvos during the critical months of July, August and September 2015 came from locally formed groups such as Agkalia (Embrace), the "Village of All Together", the "Human Social Kitchen", the Starfish Foundation and individuals such as the Kempsons – a British family living in Lesvos (Channel 4 News, 2015). Greek NGOs such as PRAXIS and METAction also played a key role, as did international grassroots groups such as Stichting Hulpactie Bootvluchtelling (Dutch Boat Refugee Foundation), Lighthouse Relief, the Octopus Foundation, Dirty Girls of Lesvos and the Humanitarian Support Agency (Menninga, 2015; Borton et al., 2016).

Why was the Initial Response by International Humanitarian Agencies So Inadequate?

It was a concern of the "activist volunteer" movement, as well as much of the public, that the larger humanitarian NGOs appeared to be absent in 2015 in what could be clearly seen to be a humanitarian crisis. While UNHCR had maintained a non-operational presence in Greece for many years, and had the infrastructure to set up camps in Europe, it was not able to gain national consents to operate fully in Greece and in other European states. They and other groups such as the Red Cross, Oxfam, IRC (International Rescue Committee) were also facing unprecedented demands across the Middle East as a result of the ongoing Syrian Civil War and the massive population displacements it was causing – of which the movement of Syrian refugees from Turkey into Europe was just one aspect. Many of these agencies considered that the scale of developing needs in Europe did not warrant a diversion of their resources, and many assumed – wrongly, as it turned out – that European governments were more than capable of responding themselves.

In addition, many humanitarian organisations were more used to working in Africa and Asia and did not have the protocols set up for field-work in European countries. Nor were such countries quick to recognise this. The economic and political situation in Greece was extremely challenging at this time, which hampered the ability of its leadership and institutions to respond to aid initiatives. In 2015, Greece was suffering from a financial crisis and the government was being forced to undertake a severe austerity programme. The country held a national referendum in July 2015 on whether to agree to the bailout conditions required by the IMF, the European Commission and the European Central Bank, and this was followed by a general election which further diverted the attention of political leaders and from the growing crisis of high numbers arriving onto the Greek islands across the summer and autumn of 2015. This meant that the UN agencies that traditionally support and work through government agencies were also hampered during this time. Also, the EU's mechanisms for providing civil protection and disaster relief assistance were focused on the EU Humanitarian Aid Office (ECHO) but its brief was to co-ordinate and fund humanitarian programmes in Africa, Asia and elsewhere outside the EU and its mandate prevented its operation within EU countries – a restriction that was not lifted until February 2016. Official aid through bilateral donors was also slow to arrive. In the case of the UK's Department for International Development (DFID), for instance, funding channelled through the Start Network of international humanitarian NGOs only began reaching agencies in late November 2015. With the closure of the "Balkan route" in early 2016 and the implementation of the EU–Turkey deal in March 2016, tens of thousands of refugees and undocumented migrants remained stranded in Greece and in countries along the Western Balkans route. Although significant funds were provided to the Greek Government and to the UNHCR and its implementing partners (ECHO, 2016), co-ordination and implementation of this assistance was poor. For instance, despite plans to upgrade tents and shelters to cope with the anticipated freezing conditions during the winter of 2016–2017, when heavy snow fell in January 2017, large numbers of refugees and asylum seekers were still living in tents on the Aegean islands and on the Greek mainland. Several refugees and asylum seekers died from hypothermia and from fires and carbon monoxide poisoning associated with unsafe heating arrangements (Howden and Fotiadis, 2017).

Established humanitarian agencies also struggled to provide effective assistance in the unofficial settlements dotted around Europe: in northern France and Paris; across Italy in cities such as Turin, Trieste, Padua and Rome (MSF, 2018); in Belgrade and near Serbia's border with Hungary and in Bosnia and Herzegovina. By their nature, informal camps develop spontaneously and are not officially recognised or designated by the authorities – which in most cases would prefer that they did not exist at all. To a significant degree, such settlements are the product of policies of deterrence and nationality-based approaches to asylum that discriminate against certain nationalities and drive them out of formal reception systems. Conditions in informal settlements were, and often continue to be, appalling, with inadequate shelter, food, water, hygiene and sanitation. People living in such conditions are often subject to frequent forcible relocations by the police, and violence and abuse are commonplace (Refugee Rights Data Project, 2019; Le Clève et al., 2016). Those staying in the settlements are often constantly on the move, staying for perhaps a few weeks before moving to another location in the hope that conditions may be better there. However, with a few exceptions, (notably MSF and Médecins du Monde), traditional humanitarian agencies rarely served these temporary and unofficial settlements. It was in these kinds of camp situations – on the Greek islands, in the post-Idomeni camps on the Greek mainland, in cities and towns in the Balkans and northern Italy, at Ventimiglia on the Italian–French border, in Brussels and Paris and in the camps and forests around Calais and Dunkerque – that grassroots groups provided essential and life-saving service on an unprecedented scale.

What Happened to Humanitarian Principles?

Within the established humanitarian sector, four documents – the NGO/Red Cross Code of Conduct, the Humanitarian Charter, the Sphere Minimum Standards in Disaster Response and the Core Humanitarian Standards – set out the principles, ethics and standards that should guide the actions and work of humanitarian agencies and have in effect formed a body of "soft law" for the sector (Mertus and Helsing, 2006). The discrepancy between the commitments made in these documents and what happened on the ground in 2015 and 2016 – and has continued to happen in different locations around Europe since – is striking. The fact that some NGOs were able to provide effective assistance in unofficial camps while others were either not able to or chose not to suggests varying levels of commitment to upholding and adhering to humanitarian "soft law". One researcher has questioned why "Agencies with long experience negotiating humanitarian access in places like Sudan, Myanmar or Syria seemed to have no idea how to negotiate with the mayor of Calais" (DeLargy, 2016). We would argue here that to provide assistance in the unofficial settlements is to *de facto* criticise and counter the policies and attitudes that have helped create them, and it seemed not all NGOs were prepared to take this step. While the reasons are complex as to why most decided not to provide assistance in particular settlements, for many it is likely to have involved the fear of risking future funding from government sources, or funding from private supporters who disagreed with helping those in the settlements.

The Response by Activist Volunteers: Antecedents

Groups and organisations working outside the governmental and "for-profit" sectors (whom academics would call "civil society actors") have been campaigning for years to improve the treatment of refugees and undocumented migrants in Europe. Set up in 1999, for example, No Borders is a loose network of activists running camps near detention centres in various parts of Europe. It also monitors police actions and Frontex operations against refugees and undocumented migrants. In Greece, Welcome to the EU (W2EU) was formed in 2009. With links to the No Borders movement, its mission is to provide independent information for refugees and migrants coming to Europe. In Germany, Borderline-Europe was formed in 2007 to conduct independent investigations of human rights violations at the EU's external borders, and advocate for greater respect for the rights of refugees and undocumented migrants.

Groups providing accommodation and support to refugees and asylum seekers had also been a feature of the volunteer landscape in many European countries for well over a decade prior to 2015. In the UK, for instance, the Boaz Trust was set up in Manchester in 2004 to help destitute asylum seekers in the city. The No Accommodation Network was established in 2006 to provide support and accommodation for refugees and migrants. The Sanctuary movement, which began in Sheffield in 2005, encourages ordinary UK citizens to demonstrate solidarity with, and provide support to, refugees. With the support of the city council and local organisations and voluntary groups, in 2007 Sheffield became the UK's first "City of Sanctuary", marking it as a city that takes pride in the welcome it offers people in need of safety. Since then, the City of Sanctuary movement has spread and there are currently over 90 initiatives in towns and cities across the UK and Ireland. In Spain, Red

Acoge was established in 1991 to promote the rights of migrants and help them integrate into the Spanish society, especially those at risk of exclusion, such as refugees; it has now grown into a federation of 20 independent organisations. In France, Auberge des Migrants was set up in 2008 to provide food and community support to refugees and undocumented migrants around the Channel ports of Calais and Dunkerque. In Hungary, Migszol, the Migrant Solidarity Group of Hungary, was formed in 2012 to campaign on refugee and migrant rights issues. In Germany, the *Flüchtlinge Willkommen* (Refugees Welcome) movement was begun in 2014, linking private individuals willing to provide a room to asylum seekers needing accommodation. It has since spread to more than 20 countries (Dearden, 2015).

The Growth of Volunteer and Grassroots Groups in 2015

Events over the summer of 2015 saw thousands of volunteers and hundreds of grassroots groups form spontaneously to provide humanitarian assistance to the large numbers of refugees and undocumented migrants entering Europe. Some groups were locally formed, others emerged on Facebook and some individuals acted on their own, travelling to an area of need and then forming a new group, or joining an existing group in that area. The scale of this upwelling of "citizen humanitarianism" was remarkable, and says much about the popular reaction to the often hostile and callous way in which many governments responded to the influx. Below is merely an indication of a tiny percentage of them, from a sample of 180 this author located from 2016 onward.

- Bezirk Jennersdorf – *Flüchtlingshilfe* – an Austrian group providing aid to refugees at Jennersdorf, near Austria's border with Hungary.
- Dirty Girls of Lesvos – providing industrial-scale laundry services for refugees (blankets, bedding etc.) on Lesvos and mainland Greece.
- Cars of Hope – formed in Germany to take food by car and truck convoys to refugees in Greece.

- East Midlands Solidarity – providing clothes, supplies and funding to refugees and vulnerable migrants in northern France, Greece and Syria.
- Proactiva Open Arms – a Barcelona-based group that provided search-and-rescue services initially around Lesvos and subsequently in the central Mediterranean.
- Rastplatz Project – a Swiss group providing food and general support to refugees along the Balkans route and subsequently in Dunkerque.
- Refugee Rights Data Project (RRDP) – a UK-based group undertaking censuses and surveys to support policy-making, starting with a major survey in Calais in February 2016.
- Stichting Bootvluchteling/Boat Refugee Foundation – a Dutch group providing search-and-rescue services, supplies and a medical mission on Lesvos, Leros, Kos and Samos, and in Athens and on the Greek mainland.
- Utopia 56 – a group formed by French citizens managing volunteers supporting refugees in Calais, Dunkerque and across northern France. By 2018 the group had more than 9,000 members.

To fully identify all the voluntary grassroots groups that have been established to respond to the needs of refugees and undocumented migrants would be a challenging task. Many were formed at a very local level and operated by using social media, some preferring closed groups. While some did set up websites and went on to become established organisations and charities, a proportion never moved beyond Facebook groups and existed only for a specific period to address the needs in specific situations. For instance, Hot Food Idomeni was formed to provide cooked meals for those stranded at the Idomeni border crossing between Greece and what is now known as North Macedonia in March 2016; after the May 2016 closure of Idomeni and dispersal of the refugees to smaller camps across northern Greece the team moved with them, providing meals at several of the new smaller camps, and then relocated to Serbia, where it continued providing hot meals during the harsh winter of 2016/2017 and then in May 2017 passed the responsibility on to a newly formed group, the BelgrAid Kitchen.

Estimating the monetary value of the assistance provided is also problematic. While established aid agencies purchase material assistance and pay their staff, much of the material assistance (largely food, tents and clothing) provided by the volunteer groups was freely donated, as was the time given by the volunteers. The monetary value of the time of volunteers is particularly hard to estimate as it involved skills and tasks ranging from clothes-sorting and loading trucks to doctors and lawyers giving their time completely voluntarily. And travel costs were a major factor; both individuals and groups made frequent trips across Europe to volunteer, and to get large aid supplies to where they were needed. Robust estimations of the monetary value of the contribution made by volunteers and grassroots groups have yet to be attempted. In the meantime, the scale and value of the contribution they made is likely to be severely underestimated by established humanitarian agencies and governments. It is hoped that this collection will contribute to filling in some of the gaps in knowledge and raising public awareness of what was achieved by this transient and responsive movement.

Let us take Lesvos as an example of grassroots operations. On Lesvos, local people provided water, food, showers and places to sleep to refugees and asylum seekers for several months before international NGOs began to appear. In 2010, local people in the village of Molyvos in the north of the island established a group to provide assistance to refugees from Turkey. The collective became more organised in early 2015, with volunteers working in shifts to provide food and water to arriving refugees. As the numbers passing through the town increased in August 2015, a car park outside a nightclub was turned into a volunteer-run transit site. The following October the collective formally established itself as a nonprofit organisation called the Starfish Foundation (Eggink and McRostie, 2016). Fishermen rescued numerous people from unseaworthy and overloaded boats, and local residents organised a watch system to spot boats leaving Turkey, to give reception teams advance notice of their likely landing point. Volunteers and grassroots groups such as the Lighthouse Project played a key role in beach rescues and supporting arriving boats. Once landed, local people drove new arrivals to the registration point at Moria, some 50–70 kilometres from the landing points on the north shore, in defiance of anti-smuggling laws that made it illegal to offer transport to unregistered refugees and asylum seekers (Kingsley, 2015). The extraordinary efforts of the people of Lesvos were later recognised in a number of international accolades given to local groups and organisations, including the 2016 Olof Palme Prize, won jointly by the mayors of Lesvos and Lampedusa in Italy; the 2016 Nansen Refugee Award, given to the Hellenic Rescue Team and Efi Latsoudi, who set up Pikpa camp (now Lesvos Solidarity); and the Raoul Wallenberg Prize, awarded by the Council of Europe to the volunteer-run local NGO Agkalia.

In Rome, the sight of refugees and undocumented migrants arriving from Sicily and southern Italy sleeping on the streets, in parks and in derelict buildings, with no support from local or national authorities, prompted a group of volunteers to set up the Baobab Experience in June 2015 to provide basic assistance. Members of the public and shop owners contributed food, medicine, sanitary items and other donations, and priority needs were posted on Facebook. Volunteer groups from France and the UK were very active in the "Jungle" camp near Calais, particularly from mid-2015 onwards. In the UK, a Facebook post written by Jaz O'Hara describing what she had seen during a visit to Calais was shared over 60,000 times in the space of a few days. In response to the post, vanloads of clothes were donated and over £130,000 was raised. The post prompted others around the country to visit Calais or set up groups in their local areas to collect clothes, food, tents and camping equipment (Borton, 2016b). One early example of the countless local UK groups that were established is Derbyshire Refugee Solidarity, which was set up in the summer of 2015 organising aid convoys to the warehouse in Calais operated by L'Auberge des Migrants, and raising money to send volunteers to help with the sea-rescues on Lesvos. Help Refugees, a group formed by three well-connected friends in London towards the end of August 2015, has grown to become a quasi-NGO, supporting or partnering with 38 other organisations (including NGOs such as Médecins du Monde) working in refugee camps in Greece and in camps and settlements in

France, Italy, Turkey, Syria and Lebanon. The group played a central role in organising the construction and provision of 1,500 insulated shelters in Calais, and funding 7,000 hot meals a day at the camp at Idomeni in northern Greece. Help Refugees' fundraising effectiveness has come from innovative branding (notably its "Choose Love" merchandise and central London shop) and the group has managed to achieve a high profile through its effective and well-financed PR campaigns.

Characteristics of Volunteer and Grassroots Groups

Looking at who these activist volunteers were in any depth, what do we know about their backgrounds and motivations? There has to date been little formal or academic research done on the age, class, gender, educational background and political views of the volunteers, or the specific reasons or triggers that caused them to make what for many was often a gruelling and intense commitment. Hopefully this present study, with its broad sample of volunteers, both local and international, from across Europe will be a useful contribution.

For many volunteers a highly influential moment was the publication and global dissemination of the shocking images of the body of three-year-old Alan Kurdi lying drowned on a Turkish beach on 2 September 2015, following the sinking of the dinghy in which his family were trying to cross to the Greek island of Kos. According to a team of media specialists who have researched the impact of the images:

> [T]hey represented the atrocity of the Syrian refugee crisis in a way that instantly and substantially affected individuals and societies. The unprecedented degree of mobilisation of people responding to the crisis was a direct effect of the images, and as their circulation gained momentum, it seemed that a change in political response was possible and forthcoming.
>
> (Vis and Goriunova, 2015)

For some volunteers their trigger moment had come six months earlier in April 2015, when over 1,200 migrants and refugees lost their lives in the central Mediterranean in a single week (Grunau, 2016).

Besides the effect of such tragic events, it appears that the use of pejorative terms by politicians also spurred people into becoming volunteers. In July 2015, when asked about the refugee and migrant situation in Calais that was causing travel delays for British tourists, UK Prime Minister David Cameron spoke of a "swarm" of people wanting to come to the UK. Over the following 24 hours, "Calais People to People Solidarity – Action from the UK", a Facebook group that had only had about 100 followers up to that point, saw the number bump to 600 in 24 hours as people, mostly British, took offence at how their head of government was portraying the situation (Borton, 2016d). UK Action for Refugees, which began as a grassroots group in 2015, summarised the process as follows.

> We began as a group of like-minded individuals who realised that the governments and main NGOs seemed unable to respond to a humanitarian crisis that was happening in their own backyard. What we could never have imagined was that there were thousands of other people who felt exactly the same way, disempowered and desperate to help, but unable to figure out how. Through the power of social media, we reached out and they reached back, and through our combined efforts we have been able to become an organisation that can and does make a difference.
>
> (UK Action for Refugees, 2016)

These new grassroots groups formed as start-up organisations as volunteers tried to organise themselves at the same time as responding. Most of the volunteers were juggling jobs, education, caring for others (including doing full-time childcare) while also somehow fitting in the time to sort donations, make trips and raise funds. These were organisations being formed in a spontaneous and improvised manner that was at the same time creative and flexible.

Research on the organisational characteristics of the grassroots groups is very limited. One of the few studies available was by MSF Belgium, which concluded:

> While the principal strength of many civil society initiatives is their flexibility, informality, commitment and self-organisation, fragility and instability are an inherent part of their make-up – in effect two sides of the same coin.
>
> (Francart with Borton, 2016)

The same report noted that "staffing is typically 'fluid and unpredictable'" and funding "unpredictable and often precarious". Volunteer work supporting refugees and vulnerable migrants, at times in very difficult circumstances, can also take a toll on volunteers' physical and mental health (Francart with Borton, 2016) – something this collection considers in Chapter 7. These results resonate with the existing literature on the voluntary sector more generally. For instance, the UK Community Development Foundation lists the following positive characteristics of community groups: flexible, needs-based, holistic, trusted, connected, value for money and committed. Interestingly, the Foundation also identifies the limitations of the community sector, and these closely accord with the issues faced by grassroots groups assisting refugees and undocumented migrants – uneven coverage, lack of institutional influence and lack of formal accountability.

For the most part the flexibility of grassroots groups has enabled them to identify areas that were poorly covered, and develop and/or relocate their activities accordingly. For instance, a number of grassroots groups shifted their activities from Lesvos to Idomeni in early 2016, and subsequently to the camps established following the closure of the Greek–North Macedonian border and the subsequent movement of people from Idomeni in May 2016. More recently, some groups have moved back to Lesvos as the number of arrivals and those living without adequate shelter increased in the summer of 2019. Similarly, individual volunteers and small grassroots groups relocated to Serbia in the winter of 2016–2017 and then in the summer of 2018 to deal with the build-up of some 3,000 refugees and undocumented migrants in Bosnia and Herzegovina, where the state was providing only 150 places in a single centre near Sarajevo (Are You Syrious?, 2018) – grassroots groups such as the Aid Brigade Sarajevo formed and provided two meals a day for an average of 285 refugees between March 2018 and May 2019, when the group was forced to close by the authorities of Bosnia and Herzegovina (Aid Brigade, 2019). For many of these volunteers and newly formed groups, their efforts were wholly focused on "the doing" – getting the pallet, van or container of supplies loaded and despatched, or running the service or activities in a particular camp – which allowed little time or energy for influencing and advocacy activities beyond those required for fundraising purposes. Nevertheless, several groups have successfully combined concrete action with advocacy and lobbying for change at the political level. In the UK, for instance, Help Refugees, Calais Action, Care4Calais and others have led and supported public campaigns, undertaken parliamentary lobbying and provided close support to initiatives such as the "Dubs Amendment" to the 2016 Immigration Act, which required the UK Government to provide protection to up to 3,000 unaccompanied minors who arrived in Europe before March 2016 (discussed more fully in the UK Flashpoint section of this book). Thus, even if they did not begin with a critique of the state and the status quo, many groups quickly developed a political critique and undertook initiatives for challenging existing rules and norms and changing the discourse. Such initiatives included pro-refugee protest marches and demonstrations across Europe (e.g., the 2 June 2018 march in Paris), sleep-outs, rallies and many other forms of non-violent protest. There were also direct challenges to politicians, such as Maltese activist Kristina Quintano's open letter, headed "A Dead Child Weighs Almost Nothing", to the Norwegian justice minister after he announced that he did not support Doctors Without Borders sailing the Norwegian-flagged ship *Ocean Viking* to the Mediterranean to save lives, and that Norway would not take in any of the refugees saved (Quintano, 2019). Of the testimonies provided in this volume, a strongly felt concern of many volunteers was that they wanted to do more advocacy and awareness-raising but felt that they had to prioritise their time on vital "aid basics".

Grassroots groups operate on the basis of a high degree of trust between volunteers, and with this and the highly pressured time-frames and emergencies they faced, systems and procedures to ensure financial and personal accountability were often kept to a minimum. Though the number of known incidents of where trust has been abused appears to be small, it is a recognised concern that has led many groups to seek formal charitable status, despite the administrative burden this put on them. Another area where grassroots groups can be vulnerable is that of what in the UK is termed "safeguarding" – meaning measures to protect children, young people and vulnerable adults from abuse, harm and neglect. Safeguarding is an issue partly because many of the temporary camps are open, and literally anyone is able to enter and leave at will. But it is also an issue for many of the smaller grassroots groups that do not have the capacity or means to run identity and security checks on those that offer themselves as volunteers. Thus far, no significant abuse scandals of the type that so damaged Oxfam in 2018 have emerged in relation to grassroots groups, but this is another issue that, going forward, the volunteer groups are aware they need to address.

Activities and Roles

Aiming at the near-impossible task of filling the numerous gaps in provision by states and established humanitarian agencies, the range of roles volunteer and grassroots groups played was, and continues to be, extremely wide. Below are some further examples, by no means exhaustive, that show the range and ingenuity of volunteer initiatives in the years from 2015 onwards. On Lesvos, volunteers monitored the approach and arrival of incoming dinghies and boats in a system set up by British residents Philippa and Eric Kempson, who founded the Hope Project, and other volunteers and grassroots groups such as the Lighthouse Project played a key role in beach rescues on the island. Local and international volunteers provided food and water to refugees and undocumented migrants on their arrival on the Aegean islands and throughout much of their journey northwards. Grassroots groups including Khora, the Bristol Skipchen, Hot Food Idomeni and Help Refugees provided 7,000 hot meals a day at the camp in Idomeni, 2,000 on the island of Samos and two meals a day for refugees arriving on Chios. In Sicily, Mayor of Palermo Leoluca Orlando took a stand against growing anti-refugee sentiment, leading the development of the 2015 Palermo Charter on International Human Mobility and declaring Palermo to be an Open City. This leadership has created space for groups such as the Astalli accommodation centres and various art and language projects to develop their provision of assistance to refugees and migrants on the island. In the Calais Jungle, the locally based Auberge des Migrants was already active by 2015. Many of those volunteers and grassroots groups based in the UK that began providing tents and supplies in 2015 channelled their support through Auberge des Migrants. Huge numbers of used and discarded tents were collected from music festivals in the UK by groups such as Aid Box Convoy (now Aid Box Community). The British group Jungle Canopy provided second-hand caravans with funds raised by schools, churches and Women's Institute groups (King, 2017). In all, 140 caravans were delivered to the Jungle. Help Refugees put out a social media call in late September for carpenters, builders and potential donors of timber and insulation materials. By May 2016, 1,500 shelters had been built and installed (Borton, 2016c; O'Boyle, 2016). In an attempt to inform policy, the UK-based Refugee Rights Data Project (RRDP) has published a series of surveys on conditions in Calais, Dunkerque, small informal settlements in northern France, Paris, Greece and Berlin, on female refugees in Europe and on the situation of refugees and undocu-mented migrants at a key crossing point between Italy and France. A vol-unteer-run Facebook page, "Phone Credit For Refugees And Displaced People", aims to put refugees in touch with others around the world who can provide them with direct and practical support in the form of phone credit top-ups. Established in February 2016, by March 2017 the group had provided 22,000 top-ups worth £400,000. After an initial focus on Calais and northern France, coverage has expanded to refugees and undocumented migrants in Belgium, Italy, Greece, Serbia, Croatia, Lebanon, Jordan, Syria and Afghanistan (Pearce, 2017). Many grassroots groups (and humanitarian agencies) set up phone-charging facilities and free Wi-Fi services to refugees and undocumented migrants from Lesvos and other Aegean islands and at key points such as border crossings, right through to their destination countries. In the Calais camp, Refugee InfoBus, a small grassroots group, installed power, Wi-Fi and laptops in a converted truck, enabling people to communicate with loved ones and access legal and human rights information.

The Relationship Between Grassroots Groups, Government Authorities and Humanitarian Agencies

In the context of government strategies, such as the UK's declared "hostile environment" policy, that seek to deter refugees and undocumented migrants as part of broader policies of deterrence, it is no surprise that the relationship between state authorities and volunteers and grassroots groups aiding refugees and undocumented migrants has often been fraught. As shown in Chapter 9, there are numerous examples of the criminalisation of assistance to refugees and undocumented migrants. For instance, in several European countries it is illegal to provide transport for people who have entered without proper documentation. In Hungary, the police and the military have the authority to search private homes if they suspect someone of harbouring illegal migrants (National Public Radio, 2015), and such measures were also threatened in Brussels in 2018, where large numbers of local people began housing refugees. In France, facilitating the "illegal entry, movement or residence of a foreigner" carries a jail term of five years and a fine of Eur. 30,000. In January 2016, the authorities on Lesvos arrested five Spanish and Danish volunteers working for search-and-rescue teams and charged them with attempted human trafficking and smuggling. They were subsequently released after a period of detention and the payment of warranties (Brown, 2017). In August 2018, two foreign volunteers (one a Syrian refugee living in Germany) and two Greek nationals who were all working for the nonprofit organisation Emergency Response Centre International (ERCI) providing search-and-rescue and medical and educational services were arrested and charged with money laundering, people smuggling and espionage. Though released on bail after more than three months in detention, they remain awaiting trial and potentially face up to 25 years in prison if found guilty (Mardini, 2019). In June 2019, following a standoff between Italian authorities and the volunteer-operated rescue vessel *Sea-Watch 3* that had 40 rescued migrants on board needing to be brought ashore, the ship's captain Carola Rackete docked the vessel in Lampedusa and was promptly arrested. She was exonerated by the court, but, had she been found guilty, could have faced up to 15 years in prison.

Legal specialists operating on a gratis or volunteer basis have played a vital role in challenging the policies and practices of EU member states. In September 2015, solicitors at the Migrants' Law Project visited Calais and were shown around the Jungle camp by activists linked to Citizens UK. Meeting children with family members in the UK, the lawyers realised that these children had a right to be in the UK under the EU's "Dublin Regulation". Working with a wider group of activist volunteers and legal specialists from the Migrants' Law Project, the Islington Law Centre, Bhatt Murphy Solicitors, Syrian community leaders and the recently formed Safe Passage, a process was begun to gather robust information to develop a legal case to assert the right of the children to enter the UK to join their families. A barrister was appointed to take a test case to court and in January 2016 the case was won in relation to three Syrian boys and a dependent older brother (Travis, 2016). The case consumed 1,400 *pro bono* legal hours. In a subsequent case relating to the "Dubs Amendment" to the UK's Immigration Act of 2016, the legal firm Duncan Lewis was invited to the Calais Jungle by Sue Clayton, the author of this book, and brought a legal challenge to the Home Office for failing to accept the number of unaccompanied children without family as agreed under the Amendment. The High Court ruled that the Home Office had acted unlawfully on two counts.

Generalisations about the relationship between established humanitarian agencies and grassroots groups are risky, as much depends on the context in which they encounter each other and work, if not together, then at least alongside each other. Research conducted along the Balkans route in early 2017 found that the larger international NGOs were often seen as bureaucratic and conservative in their advocacy, while volunteers were perceived by NGOs to be helpful, flexible and responsive to urgent needs but with few or no structures of accountability (Martin and Nolte, 2019). In many places such as Lesvos, Samos, Macedonia and Serbia, volunteers and grassroots groups had been responding for significant periods of time before the more established humanitarian agencies set up effective operations. This inevitably led to feelings among the volunteers that they had been "covering" for agencies that were either absent or had arrived late. Wherever in Europe they were working, volunteers frequently expressed disdain for the larger international NGOs and their claim to be "humanitarian" agencies. In Lesvos, a Greek volunteer who had worked with local groups on the island for four months said that some NGOs had come across as arrogant, effectively claiming, "we are here now and we are going to operate everything", even though local people had been providing many services as best they could for months before the NGOs appeared. And yet, even once NGOs had begun operating, this same volunteer found that most of the frontline work continued to be done by volunteers and that the NGOs' communication with the local population and existing volunteers had been poor (Karpodini, 2015). An international volunteer working for the Starfish Foundation in another part of Lesvos observed that volunteers did not take kindly to being criticised by professionals who failed to recognise that the systems in place had been born in the midst of a crisis and had developed precisely because the large NGOs had been absent. Where there was friction between professionals and volunteers, this volunteer felt that it was mainly a result of volunteers' eagerness to respond to needs rapidly, while professionals worked on setting up systems that would enable an efficient response in the long term (Eggink and McRostie, 2016). The fact that volunteers were unpaid, many drawing heavily on their own funds, was often felt to have gone unacknowledged by salaried agency staff.

Where established humanitarian agencies and grassroots groups worked in the same locations, as in the post-Idomeni camps on mainland Greece, stark differences in the funding levels of agency projects and the roles being undertaken by grassroots groups were also a source of tension. Agencies also could not subcontract grassroots groups if they were not established organisations with which contracts could be entered into. Another source of irritation expressed by grassroots groups working in Lesvos, Athens and Thessaloniki were the working hours of agency staff, which often saw them withdraw from camps at the end of the day, leaving the volunteers and grassroots groups to deal with any incidents during the night, such as new arrivals to the camp or medical emergencies (Borton, 2016e). But there were also positive encounters. As referred to earlier, the opening of the transit camp on Lesvos by the Starfish Foundation allowed established NGOs to pro-vide Starfish with logistical support and training to develop systems that significantly increased the capacity of Starfish's volunteers. At least one major NGO recognised the important role being played by volunteers and grassroots groups and the need to improve co-oper-ation with them. In late 2015, MSF Belgium launched a "Civil Society Networking Project", mapping grassroots groups across Europe to enable MSF teams to link up with them where appropriate. The project supported MSF teams working in the Idomeni camp and elsewhere in Greece, enabling them to work more effectively with volunteer groups (Francart with Borton, 2016). However, few other agencies appear to have invested in this sort of initiative.

The Evolution of Volunteer Groups after 2016

The terms on which grassroots volunteer groups had sprung into exist-ence in 2015 were fundamentally changed in early 2016 by the closure of borders along the Western Balkans route and the EU–Turkey deal of March 2016, under which Turkey undertook to prevent boats leaving its shores for Greece, while the EU undertook to return newly arriving migrants to Turkey and to provide funding and resettlement for refugees in Turkey. What had been characterised by movement and dynamism requiring quick thinking and organisational flexibility very quickly became static, ordered and procedural. The newly created camps for the

60,000 or so refugees stranded in Greece required investment in infra-structure and systems, and refugees required legal advice and support in submitting their applications for asylum and social and culturally spe-cific support to cope with their being stuck in a country that for most was not their preferred destination, and where few had any links. In Germany, Sweden and other countries, priorities shifted from receiving and accommodating to the provision of language training and routes into education and employment. And to make things even more challen-ging for the activist volunteers, this was against a backdrop of hardening social and political attitudes towards refugees and undocumented migrants. In October 2016, the demolition of the Calais Jungle dramatic-ally, and also traumatically, removed what had become a focal point for the efforts of British and French volunteers and grassroots groups.

For some volunteers and a handful of grassroots groups, the funda-mental shift that occurred during 2016 proved the point at which they decided to stop their international volunteering. Some returned, as best they could, to their previous roles and livelihoods. Others focused their attention more on welcoming new arrivals nearer home, or on longer-term campaigning and political actions, building solidarity with campaigns such as, in the UK, the Justice4Grenfell campaign, and support for Windrush victims. However, it would be quite wrong to see this as signalling the demise of the grassroots groups and activist volunteers that sprang up across Europe in 2015. The reality is that the vast majority of European groups are still going and still responding to the needs of refugees and undocumented migrants, though generally now with a greater emphasis on establishing their sustainability and supporting those refugees that have arrived and are settling in to their new lives in Europe.

Although there may be precarity at the level of individual groups, there is significant stability and continuity within the grassroots com-munity as a whole. Some UK groups are opting for more orthodox modes of development by gaining full charitable status, with its resulting requirements for the governance structures and adherence to finan-cial management and other practices stipulated by the UK Charity Commission. In effect, these groups represent a fresh cohort of NGOs, and it will be interesting to see how they develop and the extent to which they will come to resemble more established NGOs working on refugee and asylum issues – or what new knowledge and practices they may bring to the table.

The overwhelming evidence from the testimonies in this collection is that volunteers radically shifted their political views as a consequence of their engagement with this issue. And as well as campaigning for better treatment of refugees travelling through Europe, grassroots groups have also focused on welcoming and securing permanent rights for those who are resettling in their home countries. Though the number (20,000) of Syrian refugees coming to the UK through the UK Government's Syrian Vulnerable Persons Resettlement (SVPR) programme is very small in comparison with the number of Syrians resettling in Germany, the reality is that many cities and towns, and even some villages, across the UK are hosting Syrian families who have arrived through the scheme, and supporting them is providing a new focus for some of the local grassroots groups that had begun by sending donated goods to Calais and Greece (UNHCR, 2019).

A key question in relation to grassroots groups helping refugees and asylum seekers is the extent to which they represent a mobilised and politicised section of the population. Although many were formed with humanitarian motivations, volunteers have become all too aware of the inhumane policies of some EU member states, and of the hostility being shown towards refugees and asylum seekers by parts of the mainstream media and large swathes of the population across Europe. Many volunteers have become more politically aware and politicised by their involvement in grassroots groups. The extent to which such groups can be linked up and brought together to form a politicised movement remains to be seen. Many groups collaborate on logistics (jointly filling containers, for instance) and campaigning on topical issues such as, in the UK, the Dubs Amendment. In Germany, there is evidence that refugee organisations and groups recognise their power in a context where the federal and state governments are dependent on their support for the implementation of programmes to integrate huge numbers of Syrians and other refugees. In Bavaria, refugee helper organisations and groups participated in a 24-hour "strike" in October 2016 by withdrawing their voluntary labour in protest against the increasingly xenophobic rhetoric being used by some Bavarian politicians. A threatened second strike in February 2017 resulted in representatives of refugee groups being invited to meet the state authorities (Borton, 2016a). The group has since formed a Federal Association of Volunteers under the banner of Unser Veto (Our Veto) and currently has over 8,000 members spread across two-thirds of all German states.

It remains to be seen what course the current tide of nationalistic, anti-refugee politics and policies will take and whether the activist volunteers mobilised since 2015 will be able to link up and influence developments. What is certain is that the tens of thousands of volunteers who were mobilised during 2015 and who have remained committed to an internationalist, welcoming vision will not abandon their principles but will continue working to improve the hostile policies of their governments, and change widely held negative attitudes towards refugees and migrants.

References

Aid Brigade (2019) "Aid Brigade Closedown – Public Statement". www. donate4refugees.org.uk/blog-master/2019-05-aid-brigade-statement.

AIDA – Asylum Information Database (2017) "Country Report: Hungary 2016 Update". www.asylumineurope.org/sites/default/files/report-download/aida_hu_2016update.pdf.

AIDA – Asylum Information Database (2018) "Country Report: Hungary 2018 Update". www.asylumineurope.org/sites/default/files/report-download/aida_hu_2018update.pdf.

Amnesty International (2018) "Greece and the EU Must Move Asylum Seekers to Safety", 6 December. www.amnesty.org/en/latest/news/2018/12/greece-and-the-eu-must-move-asylum-seekers-to-safety/.

Are You Syrious? (2018) "More than 3,000 People Came to Bosnia since January", AYS Daily Digest, 11 May. https://medium.com/are-you-syrious/ays-daily-digest-11-05-2018-more-than-3-000-people-came-to-bosnia-since-january-67ea45ec12d7.

Associated Press in Lesvos (2020) "Police and protesters clash on Greek islands over new migrant camps", *The Guardian*, 25 February. www.theguardian.com/world/2020/feb/25/police-and-protesters-clash-on-greek-islands-over-new-migrant-camps.

BBC News (2015) "David Cameron Criticised over Migrant 'Swarm' Language", 30 July. www.bbc.co.uk/news/uk-politics-33716501.

Borton, J. (2016a) Interview with Rafael Sonnenschein, founder of Integrationshilfe Lläuft e.V., 15 November.

Borton, J. (2016b) "The Humanitarian Impulse: Alive and Well among the Citizens of Europe", *Humanitarian Exchange*, 67. London: Overseas Development Institute. https://odihpn.org/magazine/humanitarian-impulse-alive-well-among-citizens-europe/.

Borton, J. (2016c) Interview with Josie Naughton, co-founder of Help Refugees, 20 May.

Borton, J. (2016d) Skype interview with Clement Blain, former administrator of the "Calais People to People Solidarity – Action from the UK" Facebook page, 29 June.

Borton, J. (2016e) Personal communication with Sumita Shah, administrator of the "Athens Volunteers Information and Co-ordination Group" Facebook page, 27 May 2016.

Borton, J. (2017a) Personal communication with Dave King, 13 March.

Borton, J. (2017b) Personal communication with James Pearce, founder of Phone Credit for Refugees, 13 March.

Borton, J. and Collinson, S. (2017) *Responses to Mixed Migration in Europe: Implications for the Humanitarian Sector*, Humanitarian Practice Network Paper 81. London: Overseas Development Institute.

Borton, J., Niland, N. and Rantsiou, F. (2016) "Humanitarian Europe? Report on a Roundtable Meeting on the Humanitarian and Policy Responses to the 2015 Refugee and Migrant Movements through Lesvos, Greece and into the European Union", Humanitarian Practice Network. https://odihpn.org/resource/humanitarian-europe-responses-to-the-2015-refugee-and-migrant-movements-through-lesvos-greece/.

Brown, K. G. (2017) "France Prosecuting Citizens for 'Crimes of Solidarity'", Al Jazeera, 25 January. www.aljazeera.com/indepth/features/2017/01/france-prosecuting-citizens-crimes-solidarity-170122064151841.html.

Brunner, K. and Rietzschel, A. (2016) "Jung, Weiblich, Gebildet – Flüchtlingshelfer in Zahlen", *Süddeutsche Zeitung*, 24 August. www.sueddeutsche.de/politik/engagement-jung-weiblich-gebildet-fluechtlingshelfer-in-zahlen-1.3118324.

Channel 4 News (2015) "The British Family Helping Thousands of Refugees on Lesbos", 17 September. www.youtube.com/watch?v=7UWa9u-W6eU.

Dearden, L. (2015) "Refugees Welcome: 'Airbnb for Asylum Seekers' Started by German Couple Spreads around the World – and the UK Could Be Next", *The Independent*, 2 November. www.independent.co.uk/news/world/europe/refugees-welcome-airbnb-for-asylum-seekers-started-by-german-couple-spreads-around-the-world-and-the-a6718321.html.

DeLargy, P. (2016) "Refugees and Vulnerable Migrants in Europe", *Humanitarian Exchange*, 67. London: Overseas Development Institute. https://odihpn.org/magazine/refugees-vulnerable-migrants-europe/.

Delcker, J. (2016) "The Phrase that Haunts Angela Merkel", Politico, 19 August. www.politico.eu/article/the-phrase-that-haunts-angela-merkel/.

ECHO (2016) "EU Emergency Support for Refugees and Migrants in Greece: 1 Year On", 16 March. https://ec.europa.eu/echo/news/eu-emergency-support-refugees-and-migrants-greece-1-year_en.

ECRE (2017) "Asylum Statistics 2016: Sharper Inequalities and Persisting Asylum Lottery", *Asylum and Information Database* (AIDA). Brussels: European Council on Refugees and Exiles.

Eggink, E. and McRostie, M. (2016) "The Starfish Foundation: A Local Response to a Global Crisis", *Humanitarian Exchange*, 67. London: Overseas Development Institute. https://odihpn.org/magazine/starfish-foundation-local-response-global-crisis/.

European Commission (2016) "EU–Turkey Statement: Questions and Answers", 19 March. https://europa.eu/rapid/press-release_MEMO-16-963_en.htm.

Francart, E. with Borton, J. (2016) "Responding to the Needs of Refugees and Vulnerable Migrants in Europe", *Humanitarian Exchange*, 67, September. London: HPN/ODI.

Greek Council of Refugees (2019) "Types of Accommodation: Greece", Asylum Information Database/European Council of Refugees and Exiles. www.asylumineurope.org/reports/country/greece/reception-conditions/housing/types-accommodation.

Grunau, A. (2016) "The Tragedy of the 2015 Catania Migrant Shipwreck", *Deutsche Welle*, 13 December. www.dw.com/en/the-tragedy-of-the-2015-catania-migrant-shipwreck/a-36729526.

Howden, D. and Fotiadis, A. (2017) "The Refugee Archipelago: The Inside Story of What Went Wrong in Greece", News Deeply, 6 March. www. newsdeeply.com/refugees/articles/2017/03/06/the-refugee-archipelago-the-inside-story-of-what-went-wrong-in-greece.

Humanitarian Practice Network (HPN) (2016) "Refugees and Vulnerable Migrants in Europe", *Humanitarian Exchange*, 67, September. London: HPN/ODI.

Human Rights Watch (2019) "No Escape from Hell: EU Policies Contribute to Abuse of Migrants in Libya", January 21. www.hrw.org/report/2019/01/21/no-escape-hell/eu-policies-contribute-abuse-migrants-libya.

Karpodini, M. (2015) "Presentation to a Roundtable Meeting on the Humanitarian and Policy Responses to the 2015 Refugee and Migrant Movements through Lesvos, Greece, and into the European Union", Humanitarian Practice Network, 9 December. https://odihpn.org/resource/humanitarian-europe-responses-to-the-2015-refugee-and-migrant-movements-through-lesvos-greece/.

Kingsley, P. (2015) "Greek Island Refugee Crisis: Local People and Tourists Rally Round Migrants", *The Guardian*, 9 July. www.theguardian.com/world/2015/jul/08/greek-island-refugee-crisis-local-people-and-tourists-rally-round-migrants.

Kirkup, J. and Winnett, R. (2012) "Theresa May Interview: 'We're Going to Give Illegal Migrants a Really Hostile Reception'", *The Telegraph*, 25 May. www.tele-graph.co.uk/news/uknews/immigration/9291483/Theresa-May-interview-Were-going-to-give-illegal-migrants-a-really-hostile-reception.html.

Le Clève, A., Masson-Diez, E. and Peyroux, O. (2016) "Neither Safe nor Sound: Unaccompanied Children on the Coastline of the English Channel and the North Sea", *Humanitarian Exchange*, 67. London: Overseas Development Institute. https://odihpn.org/magazine/neither-safe-sound-unaccompanied-children-coastline-english-channel-north-sea/.

Mardini, S. (2019) "I Dragged My Migrant Boat to Safety – Now I Face Decades in Jail for Helping Others", *Metro*, 10 December. https://metro.co.uk/2019/12/10/i-dragged-my-migrant-boat-to-safety-now-i-face-decades-in-jail-for-helping-others-11245438/?ito=cbshare.

Martin, E. C. and Nolte, I. M. (2019) "Might Less Accountability Be More? INGO-Volunteer Relationships in the European Refugee Response", *Public Management Review*, 22(3): 408–431.

Médecins Sans Frontières (MSF) (2015) "Obstacle Course to Europe: A Policy-Made Humanitarian Crisis at EU Borders", January. www.msf.org/sites/msf.org/files/msf_obstacle_course_to_europe_0.pdf.

Médecins Sans Frontières (MSF) (2017) "Hungary: Widespread Violence against Migrants and Refugees at Border", 8 March. www.doctorswithoutborders.org/what-we-do/news-stories/news/hungary-widespread-violence-against-migrants-and-refugees-border.

Médecins Sans Frontières (MSF) (2018) "Out of Sight: Informal Settlements", second edition, 20 February. www.msf.fr/communiques-presse/out-of-sight-informal-settlements-2nd-edition.

Menninga, A. (2015) "Lesvos: Playing Hide and Seek with NGOs", blog. https://alfardmenninga.nl/en/lesvos-playing-hide-and-seek-with-ngos/.

Mertus, J. and Helsing, J. W. (eds) (2006) *Human Rights and Conflicts: Exploring the Links Between Rights, Law and Peacebuilding.* Washington, DC: US Institute of Peace Press.

Migration Aid (2016) "Our Activities in 2015–2016". https://migrationaid.org/en/our-activities-in-2015.

Missing Migrants (2019) "Missing Migrants: Mediterranean". https://missingmigrants.iom.int/region/mediterranean.

National Public Radio (2015) "Risking Arrest, Thousands of Hungarians Offer Help to Refugees", 29 September. www.npr.org/sections/parallels/2015/09/29/444447532/risking-arrest-thousands-of-hungarians-offer-help-to-refugees?t=1572444450459.

O'Boyle, B. (2016) *Mud, Sweat and Tear Gas: Volunteering in the Calais Jungle.* Wheathampstead: I2F Publishing.

Quintano, K. (2019) "A Dead Child Weighs Almost Nothing", *Times of Malta,* 21 August. https://timesofmalta.com/articles/view/a-dead-child-weighs-almost-nothing.729898.

Refugee Rights Data Project (2019) "The State of Refugees and Displaced People in Europe: A Summary of Research Findings across Europe 2017–2018". https://refugee-rights.eu/wp-content/uploads/2018/12/RRE_SummaryReport_2017-18.pdf.

Spindler, W. (2016) "UNHCR Expresses Concern over EU–Turkey Plan", UNHCR, 11 March. www.unhcr.org/uk/news/latest/2016/3/56dee1546/unhcr-expresses-concern-eu-turkey-plan.html.

Travis, A. (2016) "Four Syrian Refugees Must be Brought from Calais Camp to Britain, Judges Rule", *The Guardian*, 20 January. www.theguardian.com/uk-news/2016/jan/20/four-syrian-refugees-must-brought-calais-camp-britain-judges-rule.

UK Action for Refugees (2016) "About Us". www.ukactionforrefugees.com/about-us/.

UNHCR (2019) "UNHCR Welcomes Meaningful New UK Commitment to Refugee Resettlement" 17 June. www.unhcr.org/uk/news/press/2019/6/5d07830e4/unhcr-welcomes-meaningful-new-uk-commitment-refugee-resettlement.html.

United Nations (2017) "Security Council Presidential Statement Condemns Slave Trade of Migrants in Libya, Calls upon State Authorities to Comply with International Human Rights Law", Presidential statement S/PRST/2017/24, 7 December. https://reliefweb.int/report/libya/security-council-presidential-statement-condemns-slave-trade-migrants-libya-calls-upon.

Vis, F. and Goriunova, O. (eds) (2015) "The Iconic Image on Social Media: A Rapid Research Response to the Death of Aylan Kurdi", Visual Social Media Lab, December. http://visualsocialmedialab.org/projects/the-iconic-image-on-social-media.

Witte, G. (2018) "Conditions are Horrific at Greece's 'Island Prisons' for Refugees. Is That the Point?" *The Washington Post*, 16 January. www.washingtonpost.com/world/europe/conditions-are-horrific-at-greeces-island-prisons-for-refugees-is-that-the-point/2018/01/15/b93765ac-f546-11e7-9af7-a50bc3300042_story.html.

Notes

1 Permission from HPN and Sarah Collinson to reuse the material is gratefully acknowledged.
2 The Dublin Regulation provides for asylum seekers to be returned to the state of arrival to process their asylum application, unless their application qualifies for consideration in another member state as a result of either family connections or recent visa/residence criteria.

THE GREEK ISLANDS

For two decades, Greece's islands in the Aegean Sea – chiefly Samos, Lesvos and Chios – have seen regular arrivals of smuggler boats carrying people from the Turkish coast.

In 2015, the number of arrivals rose sharply, provoking a large-scale response from volunteers, humanitarian workers and others to bring people safely to shore and accommodate them.

Greek coast, 2016. Guests of the volunteer rescue ship *Sea-Watch 2* recover after their ordeal at sea.

Image credit: Judith Buethe.

3

Testimonies from the Greek Islands

Sue Clayton

For two decades, the Greek islands of Lesvos, Samos and Chios had seen small numbers of arrivals by boat from Turkey. I will start the volunteers' stories with those older people, older women, who already had a perspective on this crisis.

Katina, now in her sixties, is a Greek woman living on the island of Samos but in a twist of fate had herself been born in Syria; her family, like tens of thousands of others, had fled to the safety of Syria when German and Italian troops occupied Greece during the Second World War. Her son Yannis translates.

> She was born in Syria actually. They went as refugees during the war to Syria, so she was born there. Her father was in the Greek army and so he felt his life was in danger, so they left during the Second World War. From Greece to Syria, so the other way around. A lot of Greeks did that. She was two years old when they came back. She always had it in her, she always wanted to help people. She always helped when the first refugees came from Iraq, from Pakistan, she was always helping. But she feels that she had a different connection with Syrians. She had drunk from the same water, she sat under the same sun, she stepped on the same earth.

He goes on.

> After 1995, they started first arriving. She remembers it was this time of year because they were celebrating Samos becoming part of

Greece. So they were celebrating that and that's why she remembers clearly when it was. They came up from the beach, they were 42 people, carrying the children on their shoulders. She didn't understand at first, she thought they were people on an excursion or coming to the party, didn't understand what it was in the beginning. But then she understood when she went to say "good morning" to them. They thought they were in Italy and she said "No, you're in Greece". She made whatever she had in the house for them. She gave them clothes to change into, whatever she had. There was no telephone at the time, so she went to the next village to use the telephone to call for help.

Soon there were more arrivals.

There was no food, so she brought food as well. She was cooking back then and bringing food to the refugees. Back then they also put them in the old nursing home, and they would stick their hands out of the window asking for help until she went and helped. The first group were coming from Iraq ... Then in 2015, 2016, it was a lot of people. One time, 22 boats came in one day here. Each boat with 60 people in it. The beach was full of life vests. She – Katina – always had an open heart, and would always offer welcome to whoever came. She had very bad experiences also. When they would come in the nighttime, the boats would overturn coming in, they were crying for help, so it was also traumatic. The most terrible thing was the big shipwreck that happened. She always slept with the window open so she could hear the people coming in. It was 2:30 in the morning, she heard them blowing the whistles, calling for help. Her sister was also here so they got up. "We have to get down there", she told her sister, "something is not right... Take whatever you find, clothes and blankets, and we will go down". There were a lot of big waves. One little girl was left alone, calling for her mother, who never came. A man came to Katina with a baby in his arms and he gave the baby to her, and then he went to search for the rest of the family. She took the baby up to the house. The baby was very cold, very blue, very small. She put the baby in the shower – it was hardly breathing, she didn't think it would survive – but when he got warm – slowly, slowly, it was like seeing a miracle ... 11 people survived the wreck but 13 died, all of them in one small boat and most of them women and children. One body was washed up on the beach, the rest were in the boat. She always picked up the clothes that she found on the beach to wash and dry them so somebody else could wear them after.

Another day, Katina went down to collect clothes and she found a dead child on the beach. "It was very hard. She did what she could." Though Katina lived in a close community, she did this work alone. "She would go down and bring them whatever she could – milk, water, cake, biscuits. Back then, from the municipality she also got some croissants and cereal and she helped that way." Were there no services to help? "In the beginning she would try the police, the coast guard, but they usually never came. And after that it was Doctors Without Borders."

The day of the shipwreck she didn't have signal for her phone. She called from the neighbours' house, but no services came until 8 o'clock in the morning. Nobody asked her, 'Do you need help?', nobody asked her anything. Since Doctors Without Borders came to the island, she got their number and she called them to pick up people. She doesn't get any other support, so she always helps alone, not from the neighbours either because they are afraid.

How does she stay strong after seeing so much tragedy? "She says 'There is just no way I could not help them. They needed help and you have to have a heart of stone not to." Does it affect her still? "She feels good that she did something. She says she opened up her house, her bed, her heart, her everything." Is she still waiting for them at night? "Yes, she is always aware." Have you spoken to your neighbours about this? "Yes, they don't care. They cannot do it. They are afraid, don't want to get close. From far away they throw a biscuit or a crust of bread."

It is hard not to read Katina's story as emblematic of all those that will follow here: the instinctive empathy, the explaining of which, though eloquent, is almost an afterthought to the action itself; the dogged acceptance of others' suffering; the resigned knowledge that neighbours and associates may not help – though there is in her final comment a sense of anger and disgust that they don't. All these are themes that we will see in further testimonies, as those urges – of empathy, of tireless commitment, of astonishment that this is happening at all and of anger at those who do nothing – play out time and time again.

Another early responder, **Pepi Lourantou**, who has since passed away, is remembered by her son Evangelos.

> Pepi started her actions in Autumn of 2015 in Lesvos island where she was born. In her sixties, she volunteered to assist the Agkalia (Embrace) project. Having basic first-aid knowledge, she dealt with fixing wounds but also helped with the provisioning of food and other everyday needs. Her initial motivation was the cry for help that was clear from the things she saw through the media and social networking. But even this was nothing compared to the reality the refugees were facing on that island every day. The challenges she faced were many. From every broken foot she mended, caused from the shores and long walking distances, to the lack of communication and shared language, and the eyes of the people that showed both relief for where they were and uncertainty for what was next to come ... She shared this hope for the new beginning in the lives of those people, not knowing at the time that for some there would be no new beginning, only an endless waiting.

Pepi moved to Athens where by now many of the people who had arrived through Lesvos were trapped in overcrowded centres, unable to move on.

> In Athens she continued as a volunteer, always independently, helping out in Elliniko, Faliro, Piraeus and Galatsi. Even though she tried to avoid it, she started bonding with some of the refugees she met. She invited families into her home for food, a warm bath and a few hours of ordinary living. We heard stories of their lives before the war that sounded so similar to our lives. And then there were the stories of loss. Loss of lives, memories, history, dignity.

The moment of separation, every time that these families had to return to the camps, was a moment of awkwardness, embarrassment and shame for taking back what was given only for a few hours. Pepi made every effort as just one person, but most times people joined her. The refugee crisis was one of the most important periods of her life.

Again, we see themes here – of how this engagement has been transformative for so many who have become involved, both on a personal level and on a political one. I argue throughout this book that the "refugee crisis" has redefined for many of us what citizens must do when faced by blatant failures in our governments and institutions. It brings a new understanding to what we mean by humanitarianism – what before may have seemed a rather lofty idealism, a kind of individual moral complexion, now with this new context appears instead a galvanising force for re-appraisal and political change.

As described above in Chapter 2, many of the initial local responders on the Greek islands went on to form civil associations to support the rising numbers of arrivals: the Agkalia (Embrace) project, which has offered support to 17,000 refugees, later won international recognition. Meanwhile, by late summer 2015, spontaneous aid donations were being sourced and arriving from outside Greece, and a new sector of transnational activism was feeling its way into existence. UK volunteer **Jess Coulson** writes:

> My mum had always been pretty anti-refugees, but after a lot of conversations we decided to get some donations together to send to Lesvos. We ended up sending containers out, my mum raising funds and arranging donation collection and shipping. The word "volunteering" doesn't quite encompass the nose-to-the-grindstone graft that went on. I set up our website and social media and helped with the collections and sorting. My mum lives in Cornwall – so we started a campaign there to collect old wetsuits for the volunteers going into the water. And we got bulk energy bars donated. Later I went to Lesvos with more aid and visited the Moria camp. That was very difficult for me because of how

hopeful everyone is when they arrive, how happy they are to be in Europe. By then I had already seen people at the other end of their journey in Calais, how they had been battered and bruised by our European nations and I really struggled knowing what was in store for everyone. I found the whole situation extremely challenging. Also, the backlash from British people towards us on social media. Complete hatred directed at us through Facebook and on our message board. We were accused of funding terrorism, of being responsible for deaths that occur because of terrorism and (as far as I can gather) the downfall of British society.

It was clear that this kind of engagement was something beyond the older style of casual donating to the Oxfam shop or to Live Aid. Sending aid to people without the umbrella of a charity or celebrity call-out was crossing a line – one that was not always discernible to the first international volunteers. **Meghan McIver** experienced this sense of stepping into the unknown in the early days of international volunteering in Greece.

I first went to Lesvos in the autumn of 2015. Like most people I'd been deeply shocked by the photo of Alan Kurdi, the Syrian boy who drowned off the coast of Turkey, but I was hesitant about if I could be of any use. When I arrived I rented a car and just drove around. Suddenly the sky darkened and it began to rain. I parked on the highway and spotted a group of refugees and UNHCR personnel. Someone hustled me into a container unit and told me to hand out dry clothes. Hundreds of women and children began to line up outside. I didn't have time to think – I just dug into the clothes and started to work. Never in my life was I more grateful to open a box and find 100 little colourful socks all tucked carefully inside each other. I gave out clothes until 4 am. The rain never let up, so the container became a makeshift place for people to gather. The UNHCR didn't have flashlights, so I asked some Syrian men to hold their mobiles over their heads to light us, while women and children picked out clothes. People seemed overjoyed just to be on land, and everyone pulled together to remain calm, and even hopeful. Next day the storm was worse. I texted a volunteer I'd met online and she told me that boats had capsized in the night. I looked outside my window and saw clusters of refugees covered in the standard grey UNHCR-issue blankets trying to hide under bus shelters as the rain pelted down around them. I texted my online friend that I would try to find some tarps before meeting her later at a camp. But first, I put a post on social media about what was happening: While "Big Aid" organisations – the UNHCR and others – had been on Lesvos for months, none of them had bothered to put up any decent shelter for the winter, and now the storm was doing people in. For a whole week the rain did not let up, and at times it felt completely overwhelming. Random tourists had taken it upon themselves to transport people around the island, and several times I nearly got hit by erratic drivers. The campsites were wet and muddy and miserable, with crying children and people swarming around small, smoky fires that were too weak to withstand the weather. Human faeces was floating in puddles, and angry, screaming men banded together to tear down the gates of the camps. Honestly, it felt like the most logical thing to do was to walk away from it all. But I didn't. Neither did a small handful of people. We had no choice but to keep going in the face of an overwhelming tragedy unfolding in front of our eyes.

International volunteers are sometimes accused of rushing in with a sense of entitlement, ignoring what is already on the ground. But what I see across the testimonies is that the immediacy of the issues very much dictates behaviours: in emergencies, practical aid had to be put first, and sorting out community relations and protocols would take longer. Meghan continues:

When I look back, I see that we didn't wait for anyone's permission. We just did what we could with the situation in front of us. Someone wrote an article about what we were doing, and it went viral and we raised a lot of money overnight. Literally millions of people were helped by independent volunteers. And from that first trip, my own involvement grew; by 2016 I had co-founded the Information Point for Lesvos Volunteers and we held a conference of local and international grassroots organisations to co-ordinate the work further.

On the smaller island of Samos, **Pru Waldorf** and her colleagues initially worked at the invitation of local government, which had become overwhelmed by the scale of numbers.

In 2015, Samos had thousands of people arriving each month and the local authority didn't have the resources to cope. There were very few volunteers going there and we responded to an appeal from the local municipality. There was no official provision of anything; a small team of local women had been doing their best to feed and clothe everyone, but the situation had escalated beyond their control and they had to cease for fears for their own safety as people became desperate and panicked. They were doing the best they could, but they were massively overwhelmed. We arrived in the midst of all of this. Thousands were being forced to sleep on the concrete floor of the ferry port. Many had no coats or shoes, and the temperatures were dropping and there was torrential rain most nights. There was one Portaloo at the port and at one time there were 3,000 people there. It was filthy and completely shocking. Small children played on the edge of the quayside beside water deep enough for ocean liners to dock and they slept on the hard concrete with no shelter. There was no government-funded provision of food, water, or shelter, and no routine medical care was being given to the refugees, let alone psychological screening or support. No social support or child protection measures were in place. There were no NGOs, INGOs or any UNHCR presence on the island then – just a handful of volunteers, some who stayed for months, others who came for a matter of days or weeks. I was in a team in charge of co-ordinating distributions of clothing and essential items to people arriving on the island. Rather than people arriving getting processed, getting some clothing and moving on by ferry to Athens, numbers were building up as the ferry failed to leave and arrivals kept coming. It was a truly terrifying time and my feet didn't touch the ground for about three weeks. We worked from a small Portakabin at the port and days consisted of literally running back and forward stocking and re-stocking the cabin in a desperate attempt to meet the growing need. We also helped with food distribution. In November of 2015, the anarchist No Borders Kitchen arrived and began providing hot food to the refugees that they cooked from the makeshift camp on the edge of the port, and we worked with them to manage the food distributions in the evenings. Night after night thousands of bemused-looking people queued in the worsening weather long into the night to receive a bowl of stew and bread from a group of punks, accompanied by pounding techno music. It was quite a surreal scene, and sometimes there were moments when everyone relaxed a little and had fun interactions, laughing and dancing and just for a moment these wonderful scenes of human connection were more reminiscent of a festival than of a humanitarian disaster. We created a play area for the children and played circle games in an attempt to give the parents a little bit of respite and to try to provide some semblance of child protection and safety to an otherwise chaotic system.

My initial two-week "recce" quickly became three months before I had even realised that the time had passed. I arrived in September and reluctantly went back home for a break in December to organise a large collection of aid and a panel discussion evening. The event was a success and lots of funds were raised – and we had a container of pre-packed rucksacks bound for Greece. By 2 January 2016, I was back on Samos again and I was there for the rest of that year.

Majida Alaskary also went to Samos, in very different circumstances: from Syria herself and with experience of camps there, she was a refugee living in the newly established Vathy camp, where she began to volunteer with Friendly Human and later the Red Cross. She says, "I offered translation services, and to teach the children in the camp, and I did entertainment for children." Like Pru, who she later worked with, Majida was inspired by collective moments and by the random coming together of diverse groups. She says:

My best activity was coffee night where all people sat and talked to each other in a friendly way, with a cup of tea or coffee. They listened to their favorite music. We made a creative project with Max, an

artist from America. That was very amazing and creative experience for me, because I was equal to them and we gave to the people
some power.

It is clear how vital this human-contact side of volunteering was to
her own sense of survival, as well as others'. She goes on.

Every day is challenge for me, to learn how I can became stronger
and I don't lose my mind or my life, for my mother's sake, before
everything in my life... The worst challenge was in Syria when I was
taken to the jail and I met somebody who was torturing prisoners; he
was absolutely unforgettable. What made me want to help was my
craving to heal from what I had been through when I was in Syria.
Pain, grief, scarcity... to feel that I even still had a life. When no one
and nothing can help me, only myself, then giving the others what
they need helped me to carry on living. Because I identify myself
with them. We came from the same pain, the same wars. We are
mirror of each other.

Majida, like a number of other refugees after they finally get status, chose
to stay on the islands and continue the work she began there when herself a refugee. She continues on Samos and works as a translator and
supports refugee families.

Gradually through 2015–2016 a kind of mixed economy was
established with international volunteers plugging the gaps where the
local islanders could not cope. It took much longer for NGOs to arrive.
Merel Graeve describes how gradually on Lesvos, local and international
systems were set up to cope with the rising numbers.

Lesvos has always known refugees arriving by boats, but I don't
think any of the Greeks could have imagined the thousands that are
arriving each day by now. Sometimes 5,000, 6,000, sometimes 10,000
people in one day. In the morning we arrived to Pikpa refugee camp,
which by the standards of all other camps on the island is an absolute safe haven. It is a camp run by 40 or more Greek volunteers, no
NGOs involved, purely the goodness of peoples' hearts. It's set up
as a transit camp for new arrivals to recover from severe illness or

injury before continuing their journey into Europe. When we arrived we saw families everywhere, and many older people in wheelchairs and on crutches. Inside one of the buildings they have made a make-shift kitchen. We started making a massive stew for around 1,000 people to take to the port. We chopped hundreds of vegetables and potatoes, sliced hundreds of pieces of bread. In charge is volunteer Jason from Australia who was backpacking but ended up based here to use his professional chef skills. At the port, thousands of people are waiting around to catch the ferry to Athens which comes twice a day, for which they pay Eur. 60 per person rather than the standard Eur. 45 for tourist prices. From Athens they continue their journeys further into Europe. When our van filled with massive pots of stew pulled into the port, I couldn't believe my eyes. People with tiny children everywhere with absolutely nothing but the dirty clothes on their backs. I still don't know how to describe the scene, but the only thing it reminded me of are the scenes you see in Second World War films where thousands of Jews are waiting on a platform to board the trains: the feel of disease in the air, the desperation, thousands of traumatised and war-torn people who have nothing, and the uncertainty of where they are going and what's going to happen to their families. I was giving out plates to the women and children. I tried to say hello and smile to everyone, but some of the people, especially the children, you could see they had fever and were very weak and ill. Some told us they hadn't eaten anything in three days, and nor had their children. But we managed to feed everybody, about 1,000 people.

Many of the volunteers who went to Greece in those early chaotic days were trained in their fields – but this did not necessarily prepare them for what they'd be asked to deal with. **Kester Ratcliff**, an academic with legal expertise, said:

From March to August 2016 I worked on Lesvos and Chios, doing mostly legal information provision and asylum interview preparation sessions with Chios Legal Info Point. At some points I found listening to the refugees' stories while doing the preparation sessions was quite overwhelming. I remember an asylum interview prep session on Chios with a man who had the strongest case for admissibility I'd ever heard, but was the most worried about it, and I had to pause for a couple of minutes to compose myself to avoid crying, which I thought would have been insensitive as he was not.

Michael d'Arata, a nurse-practitioner from the USA working at a clinic in Lesvos, had a similar reaction.

One man from Syria, who I saw for a respiratory infection, sat in the chair opposite me stone-faced and impassive. As he was telling me about his cough and fever, his face started to crack as he tried in vain to hold back his tears. Through our Arabic translator I asked him what was wrong. The man started to sob uncontrollably. He told me of a day seven months prior when he and his son were sitting in their living room watching TV, and they heard the thump-thump of a low-flying helicopter outside. Before they could get up to run for cover, a blinding explosion occurred causing part of the roof to collapse and the walls to blow in. In the chaos and panic that ensued, he found his son lying peacefully on the floor with his head tilted to the side as if sleeping. Debris covered the lower part of his body. As the man frantically began to pull off the debris and shake his son to see if he was alright, he saw that his body had been completely severed in half and that the rest of his body lay several feet away over pieces of shattered furniture... As the man spoke, our Arab interpreter Mohammed, also Syrian, became distraught as well and began to sob, as he had his own stories of the barrel bombs and had witnessed similar attacks.

These extremely painful and traumatic stories were something that all volunteers had to learn to deal with and respond to as best they could, and somehow find a way to maintain their professional roles while at the same time showing empathy and solidarity.

One account known to many UK volunteers is that of firefighter **Brendan Woodhouse**; he was later awarded for his bravery for the rescue described below, but I also quote it here as it highlights his struggle to weigh "professional" training – the safety of himself and others – against his instinctive humanitarian responses.

In December 2015, I took a week's leave from work and went to Lesvos. I met some people in a café who said Lighthouse Refugee Relief needed a volunteer medic, and that was it, I didn't see my room again until the day I left. On my last night, I was on lookout at the lighthouse. The sky was awash with stars as I sat looking across at Turkey on the horizon, waiting for sunrise. Then at 5:50 am I saw a boat coming in fast. It was still dark, but I could see tiny lights of phones come on as they tried to guide themselves to shore. I had no time to warn them, just raise the alarm. I woke Hekla, our Dutch team leader, pointed at the boat and then boom! The tubes of the rubber boat had hit the rocks and exploded, causing it to capsize. There were piercing screams as the lights from their phones flew through the air. Then darkness and silence as the precious cargo of the boat hit the water. "What the fuck, what the fuck!" shouted Hekla. Oh shit! No time for conversation. I zipped up my wetsuit and flew down the cliffs. Hekla went back to get the others. Against everything I know about water-rescue I waded in, knowing that here, the rules would save nobody. I could hear names being yelled out. Desperate families trying to find each other. Children just screaming. It was unforgettably horrible. Soon I was out swimming. A woman was screaming over and over and over. A really anguished wail. When the boat had capsized, she like the others had been catapulted into the air and then thrown down into the sea, and in that moment, she'd lost the baby she'd been holding. A woman, her sister, was trying to drag her back to the shore, but she wouldn't move to safety, her arms were outstretched to the sea. There was a floating stack of possessions on the sea: bags, ripped-off life jackets, blankets, all in among spilled fuel. I swam at the things floating away, not having a clue what to do. Thankfully the first bag I came to, that was it – a small baby. Her eyes were in the back of her head, her lips were blue. My heart even today, four years on, is racing when I think how terrible that felt. I swam on my back, baby on my chest. I did little compressions quickly on her chest as I swam, thinking that it might just do something. I shouted at a God I didn't even believe in, "Fucking help me now, this baby does not deserve this!" I was momentarily pulled under, gulping the sea, thinking I was going to die, but just getting closer to the cliffs at the bottom of Korakas. At last my head was out of the water, and I held the baby up and tilted her mouth towards mine. Five rescue breaths for infants, I remembered. I blew the first, nothing. On the second, sea water came out of her nose and mouth and then she screamed. I still can't believe it happened. The little sound of bubbles in her scream. A slight froth on her face. Hekla was wading towards me, her long dreadlocks bouncing as she came. She was angry with me for swimming so far out, but also she was crying, because she told me after, she thought I'd been pulled under and not made it back. "We need to keep going!" she said, but I was done, so she told me to go to help the doctor. She turned and went off pulling people out of the sea. Hekla was only 19 years old herself, but she led us all really well and we trusted her. I dragged myself up the cliff path to the medical room, a battered old building that our team had tried to make into something usable. I remembered how my own daughter had donated baby hats and blankets to me for my early Christmas present before I left, and quickly wrapped the baby up. The volunteer doctor, a Dutch woman called Freeha, was able to cannulate the baby and get her more oxygen. I looked down at this tiny baby, wrapped in blankets and a hat donated by a girl in Derbyshire. The oxygen had been bought with money donated by Derbyshire Refugee Solidarity. I thought about how the baby was here because someone had paid for my flights and accommodation just to get me there. The glass jar in The White Lion in Beeston had collected change from peoples' drinks. Little things like that had made all of this happen... The baby's mum and her sister arrived – they'd heard a baby had been found and when they saw her with the mask on, they broke down, thinking she was dead. I pulled the mask off for a minute and let them cuddle. Then I realised my flight was due to leave and someone bundled me into a car to the airport. On the plane I sat down in shock. I put my head in my hands – my hair was still wet from the rescue. I'd left my mobile phone in the pocket of a coat I'd given to someone, but Matt, who arranged so much transport on Lesvos, called a woman volunteer who was on my flight to pass on the message that baby Sewin was with her mother and they were in hospital together. She'd made it. We both cried and hugged each other.

These were abnormal conditions even for professionals. Many like Brendan were volunteering in their down-time from already demanding jobs – Brendan is a firefighter – parachuting in and out of extreme conditions with no time for briefings or debate. They faced lack of equipment and facilities, as well as unresponsive NGOs and hostile police. The scale of arrivals was massive – thousands arriving daily to small and under-resourced island economies. And there runs through so many volunteer accounts, whether "professional" or not, an abiding shock and disbelief that this was happening, that people were dying without anyone to witness, let alone aid them, in "civilised" Europe. **Anne-Marie Brennan**, a midwife who volunteered on Lesvos and Chios, said:

> After Lesvos I went to Bangladesh in the wake of the Rohingya crisis. I was amazed at how the Bangladesh Government stepped up and organised the accommodation of more than 800,000 people in a very short space of time. It puts Greece and the EU to shame. And it's interesting to compare how small grassroots NGOs and individuals work, compared to the large international NGOs. They all have their strengths and weaknesses. The individuals and small NGOs alone could not have coped with the Rohingya crisis, but in Greece they were essential.

Ariel Ricker, a legal volunteer, echoes this sense that more could have been done in Europe, and faster.

> I moved to Lesvos, because when I was working in Izmir, Turkey, as a legal volunteer, I'd be called from Lesvos by people who'd arrived there from Turkey and needed help. I'll continue doing

legal volunteering for as long as volunteering is needed. I strongly believe that camps such as Moria are not Greek creations, they are EU Hotspots of prejudice, fear and racism, and all of this comes out – regardless of how hard the camp managers and the volunteers and NGOs work, this prejudice and racism all still comes out.

After the EU–Turkey deal in March 2016 (see Chapter 2), optimism about rescues, setting up new camps like Pikpa and co-operation with the late-arriving larger NGOs gave way to despair as refugees realised they may be interned on the islands for years, and volunteers saw that European states were not going to relieve the pressure on collapsing local Greek infrastructures. This brought to the fore a common theme in volunteer debates: were all of us who volunteered simply doing the unpaid work of the state, and making it easier for the establishment to cover up its dirty and macabre secret – that 35,000 people would die in European seas, many within sight of our beaches, and those who made land, living or dead, did not merit expending official resources, but could be left to our unofficial and unauthorised, ever-available, ever-willing care? This was reflected very clearly at the official Vathy camp on Samos in 2016, when the UNHCR team pulled out from supplying vital food and aid in protest when Vathy became a place of permanent detention. Grassroots volunteers working there were torn between wanting to make the same protest, and continuing the never-ending aid supply. They chose the latter. I believe much of the depression and mental health issues volunteers have encountered, of which we will talk more later, stems from a concern that our best instincts, our best attempts at "helping", might not challenge oppressive regimes but simply aid them to manage or contain their "crisis". This constant tension – between providing aid and seeking change – left many feeling powerless and exhausted.

The testimonies below are hard to read, but they must be acknowledged by anyone who really seeks to understand this crisis – and out of respect for those refugees who suffered and the volunteers who were prepared to bear witness. **M**, a volunteer from Italy, says:

I was a volunteer on Lesvos in late 2015; I worked as a first responder. Some days, we would witness the arrival of more than 100 boats, each carrying 60–70 people. I worked mainly at nights, in the dark, which made the work harder and more dangerous. Smugglers were drugging the children to prevent them from crying, and we never knew whether they would wake up again. I never got to know if they did; the flow of arrivals seemed unstoppable and there was never the time to follow up on those you welcomed the hour, the day, the week before. We all were seeing things that we would never see in normal life; there, it was normal. You would see CPR done on small babies – five, six, seven children dying before your eyes. Yet, there was no stress or shock; when you are there, your reaction is different. We would get a cup of coffee and get back to work. Sometimes you would pick up the garbage after the latest arrival, and find that one life jacket was too heavy. I did not find it hard to return to my normal life. I functioned just fine; no nightmares or anything. After three days, I went back to my normal job. What changed is that I no longer had a reaction if I saw a car crash or a dead body; and I guess that is not normal. But my own problems are no longer problems, really. How could they be?

Dillon Savala, an American medic working on Lesvos, describes his time in early 2016.

Urgent messages were circulating on the e-message boards connecting volunteers across Europe: Greece was overwhelmed with arrivals, and Lesvos was getting the worst of it. They desperately needed medical personnel. I posted my experience and the work I had been doing. By evening I was in transit to Lesvos's capital Mytilene – a British nonprofit asked me to jump on board with them. I was blessed to work with a real medical team, including three doctors. The situation was desperate. We were working nights in Moria, the migrant camp there, to register non-Syrian arrivals from Turkey before they could continue on into Northern Europe. There were almost no shelters. Women slept with their infants on dirt grounds. People were burning plastic and dismantling olive trees for firewood. It was truly the worst humanitarian situation I had ever found myself in. There were between 2,000 and 2,500 people arriving on Lesvos every day. It was overwhelming. Our team had a constant flow of medical emergencies, injuries, as well as people needing medication to treat chronic conditions, like diabetes. The doctors saw medical cases as I triaged and provided care within my scope of practice. Our shifts were long, stressful and exhausting. We made it a point to process with each other the traumas we were working with, in an effort to mitigate the impact on our own mental health, but still, the toll that every single shift took on all of us was exacerbating. By the time I had arrived in Greece, nearly 2,000 people had drowned making the journey from Turkey to Lesvos. The Lesvos municipality had run out of burial space for people that had drowned on the journey, and commissioned a refrigerated shipping container to store the bodies until burial. We were asked to help move more bodies. I walked into the container to be surrounded by dozens of corpses... men, women and children, all wrapped in a single sheet, with their internal organs removed to slow the effects of decomposition. Their faces were frozen in time with the expressions with which they'd died and been pulled from the water, not altered to look restful, as would normally be prepared by a mortician for a funeral. I will never forget those few minutes in the shipping container. The day after, I found myself in a deep depression, and was nearing the end of my visa-free time in the Schengen Zone. I made arrangements to leave Lesvos before returning to America. It was a long time before I could do this work again.

Kristina Quintano, a resident of Norway working in Lesvos, posted on social media in 2016:

Today I received an inquiry from one of the Norwegian tabloid papers: a Syrian grandfather has reached Norway and hasn't heard from his grandchildren since they left Turkey. The Norwegian journalist would like to know if we have seen the children – if we could help? My silent answer is yes, we have seen the children. On my phone I have a picture of eight of them – all little children. One has a braid that hangs loosely on one side, just like me. It has become wet, and she has lost her ribbon. Her skin is beautiful, almost porcelain. She looks like a doll, almost transparent. One of the boys has his jacket glued tight against his body, and around his arms he wears a pair of arm-floats meant for a kid's pool. He has lost his football. He won't be needing it. Never again will he get to play football. I know this; his grandfather doesn't. The newspaper insists: Have I seen the children? Are they safe? Together? Yes, they are together. They are beautiful, they are small, they are cold, they are wet – they are dead. All of them. Everyone on that damn boat is dead.

Her posts were part of a broader campaign. In December 2015, she had written an open letter to Norwegian Minister for Immigration Sylvi Listhaug, who wanted to restrict immigration to Norway. It went viral in hours.

Dear Sylvi ... If you do not want to see them in Norway, then have the decency to tell them face to face, because we feel like messengers from hell on your behalf, and we are speechless every time they ask through their tears where they are supposed to go next.

UK volunteer **Ruhi Akhtar**, who works with the group Biryani and Bananas, says:

One of my friends from Iraq trying to seek asylum in Greece always says "Mako Rahma" and he says it over and over again as if in a traumatic trance. Meaning "No mercy, No mercy." All I know is that I have never seen devastation like this, and if nothing else I will tell the world their stories and I will do my best for it to reach as many people as possible. We have been buying supplies, making food packs, new-arrival clothes packs and constantly distributing the last ten days – providing for almost 2,000 people now. Funds are at an all-time low and our warehouses either don't have enough of – or the right – aid. But what I saw today means I don't get to be weak. I don't get to give up.

And nor will we.

Flashpoint: Lesvos and Chios

Kester Ratcliff and Sue Clayton

Figure 3.1 Lesvos, Greece, 2016. Near Korakas, a team from Lighthouse Refugee Relief guides a refugee boat to safety on the rocky shore.

Image credit: Brendan Woodhouse.

The arrival of refugees to the Greek islands began in summer 2015, and was at its height from August 2015 until March 2016. In winter 2015–2016, most of the Syrian refugees came from Aleppo and the surrounding rural areas, since the Russian regime began direct and major military intervention on 30 September 2015, first targeting the biggest city with a majority-opposition population, Aleppo. Most of the

Syrian refugees who arrived at this time were young men. That was because the most common final reason for fleeing Syria was to avoid persecution for conscientious objection to being conscripted to fight for the regime, knowing that the regime did and would order them to commit war crimes, crimes against humanity and genocide crimes. Also, knowing that the route to Europe was dangerous and uncertain, many young men went first, hoping to bring their families later or to send back remittances to support them. Along with the Syrians, refugees and migrants of other nationalities took the opportunity to join the mass migration to Greece and onwards further into Europe: mainly Iraqis, Palestinian stateless secondary refugees who had been resident in Syria, Afghans and Iranians. Smaller numbers of people came from Pakistan, the Maghreb countries, Egypt and Ghana. In total in 2015–2016, at least 1,032,408 people arrived by sea, according to the UNHCR's data. In 2015, it was probably the world's most dangerous irregular migration route. Some of these individuals had valid asylum claims, but European asylum systems in fact operate much by general presumptions about nationalities, so it was (and is) extremely difficult for refugees of nationalities not widely understood to face persecution or war to get their asylum claims recognised.

The three main islands in the Aegean where refugees arrived were Lesvos, Chios and Samos. Most refugees arrived on Lesvos, probably because the departure points on the Turkish side, in the forested bay south of Ayvalık, near Izmir, a major city and transport hub, and patrolled by fewer Turkish police than the departure points around Cesme towards Chios. Also, the strait between Ayvalık and Lesvos is relatively calmer due to its shape, which protects it from high waves.

Lesvos is a large island – it takes at least two hours to drive from end to end, and refugees only arrived on the easterly half of the coastline, so volunteers and NGOs divided up that half of the coastline into four sectors: "North" is from Eftalou to Korakas, with the main base of operations at Skala Sikamineas; "North-East" is from Korakas to Palios, based at Korakas; "South-East" is from Palios to Mytilene city centre; and "South" is from Mytilene to the airport, near to Mytilene

city. Most refugees arrived in the North and South sectors intention-
ally, because those are the safest to land in – long, smooth beaches
and easy access for rescue and assistance. Fewer refugees arrived
in the North-East sector but because it is the most rocky and remote,
with the worst roads, it was disproportionately dangerous. Korakas is
a rocky outcrop with a semi-ruined lighthouse owned by the Greek
Navy, which granted permission to volunteer groups and a few small
NGOs to use it. Korakas hilltop was a useful look-out point for the
range from the North to South-East sectors, and eventually it was
equipped with night-vision goggles and a telescope. Unfortunately,
refugees piloting a boat often for the first time in their lives tended to
steer towards the lighthouse instead of understanding that the lighthouse is a warning signal about rocks.

Figure 3.2 Lesvos, Greece, 2016. A Co-ordination Korakas volunteer installs
steps and LED light ropes to help those arriving weak and with hypothermia to
more safely navigate the cliffs.
Image credit: Patrick McBride.

The main camp on Lesvos is at Moria. During the peak of arrivals in August 2015–March 2016, there grew an unofficial outer camp supported mainly by volunteer groups and small NGOs, which provided aid and services mostly not available inside the official camp. After the EU–Turkey deal was imposed in March 2016 (see Chapter 2), the outer camp – called "the Olive Grove" – was demolished. It has, however, since been re-established by the refugees who cannot fit inside Moria, and who have made makeshift shelters out of tarpaulins, rope and sticks. These freeze in winter, get flooded in spring and catch fire regularly, more often in winter when people improvise potentially dangerous methods of heating and cooking.

On Chios, the official camp Vial is a 1.5-hour walk from Chios city. Food is nutritionally inadequate in calories and nutrients, unpalatable and sometimes rotten on delivery. Mostly it consists of slices of boiled potato. Tensions between Arabic and Afghan speakers became so bad in early March 2016 that most of the Arabic refugees walked to the port one night and stayed there for a week, until the municipality conceded to allow them to camp at Souda, near the port, and at Dipethe, in some abandoned buildings near the city centre. The discord arose because Afghans resented what they saw as preferential treatment given to Syrians, and because of their inability to communicate in a common language to resolve minor conflicts due to living in overcrowded conditions, with very little privacy and because almost everyone was more or less traumatised, and therefore over-sensitive and reactive. The camp at Dipethe was closed in June 2016, and that at Souda was demolished in September 2017.

Since the EU–Turkey deal, the Lesvos camp at Moria has been populated at around three times over official capacity, with nearly 10,000 people; Vial is also running at around three times over capacity. According to SPHERE Humanitarian Standards, the water, sanitation and health provisions at Moria and Vial are grossly inadequate – the ratio of toilets and showers to people is a quarter to a third of what it should be, and the security and privacy arrangements for women are so frightening that some women use adult incontinence pads to avoid

Figure 3.3 Chios, Greece, 2019. A volunteer and an Afgan woman make friends.
Image credit: Mary Wenker.

having to go to the toilet alone in the night. Overcrowding also makes fires more frequent and much more devastating when they do occur. Fires also tend to coincide with unrest, but the Greek fire brigade will not go in to the camp until the riot police are also ready, which always takes too long.

By December 2015, upwards of 600 people per day were arriving most days on Lesvos, Chios and Samos, the three islands closest to Turkey. People were mostly arriving in the night between 1 am and 8 am, to avoid the Turkish Coastguard's patrols, which would have forced them back if they had been caught (and it is really capture, not "rescue"). The refugees frequently reported and showed us videos of brutality and reckless endangerment by the Turkish Coastguard. The first time I met three boatloads of refugees at Tsonia harbour, they told me about how the Turkish Coastguard had aimed a water cannon at them – which could knock them out of the boat, without proper life jackets on – and hadn't stopped even when they had held their babies up.

Since arrivals were mainly from August until March, hypothermia was the biggest danger. Several times refugees arrived alive and then died of hypothermia or complications arising from it. The Aegean islands in winter are surprisingly cold if you are used to living on the west coast of Europe with the Gulf Stream: temperatures were around -7 to -4°C for a week in Lesvos in January 2016. Men usually sat at the front of the dinghies, thinking that they were being chivalrous by sitting in the spray, but because the boats were typically threefold-overloaded, the women and children at the back were usually in water up to their armpits. We received people of varying ages, from two-week-old babies to 80-year-olds, with only one or two plastic carrier bags of things left of all the belongings they'd ever had in their lives.

Lack of lifejackets and worse-than-useless fake lifejackets are also a major danger. Fake lifejackets contain packing foam, which absorbs water so fast it becomes heavier than water within 30 minutes; further, the buoyancy is distributed wrongly so that they flip people face-down in the water instead of keeping them face-up.

Following Germany' decision at the end of August 2015 to suspend Dublin Regulation admissibility tests (see Chapter 2), other EU states on the route from Greece to Germany allowed Syrian and some other refugees to travel through. Thus, from August until late December 2015, refugees arriving on the Aegean islands were mostly moving on again within a month. The situations in the official camps at Moria and Vial were quite degrading, but people were not exposed to their conditions for so long, and they had the hopeful prospect of reaching Germany, or another target country where they already had family. But, starting in November, Austria and Hungary gradually closed their borders, which triggered other states on the Western Balkans route to restrict or close their borders. As more Balkan borders closed, families were less inclined to risk the long journey north, so the numbers of refugees on the islands increased and the inadequate provisions in the official camps became even more degrading due to increased overcrowding, duration of exposure and lack of hope.

The number of refugees who arrived in 2015–2016 was close to the number of people who had been forcibly displaced by the wars

Figure 3.4 Lesvos, Greece, 2015. A volunteer surveys the abandoned life jackets of new arrivals at Eftalou. Almost all of these are fake, and offer little or no protection at sea.
Image credit: Jess Coulson.

and ethnic cleansing in Yugoslavia in the 1990s. The official term for arrivals on such a scale – "Mass Influx" – is significant because such a situation should allow EU protocols to be brought into play. Yet the arrivals of 2015 and onwards were never officially acknowledged publicly as such by European governments; had they done so, it would have been even more obvious that EU states were not executing the EU laws made exactly for such events. That is, in the event of a Mass Influx of persons likely to be in need of international protection, according to Article 78.3 of the Treaty on the Functioning of the EU, all EU member states should have committed to share responsibility proportionally according to their socioeconomic integration capacities.

In the meantime NGOs and volunteer groups continued to provide aid, housing and medical services – and increasingly in Lesvos these functions were left to grassroots groups as NGO presence waned and the unofficial camp around Moria continued to grow.

In 2018, UK charity Help Refugees reported on the following groups it was funding in and around Moria camp. The Timber Project, over the winter of 2017–2018, had installed insulated and raised flooring in over 80 tents, to lift the bases away from freezing ground-water and sewage. Given that three people died in Moria in the winter of 2017 due to the cold weather, this has been very important. The community centre One Happy Family, which ran at some distance from the camp, was managed in collaboration with residents, and its work is ongoing (in Chapter 10, we describe the challenges it has gone on to face in 2020). Its buildings included a clothes shop, school, doctor's clinic and gym, plus a vegetable garden, a playground and a mobile library. There was also a women-and-children's space, a tailor and a barber – largely staffed by members of the community. Moria Medical Support (MMS) filled a gap following the departure of NGOs that had previously been providing evening and night-time medical

Figure 3.5 Lesvos, Greece, 2016. At Moria outer (unofficial) camp, a Co-ordination Korakas volunteer talks with a mother.

Image credit: Patrick McBride.

support for the residents of Moria. Together for Better Days was set up to provide support for women and children, and cultural and entertainment activities, with their mission to "bring dignity and hope to many displaced people living on Lesvos."

Volunteer organisations often found themselves in tension with state governments and the state-dependent humanitarian NGO sector. For instance, International Rescue Committee (IRC) built a high-spec and expensive transit camp at Eftalou on Lesvos, which reportedly cost around Eur. 5 million, but was almost never used because IRC had not co-ordinated with Médecins Sans Frontières (MSF), which had moved much faster and built a transit camp in a more practical location at Mantamados; by the time the IRC camp was ready, it was no longer needed at Eftalou. Often, the bridge between the larger NGOs and the grassroots groups was MSF, which refused Greek state funding in order to conserve its political independence and freedom to advocate, and generally was faster and much more flexible in responding to, and co-ordinating with, volunteer groups.

Figure 3.6 Lesvos, Greece, 2016. Protesters gather outside the port of Mytilene as the authorities begin the process of deporting people back to Turkey following the EU–Turkey deal.

Image credit: Brendan Woodhouse.

Thus, the camps such as those on Lesvos and Chios were terrible places for a temporary stop, but after the Turkey–EU deal and the closure of European borders further north became truly intolerable as long-term homes by default for thousands – made only a little more bearable by the grassroots volunteers, both local and international, who continued to provide food, medical care and legal support in the face of ever-growing hostility from the Greek police. As discussed further in this book, in November 2019 the Greek Government announced that it would close all the Greek island Hotspots and transfer the arrivals to "secure" prison-like detention centres on the mainland. Grassroots groups continued to supply aid and support, facing increasingly high levels of state resistance as they did so.

Then on 8 September 2020, the entire Moria camp on Lesvos was destroyed by fire leaving 13,000 people, including families with babies and young children, without any provision or shelter. In the final Flashpoint "Returns to Lesvos, 2019–20" we will reflect further on this devastating event, the responses of volunteer groups, and what it means for the future of asylum on the Greek islands.

Flashpoint: Samos

Pru Waldorf

Samos is a small Greek island in the eastern Aegean Sea with a population of around 30,000 people, separated from the Turkish mainland by a stretch of water just 1.6 kilometres wide. In October 2015, there were over 25,000 arrivals to the island. Those who made it across were rounded up by police and taken to a facility in the town of Vathy to be processed by the authorities. Thousands slept on the concrete floor

Figure 3.7 Samos, Greece, 2019. Two boys sit overlooking Vathy refugee camp. Image credit: Ruhi Akhtar.

there, with no shelter, food or toilets. Local people responded as best they could, providing dry clothes and food to those arriving. Two Danish women living on the island formed a group called Friendly Humans and worked with local Greek volunteers to provide meals for to up to 800 people a day from June 2015 onward. But the numbers kept rising, and local groups struggled to keep pace. International volunteers began travelling to the island, providing assistance and raising funds through people-to-people solidarity networks. The UK group Calais Action set up an aid shipping and distribution system, working with a local shipping firm, and volunteers and local people collaborated to build a supply warehouse near to Vathy camp. This civil society network of grassroots groups also paid for local Greek women to provide breakfasts at the port, and a kitchen set up by German group No Borders began pro-viding hot meals every night for thousands of people. Volunteers distributed food, water, clothing, footwear, tents, sleeping bags, baby buggies, wheelchairs and all other essential items to people arriving on the island. This continued until the end of 2015, when the larger NGOs, such as the UNHCR, Save the Children, Médecins Sans Frontières (MSF) and the Red Cross eventually arrived and began to co-ordinate their operations with the volunteers.

Until March 2016, the refugee population in Greece was tran-sient and temporary. For the most part the refugees arriving in Samos were, after being registered by the Greek authorities at Samos Port, able to cross to the Greek mainland. However, everything changed on 20 March 2016, with the introduction of the hastily arranged EU–Turkey deal. Under this agreement, Turkey agreed to prevent refugees trying to cross from the Turkish mainland to Greece – the "Gateway to Europe" – and agreed to take back those whose claims for asylum in Greece had been rejected. For each failed asylum seeker returned to Turkey, one Syrian refugee would be accepted into the EU. In return, Turkey would receive up to Eur. 6 billion in payments and the EU would provide visa-free travel to Europe for Turkish citizens.

At the beginning of April 2016, the Greek Parliament adopted a law imposing blanket "restriction of movement" on new arrivals inside closed facilities at border entry points for up to 25 days during the reception and identification process. All new arrivals on Samos were therefore immediately detained and held in the detention facilities at Vathy.

All onward travel to the Greek mainland was prevented until the outcome of asylum applications had been decided. The Vathy camp was designated an EU "Hotspot" (officially termed a Reception and Identification Centre – RIC). Staff from Frontex (the European border and coastguard agency) and the EASO (European Asylum Support Office) were deployed to the island to introduce more rigorous systems for screening and fingerprinting the new arrivals. Almost overnight, the status of the island changed from being a "staging post" to a place of containment, uncertainty and suffering.

Responsibility for the provision of services for those seeking asylum was handed from local municipal control to the Ministry of

Figure 3.8 Samos, Greece, 2016. A child faces indefinite detention in the Vathy camp in April 2016 after the EU–Turkey deal freezes refugee movement.
Image credit: Pru Waldorf, with parental permission.

Migration for Greece, and so the army and the police assumed control of security of the Vathy camp. Its capacity of 640 had already been exceeded before the EU–Turkey deal, but in March 2016 it rapidly became severely overcrowded as all refugees on the island (at that time numbering around 3,000) and all subsequent new arrivals were detained inside. Within weeks the UNHCR Samos mission, opposed to the forced detention of asylum seekers, suspended all activities at Vathy, making a press statement on 22 March saying: "Under the new provisions, these so-called 'Hotspots' have now become detention centres." Médecins Sans Frontières (MSF) also withdrew its teams from the Aegean islands after its head of mission in Greece made a statement, also on 22 March, saying, "continuing to work inside a closed facility would make us complicit in a system we consider to be both unfair and inhumane". As a result of these withdrawals, all local NGOs funded by the UNHCR were left without contracts to operate and were unable to provide services in the Vathy camp. In the absence of any responsible agencies, it fell to the volunteer groups to devise systems once again. So, with no support from official agencies and working in an increasingly more hostile environment, they began covering all kinds of social support, trying to help rebuild shelters for people and conduct a census of who was in the camp, as well as a needs assessment. They provided all essential items, including clothing, baby milk, nappies, toilet paper, sanitation products, personal hygiene products and medical care, even though this was an EU-funded facility. They did this for a three-week period.

EU funds were later spent on the facility, but most went on security measures rather than improving the capacity of the centre or its facilities. Bigger fences went up and large bale-like rolls of razor wire were put into newly created "dog run", which ran along the perimeter of the camp. The police and security presence in the camp was doubled and the army took official control of basic provisions such as food and water. A large EU sign went up outside the camp claiming that it was an EU-funded facility – a sign duly photographed and circulated by the EU – but there remained no provision by them of tents or clothing, nor psychosocial activities or safe spaces for

Figure 3.9 Samos, Greece, 2016. The *ad hoc* cinema run by volunteers every Friday and Saturday night in the early years of Vathy camp.

Image credit: WeAreOne:collective.

children. During this time the UNHCR staff "lost visibility", as they called it, removing their official UNHCR bibs. They were still present on the island, "observing and advocating", visiting the camp and in the surrounding area daily, but they declined to support volunteers by providing personal or essential items.

To compound this, tensions over asylum processing and the preferential structures built into the process of assessment were rising. Other nationalities complained that Syrians were often given access to food and medical services while they had to wait. Rumours about certain groups being "sent back" to Turkey began to circulate. As numbers continued to grow, things reached breaking point. In May of 2016, sporadic fighting broke out between several groups of men and escalated over the course of two days. Dozens of people were injured, and hundreds lost their few remaining possessions when their meagre shelters were destroyed in a fire that started during the riot.

According to volunteers, the aftermath of the rioting and destruction of the camp was dreadful. In the midst of the chaos vulnerable unaccompanied minors, left alone and afraid at the prospect of being harmed in the violence or returned to the "first safe country" under the EU–Turkey deal, fled the camp and went underground, taking their chances at crossing to the mainland. This left them undocumented and therefore vulnerable to exploitation and abuse. Other camp residents doused themselves in petrol and set themselves alight in desperation. One man was very badly burned and was hospitalised and eventually sent to a secure psychiatric hospital in Athens.

Following this event, volunteers on the island contacted Human Rights Watch, which prepared a report in May 2016 which found the Vathy camp to be "severely overcrowded with a lack of basic shelter and filthy, unhygienic conditions. Long lines for poor quality food, mismanagement and lack of information contribute to the chaotic and volatile atmosphere".

After the rioting and the increased press attention, the UNHCR officially resumed activities in the camp, doing so in the capacity of "supporting" first reception. In 2017, MSF issued the results of a survey that described the situation on Samos and Lesvos as a "dramatic

Figure 3.10 Samos, Greece, 2017. Maggots are common in the one imported meal a day officially served in Vathy camp – noted in a sustainability report carried out by WeAreOne:collective.

Image credit: WeAreOne:collective.

mental health emergency". In Samos, the survey found that close to a quarter of people surveyed had experienced violence in Greece. Half of that violence was described as beatings, 45% of which were committed by the police or army. The survey found that people who had arrived on Samos after the EU–Turkey deal reported more violence in Greece than people on the mainland, who had arrived in Greece before the deal.

Due to a continued focus by the EU states on "detention and security", a lack of priority was given to humanitarian support, and no one held the Greek Government to account for its lack of adequate service provision. The processing of asylum claims was also incredibly slow, and consequently numbers detained on the Greek islands continued to rise while conditions on Samos grew steadily worse. In February 2019, a team from the European Court of Auditors highlighted the situation faced by the unaccompanied minors.

> We visited the minors' section of the "Hotspot". It had seven containers. Some had no doors, windows or beds. The official capacity of each container was eight to ten minors, but around 16 minors were staying in each, even sleeping on the ground; 78 more were in tents or derelict buildings outside the Hotspot, in unofficial extensions to the facility. Nine unaccompanied girls were sleeping on the floor in a ten-metre-square container.

By the autumn of 2019 there was a new spike in arrivals on Samos, with between 40 and 75 people arriving each day. The appalling conditions led to increased tensions resulting in frequent violent disturbances and reports of crime – mainly stealing food – within the town of Vathy. The numbers in the camp and surrounding area were more than 6,000 by October and the facilities were completely at breaking point. In October 2019, after one more protest, a fire broke out in the "Jungle" area surrounding the camp. It destroyed hundreds of tents and wooden constructions that had been the only source of shelter for more than 700 people, who were then forced to flee into the town.

In October 2019, Giorgos Stantzos, Mayor of East Samos, warned that the fire had brought Samos to breaking point as hundreds of people were now having to sleep in the streets and public squares and that "the island has become destabilised". In November 2019,

Figure 3.11 Samos, Greece, 2019. Syrian Kurds at Vathy protest that they are not being allowed their legal right to claim asylum.

Image credit: Pru Waldorf.

Human Rights Commissioner of the Council of Europe Dunja Mijatović severely criticised the Greek Government for the conditions faced by the refugees on the Aegean islands, stating:

> It is an explosive situation. There is a desperate lack of medical care and sanitation in the vastly overcrowded camps I have visited. On Samos, families are chipping away at rocks to make some space on steep hillsides to set up their makeshift shelters. This no longer has anything to do with the reception of asylum seekers. This has become a struggle for survival.

In the Postscript of this book (Chapter 10), there is an update on current conditions in Samos in March 2020 as the situation continues to escalate.

THE CENTRAL MEDITERRANEAN

In late 2013, the Italian Navy launched a large-scale operation, Mare Nostrum, that went out into international waters to look for refugee boats in distress, most of which had departed from Libya. The hope was that the EU would take over the funding. However, the EU replaced Mare Nostrum with the controversial Frontex operation, far more limited in its scope and much criticised for its practices, and so much of the sea-rescue work fell to NGO and volunteer crews. The Italian island of Lampedusa, close to the North African coast, has for many years been a focus of boat arrivals; as the rescue operations changed, Sicily and Malta also became key areas for new arrivals.

Central Mediterranean, 2019. The crew of the *Sea-Watch 3* on Mission 18: the rescue of shipwrecked refugees taken to a port of safety in Italy.

Image credit: Doug Kuntz.

4

Testimonies from Southern Italy, the Sea-Rescues and Malta

Sue Clayton

While international volunteers poured to the Greek islands relatively quickly, the situation in southern Italy was rather different. Numbers of arrivals by sea were very high – particularly to Lampedusa, as it was relatively close to the African coast. Compared to Greece, local and government authorities were more visibly present in organising immediate material concerns like accommodation. However, on Lampedusa this provision was still limited. **Lillo Maggiore** speaks for those Lampedusani who wanted to do more.

> We are a family of five in total; we have two daughters and Seidou, who arrived in Lampedusa from Senegal six years ago. First, we were his foster family then he chose to remain with us when he turned 18. "I would like to stay, if you want me", he told us. I said "We are your family. You are free to leave, if that is what you wish, but this is your home and we could not be happier if you stayed." Now he is 22 years old; he works for a clothing chain, warehouse work and fabric printing. Did we face problems? Yes, at the beginning; Lampedusa is a small community, and we represent Italy a bit – we have those who are in favour of welcoming and those who are not. When Seidou came to live with us, there were people who said "What are they thinking, taking him in their own house, knowing nothing of his story!" Now they know him; he himself is part of the community.

Racist incidents? No, never. Sure, there are debates. And yes, you raise your voice sometimes. But aggressions? No. Though we heard about an incident in Cosenza, Calabria in September 2019 – a man attacked a three-year-old child from North Africa who came close to touch his baby on the street in Cosenza. Passers-by stopped the man and called an ambulance. Shameful. Maybe we are not exactly like the rest of Italy.

Lillo has become increasingly unhappy about the lack of state-provided facilities.

The Hotspot facility is not good reception. Men, women and children share overcrowded facilities that are barely tolerable for an adult, let alone for a baby. The official capacity is 95; the average number of "guests" is 300–350. Since 14 October (2019) about 400 people have been staying there, many of them women and minors. They wait weeks, sometimes months, to be transferred to Sicily or to the mainland and be assigned to a reception centre.

Lillo's anger about the broader picture is clear.

Europe speaks, but does not act. We need more democracy and fewer walls; respect for human life. The world is property of nobody; every individual has the right, must have the right, to migrate through legal ways, without putting their own life at risk. But things are going in the wrong direction. We need better media reporting, neutral and committed journalism. We need to push education towards a more welcoming culture. The biggest challenge we face is bureaucracy. It is one thing to receive arrivals at the port; you hand them a tea, a blanket and a smile, let them know that they are welcome. Emotional and physical support, in response to their immediate, most urgent needs. Entirely different is to deal with the challenges posed by the current legislation. My family owns two apartments; the second one we keep for guests and sleeps four. We would be happy to host some of the arrivals when the Hotspot is full, which is almost always, but the law forbids that. All we can do is to offer them a warm meal in our house, a shower, some fresh clothes. Even becoming a foster family is not easy; documents, permits, passports – it takes a lot of energy, time and commitment. And sometimes that is not enough.

He has clearly made strong attachments to the new population.

I will tell you about Bakeri. I met him on the main road of Lampedusa. He was alone, he was ten years old and came from Eritrea. He had a throat infection and struggled to speak. I said "Come home with me, you need warm liquids, my wife will make you tea and a soup." He accepted right away. For about 20 days, he came daily to our house. He was showing affection and the feelings were mutual; so we asked him whether he would consider staying to live with us. He was thrilled; a life with Papà Lillo and Mamma Piera and the possibility to go back to school! We contacted social services to become his foster family; we presented our case to the Tribunal of Minors of Agrigento. We managed to stall his transfer from the Hotspot to the mainland to buy time, while waiting for the court to process our application. But one Sunday morning he was forced to board a ship; witnesses reported his resistance and desperation. The authorities ignored his protests. He was taken away from us without a word; we never knew exactly what went wrong or where he was taken. Some time later, I was in the countryside, my cell phone rang. I could not believe I was hearing his voice! Somehow he had managed to track down my number. He had been staying at a reception centre, but he let me know that he decided to try to reach Sweden. We were not in touch again until one year later, when I found him on Facebook. He accepted my invite to connect instantly! He now lives in Sweden with a foster family, goes to school and is doing well. But he looks forward to becoming 18 to return to Lampedusa to see us again. Many pass through our house; when they leave to build their own life, or to join their relatives in other countries, they never forget us. We speak often through Skype. Sometimes they come to visit. Alex and Teame are two survivors of the shipwreck that occurred on 3 October 2013 in which nearly 400 people lost their lives. They were with us for four months before leaving Italy for northern Europe. Now Alex lives in the Netherlands and Teame in Norway; they both

got married and have children. But every year on 3 October, they
return to Lampedusa to commemorate those who did not survive.
During their stay, we are reunited at our house.

This last point is particularly remarkable; the marking of anniver-
saries, and mourning and respecting the dead, is hugely important
here, both for those who survived the journey and those who have
borne witness. (This is discussed further in the Flashpoints on Sicily and
Lampedusa). It is one of the factors that has driven the work of artist
and activist **Giacomo Sferlazzo,** who co-founded an art and museum
collective.

> Collettivo Askavusa in Lampedusa was born in 2009. We have
> done many things in different areas. We dealt with the recovery of
> objects belonging to migrant people passing through the island –
> objects that were inside the boats used for the crossing from Libya.
> The boats were first seized and then were to be destroyed with
> everything left inside. The Italian state has been destroying an
> enormous historical and cultural heritage that has very strong pol-
> itical implications. We have found many of these objects including
> photos, letters, and sacred texts – and these are now on display at
> PortoM, our museum and headquarters. At the exhibition we get
> many visits and after "the meeting with the objects", people can
> stay to discuss, and we try to give our vision of migrations starting
> from two questions: "Why do people have to leave their country?"
> And "Why can't they travel in a regular way?" We have carried out
> direct activities with the "migrants" giving support both for material
> needs and for political reasons during protests, for example against
> the living conditions and the forced detection of fingerprints inside
> the Hotspot. Here we are not only dealing with migration but also
> with many issues relating to the island on which we live, and issues
> that are often never associated with migrations but that instead
> are closely related to the militarisation of borders. Lampedusa is a
> militarised island [with a] strong presence of radars, antennas and
> pylons for telecommunications in addition to several barracks and
> inaccessible military areas.

As in other places this book surveys, the "refugee issue" is a layer among further layers of history and culture, that need to be unpicked to make sense of the present. Giacomo goes on.

> I do not feel European, I am a child of the Mediterranean. I do not "support" refugees – I fight together with them, and with those who want to overturn centuries of exploitation, colonisation and imperialism that have seen European states act as the bloody protagonists who have practiced violence and exploitation of man on man and man on nature. What I do together with the Askavusa collective is the result of a vision we have of the world, in which a minority has too much and a majority is reduced to slavery and hunger. I believe that the migration issue must be handled starting from a new anticolonial and anti-imperialist consciousness, otherwise we risk self-referencing and unnecessary quarrels. And, even worse, we risk playing the game of global capital, which sees migrants as goods and commodities to be used, and in the migration issue an ideological weapon, a political bargaining tool.

Local Lampedusan people were also directly involved in boat rescues, sometimes through pure chance. Carmine Menna, his wife Rosaria and some friends were out sailing on 3 October 2013 when they witnessed one of the biggest Lampedusan shipwrecks, which had 366 fatalities. Carmine fearlessly organised the rescue of many from the sea, and he and his group offered help and comfort to those who finally got to land, injured and bereaved. His story was spread by international media and has been documented by UK author Emma-Jane Kirby as a memoir, *The Optician of Lampedusa*. It is worth noting that Menna rightly received universal respect for his actions, where by contrast the voluntary rescue ships – committed to patrolling Mediterranean waters since the EU ceased funding the Italian Mare Nostrum operation and replaced it with the essentially hostile Frontex force – are increasingly met with open hostility by both media and governments, and their crew members subject to heavy fines and threats of imprisonment. Below, I record testimonies from some of the rescue crews working in the triangle of sea between Tripoli, Malta and Lampedusa, where wreckages of the boats leaving Libya are most likely to occur. These accounts, though some-times painful to read, are stories volunteers want to be known, so that people understand the true horror of deaths at sea – horrible perhaps most of all because they are for the most part preventable even after those craft have left port. It is widely known in the volunteer and NGO sector that as many as 90% of life jackets purchased by those in Izmir for the Turkey–Greece crossing, and in Tripoli and Sabratha for the Italy–Malta crossing, are fake, padded only with water-absorbing foam or even newspaper. Many of the vessels, too, that are sold or offered to those risking the crossing are made of cheap substandard materials, and are not remotely seaworthy. Thus, shipwrecks are doomed to happen all the time, and are not just occasional mishaps caused by bad weather or poor navigation. And it is why the volunteer missions place great importance on proactively patrolling the sea rather than simply, as Frontex forces do, docking hundreds of miles away until a distress call is put out. It is a question worth considering – why many publics can accept the idea of serendipitous rescue, like Carmine Menna's, but see systematic patrol missions as somehow pandering or giving in – "providing a taxi-service for refugees" as one right-wing pundit called it. As Giacomo discusses above, and as people on Lampedusa understand, the causes of mass migration must be tackled at source, by addressing global inequalities, and no one should even be entertaining the obscene debate over why human beings, including babies and children, should not benefit from rescue patrols, or whether those that provide such rescues should face lifelong jail sentences.

Arturo Centore describes himself as a true European – "I am an Italian citizen living in Ireland, working between UK and Germany." He has completed several missions with Sea-Watch and describes a recent mission here.

> I joined Sea-Watch in March 2019 as one of the captains of the *Sea-Watch 3* vessel. In my last mission in May–June 2019, we did a rescue off the coast of Libya; 65 lives were rescued, and the survivors taken to the closest port of safety, Lampedusa. As a result of our docking, legal and political problems arose for myself, the vessel and the

Sea-Watch organisation. However, the priority of our mission, the rescue of people at sea, was achieved. This last mission was of a high significance for me, every moment was very intense and emotional. Even though I had served on another of the search-and-rescue (SAR) Coast Guard vessels a few years ago and rescued people in distress before, this time was different because I know the people we rescued are unwanted by everyone.

Arturo remembers the moment he met those they rescued.

For me, the most important and most remarkable moment was at the completion of the rescue. I saw desperation and suffering but also happiness and joy in their eyes. A mix of feelings and a different perspective on life. It was very emotional. When you see them in the newspapers they are just numbers, you are not connected, but those 65 were humans, like me. Each of them with a story to tell, a relation, a family for some, with dreams and hopes. When you are there in person you start to think with your heart more than your brain. And thanks to them, you even forget that mostly we on shore don't want them – that people who have not met them, hate them. The other moment that stays with me was when an Italian military vessel came alongside ours to notify me that I was under investigation for human smuggling and that our ship was confiscated. But at the same time, when the military vessel took me on to their ship and I was looking at the rescued people, I thought "This was all worth it, and no one should be blamed for saving lives". In that moment I understood what was important to me. And even now that I am under investigation I think I could not have done any differently, not even in respect of the humanitarian and international laws. I just did like any other human being would have done. If we had not done it, they would be dead. And from off the coast of Libya, the only closest places, safe to reach, were Italy and Malta. But because Europe is implementing policies that are closing borders, it is not easy and is legally challenging – especially in Italy with the new rules on immigration, is becoming a real challenge. I am a convinced Europeanist and I believe in Europe and its foundations. I feel part of a great community, that even without a common language shares the same roots. But at the same time, I was surprised and felt let down by the European countries' response to the migration problem. In my case, no European country has seriously taken the lead in the situation, they all just replied that we were not welcome in their territory with our cargo of illegal immigrants. Very sad indeed, but this is the result of modernity. A fake globalisation, a fake modernity. Since centuries we are exploiting African soil and we have humiliated indigenous people through colonisation – and now that we should give something back, we turn away.

Arturo is also very clear on the politics of what they see on the Libya–Italy route. Many of those using it are African migrants, who often face racism and discrimination. Arturo goes on.

Very often people living in Europe do not understand the reasons that lead Africans to jump on a rubber boat as their last hope towards freedom and maybe a better life. Politicians describe them as another problem we need to get rid of, instead of encouraging people to embrace diversities and offer help. And not forgetting that many of the African issues came with the "developed" countries' colonisations. We spoiled and continue to spoil their resources through our multinationals to the benefit of few and the suffering of many African citizens.

Another Sea-Watch volunteer, **Merlin Koetz**, says:

I am a volunteer for Sea-Watch and have been conducting search-and-rescue (SAR) operations in the Central Mediterranean off the coast of Libya. I am part of the medical team within the ship's crew, being a registered nurse, and an occasional cook – and went on three missions over the last three years. Some memories for me stand out quite heavily: the first was spotting a migrant boat for the first time. That was when reality hit me, realising that it is actual people in actual distress situations, and that it is truly happening. I have read countless articles, seen footage and heard first-hand experiences from my wife who participated in SAR operations prior to my own first mission. Apparently, somehow I still managed to look at it from a certain distance that allowed the illusion of it all still having been "made up". The second was taking guests on board for the first time. I remember a young woman falling to her knees, crying. That was the second time reality hit me – this stuff is real, happening, and totally incomprehensible. How are any human beings able to treat their own kind like this? To abandon someone to their fate like this? Another memory that will be with me forever is the near-miss with a patrol boat of the so-called Libyan Coastguard. It was 10 May 2017. The footage is well-known: you can see how the patrol boat crossed the bow of *Sea-Watch 2* by only a handful of centimetres. I was in the galley at that time and saw the boat taking over from our portside and the white stern wash, and I immediately held on to what was within reach because I was certain that we were going to crash into each other. Such behaviour symbolises the recklessness of the "coastguard" ... Another thing I would like to mention is something that fills me with delight. The gratefulness of our guests! We may play it down afterwards, we can hardly imagine what hell and fears they had to go through, but when they realise that they reached safety and that they did so thanks to the efforts of the SAR crews, the amount of instantly materialising love is overwhelming. It forms a bond that is beyond regular acquaintances. I do not mean to sound like bragging about it. It is just different, very genuine and wonderful.

But Merlin was very aware that after the first reactions, skill was needed to relate to people in an appropriate way.

After days with guests on board, they started to fear we would bring them back to Libya. They all were – without exception, and that includes Libyans as well as everyone else – ready to die rather than go back. People from my orbit, when they talk about fear, they mean stuff like fear of heights of losing their jobs. Which is all right; it is perfectly fine to have those fears. But the fear you could see in the faces of our guests, though, was different and more sincere, if you can call it that. It was fear for their lives. At first I myself found it hard to make contact that went beyond the initial small talk. I felt as if I was not worthy enough to get to know them better. I mean, what was I going to tell them? My life has been ridiculously easy compared to theirs, and I felt shame and guilt for that. Who am I to tell them how strong they are for having made it that far, without ever having had to be that strong myself? On the other hand, the situation is not about me, and I am very grateful for my fellow crew members who always did an incredible job with the guests whenever I could not. This is one major thing I have learned about myself – I will do my best to pull myself together to be there for the guests.

Like Arturo, Merlin sees this as a sort of front line of politics.

It amazes me how ignorant and pure evil Europe seems to be in the ways they are handling the situation (or their lack thereof). But I think that after roughly four years of work by Sea-Watch and similar NGOs (Sea-Eye, MOAS, Jugend Rettet, SOS Mediterranée, MSF...) a certain public awareness of the matter has been established. Although there are both opposing and supporting positions, I have a feeling that it is slowly shifting towards the better, the rather supporting end of the spectrum again. We have to keep up the reports so as to never let the matter fall into oblivion. We are on the right track, and we need to carry on, in the name of humanity and for people worldwide.

It is of course the medical staff who are at the very rough end of the rescues. Many are able to do one or two missions a year in their leave from full-time jobs. **Yanick Bonichon** is a paramedic from Hamburg in Germany. He says:

I took part in several missions with the *Sea-Watch 1* and *Sea-Watch 2*. Since I'm a medical student and paramedic I know about the good conditions in Germany concerning our health system and medical care. Being on your own and with very limited access to proper medical equipment, it was quite challenging to just stick to the basics and sometimes hope for the best. In one case, we had four minors with horribly infected wounds from scabies. They had been held for months with about 100 others in a basement building while in Libya to extort more money from their relatives. This was the first and only time in my career as a paramedic that I had to breathe through and calm myself before getting to work. Parts of their clothes were fused with their wounds so it took hours to get it all out and to properly cover them up. All of that while an Italian navy vessel was close by with much better medical facilities, refusing to help us. Doing this work has changed me a lot. In the summer I go to festivals to sell Sea-Watch merchandise and raise awareness about what we do. While we were at the Wacken Open Air Festival talking about our work, I came in contact with a lot of right-wing people. They were eager to tell us how bad we are, and that in fact we worsen the problem in the Mediterranean. It was interesting to see what these people actually believe and what kind of news and information they consume. Even when I was talking about my experiences onboard, they would still call me a liar and refer to some obscure fake news about deals with the smugglers. They wanted to see us in prison, our ships should be wrecked and so on. Telling them about all the official investigations without any proof of wrongdoing in the end – court rulings in our favour – wouldn't change their mind. It feels like an impenetrable wall of arguments built around their minds to shield their racism. And of course none of them was a racist, just a *besorgter Bürger* – "concerned citizen" – as they are called in German. One guy in particular told me that he took part in the operation "Defend Europe" [a far-right group that chartered a ship in the Mediterranean in 2017 to try to stall the volunteer rescue missions] and that he is very skilled in martial arts. He then took photographs of our faces and walked away.

He goes on.

My family is always very concerned about the effect this work might have on my mental health. I had to persuade them that there will be professional care in case I get traumatised. Which of course didn't help very much. After my second and third mission with Sea-Watch I felt quite alienated being around all the very rich people on Malta while there are people fighting for their lives just some 100 kilometres away at our borders. We had to drive through the Grand Harbour, passing by the super-yachts. I just couldn't believe what people value in their life and their urgent need to show it to everyone. It took me some time to forget about these things and feelings and to blend in again. I am a lot more introverted than before and I donate much more money to small NGOs.

I hesitated to include some of the text below for fear the graphic detail somehow objectifies people who have died, and disrespects them. But these are testimonies I was sent, and like the yearly memorials on Lampedusa, the very least we must surely do is bear witness to this reality. **Barbara Held** is a medic who has done a number of missions with Sea-Watch. These are her some of her diary entries.

22 October 2016. After the attack of the Libyan Coastguard. For 59 hours now, we have been working almost continuously, far beyond our physical and psychological limits. None of us have slept more than six hours during this time, and most of the time only in a niche with the radio on our ears. It started well. On the first day, together with the *Bourbon Argos* ship of Médecins sans Frontières, we rescued more than 600 people from wobbly rubber dinghies. We were all exhausted, but happy. About 10 pm we were finished with the clean-up. Around 1 am we were called to a rubber dinghy in distress. A boat of the Italian Coastguard should be taking up those in distress. I was on the tender boat. It was our first rescue at night. Antonin and Melanie communicated super-professionally with the people who sat crowded on the boat. Although they were very restless and anxious, we had the situation under control until the so-called Libyan Coastguard came and pushed us away from the boat as we were about to start distributing life jackets. One of the coastguards went on the boat, insulted and beat the refugees and trampled over people, of whom many were lying on the ground, up to his goal, the engine (engine-fishing is a popular method in the Mediterranean to earn something in addition; however, most fishermen and also the other Libyan Coastguards wait until we have recovered the boat before they get to their prey). The refugees panicked, and the first one jumped into the water and swam towards

us. In such a case we drive backwards, in order not to encourage further people to follow his example, because otherwise such a boat capsizes faster than we can deal with. But more followed, and when we saw that they had big problems keeping themselves afloat, we – Bastian and Melanie – pulled the people out of the water in the second tender boat. At that time I didn't see exactly what was happening on the boat, but the panic grew audibly. On the radio we learned that the Italian Coastguard ordered us to leave immediately, as the situation was too risky and the Libyan Coastguard was aggressive. At about the same time we saw the boat capsize. Nobody was wearing a life jacket. Our captain refused to obey the order and I heard him scream: "There are people drowning! We are not going to leave the scene! Fuck off! Mayday Mayday Mayday!" And also Antonin, Melanie, Bastian and Bianca would never have left while seeing the people drown. The *Sea-Watch* turned on, the whole crew on the *Sea-Watch* and the tender boats threw life jackets, life rings and CentiFloats into the water. We pulled people out of the sea one by one, or provided them with life jackets. Then we had three people by our side who panicked, grabbing for the rib. Two had made it, one was shortly behind. Melanie and I reached for him, hung far overboard, but couldn't reach him. A few minutes later he was right in front of us again. We pulled him out lifeless, I tried to resuscitate him, alone because Melanie and Antonin were rescuing more people – doing cardiac massage on a rubber dinghy with soft ground and an Ambu bag without oxygen. I soon had to realise that it made no sense and that others needed my help more. I pulled living people gasping for air onto the corpse. Eventually we had 120 completely exhausted, salt-water-vomiting people on board and four dead bodies. We showered the young men, because the petrol burned into their skin. Some searched desperately for friends and relatives, but they could not find them on the ship; 20 to 30 other people had drowned, but we could not find them because the Libyans were threatening us and the next emergency was already announced. And – I think – seven more that day. But I'll write about that later... I have to go back on deck.

She continues.

24 October 2016. When Noëmi woke me up at 5 am and I realised that I had slept for six hours, I felt guilty for a moment because I was afraid that the others were still working. But that day and night other crew members could actually get some sleep as we had no more rescue operations. We still had a lot of rescued people on board though, so I patrolled over the ship to help here and there, and see if everyone was all right in the cold, on the metal floor, wrapped in silver-gold rescue blankets. I prepared baby bottles, led the weakest to the toilet and greeted the sunrise and the people slowly waking up around me. I played the Pippi Longstocking game "Don't touch the ground" as I cautiously climbed over the railing, life rafts and stair railings to avoid stepping on the sleeping people lying everywhere. At some point I sat in the sunshine on Monkey Island, our lookout, and watched the scenery. Exhausted but relieved faces everywhere. Every now and then laughing and singing. "God bless you, Mam," "Merci beaucoup"... And suddenly I was sure that I wanted to ride on the *Sea-Watch* again next year. After I had thought one day before: "Never again, I can't do it anymore!"

I can hardly tell chronologically what happened in the last days. The events mix, I don't know any more when what happened. So here are just a few mixed impressions from my personal colour-book of nightmare and hope... With my rib crew I shuttled several hundred people from rubber dinghies to a Romanian tanker and watched with a pounding heart as they climbed up a 25-metre-high ladder. The weaker ones – and I – were then allowed to climb up a shaky gangway. I provided them with makeshift medical care and got to know two wonderful people – Captain Gabriel from Romania, who with enthusiasm and calmness took over more and more arrivals – in the end more than 900! – Gerry from Cameroon, who was there with his wife and baby, organised everything and looked after the people. I was allowed to rest for an hour on the bridge and in the Officers' Mess and was provided with food, sweets and coffee before

I paid expensively for it.... All of a sudden I was involved in a conversation with two Romanian officers who asked me blankly why we were doing this and, in the course of the conversation, confronted me with the crassest and most disgusting ultra-right beliefs I had ever experienced live: about the genetic inferiority of Africans, about the hordes of refugees marauding and raping in Europe, about the guilt of the Jews in the Second World War, about the Jewish World Conspiracy and about the Illuminati. I was glad when I got away from this tanker again, not without cordially saying goodbye again to Gabriel and Gerry.

I cooked rice with vegetables for almost 200 people. I packed the four dead boys in the body bags with Ingo, René and Alex. I accompanied three brothers as they said goodbye to their youngest dead brother. I cursed and yelled at the Frontex people who were picking up the bodies after I learned that they were taking the 900-plus people from the tanker to another ship in an overnight action, which was absolute and senseless madness. I was on a refugee boat full of women when the *Sea-Watch* took it to the tanker, standing ankle-deep in the soup of gasoline, urine, vomit and salt water in which these women had spent hours or days. I took crying babies from a rubber dinghy and held them in my arms and sang "Bella Ciao" to them. I have administered a series of infusions to dehydrated, partially unconscious people. For an hour I scrubbed away the dried body fluids of the dead in the hospital. I ate the best apple pie of my life – the scent alone was a delight after the cleaning action (thank you, Friedrich!). I laughed and cried. And this morning I took a long shower, groomed and sorted my completely filthy hair, washed laundry, fed our little ship birds and enjoyed a peaceful sunrise on a tidy ship.

Me, me, me... that's wrong, it is of course a big "WE", but each one of us has experienced this madness differently, and I am also happy about the reports and photos of our journalists on board, who not only report, but are right in the middle of it and tackle it just like everyone else.

Today we decided to stay outside the search area in order to regenerate and make our small, rocking workplace operational again. It was a great relief to hear that yesterday only a few boats were on the way and were well taken care of. We hope it is the same today. Because despite the exhaustion of the last days we want to continue. The thought that people are dying because we are not there, although it is our mission, is stronger than the desire for a sofa and a glass of red wine.

Barbara goes on.

26 October 2016 – The Ship of the Dead. We were just exhausted. Our operations since the deadly intervention of the Libyan Coastguard had lasted about 60 hours. We spent our much-needed break 90 nautical miles off the coast cleaning, washing and sorting life jackets, but finally also sleeping and talking about what we had experienced. But when we were just about ready to be able to look into the mirror without being scared and our jokes weren't all raven-black anymore, we learned from the Sea-Eye ship that in their search-and-rescue area with 14 rubber dinghies there was a hell of chaos again, and our friends were completely overwhelmed. But instead of saving human lives, we had to recover corpses in the following two days. After we had explored and stretched the limits of our resilience, we had to cross completely new borders during these days.

When I was 12 I saw a film about concentration camps on television. In 1945, American soldiers forced the people who lived near the concentration camps to look at the piles of corpses they did not want to know about. What must have happened in the young American men's minds when they had to see, smell and feel the crimes of the Nazis with their own eyes? When they saw the survivors, the tortured before them? Were they grasped by cold outrage? Did they want the German look-aways, the blind followers, comfort-zone Nazis to feel the same disgust and horror that traumatised these young Americans? As a child, I could not believe how terribly people had treated people because they regarded them as inferior. I can't do it today either.

It is clear how strong a sense of camaraderie and solidarity there is on the independent rescue ships between volunteers and their new guests, that supports the immense bravery that they show. But as Arturo points out above, after the at least partial euphoria of rescue, the next issue for the new arrivals is, as he says, the fact that "Nobody wants them". We look now at some arrival situations in Malta and Sicily, to test whether that is true.

Kristina Quintano is an activist working in Norway and originally from Malta. She says:

> On a bench outside the cloisters, Lilliana is sitting. She has just been released after almost two months in custody in what she herself describes as a prison. When refugees arrive in Malta they are placed in closed medical custody. There they go through physical, identity checks and possibly vaccinations if necessary, but the open receiving area where the refugees preferably should be transferred to and live the first year is full now. The countries that have said they are going to help often spend a long time to "pick up" their allocated refugees, and many will be sitting too long under miserable conditions in the first receiving area. When I meet Lilliana she doesn't have shoes; the pink sandals she's been wearing are trampled flat. This is the first time since she left Eritrea that she has got new shoes. Relief over the freedom that new shoes gives is something we rarely think about. "Now I can walk forever", she smiles with a wide grin. Lilliana, who like so very many who pass though Libya, had never thought about Europe. Her dream was working in Libya, where she had heard that there were jobs to get. But when she came to Libya, she realised that she was on an inhuman route filled with smugglers and traffickers in a life I don't understand how you can survive. She was only one of at least 500,000 people from the sub-Sahara who were stuck in Libya after 2011, without any opportunity to get out again, any other way than across the sea.
>
> "If you try to get out of Libya again you get shot", she tells me – the border guards there are relentless. She wouldn't have been able to travel back to Eritrea over borders even if she would have wanted

to. Lilliana says that she could choose between dying slowly in a camp in Libya, or die on the sea heading towards a future. She chose the last. The scars on her soul are clear in her appearance – all her movements are slow and I almost feel helplessly stupid with nothing else to offer than shoes, pots and coats this time. Here in Malta she gets temporary residence. People from "Africa" are safe here; the politicians in Malta have something that the Norwegian politicians have not – they do not return people to lands with dictators, driven by militias and torture.

But, in return, Malta does not have much to offer and people are almost without a sensible future in the smallest country in the EU. The centre that has been run by an old nun ever since 1992 is almost without means, and everything is dependent on volunteers and donations. Here come single, vulnerable women and very vulnerable families with small children. But this will be one of my favourite places in Malta in the future, because this is as "direct-assistance" as it can be; the nuns are of course working for free and live here, and the volunteers live in the small village. No bureaucracy anywhere. The families get to stay as long as they want but they are encouraged to find a job and manage themselves eventually. And today, the 100 pairs of new Norwegian Bibba shoes have been opened, 51 more parcels have received new small owners, enough pencils and stationery to fill up the cabinets in what they call "the classroom" and all the children got at least one "new" item of clothing each. All the different families have today got their own pots so they can cook without waiting four hours in line for a casserole dish. But the joy a pair of new shoes gives is almost everything.

Angelo Lo Marco teaches Italian to recently arrived refugees in Palermo, Sicily. He says:

I will not talk about happy things here. Not because there were none, but because the stories I am about to tell made me question myself about a lot. Three in particular are still vivid in my memory, as if they just occurred. All those things made me feel ashamed and I really was not able to feel comfortable with myself for days. And what do they say about us as a host country... One day, a child came to my office to be tested for language classes. I was there, talking to his mother, filling in the form needed to enrol him. I asked his mother about their nationality and the boy said, "I am Italian, I was born here". How can you explain to a child that even if he was indeed born in Italy, he was not like the other children? How can you tell a child that his rights will not be quite the same as another child's just because he was not "lucky" enough to be born to someone who had citizenship? How can you explain to a child that for at least 12 years from that day, his family has to prove they possess the rights to live in a country in which they have now lived and worked for years? How can you explain to a child that at any moment someone could deny his right to live with his mother or to live in the place in which he was born?

Another day I was testing some girls from Nigeria. They were hosted in a refugee camp and the eldest was 17. I am usually good at helping people feel comfortable to talk and open up with me. That time I gave a pen and the test sheet to one of those girls. I suddenly noticed that her hand was trembling. At first, I thought it was maybe because she could not read and write and so she was embarrassed by that. But then I noticed that every time I was closer to her, her trembling intensified. She could not even bear to look at me in my eyes. I asked a female colleague to switch with me and the girl relaxed. Later that day I discovered that she was not able to be near a man, thanks to some beasts from back when she was in Libya.

It is clearly this last story that makes Angelo angry.

Have you ever heard someone saying that all black people look the same? Another time, a girl accused one of our former students of robbery. She "recognised" him to be the person who had stolen her mobile phone at the station. He was put on house arrest for three months, waiting for the trial. Funny thing is that a couple of surveillance cameras had recorded the scene and this boy was innocent. The collateral damage of this misfortune is that he felt he had no chance to have a life here anymore, and he ran away after falling into a spiral of bad decisions.

Angelo talks as others have, about navigating the power relations of working with especially young refugees, in a way that does not objectify them.

> Speaking from the point of view of a school, I could see our obvious challenge was to try to make them learn a new language or to learn how to read and write. But I think that in the end, the most challenging thing was to try to not be driven by pity when having to deal with some of the refugees. I say pity because after you hear their stories, you cannot help but sympathise with them, you want to correct that wrong. You want to treat them as equal to other people but, when you act in a certain way due to pity, you are implying that they are not normal people. Personally, I do what I do because I hate when people struggle to be recognised as human beings.

This is a specific tension I believe was felt by many volunteers. There is a yearning to help, to dive in, to follow an emotional connection in the way such connections would flow in our own social worlds, from, for instance, helping a friend or colleague in trouble. It is how our societal emotional bonds are built. There are times in this work when surely "rushing in" is justified – after moments of extreme danger, or when comfort for a child is needed. But in longer-term social relations, there is a form of respectfully holding back which many of the testimonies in this book talk about as something that we must practise and learn. Of not making what another has suffered define them, or our behaviour toward them. Of leaving a space for a new relation or connection or identity, in this new country, to be built. To achieve this more nuanced responsiveness, I see that we as volunteers need to engage in a sort of constant dance – of rushing forward when the emergency or the distress is very real and no one else is there, but then learning to pull back so as not to overwhelm. I, for one, fear that I make mis-steps in this complex dance much of the time, and I get the sense that Angelo here is saying the same thing – as is Merlin earlier in this chapter. Here, Angelo also recognises that we need to manage our own responses and our own mental health if we are to continue to be of use. He says:

> It might seem a little bit extreme to say this, but the way I decided to "live my work" almost destroyed me. I have heard too many tales and, even though I had experienced none of them personally, I could not cope with all of that. I heard the stories of almost 1,000 people. I started alienating myself from my family and acquaintances. I wanted to be present in the lives of those I was trying to help, because I realised that they did not have that many people to rely on here. That led to a downfall due to the self-imposed pressure I was experiencing. I lost control over myself and I started overeating, I became more prone to anger, I developed hypertension, panic attacks and everything else seemed so unimportant. Now almost everything is again fine, and I found out that I am able to help without risking my mental health. But my vision of the world has never changed. The world is not the good place we used to think when we were "First-World" children. People are usually not good and they usually do things to satisfy their own interests. So others suffer every second and we build walls instead of building human connections. But there is always hope. As long as there are people willing to co-operate to ease the burden on someone else's shoulders, we can build a new and better world for our children to live in. About Europe, I hope it lives up to the expectations we had when as teenagers we first heard that freedom, fairness and mutual support were some of its main values.

Emanuele Cordella began volunteering at Centro Astalli in Palermo, Sicily, over ten years ago, and has since given up his planned "First-World" career to work in refugee support. He says:

> Centro Astalli is a voluntary association that is part of the Jesuit Refugee Service network in Italy. The group is committed to the defence of rights, integration and inclusion of immigrants, refugees and asylum seekers. It opened in the historic Ballarò district where, with the help of people who made their time and skills available for free, they offered users first- and second-reception services. Since

then, in spite of my family's reluctance, I decided to leave the university course I started at the Faculty of Statistical Sciences to dedicate myself to this work. I continued my training through some specialised courses, such as intercultural mediation and foreign languages.

He talks about his Christian perspective, and I see again here someone trying to tread a line between supporting someone in a necessarily intimate way, and paying them respect.

Throughout this time there have been many events that have left a profound mark on my life. The most significant event was to meet Rachel, a 16-year-old Eritrean girl, whom I looked after in her last days of life. When she arrived in Italy her body was devastated by very serious burns due to the explosion of a gas cylinder in one of the Libyan prisons where she had been for several months. She had been abandoned by traffickers and torturers, on a boat left adrift for several days. After the Italian Coastguard found her, although immediately hospitalised in a city hospital, she was unable to survive. She died alone in a foreign land and was deprived of being with her loved ones. Witnessing her last days of life, helplessly, the unspeakable physical and psychological sufferings and, above all, reading in her eyes the hopes of a better life broken by a never-ending journey of salvation, made me understand, as a human and as a Christian, how concretely important it is not to close our eyes to this reality which, for convenience, we often persist in ignoring. This job for me is a real mission, despite the frustrations of having to face an increasingly dehumanised, closed and xenophobic society.

Next, in the Flashpoints we explore more how European authorities from 2016 onwards turned their attention from rescue to repelling the new arrivals at sea, how the independent rescue ships became even more critical in saving lives and how the front-line Mediterranean ports – in Lampedusa, Sicily and Malta – dealt with the new arrivals.

Flashpoint: Lampedusa

Sara Creta

The destiny of Lampedusa is marked in its geography. The small fishing island is an isolated white rock in the Mediterranean, marginal and inaccessible, bleak and arid, scarcely more than 20 kilometres square – so hardly imposing in size, and yet so well-known over the years. It made its debut in the international media in 1986, when despotic Libyan leader Colonel Gaddafi ordered the firing of two missiles towards Lampedusa,

Figure 4.1 Lampedusa, Italy, 2016. A Senegalese man gives thanks for being saved, moments after stepping on board MSF's rescue vessel.

Image credit: Sara Creta.

which at the time hosted a US Coastguard navigation station. This came in retaliation for the American bombing of Tripoli and Benghazi, and the alleged death of Gaddafi's adopted daughter. The two missiles never hit Lampedusa, but after that episode tours started to flourish on the island, as curious visitors wanted to know where the missiles had blown up. A few years later, worldwide headlines were multiplying as the island was again catapulted to the front pages, turning into a political stage for a myriad of public-figures visits, from the pope to high-ranking officials from the European Union, transforming the small, touristic strip of land, known as "the Mediterranean gem", into a "border spectacle". Lampedusa, only 130 kilometres from the edge of Africa and at the veritable centre of the Mediterranean death-scape, entered in the collective imaginary as the "door of Europe".

The phenomenon of sea arrivals started to become visible in the 1990s, with some 50,000 people landing in Italy in 1999, the majority from Albania, and only 356 arriving in Lampedusa. No institutional assistance was provided on the island and food, shelter

Figure 4.2 Lampedusa, Italy, 2017. Syrian families getting some rest after their perilous journey at sea.

Image credit: Alberto Mallardo.

and clothes were offered only on a voluntary basis; the majority left with the first available ferry to Sicily. In 1996, the first centre for assistance was established, initially run by Red Cross volunteers. In July 2002, under the supervision of the Italian Government, the brotherhood Misericordia (a Calabrian religious charity which was under investigation by the anti-Mafia police) replaced the Red Cross, turning the Lampedusa centre into the only *de facto* detention centre on an Italian island. From then, transfers were slower, with migrants detained for longer periods. Since 1999, according to the Italian Ministry of the Interior, over 230,000 people have arrived in Lampedusa, and everyone on the island – from fishermen to housewives, from activists to military personnel – has been playing a role and has had an opinion on Europe's so-called migrant crisis. Among the symbolic places of Lampedusa, there is the "Cemetery of Boats" (an open-air dump for vessels that have arrived from Tunisia and Libya), and the numerous nameless graves dotted around the island's cemetery. The local graveyard is too small; even today, when the Italian Coastguard finds bodies of migrants who drowned at sea and brings them to the island's harbour, the corpses are not buried in Lampedusa but have to be sent to other towns, mostly in Sicily, but sometimes in other southern regions.

If bodies have to leave quickly as there is no space in the local cemetery, symbolic testimonies are collected by the Askavusa collective, which in February 2014 inaugurated a grassroots migration museum, "Porto M", doubling as a space to witness the stories of thousands of people who crossed to the island.

Lampedusa, twice as far from Italy as it is from Africa, was for centuries left alone, its inhabitants living with the absence of the state in their daily lives. But through the years, migration emergencies have been artificially created on the island as migrants that have been disembarked at Lampedusa have been held in the centre by the Ministry of Interior for weeks and even months; the local people have seen their island transformed into a heavily militarised zone, and slowly converted into an immigration warehouse. Against this, Italian civil society, associations of secular and

Figure 4.3 Crossing to Italy, 2016. A phone number on a t-shirt might be the only way to inform your family if you don't make it.
Image credit: Sara Creta.

religious volunteers or solidarity groups like Lampedusa Solidarity Forum or Mediterranean Hope have kept the identity of Lampedusa as a place of reception and welcoming. They play a significant political role also within the complex dynamics on the island, addressing concerns including the increased militarisation and the rampant corruption; many scandals linked to the institutional mismanagement of the centre have come to the surface.

The number of arrivals fell sharply in 2009 and 2010 – from 300 to around 500 – following the accord between Libya and Italy in order to stop migration. The 2008 agreement, also known as the "Treaty of Friendship, Partnership and Co-operation", was centred on *respingimenti* – so-called "pushback" – and the signing of lucrative business contracts between the two countries (including Eur. 5 billion to Libya as compensation for damages inflicted during the colonial era). The new policy, which resulted in the return to Libya of nearly 1,000 migrants, was later suspended and in 2012 Italy was "historically" condemned by the European Court of Human Rights in Strasbourg for violating international obligations.

A further humanitarian emergency was declared in 2011, when the population of the tiny island multiplied quickly, as more than 52,000 people landed due to revolts in Tunisia and escaping violence in Libya. Many Lampedusani volunteered with their own food, blankets and whatever hospitality they had to offer. In many cases, people had been forced to flee Libya by boat, as part of the "invasion" Gaddafi promised should his rule come under NATO attack. At the end of March 2011, former Italian prime minister Silvio Berlusconi made a formal visit to Lampedusa, which was nationally described as a "show", where he promised rapid migrant transfers to the mainland. Riots had continued on the island, with both locals and migrants having been involved in violent protests. Following the tensions, with hundreds of Tunisians imprisoned without access to a judge, and the consequential effects on tourism, the Council of Europe's Parliamentary Assembly organised a visit to the Island. In their report, the *ad hoc* sub-committee called on the Italian authorities to guarantee the rapid transfer of new arrivals to reception centres elsewhere in Italy, stating that "the inadequate and belated management of the crisis in early 2011 as well as the recent events will unquestionably have irreparable consequences for the inhabitants of Lampedusa".

In 2012, Lampedusa's new mayor from the centre-left Democratic Party, Giusi Nicolini, released an open letter to the European Union to ask for a change in the asylum policies: "If these dead are only ours, then I want to receive telegrams of condolence after every drowned person I receive. As if he had white skin, as if he were our son drowned during a holiday." Her call for help went unheeded until the tragedy of October 2013. On the morning of 3 October, so early that the sun had not yet risen, a boat carrying over 500 people – almost all of them escaping from Eritrea's dictatorial regime – caught fire just 800 meters off the coast of Lampedusa and 366 men, women and children drowned. Pietro Bartolo, a doctor who was later elected as a Member of the European Parliament, has worked in Lampedusa since the first boat arrived in 1991, helping migrants and fighting to give Lampedusa a permanent airborne medical service. He was a witness, and later co-authored a book, *Lampedusa: Gateway to Europe*, which describes this tragedy, including one of its very few redeeming moments. "Firemen were busy putting the victims into bags and I found a girl suffering from hypothermia. I thought I felt a pulse, a weak pulse. Later she was resuscitated then hospitalised. Her name was Kebra. She survived." Recovered bodies of the drowned migrants were proclaimed to be Italian citizens. In the end, victims neither received Italian citizenship nor a state funeral but instead were quietly buried in cemeteries across Sicily, often with only numbers marking the grave, and shipwreck survivors and relatives were denied permission to attend the funerals. Furthermore, as a result of this tragedy – as well as of a second sinking that left 268 Syrian refugees, including 60 children, dead just a week later – the Italian Government in 2013 launched Operation Mare Nostrum, a "military and humanitarian" search-and-rescue operation under the authority of the Italian Navy and supported by the European community.

Europe's conscience was pricked by the sight of the bodies of hundreds of migrants shipwrecked at Lampedusa, and new debates and civil-society actions were triggered. Grassroots organisations, civic associations and individuals made calls for a comprehensive overhaul of European migration policies known as the Charter of Lampedusa, with intense collaboration by a diverse array of activists to support freedom of movement and freedom to stay. In the aftermath of the 2013 tragedy, another group of journalists and activists, consisting of both Italian and refugees, created the Comitato Tre Ottobre (October 3 Committee), which pushed the Italian Parliament to recognise 3 October as the National Day in Remembrance of the Victims of Immigration.

Operation Mare Nostrum was politically controversial, especially given the high costs and the fact that so many of the arrivals to Europe became the responsibility of Italy. This search-and-rescue operation ended just one year later, in October 2014. As of 1 November

Figure 4.4 Lampedusa, Italy, 2014. "Gate of Lampedusa – Gate of Europe".
A monument to the migrants who died and were dispersed in the sea, by Mimmo
Paladino. Printed in black and white.
Image credit: Vito Manzari.

2014, EU partners launched Operation Triton, followed by Operation
Themis in 2018, both run by the European Border and Coast Guard
Agency, also known as Frontex.

With the intensity of rescue operations and arrivals in Italy, the
Italian authorities were identifying and registering arrivals in active
Hotspots (Lampedusa, Pozzallo, Taranto and Trapani), supported by
Frontex and European Asylum Support Office (EASO) staff. Many
people were hosted in the Lampedusa Hotspot, including those who
had refused to register for asylum. For instance, between November
2015 and January 2016, a group of 200 Eritrean, Sudanese and
Somali asylum seekers were not allowed to leave Lampedusa
for refusing to have their fingerprints taken, as, given the Dublin
Regulation, migrants and refugees have to be fingerprinted in their
country of first arrival. Horrific stories continued to come out from the

Lampedusa Hotspot reception centre, which migrants have set on fire three times, exasperated by their living conditions.

Every year since 2014 has been deadlier than the previous. The twin shipwrecks in the central Mediterranean in April and June 2015, which left an estimated 1,200 people dead or missing, marked a further turning point, compelling EU foreign ministers to launch an anti-smuggling mission, "EU NavFor/Sophia". Humanitarian NGOs including Médecins Sans Frontières (MSF), Migrant Offshore Aid Station (MOAS), Sea-Watch, Sea-Eye, SOS Mediterranée, Jugend Rettet, Save the Children, Lifeboat, BRF and Proactiva have also stepped up their search-and-rescue operations around Lampedusa, providing a crucial contribution to rescuing migrants at sea and going further south than the EU, NATO and merchant vessels. By rescuing over 100,000 migrants between 2015 and 2017, these NGOs became the largest provider of search-and-rescue (SAR) operations in the Mediterranean.

However, in May 2017, Interior Minister Marco Minniti asked NGOs to sign a code of conduct which imposed several limitations on rescuing operations and threatened the closure of Italian ports to non-signatory organisations. Soon after his appointment, Matteo Salvini, leader of Italy's League party and Minister of the Interior until September 2019, seized the opportunity to implement a closed-port policy to NGO ships and foreign-flagged merchant vessels carrying migrants rescued off the shore of Libya. Since 2013 all distress calls in the central Mediterranean had been systematically directed to Italy, which had been co-ordinating the majority of all SAR operations off the coast of Libya. In this difficult context, many NGOs operating in the waters of the Mediterranean found themselves involved in violent accidents with unidentified Libyan Coastguard vessels. In June 2018, the Libyan Search-and-Rescue Region (SRR) was formally recognised after quietly submitting details of its new maritime SRR operations to the International Maritime Organisation (IMO), the UN agency responsible for regulating shipping. Libya started to assume primary responsibility for SAR co-ordination in an area extending to around 100 miles from its coast. The plan has been pushed ahead by Italy, with the aim of bolstering the Libyan Coastguard in migration control. Compared to 2018, arrivals to Europe from Libya fell drastically according to United Nations figures in the first months of 2019, with Europe subsequently relying on Libyan capacity and EU member states unprepared to co-ordinate a response to people in distress in the Mediterranean.

But dozens of migrants are still disembarking autonomously on the island. According to the Ministry of the Interior, in 2019, almost 10,000 have been rescued and brought to its shores by humanitarian vessels – over 5,000 in the first months of 2020. A new act of the "border play" has started, with the present government incapable of recognising that, with the current political position, the stand-offs at sea will continue. Meanwhile, episodes of intolerance and anger have prevailed and thrown an unflattering light on the hospitable

Figure 4.5 Lampedusa, Italy, 2018. A group of young arrivals sleep outside the local church in protest against forced repatriations.

Image credit: Lillo Maggiore.

people of Lampedusa. Last June, the Lampedusa "migrant boats graveyard", a key symbol on the island, went up in flames and the Gateway to Europe (Porta d'Europa) monument, designed as a memorial to migrants who died making the crossing, was wrapped by vandals in plastic bags.

Flashpoint: Sicily

Simona Bonardi

The southernmost region of Italy, Sicily is also its largest island and its fourth-most populated region, with 5 million inhabitants. As of January 2019, 4% of the population – approximately 200,000 – were non-Italian; of those, 43% were of European origin, 33% African, 20% Asian, 3% American and a very small percentage were from Oceania or without a nationality.

As the first landing place of migrants from the Mediterranean for centuries and the administrative division to which Lampedusa belongs (Agrigento province), Sicily's role in today's migration flows is threefold: receiving the dead, receiving the living and functioning as part of the national reception system.

"Giving a name to the dead before burying them is a duty of civilisation that we fulfil mainly for the living. It is a matter of mental health," says Dr Christina Cattaneo who was a coroner to Melilli NATO base, Sicily, between 2013 and 2015, where she helped identify some of the 1,400 migrants drowned in the Mediterranean during that period.

International human rights law demands that no distinction be made between the death of an EU citizen and that of a non-EU one, and the procedures of retrieval and identification of the bodies should reflect that. According to official reports, the retrieval of migrant bodies from the sea involves multiple actors, including the Italian Coastguard, the Italian Navy, ships from the European Border and Coast Guard Agency (Frontex), as well as merchant ships responding to distress signals and NGO ships conducting search-and-rescue operations. Due to limited

Figure 4.6 Castellammare del Golfo, Sicily, 2014. Amid unmarked graves,
the cemetery memorial reads: "From the stormy sea of life to the calm sea of
eternity in an infinite embrace. The city of Castellammare del Golfo remembers
shipwreck victims, 1 November 2014".
Image credit: Anon.

resources, rescuing the living is often prioritised over the retrieval
of the dead, who are buried in anonymous local graves which are
simply covered with earth and marked by stones. Always without
a state funeral, often without any funeral, normally without formal
identification of the bodies, the nameless dead are scattered
around Sicily. Families in remote countries are generally unable
to confirm the death of their lost relatives, unable to leave their
own countries or face the challenges of legislation and bureaucracy when attempting to search for and identify the dead
(including having to pay for DNA tests); they are left with lifelong
doubt and "no place in the memory for our lost family members to
rest in peace".

Denied a death to be mourned, surviving family members of the victims are trapped in a life where they struggle with senseless disappearances of their brothers, children, spouses. But there has at least been progress with attempts to create an international database for missing persons, including the unidentified sea victims, and so offer some closure to bereaved families. This is the result of 20 years of work by the Laboratory of Anthropology and Forensic Odontology of the University of Milano (LABANOF), which was later joined in its mission by the Comitato Tre Ottobre and the Red Cross, IOM, Borderline Europe and diasporic communities, such as Eritreans Across Europe.

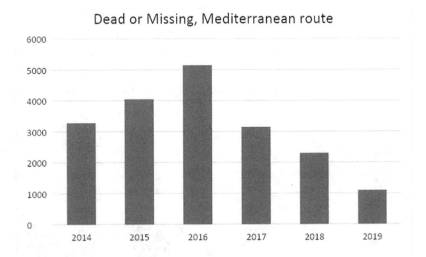

Dead or Missing, Mediterranean route

Although the years of 2015 and 2016 are commonly associated with the migration crisis, Sicily had already been seeing arrivals long before. The shipwreck that occurred on 25 December 1996 at Portopalo di Capopassero, resulting in at least 283 deaths, was recorded as the worst since the Second World War (and remained so until October 2013, when a new record number was reached). First referred to as the "ghost shipwreck", it became known as "the tragedy of Christmas" after the wreck was found in the Sicilian Channel thanks to the work of journalist Giovanni Maria Bellu, a journalist for *la Repubblica*, and fisherman Salvo Lupo from Portopalo. Authorities had given no credit to the reports of the survivors; however, identity documents and body parts were found in fishing nets near Portopalo. Consciences were shaken by the events, which were also narrated in Bellu's 2004 account *I fantasmi di Portopalo* (*The Ghosts of Portopalo*).

Since the late 1990s, right and centre-left Italian governments alike have signed or renewed deals with Libya to control the migration flow. Additional bilateral agreements were signed under Berlusconi's government, resulting in the provision of military ships to the Libyan Government for sea monitoring, and financial funds for the creation of the first Libyan "collection camps" in 2003; in the same year, the first camp for undocumented migrants was built in Libya near Tripoli, financed by Italy. Research has shown that more camps were financed in the following years. According to news reports, in just one year, between the end of 2004 and

Figure 4.7 Pachino, Sicily, 2013. A migrant boat arrives at Morghella beach where local people are bathing. Initial surprise is followed by a rush to help.
Image credit: from a video by MariaGabriella.

2005, approximately 4,000 individuals were subject to collective deportations back to Libya, in violation of Article 3 of the European Convention on Human Rights. Although numbers remain unconfirmed, the expulsions continued in the following years and resulted in the February 2012 sentence by the European Court of Human Rights condemning Italy for the refoulement of Africans to Libya. In 2011, similar bilateral agreements were sealed between Italy and Tunisia, and armed ships to the value of Eur. 16.5 million were delivered to Tunisia for the monitoring of sea waters. That same year came reports of collective deportations from Punta Raisi, near Palermo, to Tunisia; attempts to escape the deportation were met with violence by the authorities.

In June 2012, 60 migrants were collectively returned to Egypt from Catania after being denied access to the asylum procedure. At the time of the events, the Mineo reception centre for asylum seekers in Catania province was holding 1,800 individuals, more than half of them in the process of appealing their rejected applications. The news followed the European Commission for Human Rights (ECHR) judgment earlier the same year confirming that human rights violations continued before Europe's eyes.

Details of the bilateral agreements signed by the Italian Government with Libya and other non-EU countries have remained secret – and without the work of local activists and independent journalism, the deportations would have remained unexposed. There is no transparency in a system that implements and perpetuates the segregation of arrivals; so, with no access to reception centres for volunteers, witnessing and actively defending human rights requires commitment and creativity. Even more than in the rest of Italy, two opposing sides have been co-existing on the island: one of awakening consciences and bold resistance, and one of corruption and discrimination.

Corruption has been rampant and widespread. It has been reported that between 2013 and 2014, more than Eur. 3 million was billed to the prefecture of Messina for refugee management by "solidarity" businesses, now under official investigation. In

Figure 4.8 Palermo, Sicily, 2015. The "Barefoot March" – Sicilian mayors and members of civil society march in the streets of Palermo on 10 September to demand humanitarian corridors and a Europe without walls.
Image credit: Borderline Sicilia.

parallel, according to Messina police figures, of 6,800 potential asylum seekers identified in 2014, only 283 had received responses to their requests for international protection – just 4% of the total registered. Exceeding the capacity of all available centres, arrivals were assigned to inadequate structures, such as the tent city at the PalaNebiolo sports centre of Messina in October 2015. Others were effectively held hostage on the ships for up to two days after harbouring, as happened in Messina in September 2016. In this landscape, civil society – the academic world, anti-Mafia cultural associations, left-wing parties as well as human rights activist groups – wrote open letters to institutional authorities, started petitions, reported and monitored and requested respect of inter-national law and basic freedoms. Reports emerged of inhumane living conditions in the primary-reception centres, the protests of their residents, the inadequate treatment of women and minors, the family separations of pregnant women from their husbands and children and the chronic delay of the initiation of asylum applications, resulting in the indefinite detention of the individuals in the temporary centres. Since 2008, voices from civil society joined to form the association Borderline Sicilia to document the arrivals on the island, and safeguard the memory of what has happened between the two opposite sides of the south Mediterranean.

The Libyan civil war that began in 2014 triggered a sharp increase in numbers attempting to reach Italy. Against a background of chronic delays with the asylum applications of those on the island, arrival numbers rose steeply in 2015, with 3,772 dead or missing and 153,842 arrivals over the year, as they would again in 2016, with more than 5,000 dead or missing and 181,436 arrivals, according to UNHCR data. Among the nationalities of arrivals, there was a decrease in the number of Syrians as they began to use the Greek and Balkan route, but a rise in other nationalities, especially those from Eritrea and Nigeria.

As reported by local activists, denial of the right to apply for international protection became a systematic violation, when police authorities in Sicily began to summarily classify arrivals on the basis of their country of origin, issuing to those classified as "economic migrants" refusal-of-entry documents as early as the day after their arrival, and an order to leave the country in the next seven days. Fulvio Vassallo Paleologo, a professor of immigration and asylum law, reported to Al Jazeera in October 2015 that arrivals from Sudan and Eritrea would be heard, those from Nigeria would get a 50% chance, while individuals from countries like Gambia and Burkina Faso would have almost no chance. Furthermore, the continuing inadequacy of the reception centres put an increasing strain on all the Sicilian provinces, where informal reception centres offering very poor living conditions made basic human rights and the protection of vulnerable categories (especially minors) an unattainable luxury.

In 2015, at the convention "Io sono Persona" ("I am a Person"), Palermo's mayor Leoluca Orlando launched the International Human

Mobility "Palermo Charter", which aimed to establish Sicily as a place of tolerance for migrants, and initiate a cultural change for international laws on migration. In 2018, when Interior Minister Salvini decreed the exclusion of non-EU immigrants from the right to an identity card and registration with local councils, Orlando and other mayors around Italy continued to register them in an act of political disobedience.

Since 2015, activism in civil society in Sicily has grown stronger and has redefined the boundaries between volunteering, activism, nonprofit activities and entrepreneurship. The joint efforts of individuals and organisations from very different worlds – non-religious and religious, social and cultural, syndicates and political – signify strong support for Palermo's new policies. This network would be essential in the coming years in demanding political change at a European level; its call to moral and civil engagement would often

Figure 4.9 Pozzallo, Sicily, 2014. The Sangue Nostrum ("Our Blood") march for migrants' rights, which began in Lampedusa and travelled on up the coast to Turin.

Image credit: Borderline Sicilia.

Figure 4.10 Sicily, 2018. Campaign poster of IoAccolgo ("I Welcome"), a popular movement seeking to abolish ex-Home Minister Salvini's decrees and the Italy–Libya deal.

Image credit: poster by IoAccolgo, using image donated by Refugees Welcome Italia.

see independent groups and citizens marching alongside political figures such as Mayor Orlando, and would be especially loud in response to the 2018 closed-ports policy and the prosecution of Domenico Lucano, the mayor of Riace in Calabria, who faced prosecution for his pro-migrant policies which produced a successful and different type of reception and inclusion: "Model Riace", the dying village reborn through welcoming immigrants.

Flashpoint: The Sea-Rescues

Sue Clayton

To understand the extreme risk and danger faced by asylum seekers making the Mediterranean crossings, we need to look first at how EU and member state search-and-rescue (SAR) operations offshore from Greece and Italy have changed in recent years, mostly with catastrophic effect and causing thousands of avoidable and unnecessary deaths at sea. Then we will look at how volunteer rescue missions like Sea-Watch, Sea-Eye, Mission Lifeline and Open Arms have stepped

Figure 4.11 Greek coast, 2016. A volunteer from *Sea-Watch 2* greets a newly arrived RIB on which there are children as well as adults.

Image credit: Fabien Melber.

in to fill the breach as best they can, at the price of confiscation of their ships and their volunteer crew-members facing criminalisation, draconian fines and custodial punishments.

In the central Mediterranean, the Italian Government's Operation Mare Nostrum ("Our Sea") began in 2013. This was a naval and air operation put in place to deal with the increased numbers of crossings from North African countries like Libya, and in response to shipwrecks that were increasingly occurring off Lampedusa – a remote Italian island nearer to the African coast than the Italian mainland, and the first European port that all those migrants leaving from Libya would reach. During the Mare Nostrum operation at least 150,000 migrants, mainly from Africa and the Middle East, arrived safely onto Italian soil. However, in October 2014, the EU declared it would cease supporting the operation, and the following year brought sea-rescues in Europe under the control of a body known as Frontex, named from the French *frontières extérieures*, or "external borders". Frontex had been established in 2005 as the European Agency for the Management of Operational Co-operation at the External Borders, and was in no sense a rescue mission, but rather a security agency responsible for border control in Europe. In 2015, the EU expanded its remit to include maritime patrol operations, changing its title to the European Border and Coast Guard Agency, and naming its Mediterranean mission "Operation Triton". There were immediate concerns that an agency designed to protect borders, based in distant Warsaw, with lower budgets than Mare Nostrum and a track record of poor management and little oversight, would be likely to prioritise repelling undocumented vessels rather than protecting the safety and wellbeing of those on board. And indeed this is exactly what Frontex did. Rather than positioning themselves in the prospective wreck-zones north of Libya, Frontex forces would remain in other parts of the Mediterranean, and respond to distress calls by relying on a maritime convention whereby the nearest vessel to a boat in distress – be it a luxury yacht or a giant freighter – is supposed to effect a rescue. Charles Heller and Lorenzo Pezzani's report "Death by Rescue" illustrates how in 2015 two major wrecks with great loss of life occurred because the ships that had to effect the rescues were totally unequipped to do so, and actually caused more deaths by coming alongside unstable small boats and capsizing them. Even President of the European Commission Jean-Claude Juncker had to admit that "it was a serious mistake to bring the Mare Nostrum operation to an end. It cost human lives" – but the policy did not change. Frontex could not be relied on to save lives.

Figure 4.12 Off the Libyan coast, 2019. The *Sea-Watch 3* crew help rescued refugees on board one by one.

Image credit: Doug Kuntz.

Newly formed volunteer groups like Sea-Watch and Open Arms came into being, to fulfil a crucial role in responding to rescue calls. Sea-Watch is a German nonprofit organisation which conducts civil SAR operations in the central Mediterranean.

Its mission is to ensure that no one should have to die at Europe's deadly sea border. Even with limited resources and few ships at its disposal, Sea-Watch estimates it has been able to save the lives of more than 37,000 people since its founding in 2015. But in that same period there were still 12,000 who did lose their lives in these waters, trying to escape war and conflict in their countries of origin and hellish conditions in Libya. Many drowned within sight of Europe's shores and beaches. Over 500 volunteers have contributed to Sea-Watch missions in the SAR (search and rescue) zone offshore from Libya. The mission is politically and religiously independent and financed through independent contributions, and it operates within the framework of the Universal Declaration of Human Rights, the UN Convention on the Law of the Sea and the Convention Relating to the Status of Refugees. Initially, Sea-Watch bought a 98-year-old "Go-46" fishing cutter and re-named it *MS Sea-Watch*. The repurposed ship left the port of Lampedusa for its first deployment in June 2015, and rescued over 1,000 migrants in three operations. Later in 2015, Sea-Watch bought a second ship, the former maritime research vessel *Clupea*, and re-named it *Sea-Watch 2*. In 2016, *Sea-Watch 2* was attacked by the Libyan Coastguard during one of its SAR operations, which compromised the rescue, so only 120 of the roughly 150 people on the shipwrecked boat were able to be saved. Later, the *Sea-Watch 2* was acquired by Mission Lifeline, another German civil rescue group, and Sea-Watch upgraded to a much bigger rescue vessel, *Sea-Watch 3*. Built in 1972 as an offshore supply ship, this had much greater SAR capacity in terms of numbers it could accommodate, and its capacity to liaise with the civil reconnaissance plane Sea-Watch next acquired, named *Moonbird* after the migratory bird. The combined operation of the two continues to provide Sea-Watch with optimal assets for scouting, finding and rescuing people at sea.

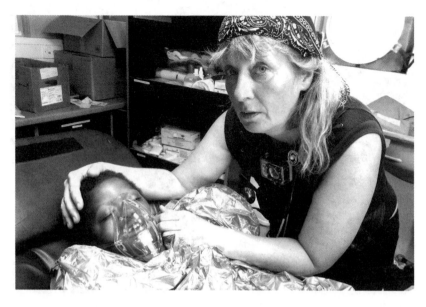

Figure 4.13 Off the Libyan coast, 2016. Volunteer medic Barbara Held works on a child rescued from a refugee boat.

Image credit: Judith Buethe.

In the eastern Mediterranean, the distance from Turkey to the nearest Greek islands of Lesvos, Samos and Chios is much shorter than from Libya to the Italian islands – but rough seas and the hostility of both Greek and Turkish forces still make rescue missions essential there too. Proactiva Open Arms is a Spanish NGO based on Lesvos. Its activities started in September 2015 on the waters around the island. The first volunteers lacked marine vessels and could partici-pate in rescue missions only by swimming. In October 2015, two Jet Skis were purchased; in July 2016, Open Arms was donated the sailing yacht *Astral*, which allowed it to expand into the central Mediterranean where migrant crossing numbers were much higher. In December 2016, Open Arms chartered the North Sea trawler *Golfo Azzurro*, which saved 6,000 people in the first three months of 2017. It replaced the *Astral* on SAR missions, and was joined next by the repurposed emergency tow-vessel *Open Arms*. As of November 2019, the Open

Figure 4.14 Off the Libyan coast, 2019. The *Sea-Watch 3* crew exchange greetings and hugs with their new guests.
Image credit: Doug Kuntz.

Arms Lesvos Mission and Central Mediterranean Mission have led to the rescue of a total of 59,696 migrants.

These independent rescue missions, as the testimonies in this collection show, have been brutal, involving not only rescuing the living, but recovering those who have drowned and doing search operations for those much longer dead, in order to have such deaths recognised and bring closure to families. However, increasingly since 2016, the rescues have faced opposition from hostile states. In 2017 there were at least five independent groups running rescue ships, but by 2018 these had been hit hard by being refused the right to dock in European ports with those they had rescued, and crews faced criminalisation as people smugglers. In June 2018, Italy's Interior Minister Matteo Salvini sparked a crisis in the Mediterranean region by refusing to allow the *Aquarius* rescue ship, operated by Médecins Sans Frontières and carrying 629 people, to dock in any Italian port.

Salvini insisted it should go to Malta instead, but Malta refused, and there was an impasse which endangered the safety of those on the ship, until it was finally accepted into Spanish waters. Only a week later Salvini barred two further rescue ships from bringing refugees to shore. "We have opened a front in Brussels", said Salvini. "We are contacting the European commission so that it can fulfil its duties towards Italy that have never been respected". As ever, Italy's anger at being, as it saw itself, left to deal with migrant numbers alone – made worse by the EU Dublin Regulation, which does not permit those seeking asylum to continue north out of Italy if they have been registered there – was now being turned on the shipwrecks and the volunteers who tried to effect rescues.

Since 2018, the independent rescue ships have continued to sail, but are constantly thwarted by being refused permission to dock, and their personnel are branded as human traffickers. *Sea-Watch 3* was detained in Malta for four months during the summer of 2018 over claims made of a registration irregularity – one which

Figure 4.15 Mediterranean, 2019. Sea-Watch crew conducting a mission off the Libyan coast.

Image credit: Doug Kuntz.

has been disputed by the Netherlands, the vessel's flag state. The ship is equipped with over 1,200 life jackets – which would have been more than enough to rescue the 400-plus men, women and children who drowned in the ship's SAR zone in that period. In June 2019, *Sea-Watch 3*, captained by experienced German navigator Carola Rackete, picked up 53 migrants whose boat was in trouble in the Mediterranean off the Libyan coast. Rackete rejected the Italian authorities' suggestion to dock at Tripoli, which is considered unsafe by humanitarian organisations, and headed instead to Lampedusa where she attempted to dock, as her passengers by now were exhausted and weak. She was immediately arrested by the Italian authorities. Salvini accused Rackete of trying to sink an Italian patrol boat that was trying to intercept her and that her ship collided with, calling the incident an act of war and demanding that the Netherlands, under whose flag *Sea-Watch 3* was registered, should intervene. A public outcry ensued and over Eur. 1 million was raised for her defence. At her trial, the Italian judge exonerated her from trafficking charges, finding that she had acted to save her passengers out of humanitarian motives, though she had to battle further state appeals. (See Chapter 10 for an update on this case.)

Because of EU states' refusal to allow docking, Sea-Eye's rescue vessel *Alan Kurdi* had to temporarily stop missions in 2019, only to restart in 2020 and face being impounded again at Palermo in Sicily, with authorities saying they had found "irregularities". Other rescue vessels are routinely detained in Italian and Maltese ports, and the threat hangs over them of hefty monetary fines and long jail sentences for any further craft attempting rescues. The only ship able to stay active for most of 2019 in the Mediterranean was the *Open Arms*; in July 2019, the Spanish Government reportedly threatened its organisation with a Eur. 901,000 fine if it continued to rescue migrants. From its location in the central Mediterranean, the *Open Arms* tweeted "We are alone here. We face people in danger of death, and we have to be prepared for the worst." The consequences are dire: people in distress are not saved but drown unnoticed. Witnesses and independent documentation of the dying, human rights violations and illegal

Figure 4.16 Lampedusa, Italy, 2019. After a two-weeks stand-off with the Italian authorities, captain Carola Rackete brings the *Sea-Watch 3* into port, defying a ban issued by Minister of the Interior Matteo Salvini, who had closed Italian waters to NGO and independent rescue ships.

Image credit: Alberto Mallardo.

pushbacks on the Mediterranean pass unnoticed on administrators' desks and in the mainstream media.

All the independent sea-rescue missions have stood firm in the face of physical attacks by the Libyan Coastguard, and constant harassment and legal challenges by ports and governments when they seek to dock with rescued bodies, dead or alive. A Sea-Watch spokesperson at the end of 2019 made the following press statement.

> As European politics appear to be increasingly motivated by right-wing and anti-refugee ideologies, these rescue missions today stand for much more than just sea-rescue. They have become a symbol of solidarity and are at the heart of the European civil society movement demanding and pushing for rescue operations by the European institutions, standing up for legal escape routes and the removal of the root causes of migration and flight. Since a political solution in the sense of a safe passage is not on

the horizon, we will continue to expand our field of operation and make new plans.

However, even these incredibly brave teams could not have foreseen the vastly increased challenges they would face with the spread of the COVID-19 pandemic where they have had to weigh yet more risk and safety factors to assess whether their missions can continue at all. We look at this troubled issue further in Chapter 10.

Flashpoint: Malta

Maria Pisani and Sue Clayton

The island of Malta is among the smallest countries in the world, with a population, along with sister island Gozo, of less than half-a-million. It is the southernmost EU state, located right in the centre of the Mediterranean, around 100 kilometres from Sicily and 300 kilometres from North Africa. Relative to its size and population, it is one of the top refugee- receiving countries in the world.

Figure 4.17 Senglea, Malta, 2018. Migrants disembark from the charity ship *Lifeline* at Senglea in Valletta's Grand Harbour.

Image credit: Darrin Zammit Lupi.

Malta started receiving asylum seekers and refugees with relative frequency in 2002. For more than 18 years now these boat arrivals, generally leaving from the coast of Libya and heading towards mainland Europe, have consistently made headline news, and the issue remains at the top of the Malta's political discourse and policy development. The circumstances of the boat arrivals have evolved during this time, reflecting a number of factors including changing conditions in the countries of origin, and the onset of new humanitarian contexts – such as the deteriorating conditions in Libya, a shift in smuggling operations, and increased efforts by the EU to prevent arrivals by preventing departures. This has led to containment and deterrence tactics and restrictions on the presence of NGO and independent search-and-rescue (SAR) vessels. More recently, we have seen the criminalisation of the independent missions, and a rise of nationalist (increasingly right-wing populist) politics of individual member states. Such realities, policies and practices have had a direct impact on the number of arrivals in Malta, the mode of arrival and how asylum seekers and refugees are processed upon arrival.

In many ways, Malta represents a microcosm of broader EU policies. The islands demonstrate ongoing and failed attempts to "manage" the "migration crisis" and the implosion of a Common European Asylum System (that never was): resettlement out of Malta and resettlement to Malta; relocation from Malta to other EU countries and back again; ongoing efforts to redistribute refugees saved by the NGO and volunteer SAR vessels; and the random and unpredictable closure of ports and impounding of rescue ships.

Groups like the US-based charity KOPIN offer support to women in the open centres, and Il-Fanal (Maltese for "Lighthouse") works with children, both unaccompanied and in families, to help them integrate into local schools and live a more settled life, but the uncertainty over their immediate futures and their longer-term status makes this difficult to achieve. Reception and detention centres in Malta, as in parts of Greece and Italy, are overflowing as more people arrive, and there remains confusion and delay around processing that ought to lead to asylum decisions and re-settlement but does not.

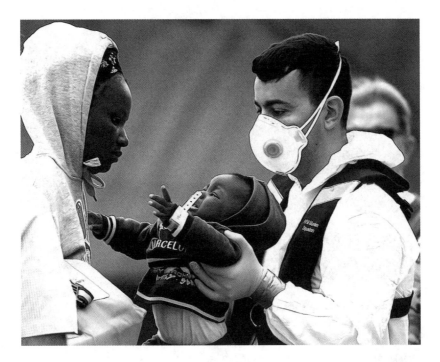

Figure 4.18 Senglea, Malta, 2018. An African woman and her child are escorted from the charity ship *Lifeline* in Valetta's Grand Harbour.
Image credit: Darren Zammit Lupi.

After the failure of German Chancellor Angela Merkel's proposed quota system for EU countries to accept their fair share of migrants, Malta and Italy proposed at least an emergency reloca-tion scheme to take pressure off frontline countries such as them-selves. A meeting was held in September 2019 between Malta, Italy, Germany, France and Finland to agree emergency measures to transfer more of those arriving into Malta. But in October, after a high number of arrivals to Malta, no offers from other EU states were forthcoming, and reception facilities were stretched yet further.

There were riots in the poorly run and vastly overcrowded Hal Far reception centre, a repurposed UK military base near the island's airport. Several rooms and vehicles were torched, including police vehicles.

Figure 4.19 Malta, 2019. A vigil organised by Integra Foundation for Lassana Cisse Souleymane, a new arrival murdered in April 2019 in a suspected hate crime.

Image credit: *The Times of Malta*.

The Malta story is also told through the country's interactions with volunteer and NGO rescue ships. From June to October 2018, the *Sea-Watch 3* volunteer rescue ship remained impounded in Malta's port as the government claimed, without evidence, that there were irregularities with its Netherlands registration. As mentioned in the Sea-Rescues Flashpoint, 400 more people drowned in the period in the rescue zone in which *Sea-Watch 3* would have operated had it not been impounded. In August 2019 another SAR vessel, the *Open Arms*, carrying 121 rescued asylum seekers, was left stranded for 19 days at sea, after both Italy and Malta refused to grant it the right to dock, despite grave concerns for the continued health and safety of those on board. (Eventually an Italian prosecutor ordered the seizure of the ship and the evacuation of those on board to the island of Lampedusa). In September 2019, the *Ocean Viking*, a Médecins Sans Frontières (MSF) ship attempted to dock in Malta – the fourth

Figure 4.20 Malta, 2020. Inmates of Safi Barracks Detention Centre protest their detention; the UNHCR claims 1,400 are being illegally detained on Malta.
Image credit: *The Times of Malta.*

independent rescue ship to do so in a week. Again, there were delays while the Maltese Government decided whether it would accept all 229 on board, and there were prolonged debates about the precise location of their rescue, as the ship had made several rescues on one mission from different points at sea. The final decision – to accept only those who were indisputably from the "right" zone for Malta to accept, drew widespread condemnation from humanitarian groups; 182 were left stranded on board because they were told they'd been rescued in the "wrong" zone. MSF reported on Twitter that these 182 survivors included a newborn baby, children and a pregnant woman. This, it said, "demonstrates the discriminatory, arbitrary and inhuman nature of a system which continues to prioritise political gameplay above human lives and dignity".

Figure 4.21 Valletta, Malta, 2016. A stateless child takes part in a demonstration of African migrants, calling for changes in the system regulating migrant workers and the protection of their human rights.

Image credit: Darrin Zammit Lupi.

With the establishment of the EU's Frontex "defence" force and its emphasis on deterrence rather than rescue, coupled with Italy's and the EU's highly reprehensible outsourcing of boat interception to the Libyan Coastguard (with systematic torture and human rights abuses facing those it returns to Libyan soil), the independent rescue ships are the last resort for those at sea. Malta, like Italy, now routinely turns away rescue ships, or impounds them if they dock. The safety, protection and rights of those on board the vessels are disregarded, as each and every European member state turns a blind eye both to these abuses and the shameful conditions of migrants held awaiting decisions for months and years.

This is Europe in 2020.

WAY-STATIONS

Migrants and refugees' journeys do not usually end once they have arrived on European shores. Faced with a lack of basic support and overstretched asylum reception systems in Italy, Greece and elsewhere, many people chose to travel onwards, despite restrictions intended to prevent them from doing so. In Italy, this led people north, via towns like Ventimiglia, by the border with France. Although borders should have been open under the EU's Schengen agreement, the new arrivals met increasingly hostile controls on their movement, which pushed them to more difficult and dangerous routes.

From Greece, people had to exit the EU and travel through the Balkan region before trying to re-enter the EU further north as they reached Croatia or Slovenia. Border controls in the Balkan region had been mainly lifted in the summer of 2015, but were progressively re-imposed from the end of the year and into 2016, creating bottlenecks at key crossing points.

Idomeni, Greece, 2016. A young boy sits down in front of Greek riot police as a peaceful protest against the closure of the border at Idomeni between Greece and North Macedonia.

Image credit: Treasa O'Brien.

5

Testimonies from the Balkan and Alpine Routes

Sue Clayton

From Sicily to the North of Italy

While many of those who landed in Italy wanted to travel on to France and other northern European countries, some settled on the way. **Laial Ben Abbou** volunteered to teach Italian in her home town of Lodi, Lombardy. She says:

It was June 2016. It was also the month of Ramadan for Muslim people, and I was teaching Italian to a class of political refugees. The class was twice a week, on Monday and Thursday, and each lesson lasted two hours. It was my first experience working closely with refugees. I tried to learn their names, to listen to their stories, and I tried to teach them the Italian language and culture. It was very difficult. The class was split in two: those who only spoke French, and those who only spoke English. Then there was a man of unknown age. Not even he could tell me his exact age. I thought that he was older than 50. M. was illiterate and he only spoke the dialect of the zone of his country, Senegal, so he understood neither French nor English. For this reason, there was almost nothing I could teach him. If M. had been my only student, surely I would have taught him something, but there were 20 more people in the classroom that I was responsible for. I wish I could have worked with some other teacher who could help me manage the course. But M. was fasting that month. And on this point we got along very well, because I, too, like him, am Muslim. We were at least able to share Ramadan and fasting.

So across language and cultures, a connection was at last found. **Mirko Orlando** from Torino also found himself navigating cultural connections to get to know new arrivals. He writes:

> I travelled to Borgo Mezzanone, a rural village in Foggia province, to meet the men employed on farms. Low pay and living conditions well below dignity; an illegal immigration status would affect your negotiating power, but would not prevent you from getting hired. I joined the activists who in summertime run Radio Ghetto, a broadcasting project that includes migrant residents of the farms. Jam sessions and politics walk hand-in-hand on air. We were supposed to be there to help – to navigate the Italian bureaucracy, to advance their awareness about their own rights, but also to help them into a life other than as labourers. But friendships were born out of this. We shared food, time, conversations, sleeping spaces. Things get tough. When it rains, for instance, everything is damp and water leaks inside the barracks. I remember one man whose tent was always dry, not a single drop would ever get in; once I asked him how. He lifted one of the sheets and showed me his secret: every centimetre of the barrack – walls and ceiling – was upholstered with thick posters of Alleanza Nazionale, a far-right-wing political party. I could not get over the irony of it; I recall thinking that they had a fighting chance after all.

Ventimiglia to La Roya

Further north, as our Ventimiglia Flashpoint describes after this chapter, is a critical border crossing, alongside the mountains between Italy and France. **Jean-Noel Fessy**, who lives in the hillside community of La Roya on the French side, says:

> Many inhabitants of my valley along the river Roya – a valley that is cut in two, the north French, the south Italian Ventimiglia – have

been helping the refugees and migrants on both sides of the border, the vast majority stuck behind it in Italia, since the 2015 flow. The migrants, mostly Sudanese, have been more than 1,000 so far. We are only a small community, 6,000 people at the most in the valley, and we couldn't have gone on without the help of other people and organisations from other valleys of the Alpes Maritimes, as well as occasionally from some Muslim associations. Finally, in May 2017, Kesha Niya showed up. They are a bunch of young Europeans, to me the pride of Europe, who keep coming here, asking how they can help. They came from Calais, professionals. Presently they are hosted at two spots, one of them being in my garden, spending winters under tents, eating and dressing like the refugees, and cooking almost daily in the open. I provide them with electricity, water and a washing machine they barely use. They also help in two other spots in Italy. Like we locals did for the first three years, they serve a daily supper to 100 or so people at a parking lot where they, we, are tolerated. Second, they welcome for a late breakfast on the Italian side of the border those who have been caught by the French police trying to cross, quite "unfriendly" sometimes. They have spent the night in prison, no food nor drink, and have 10 kilometres to walk backwards to Ventimiglia. So Kesha Niya offer a little comfort, chat and a bus ticket; they also try to document the complaints of police brutality.

Another aspect of our work is legal. Both to fight the French authorities who often eagerly flout their own laws – the Préfect has been condemned a few times – and then to defend ourselves, being often attacked by those officials. Almost no one has been imprisoned yet, but they have been spending a lot of time, energy and money trying to make that happen.

Jay Green, a UK volunteer who also began in Calais, says:

I go to La Roya whenever I can, to work with Kesha Niya. I fixed a shower in Jean-Noel's field so people can get clean. Sometimes they stay here for a week or two, just for a rest and to be treated decently, before they try to go on over the steep mountain paths into France. Worst is those who are still stuck in the Italian side at Ventimiglia before they do this climb. There were up to 1,000 living down in a kind of ravine, near the highway. It floods down there, it's steep and there is just nothing. We go over there at night as the Italian police don't allow us to feed them. All we can do is take food in backpacks so the police don't suspect us, then chuck the packages down the ravine to them. I have done that regularly. But it is such a small gesture in the huge ravine. They called back up "Not Enough, Not enough." I hear that in my mind all the time.

The Ventimiglia Flashpoint describes further what goes on at this border, where the French have overturned the Schengen Agreement that ought to allow free movement from Italy to France. In Chapter 9 we also look at other French/Italian border issues, and the risks taken by volunteers to support those who are stranded, or attacked by police. Here, we next look at another chain of often remote and little-known way-stations on the Greece to Croatia "Balkan" route.

Samos to Athens

As described in the first section of this book, almost all of those who had crossed from Turkey to Greece were hoping to move forward to countries like Germany, whose policy was still very open in 2015, or to other European countries where they had a claim. After being delayed for weeks or months on the islands of Lesvos, Chios and Samos while awaiting processing by the Greek authorities, they then headed to Athens and on from there onto the Balkan route to the EU states of northern Europe. This would be a 1,600-kilometre journey that many would make by foot, largely unsupported by the countries they would pass through – but they hoped it would be the last leg of a journey across continents with a final destination in sight. However, many in transit on that journey in Spring 2016 were tragically unaware of the news that borders were already closed further north (as is described in Chapter 2 of this book). **India Nunan** was volunteering in Greece and witnessed the increasing backlog of people who would end up being trapped in Greece. She says:

I began among the chaos of families arriving by boat to the island of Samos. The land borders were still open when I first arrived, and people then could next travel straight to Athens and across the Balkans. Later, as the winding conglomeration of tents sprang up in Piraeus port and continued to grow once the borders shut, I volunteered there too and then in Athens at both the Skaramagas camp and in the unofficial squats. During this time, I saw the way people were informed that the land borders in northern Greece were closed, and saw the hopeless slowness and inadequacies of the official NGO and government response – people had not even received correct information – as well as the lack of attention to their basic material needs. I was on a ferry from Samos to Athens, full of people moving to the mainland, sitting with refugees I had met, including some unaccompanied minors who had been incorrectly age-assessed and at that point did not have the legal advice they needed to challenge this. Some other volunteers were with us. One of them looked at her phone with a concerned expression, spoke very fast for a few minutes and gestured with her head for us to follow her into a less crowded space. In hushed, urgent tones, she passed on the news that this huge political decision had been passed; it had totally passed us by in the whirlwind of activity and arrivals on Samos. We had listened to people tell us that they were going to continue on, past Greece, and no one had told them this was no longer a possibility. They would have interacted with so many officials, from when they attended their asylum interview, collected blankets, even their papers that determined they could now travel, but at no point had this crucial information been passed on that they could not move on. It was down to us to inform them, using just our phones, and beginning with our friends who spoke English as well as Farsi or Arabic. We made our way round the boat, and held space for people when necessary as grief and disbelief began to echo around us. It was one thing that they had not received adequate shelter or food, but official bodies not having given them information was worse.

Piraeus

Those who became stranded at the port of Piraeus or in Athens relied heavily on grassroots organisations. **Negia Milian** has worked since September 2015 with a Greek grassroots group, Pampiraiki Support Initiative for Refugees and Migrants. She says:

> From September 2015 to February 2016 at the Port of Piraeus we met refugees coming from the islands in ferry boats and we provided them with supplies for their trip through the Balkan way. But in spring of 2016 the border closed and the deal with Turkey was signed by the EU. The port became an unofficial camp where at its most crowded it had close to 7,000 people and for many months close to 4,500. We as a group ran this camp, providing shelter, food and medical care. Many organisations supported and co-operated with us at this time. I myself was based at the E1 passenger station, which had close to 2,500 refugees, mostly in tents around the building. I was responsible for running this site and for co-ordinating supplies and activities in the other areas in the port. We received help and donations from Greeks and from all over the world. As these became too many to store at the port, we also started a large warehouse at the site of the old Athens Airport at Elliniko. By the end of July 2016, all the refugees had been moved to camps in Attika and other areas in the mainland and to self-governed buildings (squats). At this point the unofficial port camp closed. But we continued running the warehouse, collecting aid from all over the world and distributing to all places where refugees reside and to organisations providing services to them.

As well as these distributions, there were many in Athens who reached out in welcome and made it possible for some, especially Syrians, to decide to stay and integrate. **Eleni Melirrytou** says:

> We are a small community of Christians in a church at Omonia square in downtown Athens. From 2015, we simply responded to the need. Church building doors were opened wide and welcomed

refugees of our city. We were really ignorant as to what all these new friends needed but we started by making lots of sweet tea, stocking up with baby diapers and baby strollers, and started cooking warm meals three times a week. It did not take long to realise that communication was a big hindrance, so we started teaching them basic English language. However, the biggest of needs we realised was that they needed community. Somewhere to belong and someone to accept them as they were and love them. This was the easy part as we in our Greek culture understand this need and esteem it highly. The need for community is a pillar of the Greek culture. Now we also try to meet some more long-term needs such as job placement, education in the Greek system, housing, and all in all try to help them be independent more than depending on others. And we found out many things about their culture and ways in life. We learned how they value family, children and community. We also observed that some of the most sensitive, kind and good fathers come from Syria. They carry the babies; they tend to the young ones and make sure mum has time off. We learned from our new friends to love even more deeply and strongly. We learned from our new family more than we could ever try to teach them. In our effort to revive them as they arrived tired and desperate, they revived us. We have found a new sense of family and life in our community with our Syrian families. Our lives have been changed and we are forever grateful, not for the misery this war has caused, but the fact that they came to us. We have not been challenged once with them. Our only challenges have come from volunteers from the West. Our community is made up of both Muslims and Christians. There is mutual respect and lots of humour. All of our community's children are now in the Greek school system and speak Greek... My husband is a retired ship's captain. We have together travelled the world, but I had no idea exactly where Syria was located until I looked for it on the world map, only to find out that we share the same sea and have a very similar landscape and culture. Yes, our horizons are forever broadened, and we understand better now that we do live in a changing world and need to adjust and not resist but enjoy the new joys and adventures that are ahead of us.

This positive integration experience has not been matched for others. **Marta Lodola** was compiling a report on conditions in Athens. She found that many people were stranded there, destitute and caught in a web of bureaucracy that meant they could neither legally stay nor return home. She says:

> I was in the city of Athens in 2017. The whole situation in the streets was truly dramatic, and every day we faced several previously unthinkable situations. I was at a place called SynAthina 43, which served as a place of first aid for people living on the street: migrants, but also the homeless. The first person I interviewed came from Morocco, his name is Abdullah. For a long time, he had been sleeping on the street, without papers, without food or water (it was August and the temperature was nearly 40°C). That night he had slept in Piazza Viktoria, praying for someone to help him see his family again, who he had not seen in two years. He tells me that after business school he started travelling, until he crossed Turkey and reached Greece, only to remain stuck there. At that time Abdullah had no hope of obtaining documents in his circumstances. The people I was with immediately took action to help him, and he was subsequently hosted by friends who helped him obtain his documents and return to his country to see his family again. What he kept repeating to me was "We do not come here to steal or take something from the European people, we have everything in our country. What we lack is a country that works, and the chance to travel without restrictions. For us Africans there is no visa that lets you travel, there is no visa for us".

Athens to Idomeni

In early 2016, people were still making their way along the 550-kilometre route to Idomeni in the north of Greece, near the border with the country of North Macedonia (then known as FYROM, the Former Yugoslav Republic of Macedonia). **Simona Bonardi** was there and writes:

7 January 2016. *Kalimera*. Good morning. Once the fog starts to lift, the blue sky will be revealed. I welcome the end of the rain – and so do the other volunteers, sitting in little groups on the wooden benches in front of the clothes distribution tent, to which I am assigned, their hands hugging steaming tea cups. The fog is covering a semi-desert camp, leaving visible the crossing point, currently closed, and five young men washing clothes and shoes at the cold-water taps near the latrines. Rejected yesterday, they walked all night seeking (unsuccessfully) along an alternative route. They are smiling, a sign that they did not encounter the Macedonian police; they are tired, but have no injuries. They are covered in mud up to their waists, but we ran out of men's shoes and clothes during the night and they will have to wear their own coats, trousers, socks and shoes, wet from the laundry.

For weeks now, only Syrians, Afghans and Iraqis are permitted to continue their journey to Northern Europe: no European country is willing to welcome the other nationalities. Those who are rejected try to cross the border illegally, across mountains, rivers and lakes, or travel back to Athens without an alternative plan... The camp was cleared a month ago, the day before my first arrival in Greece. The peaceful protests of the "Forgotten in Idomeni" had occupied the rail tracks, with consequences for Greece's trade relations. At the time, about 3,000 people had been staying at the camp. They were all transferred to Athens and parked at the Athens Tae Kwon Do Olympic stadium. Adults and children slept there on the bare floor, the few toilets kept vomiting their inadequacy, and days passed marked only by meals, in a long, endless queue destined to never get extinguished, due to the many prepared to face the wait more than once, unsatisfied by a single ration. Men from Morocco (free men, I repeat to myself) protested in the court of the stadium calling for borders to be opened, and asking journalists and volunteers to bring their voice to you, European citizens afar. I saw them cry, heard them say "It is not fair". I never met the Iranians who, back in November, sewed their lips in protest. The Idomeni camp, equipped with heated tents, has been unused ever since; nobody is allowed to stay except for brief transiting prior to border crossing, which happens on foot, through a little gate that the Macedonian police opens intermittently, at irregular and mysterious times. Buses arrive one by one after waiting many hours on the motorway, parked at Polykastro EKO Gas Station, the last service station before the Greek-Macedonian border. There, people warm up by burning wood offloaded in the parking area by anonymous trucks, and eat cookies they buy at the station's convenience store (NGOs are not allowed to operate here, because *this is not a camp*). At the Macedonian frontier open fires burn, day and night, at a gas station, and children run and play on the asphalt among parked cars. A new crowd of arrivals brings my attention back to the shelves around me. The men point to the shoes behind me; they do not believe that we are out of their size. They are cold, they are tired, they want coats, hats, scarves and gloves, but the warehouse is far from the camp and the new supply of clothes is expected later this morning. With us struggling to communicate in a language that is neither theirs nor mine, frustration grows. Shoes, they want shoes, even small will do: *better with small shoes than barefoot in the swamp*, they must be thinking. Should I waste a pair of good shoes that will be worn as slippers (too small, a third of the foot destined to stick out) or save them for the next person needing that exact size? Someone gets angry and, before walking away without shoes, shouts a "thank you" like a curse. His friends in the queue apologise.

And now I am alone in the tent, heavy with the sickness of a system that gives me power to grant somebody clothes or say no in the name of some common sense. And I come to realise that this moment of stress release, of steam-blowing, this chance of blaming someone else for their misery, is, to the person in front of me, a rare luxury. For one brief moment, the problem is a pair of shoes, not the freedom of movement denied, or the condemnation to live in a state of illegality. And so, just perhaps, even to be there to receive that rage matters. And their journey resumes.

Ariel Ricker was doing legal work on the Greek islands but moved to Idomeni in 2016 as its reputation as a bottleneck was growing. She says:

> At that time, I heard of trouble in Idomeni. I decided to volunteer there and after a month spent listening to cases, it became clear that there was a need for programmes such as Advocates Abroad. Idomeni was a main border between Greece and North Macedonia. At first it was open, and people could just walk through, but then it became increasingly restrictive; guards came, started checking people, issued tickets to them to come back at a certain time, started asking people lots of questions, then started only letting people through if they had come from a city within the war zone. There was one family that I was trying to help cross, who had come from a city that was not classed as being in a war zone, and so they were rejected. They had a little boy – only six or seven years old – and he collapsed in front of the barbed wire and started sobbing hysterically. To have a child that young understand what rejection at the border meant was terrifying to me.

This book's Idomeni Flashpoint section tells in more detail how in May 2016 this border was finally closed to all undocumented migrants, how the camp was demolished, and how the thousands desperate to move forward were forcibly removed to detention centres in other parts of Greece.

Serbia, Belgrade and the Croatian Border

Those who had earlier made it through as far as Serbia did not find this trip easy; if the arrivals process onto the Greek islands had been characterised by chaos and institutional inertia, the dominant theme of this Balkan route was, from all volunteer accounts, state violence and abuse by both military and police forces. Practically none of those travelling north were looking to settle in the states between Greece and Northern Europe – North Macedonia, Albania, Kosovo, Montenegro, Serbia, Bosnia and Herzegovina, Croatia, Hungary – and many of these states such as Serbia and Hungary had openly declared hostility towards those caught in the "refugee crisis". Some countries, even if failing to offer humanitarian support, simply hastened these travellers on their way to save themselves further trouble. But others, as volunteers and human rights observers have recorded in countless cases, operated policies of abuse and harassment, frequently imprisoning those passing through, and operating what is known as the "pushback" practice of returning them to the last border they crossed, using extreme brutality and causing many to be injured or die.

A member of a UK group that prefers to be anonymous but reports under the name of "Puffi to the Rescue" wrote the following account of the early days of the crisis, when forward movement from Serbia to Croatia (an EU state) was at least still possible.

October 2015 in Preševo, Serbia. The situation is being kept calm, yet we must admit it is dramatic. Thousands of people are being put on buses in order to be brought to the Croatian border. Despite the huge amount of buses, people still have to queue for hours, exhausted, in the cold and under the rain. Police are controlling the access to the bus lanes in order to avoid crowds – they are stressed, and journalists and photographers are not allowed to enter. With Eastern European countries closing yet more borders within a couple of hours and being mysterious about their next moves, we're left in the rain here in Preševo. And at least another 2,500 people will be entering Serbia during this night. So we keep calm and just build huge tents over the queue in order to prevent refugees from getting soaked and sick. We have tried many ways of keeping people dry in the freezing rain because they are forced to walk through fields across "borders" and then wait ten hours in the open street. The rain and cold is extremely dangerous. I have seen a father's face while holding his child in his arms in the pouring rain with no waterproofs, knowing that his child is now close to death after 12 hours with no shelter. We bought big rolls of strong sheet plastic, cut them and punched holes in the middle for the heads. I have never wanted to have kids but the first night, after handing out hundreds of these black plastic sandwich boards, I realised that all the little kids now had Darth Vader black capes, giggling and running down the railway in the rain; a very cute and beautiful sight. That night I felt we had achieved something.

Every two to three hours a train arrives and offloads 500–1,000 people into the pouring rain without waterproofs. They then trudge 1 kilometre through the mud and rain to a police station just across the imaginary border. Today I dragged someone's wheelchair for an hour through it. The man had no way to get there unless I did. I am sitting now in the camper van with the rain pounding on the roof, and I know that we don't have enough waterproofs for the children, and that at some point again I will have to say that we have run out and leave 6-year-olds to walk into the storm with just a jumper on. The Serbian authorities will then make them stand in the rain, ten hours waiting in the street that looks like a war zone, trying to get papers to cross other imaginary lines. Fucking preposterous. If they live, they get a cup of tea at the other end and a bus ride to the next fascist country. Every day I break down now...

Blackout in Preševo: the registration centre is completely in the dark – this blocks the process and consequently also the queue. Many people are panicking, many others try to actually leave the queue and come back tomorrow. There is VERY LITTLE medical help around, everybody is wet and cold and lots of children are sick. At least it hasn't been raining for half an hour now. We try to help and inform – in the dark, with patience and a smile. Serbia and Macedonia are tough places. Unemployment is at 17% and 27% respectively. There are constant problems with the Mafia and those taking advantage of the refugees here, selling goods, fake registrations and taxi rides to nowhere. As a comparatively rich, white, privileged person, I must remember that these are also poor people trying to survive.

At Tabanocve in the pouring rain two men approached me, both with new leather jackets, the second, much bigger one, with a shaven head. They explained to me how I should act here in no uncertain terms. The train then arrived with another 1,000 refugees and I approached the train next to the more dominant man of the two. He stepped forward in front of me to open the train door and we both recoiled back at the stench from the inside of the train. He vomited on the ground a few metres away, but I managed to cover my face quickly enough. He walked straight back, helped the first family off the train and looked them up and down. Upon realising that the child had no socks he ran back to his stall, grabbed some socks and, kneeling on the ground in front of the mother, placed the socks on the child's feet. He placed his hands together, smiled and wished them good luck. In these extreme emotional situations, and in other cultures, one should never judge another person by body language or appearance. They were both exceptional people and I will not forget them. I will always think they are about to kill everyone they are chatting with though!

Providing help in emergency situations means constant emotional swings. You have to remain strong at all times as hundreds are counting on you. Be alert to spot those who are in danger and can't ask for help. Stay empathetic to give a smile of hope for the most vulnerable ones. Never forget to take care of your team mates and beloved, as they may be on the edge of emotional breakdown. Make sure to hug, or smile at, a volunteer passing you on the street. Remember to sleep, eat and drink enough water and give yourself the right to burst into tears whenever you have to. And keep on going again, and again, and again...

Because each time you get invited to dance with a group of people who have finally made it through the line, or receive a hug from the most beautiful child in the world, you know you're here for a reason.

Northwest Bosnia and Herzegovina

American volunteer **Jack Sapoch** was working at the Velika Kladuša transit camp with No Name Kitchen, one of the larger groups active in many of the Balkan and Greek "Hotspots". This camp was in the country of Bosnia and Herzegovina, just before the border crossing to Croatia. He says:

> I remember there was a group of maybe ten Kurdish men, young adults my age, in their early twenties. They were all from the same city in Syria, from Kobani, which had been almost entirely destroyed in the battle between SDF (Syrian Democratic Forces) and Daesh. As volunteers, we would spend six, seven, eight hours at the shower project getting the line in order, making sure the showers were operating, and cleaning them when they got dirty. These Kurdish guys from Kobani would come at the end of every day and they would wait, wait, wait; and then they, unlike everyone else, would take ten minutes to clean the showers by themselves before they went in. "What, you want me to shower in this dirty place?!" It was special. I got to know some of the guys and one of them in particular became close. He was my age, 22, and he had more physical injuries on him than anybody I had ever seen in my life. He had probably 15 bullet wounds in his body. He showed me all of them the day before he left. He had been shot through the stomach three times, he had been shot clean through his kneecap – he had no kneecap – and shot in the head. It was amazing to me that this boy was alive. He complained that it was difficult to walk all the way to Europe to get surgery for his kneecap, because he couldn't get it in Turkey or Syria. This group of ten introduced me to the beauty that can survive in these transit situations. One night they invited me to their tent in the Velika Kladuša camp, and I went, and at the end of the night they broke into song. I have the audio recording of the song on my phone. It was a Kurdish song that they all knew. One guy, Mahmo, took the lead in singing and we were sitting around this fire, and usually there is the hustle and bustle of transit camp that goes on at night – noise in the background or whatever – but in my memory of that time it was all quiet and you just had these ten men who were sitting there, singing this song that meant so much to them and reminded them of their homeland. It had such an intense beauty to it; I don't know that I ever experienced something like that before.

But Jack, like many others, was also witness to the ugliness and aggression of the "pushbacks". He goes on:

> Then on the other end of the spectrum there is the ugly, horrific nature of the transit camps. All of those guys except for one or two ended up leaving for "the game" – to attempt to transit – and they made it, but a couple of guys ended up staying behind because they didn't have money to pay the smuggler or they weren't ready to go or something. One of the boys that stayed behind was named Sami. He was also from Kobani and he was quite young – around 17 – and I ended up getting to know him a bit better. He went to attempt to transit one night in November. I remember being nervous, as you get nervous for the people you know when they try these risky attempts, and he texted me at one o'clock in the morning saying, "I need to talk to you, where are you?" I didn't see him until the next morning, and he came up to me on the street and he said, "Jack, I need to show you something". He took out his phone and proceeded to show me a video; it was a black image but there were noises in it, and to me it sounded like someone singing or being tickled so I thought it was funny at first. I said, "Sami, what are you showing me?" But his face was so serious and traumatised that I looked again, and I understood that what he was showing me was a recording of a pushback by Croatian police officers beating men, human beings, and the screams of human beings being hurt. Sami had gone on this game and he had stopped close to the Croatian border, when he saw police officers come and he witnessed a pushback in action.
>
> People would come to Kladuša and use our showers and we would give them sleeping bags and shoes to take with them so they could make these transit attempts, try to get out of these deplorable living situations and try to find stability in their lives. And they would go off on these attempts and we would hear a few days, weeks later that one of them had been taken by the river. This was never a feeling that I knew before getting involved in volunteering, what it was like to have someone you know die so quickly and so preventatively, over something like trying to cross a river when

there's probably a bridge a few kilometres away. Yet because the people attempting the routes are pushed to attempt in more and more clandestine and dangerous ways, this is a story that we have to hear often; it's become normal.

Thousands of refugees have been effectively "kettled" by the closure of the Balkan borders, unable to go forward except by clandestine routes, and knowing also that it is absolutely impossible, even if they should decide to do so, to somehow traffic themselves all the way back home. So they were trapped in a corridor reaching from Croatia all the way back to the destitute squats of Athens, with whatever status they may have had back there now nulled.

Belgrade, Serbia

As the Bosnia–Croatia route became more difficult, others attempted to travel through Serbia, though Serbia was known to be even more brutal in its treatment of refugees and of volunteers. Berlin-based volunteer **Nadine Allgeier** was in Belgrade in January 2017. She says:

> I and some others had been in Thessaloniki working with Soulfood Kitchen, a grassroots group that feeds refugees on the streets. We began to hear rumours about a tragic situation in Belgrade, where over 1,000 refugees were sleeping in an abandoned railway station in the centre of the city called "the Barracks" with no humanitarian support at all. On the official news, however, the situation was scarcely reported if at all. Four other volunteers and I formed a new group, Soulwelders, and headed off there. I remember clearly our first sight of the railway station. We came by car and parked inside the unofficial camp, which also served as a parking lot for regular citizens. The snow was falling, it was freezing. Still, the first thing I saw was two young boys outside in the snow, half-naked, helping each other to wash themselves. There was one local group who distributed a meal a day on site – the food line was a frightening vision. Outside in the cold, hundreds of refugees

stood in line, covered with snow, barely clothed, waiting for their one meal a day. For the rest of their nutrition, they had to take care of themselves. It is important to note that most of them were underage or still young. These first images of the Barracks will stick with me forever. It was so unbearable to see that it made me remember the images of concentration camps in my history books at school.

Inside the warehouses where immigrants slept, smoke was all over the place, coming from fires made of toxic railway sleepers. It was a dark and smoky place. Our first action was to build safe stoves out of barrels with pipes to make the smoke go outside. Then we provided clean wood, which we distributed each morning by truck. As simple as it may sound, these actions made a huge difference. And so our ambitions grew. Our group with other independent workers set up a washing station, a shower truck and a warehouse where provisions were kept, and a new kitchen.

As the only woman in our group, I was less able to do the heavier work so I instead started to focus on our social media, taking photos, responding to messages, reporting about what was happening. So I was more in contact with refugees themselves, talking with them, taking pictures of their routine, documenting their stories. They used to invite me for *chai*, or just for a chat. I stopped feeling useless when I realised my emotional support was also very important for them, especially when I realised a lot of them were suffering from savage tortures at the borders when trying to cross them. I've been collecting records of police abuses at the borders of Europe for a week now. The stories you hear from underage boys are unbelievable. They are being tortured by heartless police officers who treat them no better than dogs. This is happening especially at the Bulgarian and Hungarian borders. They spit on them, they make them lie on the floor and then they walk on their backs, they throw cold water on them and give them electric shocks, they call them "dogs" and "animals", they steal their money, food, mobiles and clothes. One of the common assaults they inflict upon refugees: they station six to eight police officers within a riot van, and one by one they make boys go into the van and get savagely beaten. They use tear-gas multiple times while laughing and taking pictures, they make them crawl around the floor and release their dogs upon them just for fun. They stub out their cigarettes on their bodies, and so on. When the boys try to get help, to ask for treatment for their injuries, what they hear is that hospitals are just for humans, not for dogs like them. When they ask for food, police officers put chewing gum on their hair and banana skins on their neck. Sometimes in the end, after lining them up, spraying them and beating them one last time, authorities make them read a paper which says they were not physically abused by any police officer. Filming just the faces, the dogs walking around their legs cannot be seen. Obviously, police officers always say they must not tell anyone about what happened...

I decided to focus more on the border crossing issue. I started to communicate that I wanted to report on it, and very soon I began to be informed almost every time someone came back from the borders. The stories of abuse and torture were heart-breaking. I did interviews and took photos of the clear physical traces of violence. That was the moment I was ultimately confronted with the harsh reality of the consequences of European laws. The tortures perpetrated by border police were physical and verbal, from calling refugees dogs and make them crawl as if they were so, to forcing them to swim back to the neighbouring country even if being told they didn't know how to swim. Police officers stripped refugees, kids included, naked and made them stand in water, in negative temperatures, for an unlimited time. If they moved, they got electrocuted, but then again... they would be electrocuted anyway.

Another volunteer, **Dylan Longman**, echoes the same story.

My first experience of Belgrade... frozen thick ice and snow... the hellish warehouses spewing yellow smoke from the railway sleeper fires... the amount of unaccompanied minors, many as young as seven with oily smeared faces and clothes from the fumes of the railway sleepers... Hungarian police brutality... one night 75 refugees came back from the border beaten and tortured, many broken limbs, concussions, cigarette burns on their faces... frostbite from standing for hours in line waiting to be beaten.

Not only does there need to be a rapid humanitarian solution for those who remain trapped in such hostile environments, but also clearly urgent reviews within the EU and the international community of state and police brutality. Volunteers have themselves faced police hostility, and are the only ones systematically gathering vital and heartbreaking evidence of these police attacks conducted in secret on refugees. Cases must be brought against countries that breach human rights in this way. And while volunteers are active on this front via umbrella groups like the European Council on Refugees and Exiles (ECRE) and the Global Legal Action Network (GLAN), they meanwhile have to deal the best they can with the continuing realities of abuses people face day to day, and, if nothing else, bear witness.

I will end this chapter by returning south to Idomeni in northern Greece, where **Ruhi Akhtar**, who had worked at Idomeni camp during its last days in 2016, returned to visit a year after it was evacuated. "Idomeni Refugee Camp – Paying Respects" is a blog post she wrote in 2017.

Today we visited the site and the rail tracks where the Idomeni refugee camp used to be... Today made me realise that as a volunteer there will always be a part of me that will have almost PTSD-like symptoms when remembering Idomeni. This camp gave me nightmares, and my first trip left me so incomplete and all I could do was try harder and be stronger in gathering support for these people. Even though the camp is now gone, it was almost as if I could see the ghost of Idomeni and tents still there, people still around. I could see children running past me saying "My friend, my friend..." As a volunteer, nothing is more distressing than walking among ten thousand people of all ages, men, women, children, babies, pregnant and disabled, in devastation and wanting to help, helping daily yet still being helpless. Because it wasn't enough. It still isn't enough.

Flashpoint: Idomeni

Treasa O'Brien and Dan Dowling

Figure 5.1 Kilkis, northern Greece, 2015. Volunteers sort international aid donations for refugees at a warehouse in Greek Macedonia.

Image credit: Sue Walsh.

At the end of 2015, Serbia closed its border to migrants regardless of their status. In January 2016, Austria limited the number of immigrants that were allowed to be in the country at the same time. A month later, Slovenia barred refugees from transiting through its territory. Then in March 2016, North Macedonia (then FYROM) announced the closure of its Greek border to refugees heading north, so blocking the main access route for refugees seeking to reach the northern European states. Thus the transit camp at Idomeni, managed initially by Médecins Sans Frontières (MSF) and the UNHCR in 2015, rapidly had to become a longer-term residential camp where over 1,000 people every day were arriving to be met by armed police blocking the way. On 24 May 2016, the Greek authorities began forcibly relocating refugees from the Idomeni camp to processing facilities hundreds of miles from the border.

Below, two volunteers give their accounts of the Idomeni border camps.

Treasa O'Brien

Idomeni is a small village in northern Greece with a registered population of 154 people, situated just before the border with what is now called North Macedonia. Greeks and Macedonians, workers and international tourists, pass through the border daily with ease. In 2015 and early 2016, it was also where hundreds of thousands of people who had arrived by boat to the Greek islands passed through to seek refuge in Europe. At the end of March 2016, the border was closed and it was estimated that there were 12,000–14,000 people living temporarily in an informal camp in the adjacent fields, also called a "tent city", including 4,000 vulnerable children. Everyone was waiting to move forward into northern Europe but was no longer able to do so. The migrants' Greek journey until now had been – and could have continued to be – achievable in days; those arriving at islands such as Lesvos had first been met by volunteers, then by the UNHCR, which encouraged them to present themselves at Moria refugee camp to get official papers allowing them to make the 12-hour ferry journey from Mytilene to Athens, then the 550-kilo-metre road journey, usually taken by bus from Athens, to the North Macedonian border at Idomeni. From North Macedonia, the intention was to continue on to further destinations in Europe. They could expect to be in Germany, Norway or another European country within three to four days, often joining family who'd travelled ahead earlier. Technically such journeys should not have been allowed under the EU Dublin Regulation, which states that new arrivals should claim asylum at their first point of entry, but in practice Greece – like Italy, beleaguered by the high numbers – had been issuing visas allowing onward travel out of the country.

Figure 5.2 Idomeni, northern Greece, 2015. North Macedonian military guards scrutinise refugees in groups of 60 crossing a temporary Greece–North Macedonia wired border.

Image credit: Sue Walsh.

But this all changed in March 2016 when prime ministers and leaders from the EU made an agreement with the prime minister of Turkey which drastically limited the options for especially non-Syrians. (The EU–Turkey deal is discussed fully in Chapter 2.) The deal also stipulated that Greece would no longer issue documents allowing forward travel to the rest of Europe. Human rights organisations, solidarity groups and NGOs decried the deal, calling it "a dark day for humanity". The idea behind the deal was to stop nationalities other than Syrians seeking refuge in other countries in Europe by detaining them in Greece and deporting many of them back to Turkey. As of 18 March 2016, over 50,000 people who were moving forward to other European states were detained indefinitely in Greece as a consequence of this, and of North Macedonia and several countries to the north making unilateral decisions to close their borders.

I was in Idomeni, Athens and Lesvos in the days and weeks after the deal was made. Many people were forced to remain on Lesvos in the open prison of Moria and nearby islands; this was because they could no longer get papers or board transport to Athens, as they had been able to do before. Some people made it as far as Athens and into various camps, including their own self-organised camp at Piraeus Port. Some 4,500 refugees were living in tents at the port in early April. They made their own shelters all along the tourist port and organised food and water. Greek and international activists joined them in support. As it was not recognised as an official camp, all "aid" was unofficial. A Syrian, an Afghan and an Iraqi worked together to organise the families staying there, including setting up a school, food, medical care and organising turns at showers in an apartment rented by the hour.

Thousands more made it as far as the North Macedonian border at Idomeni, where they were forcibly stopped from going further. This place had only ever been a "stopping point" as refugees left Greece and moved into North Macedonia, but was now a dead end. Groups formed together in makeshift shelters; a few tents became a sea of thousands of tents within days. The camp itself was chaotic, and attempts to improve things were swamped by the speed at which

Figure 5.3 Idomeni, northern Greece, 2016. A self-organised camp set up by refugee families at an EKO petrol station a few miles south of the Idomeni border with North Macedonia.

Image credit: Treasa O'Brien.

it grew, with huge numbers of people arriving each day. Smaller *ad hoc* support groups were fire-fighting – literally – and because of the political situation, the resources needed to address the most basic human requirements were scarce at best. I met a woman whom I had befriended when I was working on the night-time boat welcomes in Lesvos the preceding winter; she had made it over the northern border by river with a group of friends; they had been asleep in a field on the North Macedonian side, drying their clothes after the river crossing, when a farmer found them and turned them over to police, who beat them and sent them back south over the border to Greece. On 14 March, in one day, an estimated 2,000 people crossed the Greek–North Macedonian border by wading through the nearby river. It felt like a triumph over the EU border regime. However, they were met by North Macedonian police who "returned" them to the camp they had escaped. These instances highlight the precarity of those who could not get through, after already having travelled so far and so dangerously to get to this point. They also highlight their enduring hope and ingenuity at trying to move forward. Nobody wanted to stay still and nobody wanted to go back.

When I arrived at Idomeni on 24 March 2016, the border was still closed; 14,000 people were waiting. No one was getting through. Large families camped together, and children played between the tents. Some camped along the train tracks and in the fields around the border, hoping that they could cross the next day. It was overcrowded, windy and cold. Food queues stretched along the muddy fields. More queues at a medical tent. Queues for water. The waiting was excruciating.

Everyone – people seeking refuge, activists, official NGO workers – was talking about the protest that was due to happen later that day. Riot police lined up in front of the border with shields, helmets and batons. Large reinforced riot vehicles loomed nearby. People who were seeking refuge made signs, some in English, including "Don't hit us" and "Happy Easter" on cardboard. The news going around informally was that four busloads of activists and journalists were due to arrive, and would walk across the border with everyone. In this act of defiance and solidarity, the international press would be there to witness and intervene so that those seeking refuge would not get beaten and would be able to pass through. There was excitement and exhilaration in the air. I met an old man who was waiting to travel on foot to meet his family, who were in Norway. He had walked from Athens, some 550 kilometres. Now he was being told he had to turn back. As the day wore on, preparations grew. Another 100 armed riot police with shields gathered near the fence. People of all ages held a peaceful protest with signs, chants and songs… But no busload of activists or journalists arrived. Nobody tried to pass. At the same time, officials from the UNHCR were calling on a loudspeaker for people to leave the area and board the buses to official camps. But people didn't know if it was a trick, and whether leaving the camp would mean failure to cross the border for sure. However, some boarded the buses, fearing for their safety and the safety of more vulnerable members of their group. Refugee and journalist Qusay Loubani, who was there and later wrote about it, said, "The most important and most asked question in Idomeni is, what is the West waiting for? Your agreement with Turkey does not address our cause. The Europeans are using us to scare other refugees away."

Dan Dowling

Every day, 2,000 more people were arriving to the border-point at Idomeni, which had few facilities. Groups in the UK heard the Idomeni camp was in crisis, and my group, Refugee Aid Network (RAN), mobilised quickly. We ended up being there for the final eviction in May 2016, two months after the border had been all but shut down.

RAN was one of the very few groups allowed through the blockade into the camp itself. The armed riot police let us know we might not come out unscathed, and that they would not be coming in to save

Figure 5.4 Idomeni, northern Greece, 2016. Greek police push back those trying to cross the border into North Macedonia March 2016.

Image credit: Treasa O'Brien.

us. This threat was enough to keep the large aid agencies away. We went in as quick as we could and frantically began giving out food and blankets. We saw children were starving and cold, everything was wet, all firewood supplies had gone – so the acrid stench of burning tyres and tear-gas was enduring. A common ground had finally been found between all the diverse refugees in that place; people were universally tired, sick and suffering immeasurably. On the back of the horrific journey and their treatment along the way lay the huge weight of trauma many had suffered. This didn't present in the media pictures. Low-level and constant weeping, sunken eyes, the overall feeling that there was no more hope – that the huge effort, the sacrifices that had been made to have a chance of a better life and safety, all was slipping away fast. The ambition of a better life was not happening, and northern Europe had no appetite to help.

On the morning of 23 May, the authorities closed the water supply into the camp. They also stopped any agency from giving food supplies, with a clear strategy for emptying the camp: creating a lack of basic needs – food and water – to force people, particularly the vulnerable, to leave by themselves. It was working. There were several buses, always in view, and waiting for people with food packs and water on board. NGOs were not allowed anywhere near the camp after that day. We managed to do one more aid drop, out of sight of police, but then more police arrived and we had to give up.

According to CNN Greece at the time, the eviction was to take seven days and follow a strategy: on the first day, the forces were to separate the camp into several sectors which were isolated from each other. Subsequently, these sectors would be emptied over several days, outside the view of media and volunteers in order to avoid witnesses and interference. Journalists and volunteers were forced out of the camp by police officers. What happened over that week – the level of violence, the force used – could not be properly verified as it was all done out of sight. Médecins Sans Frontières denounced the forced movement of thousands of refugees, the lack of information provided about their destinations and the restrictions imposed on humanitarian assistance during this process.

Figure 5.5 Idomeni, northern Greece, 2016. Refugees make homemade signs in a peaceful protest at the Greek–Macedonian border, which was closed indefinitely as an effect of the EU–Turkey deal in March 2016.
Image credit: Treasa O'Brien.

Many refugees, and the few doctors who were allowed to witness the final days, later described the eviction. One described a well-dressed family of five who stood out in the demoralised crowd. Led by a father who was clearly resolute in his decision to remain dignified in this undignified situation, he marched with his family towards the bus. The eerie silence that had filled the air since daybreak was broken by a bulldozer demolishing their makeshift shelter behind them. Made of wood from tree branches and covered with blankets, it had been their home for three months. Other families followed. A 3-year-old girl stumbled through a field of poppies and long grass, trying to keep up with her teenage brother. Despite his size, he was struggling to balance the wheelbarrow carrying their belongings.

RAN was not allowed back into the camp. Having raced to Idomeni to help, we could do no more. We went on to Thessaloniki to help in the camps there.

Flashpoint: The Balkan States

Nidžara Ahmetašević and Jack Sapoch

Over 2 million people on the move have reached Western Europe since 2014, with likely more than half of this number having passed through what is known as the "Balkan route" – from Turkey and Greece up to North Macedonia or Albania, and then on to Serbia,

Figure 5.6 Tabanovce, North Macedonia, 2015. People heading north before borders are closed, supported here by activist group Legis, which continues this work.

Image credit: Legis.

Kosovo, Montenegro, Bosnia and Herzegovina and Croatia. While some of the routes have changed with time, the Balkan route has never completely closed. In 2014, the Balkan route was already busy with those arriving from Greece and heading towards the wealthier European countries. Limited numbers of people aimed to settle in the Balkans – one of the poorest regions in Europe. But the sudden and unexpected closure of EU borders that came after the controversial EU deal with Turkey in March 2016, accompanied by state-based violence against the new arrivals, turned the Balkans region into a bottle-neck where many became stuck in an intractable limbo. In December 2019, according to some estimates, at least 20,000 people were still trapped along various points on the route.

And along this route, places like Idomeni at the border between Greece and North Macedonia, Tabanovce and Gevgelija in North Macedonia, the "Barracks" in Belgrade and the informal settlements in Šid, both in Serbia, as well as Bihać and Velika Kladuša in Bosnia and Herzegovina – all of these are otherwise little known to the broader international public, but will forever be remembered by those who witnessed them as places where human rights were suffocated by the EU border regime. These locations bear witness to the experiences of thousands of people stopped by different means and forced to live in inhumane conditions for long periods of time. All along this route there were camps of a sort, but they mostly provided dismal living conditions, with residents deprived of their basic rights and often falsely presented to the public as the cause of their own crisis.

Macedonia to Croatia

For much of 2015, safe passage was to some extent provided by Balkan states for people coming from war zones like Syria, Iraq and Afghanistan. For example, for several months authorities in North Macedonia, Serbia and Croatia provided buses and trains in order to transport people through the Balkans, helping them to leave, and at the same time avoiding offering them shelter. However, most of the people had to walk, following roads and railway tracks to reach the larger cities. The media at the time focused heavily on showing pictures of families, babies, but also elderly people walking across the Balkan route, tired yet hopeful.

But by October and November of 2015, the atmosphere had already begun to change, and restrictions were imposed for people entering the Schengen zone, an area of 26 European states that had officially abolished all passport checks and all other types of border control at their mutual borders for their citizens. At the same time, North Macedonia, and then Croatia, followed the practice of several EU countries and imposed stricter border controls. The first results were visible across the border from Idomeni, where the North Macedonian army was deployed.

Those who were allowed, or found a way, to cross from Idomeni into North Macedonia were held in camps in Gevgelija and Tabanovci,

Figure 5.7 Šid, Serbia, 2017. Graves of those who died at EU border lines, including Madina Husseyin, a 6-year-old girl from Afghanistan, who was killed on the train tracks after a pushback by Croatian border police.
Image credit: Nidžara Ahmetašević.

where entry selection was made by local authorities following EU recommendations, with primarily people from war zones being allowed to continue. At some point in December 2015, the term "economic migrants" became more present in media and public discourse. This situation was reflected in Serbia, where by the end of the year the number of people on the move increased. At the same time, Hungarian border police introduced brutal violence, while fences and walls were being built. Still, people continued on the route.

Border Closures along the Route

It became clear that EU countries intended to close more borders at the beginning of 2016. Coincidentally, the visible presence of smugglers along the route also became more obvious during this time. For them, the closure of the borders meant an opportunity to increase prices for crossing. In March 2016, one person had to pay Eur. 800 to cross from Greece to North Macedonia, according to the independent Are You Syrious? Daily Digest. But soon after this, in May 2016, the makeshift camp in Idomeni on the Greek–North Macedonian border was evicted and the options for people to freely utilise trains and buses on their journeys was frozen as well, and smugglers benefitted further.

People continued walking and travelling in different ways along the Balkan route. Many were usually halted for some time at a camp in Slavonski Brod, eastern Croatia. Thousands continued on to make their way towards Slovenia, the first country within the Schengen zone. Often, they were met by local people from the region but also from other parts of the world who were showing solidarity in any way they could. Local people along the way would leave food in front of their doors and along the roads all over the Balkans, including Croatia, which kept its borders with Serbia open for people on the move back then. However, the rise of the far-right political groupings in the EU coincided with the stepping back of several governments in their support towards the new arrivals. Accordingly, many of those on the move became afraid that the borders would close, and began spending less time in camps and stopping as little as possible along the more remote parts of the route. By the end of 2016 and the beginning of 2017, the number of people on the streets of Belgrade was visibly increasing and local organisations, activists and volunteers attempted to respond to their needs by organising distributions and providing shelter wherever possible.

At around this time, activists and volunteers on the route began noticing and recording how people on the move became subjected to "pushbacks" – the unlawful, cross-border return of people apprehended by border authorities to the country from which they had entered. Pushbacks from Schengen-zone countries also began to be recorded. Austria started sending people – most often those from North African countries or Iran – back to Slovenia. Many people became stuck in Serbia after pushbacks from Croatia or Hungary, and from other EU countries such as Bulgaria and Romania. Large numbers of those pushed back were Afghans, whom many EU countries considered had little claim on refugee status. During these pushbacks, national border authorities often engaged in direct physical violence (in the form of punches, baton strikes, kicks, forced immersion in near-freezing water or electrical shocks), and systematic targeting of material possessions (such as mobile phones, power banks, legal documents, shoes, sleeping bags, money and backpacks).

Shifting Routes through Serbia

In 2016 and 2017, accommodation capacities in Serbia were sparse, often leaving many people out of the system and sleeping out in the open. This led to the creation of several makeshift camps and settlements, with the biggest one located in a series of abandoned buildings behind the Belgrade railway station, colloquially referred to as "the Barracks". At its height, close to 1,500 individuals would live here. The majority of Barracks residents were from Afghanistan, including many unaccompanied minors. At the same time, groups of around 200 camped out in Serbia near the border with Hungary close to the towns of Šid and Subotica, sleeping rough either in abandoned industrial complexes or in hard-to-access forested areas. Assistance to all of them was provided mostly by local and international NGOs as well as volunteer groups. However, the state apparatus was strongly against this type of solidarity, and presented obstacles to the continuation of these activities. A group called Border Monitoring Serbia reported that in November 2016, the Serbian Ministry of Labour, Employment, Veterans and Social Affairs issued an open letter to NGOs saying that their existing capacities could manage all the people, and that "assistance and support in the form of food, clothing, footwear, encouraging migrants to reside outside the designated permanent asylum centres and transit reception centres are no longer acceptable, particularly in the Belgrade municipality". At the same time, the police were increasing pressure and preventing volunteers from distributing aid in the streets. Despite this, local grassroots NGOs such as Info Park and Refugee Aid Miksalište reported that the camps were full and that people had nowhere to go. Accordingly, these local NGOs, alongside international solidarity and volunteer groups – such as Hot Food Idomeni, Soulwelders, the local No Borders chapter and No Name Kitchen – continued to operate, especially in the Barracks, providing food, heating, medical assistance and clothing. Volunteer groups such as Rigardu, Aid Delivery Mission and Fresh Response engaged in similar efforts in the border regions.

Living conditions for people were desperate in the Belgrade Barracks. The winter of 2016–2017 was particularly harsh and people faced months of sub-zero temperatures, outbreaks of scabies and body lice, food insecurity and serious health risks associated with the plastics and railroading material they were forced to burn for warmth. Reuters news agency even reported cases of self-prostitution of minors there. Despite this, however, the Barracks offered some kind of established community of support and solidarity, with many volunteers coming and staying there with people, cooking for them and providing basic care.

Figure 5.8 Belgrade, Serbia, 2017. Refugee support group Biryani and Bananas distributes clothes packs at the "Belgrade Barracks", where over 1,000 people were housed, including many minors.

Image credit: Ruhi Akhtar.

In May 2017, the Barracks was evicted, and most residents were relocated to state centres across Serbia. Many resisted these relocations and instead moved towards the Serbian border with Croatia in order to continue their journeys. Šid, a small city near this border, became an important place for people attempting to enter the Schengen zone via the Balkan route in 2017, and here they often were met by violent border authorities. The picture of this brutality will forever bear the face of Madina Husseini, a 6-year-old girl from Afghanistan who lost her life after being pushed back by the Croatian border police. The story of her death was made public by the efforts of volunteers and NGOs. Madina was buried in Šid, and it took many attempts for her family to finally manage to cross

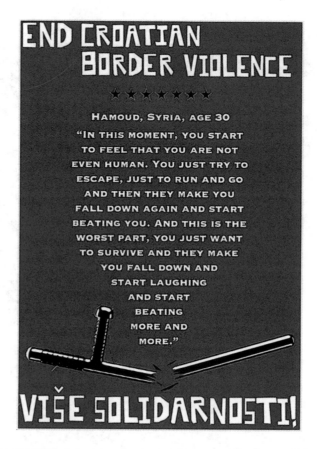

Figure 5.9 Velika Kladuša, Bosnia and Herzegovina, 2019. Poster produced by No Name Kitchen to protest violence used by the Croatian armed forces and police. Image credit: Jack Sapoch.

into the EU after she died. Madina's grave, along with several other mostly non-identified persons, will stay forever at the entrance to the EU as a reminder of the cruelty of the closed-border policy.

Madina's death, which signified the entrenched dangers of attempting to cross the Serbian–Croatian border, precipitated attempts by people smugglers and migrants to look for new, less controlled routes into Europe through the Balkans. The best remaining option to attempt to cross into Croatia and the EU was to travel further west, through the state of Bosnia and Herzegovina, a country that had not experienced a significant arrival of migrants in previous years. Even though the state authorities – as well as UNHCR and the International Organisation for Migration (IOM) offices present in the country – were aware of developments on the route, nobody was ready for the thousands of people who began arriving from November 2017. The border city of Pljevlja in Montenegro became busy during the winter, with hundreds of people crossing over the mountains in deep snow, and the only help was provided by the local feminist organisation Bona Fide. These individuals would stop briefly in the city of Trebinje before continuing towards the capital Sarajevo, then moving northwest towards the Una-Sana Canton – with its key border towns of Bihać and Velika Kladuša – where they would make perilous attempts to cross through to Croatia.

Bosnia and Herzegovina – The "New Balkan Route"

By the Spring of 2018, 1,000 people who had arrived mostly from Greece were registered in Sarajevo. Many of them were Syrians or Afghans, and others were from the Maghreb countries, Pakistan, India and Bangladesh. Large amounts of support and assistance were provided by local citizens, who showed an admirable level of solidarity, similar to the efforts seen in Greece during 2015 and 2016. People reacted spontaneously, just going out and together finding ways to provide assistance or support. A makeshift camp was formed in a city park adjacent to Sarajevo city hall, and over 300 people were soon sleeping there – in tents with no access to sanitation, but supported by local people with food and clothing. Similar forms of support developed in the cities of Bihać and Velika Kladuša, which are the closest to the EU (Croatian) border. At this time Bosnia and Herzegovina had only a single asylum centre with limited capacity for about 150 people. So even in these larger cities, people were sleeping in the open in parks, abandoned buildings or anywhere they could find a shelter. More informal camps began to spring up. In

Bihać, a disused dormitory building known as Borići began to be used by hundreds of refugees and migrants. In Velika Kladuša, an informal tent camp known as Trnovi swelled with new arrivals. In some cases, local people provided space in their own homes.

The involvement of the state authorities at this point was largely limited to registration, while large international aid organisations and their local partners proved clumsy and slow. Only later, in the spring and summer of 2018, did several independent volunteer groups such as SOS Team Kladuša and No Name Kitchen also begin providing direct assistance in transit Hotspots in Bosnia and Herzegovina, expanding on work previously being done by local people – which was considerable: local business owner Asim "Latan" Latić, for example, became well known in Velika Kladuša for his decision to open his restaurant doors to allow people on the move to eat there for free. But overall, together with the migrating people, the violence shifted from one border to another.

By February 2018, local people living in the villages around Velika Kladuša and Bihać would talk about encounters with those who had been brutally pushed back from Croatia, and how they could hear them screaming in the night, and the border authorities from the neighbouring country shouting at them. These pushbacks continue to be characterised by direct physical and material violence. Despite the spread of these very visible, violent and illegal tactics from EU authorities, institutional actors in Brussels and other EU capitals have remained unable or unwilling to critically engage with these crimes. Instead, the condemnation of these acts fell on the shoulders of volunteers and activists – including No Name Kitchen and the Border Violence Monitoring Network – who were witnessing them every day, collecting reports about them and advocating against them.

Bosnia and Herzegovina – a state with an unstable government generally lacking the capacity or will to protect the human rights of its own citizens, much less those of the new arrivals – did very little. Furthermore, Bosnia and Herzegovina has a complex constitutional status, being a semi-protectorate of the international community and represented through the country's Office of the High Representative,

Figure 5.10 Velika Kladuša, Bosnia and Herzegovina, 2019. A sticker promoting No Name Kitchen, a group active in Serbia, Bosnia and Herzegovina and Greece, whose motto is "Integration, non-discrimination and mutual aid".

Image credit: Jack Sapoch.

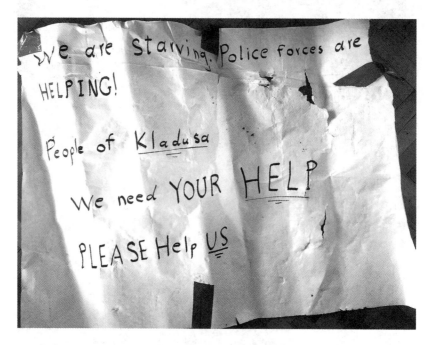

Figure 5.11 Velika Kladuša, Bosnia and Herzegovina, 2018. A note written by refugees protesting their living conditions at the border between Bosnia and Herzegovina and Croatia.

Image credit: Jack Sapoch.

which allows international actors to make policy decisions. Thus, in June 2018, the EU started channelling its relief funding towards the International Organization for Migration (IOM), UNHCR and UNICEF in Bosnia and Herzegovina, allowing those three organisations to take a lead in managing the ongoing situation. The IOM was given a leading role. This meant establishing "temporary accommodation centres", as the IOM refers to its own camps, and, in many cases, heavily influencing the decision-making process relating to people on the move, whom the IOM often frames as economic migrants. In this way, help from the EU was directed not towards the improvement of the asylum system, but rather towards border security. Activists discovered that at the border between Bosnia and Herzegovina and Montenegro, cage-like facilities had been installed, and people were

Figure 5.12 Sentilj, Slovenia, 2015. Volunteers from Slovenska Filantropija prepare aid boxes of clothes to distribute to refugees.
Image credit: Jasmine Piercy.

held inside. Authorities, supported by the IOM, explained that the facilities are "in accordance with EU standards", and that they had been donated by the EU.

Currently, many people are still moving along the route. Since 2018, more than 50,000 people are estimated to have arrived in Bosnia and Herzegovina alone, in the hope of moving further into Europe. All told, the Balkan route cannot be viewed as a static and singular entity; rather, it must be considered as a living ecosystem of transit, developing in response and relation to the shifting zones of securitisation in the Balkans. It is a violent route, and in some cases deadly. Nobody knows the exact number of deaths. In Bosnia alone, in the first half of 2019, over 30 bodies were found. Most of them were young; some were children. Many will never be identified.

So we saw very clearly that the trauma of the EU's closed-border policy – which includes severe and unchecked violence from the border authorities – remains tragically visible on the Balkan route.

Flashpoint: Ventimiglia

Mirko Orlando and Sue Clayton

The Italian city of Ventimiglia is a mere 8 kilometres from the French border and has always been a frontier for migrants in Italy crossing into France – a place where they are exposed to aggression at the hands of both the Italian police, who do not want camps growing up at the border, and the French police, who do not want to accept them on the French side, even though many have a legal claim to enter. It is impossible to provide exact data on the number of migrants in

Figure 5.13 Ventimiglia, Italy, 2018. A migrant, unable to cross to France, among tents built near the Roja river. Food is provided by local support groups.
Image credit: Mirko Orlando.

transit through the city, due to their undocumented status and to the (often illicit and unreported) police practices involved during this process; however, it was estimated that up to 2014, over 100,000 had been rejected at the border. And these numbers have continued since. The Alpes-Maritimes *Département* reports that in 2017 almost 31,000 were denied entry into France, with similar numbers in 2018 and the first half of 2019. Migrants mostly came from Nigeria, Mali, the Ivory Coast, Guinea, Algeria, Afghanistan and especially Eritrea and Sudan. Of these, about 10% were women, and – disturbingly – around 22% were unaccompanied minors.

As a border zone, it is normal for Ventimiglia to be the target of such migration flows, and it's widely known that many of the people who disembark in Italy do not intend to stay, but aim for other European countries like France, Germany or Sweden, where they may have relatives, or at least a hope of better working conditions. But it's also known that European law does not allow this transit; the EU Dublin Regulation dictates that new arrivals to Europe should claim protection in the first country in which they set foot. This is designed to keep the pressure on "frontline" states like Italy, but is made worse by the inefficiency of the current Italian system – its slowness in processing applications for status, which can take up to two years, the lack of information provided to migrants (partially due to the lack of trained cultural mediators in the workforce) and poor reception services and facilities. Reception centres at Foggia, Cona, Catania, Rome and Venice were accused of operating only to collect public funding, and a centre in Aprigliano was closed down in September 2015 after a local court found it unfit for use, with the prosecutor citing "grave danger to the safety of the immigrants hosted in this structure", claiming that management was "conducted in defiance of criminal laws and preordained exclusively to profit, with no respect for the human person and for constitutional rights". In Ventimiglia and other towns, many preferred to camp on the street rather than make use of the state-provided accommodation.

So Ventimiglia turned from a crossing point to a stopping one, and despite most migrants outside of the reception facilities lingering there for only days or weeks, their presence raised complaints from some of the local population. The situation has been worse since June 2015, when France took an abrupt decision to close its border to undocumented migrants and to impose state police checks along the Italian border. (To do this it invoked an exemption clause in the Schengen agreement – an agreement designed to keep borders open – that applied to "threats to national security".) In response, Italy, which along with Greece, Spain and Malta has borne the brunt of increased migrant numbers, accused France of lacking co-operation, and supporting the anti-European policies of the Visegrád Group (an alliance of the Central European states of the Czech Republic, Hungary, Poland and Slovakia, which has been openly hostile to new arrivals). France then accused Italy of irresponsibility in handling European funds allocated to deal with migration emergencies – funds amounting to several hundred million Euros between 2014 and 2019.

In any case, the introduction of French border checks, instead of stopping the migration flow into France, only drove the migrants to turn increasingly to *passeurs* (smugglers), or to take more dangerous routes, including the steep mountain trail leading to Menton on the French side, sadly known as the "Step of Death". (This trail, which does not appear on any maps, was formerly trodden by partisans and others persecuted by the Italian Fascist regime.) Once they reach the border between Italy and France, these travellers tend to naturally veer to the left towards France, attracted by views of Menton's seaside coast, when in fact they should bend to the right, towards the hinterland, despite this giving the impression for a moment of retracing their steps. But in turning left they risk sliding down a treacherous cliff face, which has already caused many migrant deaths.

Fortunately, since 2015, French citizens in the mountain settlements of La Roya region have extended hospitality to the trail of people who began passing through their remote communities. Meals have been cooked every night by each small village in turn; a camping space was set up with fire pits and later a shower for those who wanted a safe resting place before continuing down the tracks to France.

These local volunteers formed a group called La Roya Citoyennes which has supported countless migrants in transit on this dangerous

Figure 5.14 Ventimiglia, Italy, 2016. A woman café-owner in Ventimiglia stays open to serve refugees and provide a safe place where children can get a free meal, despite local right-wing opposition.
Image credit: Charlotte Maxwell.

route, extending their activism to sourcing legal and medical help for those passing through and organising international volunteers to support them when the numbers rose sharply in 2015–2016.

They also aided groups of migrants safely down the difficult tracks into France, and here witnessed first-hand French police violence against their guests – violence which they have continued to document and challenge to the present day. They have on record hundreds of episodes of blatant illegality including racial discrimination, physical and psychological abuse and the arbitrary detention of adults and unaccompanied minors. Many migrants recount how their shoes were taken by the French police at the border, forcing them to return to Ventimiglia barefoot. Kesha Niya (Sorani Kurdish for "No Problem") is a group originally set up in France that has been

Figure 5.15 Ventimiglia, Italy, 2017. At Gianchette church, volunteers offer legal advice to unaccompanied minors who are trying to reach other European countries.

Image credit: Andrea Panico.

tracking police violence at the French–Italian border. Extracts from the group's online briefings include the following from October 2019.

> Oct 28th: This week we met 408 people including about 15 lone minors and 7 women. A four-month pregnant woman says she was gassed in the train toilet with four other men. Three minors have been pushed back, one says he had his asylum seeker's card stolen by the French police. Oct 30th: An asylum seeker in France was pushed back to Italy and reported having been robbed by the French police of his asylum application receipt and the paper proving his appointment at the prefecture of Marseille. Several people received pepper spray on their faces as they came out of the *algecos* (Portakabins). They said that there is absolutely no procedure for leaving the *algecos*. The police open the door

Figure 5.16 La Roya valley, France, 2015. "La Caravane, L'Aventure Humaine", a sculpture by Jen-Noel Fessy, showing the migrant journey on the La Roya mountain path.
Image credit: Jen-Noel Fessy.

and say how many people they are going to release, everyone is pushing to get out of this place as quickly as possible, the police are randomly gassing inside to avoid this.

(Kesha Niya, October 2019)

The situation of the unaccompanied minors is a little different, as a clause in the EU Dublin Regulation (Dublin III Regulation, Article 3.2) allows them to proceed to any EU state where they have close family – so they should not be returned from France back to Italy. But as La Roya Citoyennes and local judicial challenges prove, this rule is systematically violated: minors face immediate forced removal back to Ventimiglia with no guardian appointed; removal documents are filled out by duty officers known to forge their birth dates to pass them off as being of legal age. The Kesha Niya blog continues.

A Pakistani minor met by Save the Children at the border at the time of his release had his birth certificate and the official translation of it in English stolen by the PAF (border police). Accompanied by the NGO to the Italian police, he was able to get registered as a minor in Italy and was then allowed back to France. Three other Afghan minors aged 15, 16 and 17 were not that lucky. They also did not have fingerprints in Europe but they were registered as adults in Italy on the basis of the false date of birth written by the PAF (border police) on refusals of entry.

(Kesha Niya, November 2019)

Once back in Ventimiglia, no transfer of responsibility for minors is organised. Back over the border the Italian police "decongests" the city by forcibly relocating migrants twice-weekly, on no apparent criteria, to the CIE ("Identification and Expulsion Centre") of Taranto or the CARA ("Reception Centre for Asylum Seekers") of Crotone, subjecting them to an exhausting and, above all, illegal journey of over 1,000 kilometres.

Figure 5.17 Ventimiglia, Italy, 2018. A young migrant waits for volunteer deliveries by Roja river camp.
Image credit: Mirko Orlando.

Thanks to the protests of volunteers and some journalists, the situation in Ventimiglia is now gaining attention, and there is hope that things will change. In June 2015, a group of migrants and No Borders activists camped on the cliffs of Balzi Rossi above Ventimiglia to protest the actions of the French national police at the border. It was the largest clash between activists and law enforcement, and went on until the area was cleared at the end of September. After negotiations between public administration, activists and volunteer organisations, a centre was created for temporary stops in Ventimiglia on property owned by the Ferrovie dello Stato (state railroad), but some of the local population protested and convinced the municipality to dismantle it, demanding any such centres be out of public sight.

Figure 5.18 Aix-en-Provence, France, 2017. Outside the Appeal Court where volunteer and farmer Cédric Herrou disputed his arrest for opening up disused state holiday accommodation to create a migrant camp.
Image credit: Association Roya Citoyenne.

Unable to find any form of shelter, migrants started camping beneath the overpass along Via Tenda, along the bed of the Roja river, in terrible conditions: no access to drinking water, no possibility of warmth during winter and no medical support in emergencies.

By early 2016, a tent city had sprung up there which by summer was home to over 1,000 people. Local volunteers did their best to provide food and clothing. A local priest, Don Rito Alvarez, opened Ventimiglia's city's Sant'Antonio church to the migrant community. It was a welcome and spontaneous gesture, but after 440 days of solidarity the priest was "transferred" to other tasks. The informal valley camp was cleared and set up again several times until finally, in July 2016, a "Roja Camp" was opened, managed by the Italian Red Cross by agreement with the local prefecture. It lies just outside Ventimiglia, hardly visible and carefully monitored. The municipality intended to have all migrants moved there – but the entry checks, the taking of fingerprints and the distance from the city centre (in 2017, two migrants lost their lives on the unlit highway leading to the camp) discouraged many from registering there. Even Mayor Enrico Ioculano, affiliated with the Democratic Party, after receiving threatening letters in which he was allegedly accused of "betraying the local citizens", signed an order forbidding citizens to offer food and drink in public areas to avoid providing migrants with the slightest form of assistance. After repeated protests from Amnesty International, Doctors Without Borders, Antigone and even Siap (Sindacato Italiano Appartenenti Polizia, a police union), the order was withdrawn.

Nonetheless, the hardline policy today continues, especially on the national level, with two "security decrees" actioned in 2018 and 2019 by Minister of the Interior Matteo Salvini excluding many migrants from reception facilities altogether. The many failures of both the French and Italian Governments and local administrations are offset by the supportive work of volunteers and activist groups. But the restoration of any kind of peaceful co-existence in a border zone such as Ventimiglia would need the municipality to co-operate with local volunteer organisations to improve facilities and to bring both Italian and French police abuses to an end, as well as providing more and better services to unaccompanied minors. Beyond this, there has to be a greater understanding of such realities, and co-operation with other European states to re-write the restrictive norms on migrant movement that were imposed by the Dublin Regulation.

THE NORTHERN FRONTIER

The EU's "Schengen area", the zone in which member states are supposed to allow open borders, ends at the English Channel. The UK is not part of Schengen, and operates its border controls from French and Belgian ports along the Channel coast. Thus, migrants and refugees trying to reach the UK and Ireland hit an obstacle when they arrive in France and Belgium. They may reach ferry ports along the coast and entry points to the Channel Tunnel, but end up stuck there for long periods. Local and national governments in France and Belgium have regularly destroyed encampments, dispersing people and preventing aid groups from operating there, and the French in particular have deployed paramilitary forces againts the settlers, approved and in part paid for by the UK Government.

Calais, France, 2016. Camp residents look on as the Jungle camp is destroyed by French riot police in October 2016.

Image credit: Rowan Farrell.

6

Testimonies from Northern France and Belgium

Sue Clayton

The "Jungle" camp at Calais has been one of the focal points of the European refugee crisis. While other European governements like Greece and Italy had – if belatedly – set up reception facilities and made agreements with the larger international NGOs like the UNHCR, the Red Cross and Save the Children, the Northern European countries did not do so. This left the French Government continuing to assert that it had no refugee camps. And it left Calais – a very visible point on the European political map, a major transit and trade hub, and under the Le Touquet treaty a British border-point – renowned for the Jungle, an unofficial settlement of up to 10,000 people with virtually no state or major NGO control or organisation at all. It was extremely unusual for us in Northern Europe to experience a settlement like one we would expect to find in Somalia, Jordan or Pakistan. The French Government provided only a requisitioned community centre near the camp for women and girls and a fenced-off enclosure for containers for families. Other than these, some piped water and Portakabin toilets, generally left uncleaned and overflowing, it was left to the refugees themselves and the grassroots groups to make a functioning, diverse community. And its prominent location, only (and shockingly, to all of us who did the journey) an hour from London St Pancras by train, made this extraordinary phenomenon highly visible to volunteers, visitors and the media.

While local French volunteer and campaign groups like L'Auberge des Migrants had been working in the Calais region for many years, trying to build longer-term alliances with local organisations and local government to accommodate the migrant population, arrival numbers in 2015–2016 increased off the scale, and international – mainly UK, Irish, Dutch and Scandinavian – volunteers, alerted by horrific accounts in the press and social media, poured in unchecked by the authorities, with vans full of donations and plans to cook, clean and build shelters. **Ali Reid**, an independent volunteer from Australia, paints this picture.

> The Jungle was a former landfill site flanked by factories of a nearby industrial estate. It was a short distance from the ferry terminal that connects France and the UK by sea, and was the temporary home to fluctuating numbers of 6,000–10,000 people seeking refuge. The Jungle was compared to the slums of Mumbai, earning it the unflattering label of "the biggest slum in Europe". In the Jungle, men, women and children were left in limbo as the UK and French Governments bickered over who should assume responsibility for them, using ever-increasing force to deter them from being there at all. The UK Government used British taxpayers' money to erect longer and higher fences around the ferry terminal on French soil, while French law enforcement units regularly made use of batons, tear-gas, rubber bullets and concussion grenades against Jungle residents who also had to resist intimidation by the right-wing French nationalist groups that often visited the camp. In the absence of any major NGO support, volunteers from around the world worked with grassroots organisations to ensure that basic human needs were met for those living within the camp.

Ali also has a realistic grasp of the elements at play in its organisation.

> The reality of volunteering in the Jungle was that if you needed clarity, structure or certainty in order to get things done, you simply wouldn't cope. I had to very quickly adjust my expectations and work beyond the frustrations that came with such an *ad hoc* situation: the lack of resources, the constant churn of volunteers (and

voluntourists), the harsh conditions, the lack of clear direction or leadership, the sometimes colourful and curious mix of people who ended up there to "save" the refugees while somehow also saving themselves. At the end of the day, it didn't matter. The Jungle was a great leveller. The only way to "be" a volunteer in the Jungle was to involve yourself: see a need, assess if you could fix or improve it and muck in. The needs were so great, so incessant, that you could work all day, every day and never keep up. During my three weeks in the Jungle I threw myself into tasks on that basis. I spent days sorting donated clothes and shoes by gender, size and category so that people could be clothed. I packed bags of clothes for children, knowing that they would only wear them for a day – because they had scabies, and the only way to treat it was to discard and burn used clothes daily to kill the mites. I filled bin bag after bin bag, up to my waist in rubbish (particularly rotting watermelon) in the mud, sleet, howling wind and driving rain to help reduce the never-ending accumulation – a side effect of both the British and French authorities failing to provide even the most basic of services afforded to their own citizens, but not to those seeking refuge. I guess that having people living in squalor served their propaganda that these people were filthy, uncivilised and certainly not deserving of a home. I helped women choose shoes in the women's centre that was set up in such a way that they felt like they were able to "shop" for items (even though they were donated and free). This was a critically important gesture towards restoring some sense of normality and agency to their lives. I chopped tomatoes, onions, radishes and garlic in a rudimentary kitchen so that we could feed 1,000 people an evening meal. I sorted medical supplies in donated caravans to support the volunteer doctors and nurses who would turn up and tend to the queues of sick people. I built one meagre shelter for Syrian refugees with the help of British charity Care4Calais and a brilliant Pakistani refugee who had the building know-how. I say meagre, because on the scale of things it was a drop in the ocean. But for the young men that moved from a soaking wet tent to a somewhat insulated and waterproof structure in the middle of the

Calais winter, this was invaluable for staying healthy and securing their few precious possessions.

Ali also recognised what many bloggers and reports did not – that while volunteers brought in incalculable amounts of food, clothing and supply materials, the refugee communities themselves were hugely resourceful in what they organised and built.

> They worked to build schools, shops, churches, mosques, kitchens, restaurants, hotels, libraries, even a "theatre" to bring hope in to a hopeless place. They were (and are) incredibly talented, qualified and often cosmopolitan people who had experienced things I would not wish on my worst enemy. They laughed, they loved, they cried, but most of all, despite all the odds, they kept on living and hoping. I have never experienced a place like it, or people like them in all my life.

Shakir from Pakistan, himself originally a refugee, talks about what he did, and also the more dangerous side of the camp.

> I am a nurse from Pakistan. I have eight years of professional experience. I was also a refugee, living in the Calais Jungle and providing a medical service for the people who were living there. There were several medical charities, including Médecins Sans Frontières, who provided services for refugees from 9 am until 5 pm. After they had finished their working day, there was no one available to help during an emergency and so this is when I was most needed. I normally did this work alone, without professional assistance. But often I had some wonderful volunteers who helped and who were able to drive me to emergencies if necessary. Regarding the police, there were many occasions when they used tear-gas against the refugees, and even rubber bullets. A big problem with this is that tear-gas is indiscriminate and spreads over hundreds of metres. Every time it is used, it affects many people in the vicinity, including families with children. This was an unacceptable use of force against innocent people. If the wind had blown the tear-gas partly away, rubber bullets would be fired. The police had no consideration for which

body part they hit with the rubber bullets, and I have treated people who have been injured in the head and in the face. I was at personal risk when I helped people in these situations, and I often had to move through the gas myself. I was also hit with a rubber bullet in my chest. I have treated people who have been beaten with sticks by the police, who have been pepper-sprayed, and who have been bitten by police dogs. My usual course of action was to give emergency treatment and then I had to hope there would still be a volunteer around to drive the person to hospital as soon as possible. I believe that the people in the police and the CRS (French riot police) have become hardened and are blind to the suffering of the refugees. They behave with aggression and force as a routine. The injuries I have seen are not part of peacekeeping, crowd control or self-defence. They are more serious and I would describe them as grievous bodily harm.

I would also like to talk about how the refugees can be supported better. People have been through trauma, first from war in their own country, and then from living in the terrible conditions of the camp, including this violence. They are likely to suffer from emotional problems afterwards. I would advise them to have access to counselling to help them get over the trauma of their experiences. Another part of this process is seeking justice for the people who have experienced police or gang brutality, and prosecuting the people who are responsible. There needs to be more enforcement of laws that will protect these people, and to make sure that this does not keep happening.

Eva Machado, a Spanish volunteer, recognised the levels of confusion that so many volunteers experienced on arrival, the listening and learning they needed to do, and the very fast adjustments required.

I arrived in September 2015, innocently thinking that I'd simply deliver a van full of donated fashion clothes from Camden Town. To my surprise there were no official NGOs, and I met the most chaotic human mess I could have ever imagined to witness in a developed country. A slum dumpster where humans were considered animals and were treated likewise, keeping them within a confined radius with the help of tear-gas and right-wing extremists. Rubbish and faeces all over, a couple of taps of water close to the ground surrounded by tents and sleeping bags buried in mud. My heart fell to the deepest pit, and in that moment I was lost. I was taken. Taken by rage and taken by a sense of self-righteous humanitarian "hero complex" that rampaged through any self-care and safety precautions that I should have followed. The mantra of all the civilian volunteers soon became: "we have no idea, but we will do what we can with what we have". Slowly learning from those who had been there since the beginning, we spent months delivering goods and building shelters for the coming winter. I realised that I was a 24-year-old child compared to the 18-year-old grown-up men who had walked through deserts, left family to die on that road and crossed the sea witnessing friends and family drown... I soon realised that it was us, the volunteers, who had to come up with a distribution system to deliver the donated goods. The endless tasks were organically carried out by volunteer individuals or groups who covered different parts of the Jungle. These included delivering cooked or dry food, water, tents, sleeping bags and clothes, and the precious mobile battery banks that would allow them to contact their loved ones back in the war zones. We didn't really know how much of what we were doing was legal or not. In the face of Europe's inefficient and inhumane response to the refugee crisis, many of us didn't think twice.

The legal issue is a difficult one. Having myself worked in the Jungle over a long period of time, what I found most frustrating was the fact that so many of those in the camp had strong legal claims for UK protection, but no lawyers to prosecute their cases nor any UK Home Office officials to process them. This was particularly true of the unaccompanied minors whose claim to UK protection I went on to defend in the UK courts. But for most, the only option to continue was by "irregular" means – stowing away onto a truck or refrigerated lorry. This required them to fight for access to particular sections of road and petrol stations nearby, an endless war of cat-and-mouse that they describe as "trying", which Eva explains.

One of the toughest tasks was the repeated hospital runs to take injured refugees from their nighttime attempts to get to England. They had to fight first against each other to get a chance, then against the right-wing extremists, then the traffickers, also the police and finally struggle with the truck or the boat, trying not get killed in the process. Many weren't lucky. Knowing what awaited men, women and children every night, all we could say was "good luck my friend".

Eva also got to grips with other aspects of camp politics. As the suppliers of goods, volunteer groups had to face ethical issues around distribution. Most groups tried to liaise with the camp residents and their communities, which was also a complicated issue. She says:

One of my first jobs was to speak all day to people begging for a shelter, and having to invent a priority system, listing families, women and young men first, and leaving the single adult men for last. These men could have got angry easily, but ended up showing more dignity than the countries that had pushed them to this hell-hole. I could spend hours describing the impact that this sense of dignity had on me. Especially the dignity that was felt from realising that everyone depended on each other even if they prayed to different gods or belonged to different ethnicities. I saw how extreme situations crossed all languages and united directly the hearts of scared humans, united in this case against the attacks of the CRS and the local right-wing who attacked them. Volunteers could be given the same treatment by the extreme right-wing groups, whose daily entertainment was to search for lonely refugees or volunteers to beat up. I too had one of those "me or them" moments I had hoped I wouldn't have to face in my life. They jumped in front of my van as I drove, trying to make me crash by blinding me with their lights and throwing stones at the van. When I realised what was happening, I stayed firmly on course and accelerated towards them, until they finally got out of the way.

There is an insight into these frequent and *ad hoc* camp meetings in what **D.E.** discusses below. This was in 2015 when the camp was growing exponentially and sometimes chaotically. The daily fluctuating issues, the fact that volunteers, particularly those from the UK, were there for irregular periods of time (as most had work or childcare commitments in the UK), the struggle to connect with the French authorities and the few French volunteers on-site; all make the meeting agenda interesting, if crazy, reading. She writes from Autumn 2015:

> We had a meeting yesterday. We've been trying to have meetings every Tuesday, 5–7 pm, for volunteers, residents, activists and helpers (from within and outside the camp)... it's a really good thing – we need co-ordination here and we need to be aware of what's going on where. I decided to take the reins on this meeting as in the last two weeks it hasn't happened because no one has led the way. That's all it needs, someone to give it a little push... or a big push sometimes.
>
> But it's kind of incredible here, how the word spreads and how things do just happen. The beauty of self-organisation. So much happens every day, every night – somewhere always someone is plotting something... whether it's a mass distribution of shoes, a night mission to the lorries – some distracting police, some jumping, plotting a protest to cry out to the Sudanese Governments or to the people of France.
>
> Anyway, the agenda for the meeting was: police violence, fascist aggression (though I wrote it on the flier as "aggressive neighbours", as some volunteers immediately close off when they hear that word) and the proposed new government housing for 1,500 people. We held the meeting in the Sudanese tent. They were very welcoming, and many took part in the meeting, which was accompanied by Arabic translations shared between three guys. It was a great meeting in loads of ways – we got through the agenda, loads was discussed, people had their chance to speak... but there were no representatives from the Kurdish or Syrian communities. There was one Afghan guy who came along who is a beautiful being who feels

and looks so much like an English friend – I can imagine hanging out with him at gigs in the UK. But this imagination feels so impossible. (Often this all feels so unreal. I know at some point I'm going to leave here, and I feel often that of course these people will continue to be my friends, and that one day we'll spend time together in a "normal" situation... but then I think, "how?!")

We spoke a lot about the French police and their violence. People saying, "How can this happen in Europe?", "Where is the UN?", and people sharing what happened to them or their friends. Last week I met a man whose jaw was broken by the police when two of them beat him up. My Iranian friend Hossa had asked me to come to see the man. He had already been to hospital where they had reinforced his jaws with metal, and elastic bands were holding them together. This meant he couldn't eat or speak. The next day I went to get him vitamin shakes, milk and soup (though a few days later his friend told me even soup was too thick for him to sift through his closed, locked jaw, so I need to get more of the vitamin/nourishment drinks). The main thing he wants is justice. He is desperate for a lawyer to follow his case. He is desperate to find the policeman who did that and ask him why. There was a freelance journalist here for a few days trying to write something on police violence for the BBC, which I think is very important as I don't think British, or even a lot of French people, know the extent of violence that is happening here. I brought the journalist to see this man with the broken jaw and she has documented it. I hope this article will get out and that people will start hearing more of the violence here. It's real and its happening and it's sick.

When I was here in September, the main injuries were giant razor-wire cuts and bruises from falling off the train or a lorry. Now it is more common for the injuries to be from police: broken fingers, a black eye, kicked stomachs. The border police are partly funded by the UK Government, and we cannot turn a blind eye to this. In the discussion on police violence a lot of people were asking "Why are the police doing this?" They were asking the European volunteers this and we couldn't answer. I told them we cannot speak on behalf of the police because they seem to be an inhuman force. They asked "Is it the UK who doesn't want us or France?" Really, with such sincerity, they wanted to know... and the painful reality is, at the moment, neither of these fortresses wants them.

A Sudanese refugee proposed a meeting with the police to talk to them about the violence. It was agreed by the majority to go ahead with this. We are looking into it. These are humans, they want to talk to the police as humans. They are not responding aggressively, they are confused, they want to understand why this is happening.

This is not a view that is representative of everyone in the Jungle. There are a lot of people full of hate for the police for their continued force. But a lot of folk I've spoken to genuinely want to have a dialogue. A lot of people even understand why police are violent at night or on the borders (i.e., when someone is jumping on a lorry and police spray tear-gas 10 cm from their face, and their face burns for two days after), because they know they are doing something "illegal". A lot of people feel ashamed at doing this. These are students, children, lawyers, doctors, linguists, artists, farmers, nurses – you, me – having to do this. No one would feel proud of it. But the extremity of violence is incomprehensible and people cannot understand why the police would be violent when unprovoked, like against refugees who are walking back into the Jungle or just cycling in town. My friend Mohammed ended the meeting by thanking everyone who was there for caring and reminding us, and the world, "We are survivors of genocide. We love our country, we did not want to leave our country, we are just looking for safety."

After the meeting I dropped off two boxes of potatoes, lemons, onions, pasta, naan bread and tomato paste at two of the houses of Eritreans who live behind the big church. I still feel very uncomfortable doing things like this out of my van (because I don't want my van to be associated with distribution, otherwise people will think I've got prized possessions in there and break the window).

Talking of broken windows, my mum has come over to visit me, and her car window was smashed in Calais town centre by a French guy (he was seen). A lot of English car windows have been smashed.

I presume it's right-wing people. They don't like English people (if you can read French you'll see on their Facebook pages) because it is mainly English people helping the refugees and they resent us.

After this I went to Abdul's to grate loads of ginger and make a big pot of ginger, lemon and sugar tea. It was quite a mission, mainly because of feeling quite stressed in the tiny kitchen where loads more people started arriving wanting to cook food and then I felt in the way. It took a ridiculously long time but luckily there was an Afghan man who was very eager to have some ginger tea and he was helping so much to make it happen.

These testimonies really get at the sense of what, especially in the early days, the Jungle was like, in all its intensity. By early 2016, more systems were set up; some of the faster-growing groups like Help Refugees, along with French organisations Secours Catholique and Utopia 56, acted as umbrella organisations and helped other groups set up infrastructures. For instance, Jungle Canopy committed to a long-term shelter-building programme and Refugee Community Kitchen acquired larger premises at the L'Auberge des Migrants warehouse, with Utopia 56 doing meal distribution. (The organisational process is described further in the Calais Flashpoint.)

Unsurprisingly, many of the volunteers who had committed to be full-time in Calais began suffering from burn-out and a form of mental health complaint known as vicarious trauma; by being so directly open to hearing so much trauma and suffering, and by witnessing further acts of violence by the police, traffickers and in the Jungle itself, a person can take on characteristics of the trauma – inability to sleep, high levels of anxiety, problems in relating to others and so on. (In Chapter 7, three therapists who came to work in the Jungle discuss this further.) What was definitely the most traumatic moment, from the volunteers' point of view, was the eventual demolition of the Jungle camp, which happened in two phases – in March 2016 and October 2016. And here I'd like to add my own testimony to those that I have collected and have collected and shared in this book.

It is almost always true of volunteers that we already understand – or we very quickly come to understand – that chopping up potatoes, then finding the right size of shoes or baby clothes, or mending leaky tents, is not the answer to the crisis that refugees are facing. Every volunteer, myself included, gets caught up in the immediacy of aid, which is a never-ending machine that must be kept fuelled, while trying to get the message out on social media or organising with other groups to make protests work, and engaging with governments and the law to make the bigger political changes that are so badly needed. When the Jungle was ultimately demolished, about a fifth of the adults and families absconded for fear of being detained or deported when the French Government finally moved to commence processing. Most of the other adults and families got onto buses with heavy hearts at being taken away from the border they were desperate to cross. Even worse, almost 2,000 unaccompanied minors were then barracked into containers behind barbed-wire fences and surveillance, for over a week, before the British Government came to finally – years late – assess their claims. I remember a group of us sitting on the bank facing into the enclosure, all the time waving, dancing about, smiling and joking across the security-fence divide to keep up the spirits of the incarcerated children. We did this even until coaches arrived to take them. I still remember this moment, when the volunteers kept smiling and waving and pointing at their phones – "Remember to call us so we know where you are!" – and the kids we knew so well were smiling and waving back. They didn't know that the coaches were taking them not to the UK as they hoped, but up to 1,000 kilometres backwards to remote mountain huts where the French Government would hold them for the winter and then abandon them all over again, and where the Home Office would later perform a travesty of assessing them and reject their strong claims to protection under UK law.

We knew we'd failed in that moment to change the infrastructure, to change the law, to make Europe protect them. Not that we gave up – indeed, I did go on to fight this through the UK courts – but in that moment we felt not only a sense of loss, but we directly felt the painful contradiction that in responding to them as humanitarians – which meant food and smiles and dry socks and phone chargers and long conversations in the middle of the night when they were upset – meant we did not also have the sheer firepower at that moment, on that sad little hill, to advocate also for their human rights.

> After the last bus was gone, I remember how many volunteers sat there dazed and shocked. One French volunteer, who had worked full-time on their legal cases, said "They're being dispersed to 64 centres in the most remote areas of France. How will I ever even find them?" None of us could move. We just sat there in the filth and mud on that bank in the eerily silent camp. Those emotions we all felt, of loss, failure, rage and despair – I think that was the nearest I came to understanding, in some tiny way, what refugees and war victims must go through mentally every day and every night of their lives. And what a world we live in, that these children must rely on us – untrained, under-equipped and ourselves now increasingly criminalised – to both care for them and to advocate for their future safety and for whole new policies in law.

The demolition of the Jungle was also the end of what had became a huge social experiment – an open refugee camp in affluent Northern Europe where anyone could and did go to "help" and for the most part made things better.

I can see that I may have failed to emphasise some of the more joyful moments of the Calais Jungle, moments that will be broadly familiar to many in the camps where we all worked. The Dome theatre; the random competing musics of 15 cultures echoing around camp; a young person looking shy and pleased after they've had a Jungle barber's haircut; refugees and volunteers together eating Afghan bread and drinking *chai* in Sami café; seeing the little shop lights on the Jungle's Main Street come on at dusk; hearing the call to prayer, and the camp quieten down in the evenings before the attempts on the road and the police battles would start. And as a rider to the story of the children above, yes, a lot of those young people who left on the coaches phoned us, and our painstaking and laborious legal work with them went on – and still does, four years later. And probably will as long as they and we are alive.

Dunkerque was a very different paradigm from that of Calais. To replace Basroch, a badly resourced temporary camp, La Linière was built, funded by Médecins Sans Frontières with the consent of the more progressive – compared to that of Calais – local prefecture of Grande-Synthe on the outskirts of Dunkerque. It had more planning and organisation built into it from the beginning. The camp was mainly for families, though increasingly became a place for unaccompanied minors after the Calais Jungle was demolished. There were more embedded relations between the camp residents and the local community. However, like Basroch before it, the camp at Grande-Synthe always struggled with the issue of trafficking, with some nationalities and ethnicities being victimised and excluded.

Maddie Harris was there in the days before La Linière and helped it come to fruition. She says:

> I first travelled to Dunkerque in Northern France as part of an aid convoy in September 2015. I had planned on staying for four days but once I arrived, I felt compelled to stay for longer – I think largely due to the shock of what I saw, the incredible people I met, I knew that this is where I needed to be. When we arrived, there were no more than around 200–300 people living in nylon camping tents around the outside of a disused football pitch in the centre of the town. Since then a whole new camp, La Linière, was built. Gradually we built up provision of basic services, working with French and international volunteers. But as time went on, I was overwhelmed by the lack of provision for those wishing to report their legal status and find out what options they had. And every day, countless basic rights were violated. I have spent time in a number of refugee camps in Greece and France and in each camp I always see a variation of the same question, "Where are our human rights?" scrawled on a wall or shelter. The reality, it seems, is that these rights don't apply to those seeking refuge, that they are reserved for the privileged, for those born into safe countries. We need to hold those responsible

for upholding and protecting these rights to account, and ensure that those responsible for violating them are held to account, and that all have access to them.

I met R in the camp. He had worked for the British military as an interpreter during the Iraq war, before leaving after sustaining a serious injury. He returned to Iraq some years later, met his wife and had a child, before his life was threatened as a result of the work he had previously done with the UK armed forces. R and I became good friends, and he was a great source of help and advice. I would consult him at various points when struggling as to what to do, and he would keep me informed of certain things he thought might be happening or about to happen in the camp. We would spend time laughing and discussing the state of things both in the camp and further afield; I also got to know his wife H well. R was fluent in English, which meant that he was invaluable in helping to interpret for others in the camp, as well as speaking with the media about his situation and the situations of others there. R was adamant that he would not attempt to return to the UK illegally, but was also unsure about attempting to engage a lawyer, as much had been promised before, and nothing had changed. I remember one evening, when I was sitting with R and his family drinking tea, he said to me that if I wanted to continue to do this work, I needed to be prepared to sacrifice other things in my life, that it was hard work, thankless work, dangerous work. Only the evening before he had warned me that a number of smugglers in the camp were planning on setting fire to the main kitchen tent – constant threats or events such as this were common in Dunkerque – as gradually the camp became largely controlled by a changing number of smugglers and their networks, vying for the business of those wishing to get to the UK in the absence of safe and legal routes.

One night, a police incident began on the road above the camp, and rubber bullets were shot by the police, many landing on the roofs of the shelters, waking and distressing the children sleeping inside. One hit R in the leg. He was badly injured on the same leg to which he had previously sustained an injury during his time serving as an interpreter in Iraq, and of course didn't receive the care that he needed in the camp. It caused him constant pain for many weeks, and he received very little in the way of medical care as a result at the local hospital. Thankfully, some months later, R and his family were able to settle in the UK. We lost touch for some time, before I received a call in November 2017 to say that R had died. He had died as a result of cancer that went untreated for so long that it became incurable.

R's story is his story, not mine, but it needs to be told, and he is no longer here to tell it. For so many reasons, not least because it illustrates how on so many levels human rights are being violated, and without full documentation of stories like this, there is no hope of justice.

Another Grande-Synthe volunteer, **Caroline Cottet**, gives her perspective on the question Maddie also raises – how to sustain long-term work, and how best to organise. She says:

My volunteer work has evolved over the years: on my first day I sorted donated clothes into men's and women's (the cruel irony for a young freshly-out-of-university activist with the fervent belief that the gender binary is bogus!). Then in September 2016, I saw a Facebook post: the Refugee Women's Centre was looking for a volunteer co-ordinator to take the reins of a day centre in the refugee camp at Grande-Synthe, in northern France. I packed up a single suitcase, initially for two months, which turned into three years. My main task was to make the day centre that existed in the camp into an official charity with a sustainable structure, that could ensure continuous support to women and families living in the camps of northern France. When I arrived, we had a physical space in the La Linière camp, made up of shipping containers in a U shape and a roof between them. There were five volunteers, but all were only planning to stay for a few weeks. We had a Facebook page and an email address, though so much time was spent organising and running the centre that we couldn't answer messages on time. We had very little communication with other organisations and with the authorities, which sadly gave us a bad reputation. The Women's Centre was unfortunately known as a mysterious, opaque place, where volunteers seemed to only speak English and had little interest in opening up to French organisations. But our relationship with the women in the camp was good, our presence and support were met with welcoming kindness and families have always been trusting. This has always been the one thing we are excellent at. To make sure we would never have to stop, I started tackling the things we were less good at: writing reports and leaving a trail of evidence of our work, fundraising, attending meetings and working more closely with local organisations and with the local authorities, as well as reinforcing welfare for volunteers to ensure their sustainability.

All of this was a phenomenal group effort. Since 2017, the Refugee Women's Centre has about 100 volunteers each year who come and help on the ground (plus many more who help at a distance with fundraising, calling for and gathering donations and raising awareness). Working with such an incredible number of people, mostly women, has been one of my favourite aspects of the work. I have become convinced that access to shelter is the single most urgent need for displaced people in northern France. It tackles a great number of needs: stability, access to warmth, access to a bed, access to water, privacy, agency, hygiene, the ability to make choices, the creation of opportunities to meet local people and a potential shift in public opinion.

As told in our Dunkerque Flashpoint, the La Linère camp was destroyed by fire in 2017. The Women's Centre and other initiatives continue, but provision of permanent housing is now even more reduced. Though governments and media generally ignore the fact, there are still hundreds of refugees along the north coast of France, from Calais to Dunkerque and beyond, living out in the woods with no shelter, and supported only by the volunteer warehouses that continue to operate.

Many new arrivals now, when moving northwards through Europe, head instead for Brussels. It has a port to the UK, Zeebrugge, and it seems to be also preferred because the Belgian police are thought to be less violent and aggressive than the French CRS – though in 2018 a small child was killed when Belgian police opened fire on a vehicle they suspected of containing refugees. As discussed in the Brussels Flashpoint section of this book, one very interesting characteristic of Brussels is how so many ordinary people have offered to have refugees stay, either temporarily or longer-term, in their own homes. This is not organised by the state but by volunteer liaison with new arrivals at the station and at Parc Maximilien, where most refugees are forced to sleep.

Mehdi Kassou, himself formerly a refugee, joined the scheme and is now its co-ordinator. He says:

> In 2015, I went to Parc Maximilien; I think it was a mix between curiosity – natural human curiosity as I knew so many people were sleeping rough – and a will to help. So I went there, and I immediately decided to provide tents. Particularly seeing kids sleeping on the ground, 3- to 4-year-old kids, young boys sleeping on the ground on plastic, actually shocked me and I decided to bring in as many tents as possible. I brought in around 150 tents but I also quickly realised that my mobilisation wouldn't be enough to answer all the needs. So I decided to join the co-ordination tent, which was the very first citizen platform supporting refugees – Plateforme Citoyenne. Now, four years later, I'm in charge of the operational management and communication, and spokesperson, and also manage the teams and the communications on a wider scale. We have a shelter offering 250 beds every night to men, we are present at the Humanitarian Hub at Brussels-Nord station where we provide services together with Doctors of the World, Médecins sans Frontières, the Red Cross and SOS Jeune (SOS Youth), which is an organisation supporting minors and unaccompanied minors. We also have another site where we provide French, Dutch and English classes, social and legal services and cyber coffee informatics classes. We started in the beginning finding places for women, the elderly, and sick people and quite quickly we actually had more families offering beds than migrants asking for them! So we decided to start to ask families to offer places

for the young men and boys. One of those families told me that at first sight, they were really afraid of hosting men who they didn't know before, having stereotypes in mind, having natural fears and fearing for their own families – kids and belongings. The day they were due to bring those migrants back to the park, they didn't – they actually kept the men two days extra, to protect them from the cold and the police. And I noticed that day that the fears were actually shared on both sides. I'd had some migrants going with a family to their home about 100 kilometres from Brussels sending me messages, asking if it was a normal for them to be driving for an hour not knowing who those Belgians were, where they were driving – and, the day after, the family told me they had all got on well, and again they wanted to keep the boys longer for their safety. I never think about this as a job actually. I think about it as a necessity, as an absolute necessity to change a society's perspectives and the way Belgian families see migrants.

Claudine B. is one of those who hosts regularly. She says:

We were moved by the lives of the migrants sleeping in the Parc Maximilien in Brussels at the end of summer 2017. We began to ask ourselves what kind of assistance we could offer them. We took up our address books and went through all of our contacts, managing to gather enough money to enable us to prepare and distribute 350 food bags. The first distribution took place in October 2017. We repeated this several times, managing to provide up to 650 food bags by spring 2019. In early November 2017, we started to house these young migrants at our house on the weekend. We haven't stopped doing so since, to the extent that today I couldn't even tell you how many young Sudanese, Ivorians, Ethiopian and Eritreans we have hosted at ours instead of leaving them to sleep outside. So many clothes washed, meals, shared evenings through which they reclaim their dignity. We appease their physical pain sometimes, but first and foremost it's their psychological suffering we attend to. These young people have faced all sorts of difficult experiences throughout the journey between home and here.

What's wonderful is to see them become teenagers again, like our kids, when they're in our homes. They forget their everyday lives – hiding out in car parks at night, facing arrest and detention with the risk of being sent back to the country to which they are "Dublined" [sent to the first country in Europe they are proved to have entered, under the EU Dublin Regulation] or to their home countries, or risking their lives to stow away on lorries headed for England. At our house they watch series for teenagers on Netflix with our kids, or decorate the Christmas tree with us, enchanted. It's moving to hear them say that the best moments are those spent at the dining table, sharing "family" dinners with us, that we show them affection with no strings attached, helping them to rebuild themselves psychologically. Many of them have told us that they arrived at ours in great distress but today have found peace. I don't feel like I took up a challenge, simply that I have risen to my duty as a citizen. I have been able to be a mother to these young people while they rebuild themselves, and have prevented children from having to sleep outside. Without your whole family's permission, you can't do this kind of hosting, but each of my family members got involved to various extents. Sometimes some of them slowed down their involvement. You need to be able to accept that not everyone can or wants to follow the same rhythm of involvement, be implicated to the same extent. Sometimes children (even though they are young adults) can show signs of jealousy. I came to realise that this was the case in other families as well. In my workplace, this involvement is either encouraged or criticised. I've come to learn that it's best simply not to talk about it. Those who show solidarity are those who come to me of their own initiative to ask for news of our friends, or to give me clothes. I realise that there really is a double-standard in the West. We never question why someone close to us goes to live or work abroad; we might even be proud of that person for doing so. However, when an African person comes here wanting to improve his or her living standards, we accuse them of taking our jobs... The notion of white supremacy is still very much alive.

Flashpoint: Calais

Tess Berry-Hart

While other important camps existed in Northern France – like those at Grande-Synthe, Dunkerque, Norrent-Fontes and Hasbrouck – what became known as the Calais "Jungle" dominated the news headlines and social media. It was unique in its sheer size, and, because it was not regulated by government or the larger NGOs, its extreme openness. This meant that, as Tess describes below, "anyone" could go there to contribute. In many ways it came to represent an experiment in autonomous grassroots organisation, and that is why many of us were drawn there, not only to offer support but

Figure 6.1 Calais Jungle camp, France, 2016. Help Refugees' iconic notice by the Banksy graffiti at the entrance to the Jungle on the Rue des Dunes.

Image credit: Caroline Gregory.

to learn how such organisation might work on a large scale. So the Calais piece here is fuller and more detailed than many of the Flashpoints, as we have tried to address some of the many ethical and political concerns that we faced as volunteers in the Jungle "experiment".

"The Calais Jungle" is infamous as a huge shanty-town camp outside the town of Calais, which survived from April 2015 until its destruction in October 2016, and at its height was home to over 10,000 people. This part of the northern French coast has always historically been a route for refugees and victims of forced migration attempting to reach the UK, and so has been home to many smaller camps and squats in and around Calais for over 30 years. In the 1990s, the number of displaced people around Calais rose sharply, with arrivals coming mainly from Kosovo, Kurdistan and Afghanistan. Though these people had been able to travel across Europe without a visa under Europe's Schengen agreement, they found themselves unable to enter the UK under new legal and security measures introduced in 1999. As claiming asylum under international law requires being physically within a country's borders, those seeking asylum in the UK are afforded no safe or legal route to do so, instead needing to resort to clandestine and dangerous modes of entry on lorries, boats and trains in order to exercise this right.

With hardly any state-provided shelter, people were forced to occupy disused buildings or set up their own small, informal camps in woods and fields – named "jungles" after the Pashto word for forest: *dzhangal*. A 1999 UK–French governmental attempt at establishing a processing centre in nearby Sangatte failed to accommodate the rising numbers and was closed down. In 2003, the Le Touquet Agreement between the UK and France effectively moved the UK border, and migrant processing, to ports on the French coast, of which Calais was one, heavily policed and fenced to prevent movement of people by "irregular" means. From 2005, with the escalation of hostilities in Afghanistan, the numbers of refugees rose again, and by 2009 there were estimated to be 1,400 displaced people in and around Calais, sheltering in squats or building shanty-towns on waste-ground or industrial estates, such as the early

Figure 6.2 Calais, France. 2016. Tents in the Afghan section of the Jungle, crowded together after the demolition of the southern part of the camp in March 2016.

Image credit: Tess Berry-Hart.

"Jungle de Calais" (also known as "the Pashtun Jungle"), which was destroyed by authorities in 2009 and its 800 inhabitants evicted. But these numbers were still tiny compared to the 10,000 and more people that the "Calais Jungle" would later house.

By now the unwillingness of European states to provide adequate shelter to refugees and expedite their legal claims was becoming more evident. Citing a "pull factor" which would encourage more displaced people to arrive, the UK Government proved unwilling to assist those in need of protection, relying instead on a policy of deterrence which involved making substantive payments – over £140 million up to the end of 2019 – to support policing of the externalised border in Calais. As well as local police, the Compagnies Républicaines de Sécurité (CRS), the paramilitary mobile riot-control wing of the French security system, was tasked with enforcing the border, adopting a campaign of evictions and harassment of camp residents. Thus the UK Government was not only funding the construction of walls and fences, but also directly financing and supporting the CRS use of tear-gas, rubber bullets and batons on all residents, including women and children, creating a highly precarious zone near the border. In response to rising numbers of refugees from African states, such as those fleeing conflict in South Sudan, Ethiopia and Eritrea, local anti-immigrant groups emerged, such as Sauvons Calais, created in 2013, which spread hostility in the local population and media. Disused buildings housing refugees were set on fire, and squats set up to shelter vulnerable people such as women and children were forcibly evicted.

By early 2015 there were various sites around Calais where displaced people congregated: the "Tioxide Jungle", on the grounds of the disused Tioxide chemical plant; Fort Galloo, a disused former factory: the Sudanese camp, behind the Leader Price supermarket; the Bois Dubrulle camp, situated in woodlands of the same name; and many other small scattered squats and camps. In March of that year, after vowing to remove the visible presence of migrants from the city centre, Mayor of Calais Natacha Bouchart opened the Centre Jules Ferry in a former leisure centre on a stretch of dunes named La Lande (or Les Dunes) outside the link-road that encircles the town. It was to provide accommodation for 400 people with priority given to women and children. This provision was of course still woefully inadequate for the approximately 2,000–3,000 people trapped in Calais at the time, but the mayor also announced the creation of a "tolerated" zone around Jules Ferry, where it was understood that residents of the various camps and squats could relocate and stay out of sight. Accordingly, police evicted the squats and volunteers helped transport residents to the zone at the end of the motorway link road which crosses over the Rue des Garennes. Residents pitched tents and built shelters on the bitter-smelling and contaminated dunes near the chemical plant, and this became the "New Jungle", as it was initially called. The camp would grow to an estimated 10,188 people by

September 2016, of which it was determined that 10% were women and nearly 20% were unaccompanied minors.

Local French citizens assisting displaced people in Calais have always been in evidence, offering food, washing facilities or phone charging at an informal level, then forming into bigger groups such as Oumma Fourchette, and into collectives of migrant solidarity groups such as C'SUR. Ever since the closure of the Sangatte facility in 2002, the French Government had been reluctant to admit to a "humanitarian crisis" of rising numbers at the border, which meant that international NGOs were not authorised to provide assistance here. Deficiencies of the government in providing food or shelter continued to be filled by voluntary organisations and charities (*les associations*) such as SALAM, Secours Catholique and Médicines du Monde. Volunteer and activist solidarity took various forms. Some French and international activists highlighted the border as a tool of state oppression and documented its countless needless deaths in the "This Border Kills" blogs of Calais Migrant Solidarity (CMS). These

Figure 6.3 Calais Jungle camp, France, 2016. Kitchen in Calais made 1,500 meals a day on-site for destitute refugees. The minors had a separate queue for their safety.
Image credit: Sue Clayton.

activists declared that "the problems in Calais will not be covered by a million blankets" and helped organise protests, strikes and solidarity camps with the camp residents, such as the No Borders week-long camp in 2009.

Many volunteer groups such as L'Auberge des Migrants and SALAM focused on providing humanitarian aid such as clothes or clean water, while others organised social events like football matches between migrants and the local community. CMS considered volunteers who helped move the residents of the camps and squats to the "New Jungle" site of 2015 to be assisting authorities with their policies of forced ghettoisation, while those helping with the move saw it as the practical way to reduce police violence, and for camp residents to be free of the constant evictions and harassment they experienced in Calais town.

From April 2015, the Jungle camp expanded around the Centre Jules Ferry, which had by now been commissioned by the state to be run by La Vie Active, a local social-care NGO. Two of the largest demographics were the Sudanese, who camped around the area by the Chemin des Dunes, and an expanding "Main Street" of mostly Afghan small businesses in the area closest to the motorway bridge. Also present in smaller numbers were Eritreans, Kurds, Iraqis and Syrians, as well as Ethiopians, Oromo, Pakistanis, Iranians, Bidoon and other nationalities who created their own areas. Homes, shops and restaurants were built from pallets and plastic sheeting bolted on to supporting stakes by bottle tops. The shops sold a variety of products, hot and cold foods and home-made cigarettes, and there were bars and barbers' shops as well as schools, cafes, mosques and churches. Scattered around the periphery of tough gorse bushes, sand dunes and craters filled with rainwater and human waste were tents housing small and large groups according to nationality and identified by their flying flags – all of them prey to rain and strong coastal winds. Residents cooked on gas stoves and accidental fires regularly occurred, destroying tents and causing injuries. On a good day – when there was sunshine and no police violence – the camp appeared as a ramshackle shanty town where residents could sit outside, eat at the restaurants, play music and get a haircut; on a bad day it resembled a nightmarish slum with dripping canvas tents, burned-out shelters, police invasions, tear-gas and seas of mud. The days started late, with camp residents going about their daily business eating, attending places of worship and restaurants or shops, while night was dedicated to concerted attempts to cut through the fences or install barriers on the roads to slow down passing lorries, find spots to hide in trucks or jump on trains. Nightly attacks by the CRS to thwart this activity usually ended in them releasing clouds of tear-gas that permeated the whole camp, affecting women, children and volunteers alike; 79% of camp residents later surveyed by the volunteer group Refugee Rights Data Project reported having experienced

Figure 6.4 Calais Jungle camp, France, 2016. Volunteers build a look-out post on the camp's central dune, also known as "Sudan Hill". It was used particularly by those on fire watch.

Image credit: Caroline Gregory.

police attacks and physical or sexual violence in camp, and 76.7% reported health issues arising from poor conditions.

Prompted by media highlighting of the "refugee crisis" in summer 2015, more international volunteers started arriving in Calais to work with or alongside local French charities and aid groups such as Secours Catholique Calais, SALAM and L'Auberge des Migrants already operating there, who were struggling to cope with ever-higher numbers of arrivals. These new volunteers, many from the UK and Ireland, would later form independent grassroots aid groups such as CalAid, Care4Calais, Side By Side With Refugees, Help Refugees, Refugee Community Kitchen and Calais Action. Smaller numbers of groups from Belgium, the Netherlands, Germany and Scandinavia also came to volunteer, for example, Ghent4Humanity and SWK Kitchenia, and individual volunteers came from other European countries and beyond, such as USA Caravans for Calais.

Shocked by the conditions that camp residents had been forced to live in, the CRS violence and the presence of hundreds of unaccompanied children in the camp, volunteers used social media and sympathetic news outlets to highlight the situation to those back in their own countries. Impromptu call-outs and hastily set-up online crowdfunding pages raised substantial funds – some generating hundreds of thousands of pounds – which were used to buy and transport food and supplies to Calais. Websites such as the Calais People-to-People Solidarity Facebook group, Calaidipedia and other support platforms helped new volunteers and groups find each other, and gave advice on what donations to bring and where to bring them. This perfect storm of social media, cheap travel in shared cars and vans from the UK and nearby countries, increasing access to information and some coverage by the largest media channels, greatly expanded the number of volunteers beyond those Europeans and local French already volunteering. People across Europe became aware that they could get involved rather than passively watch their Facebook feed or send money to large NGOs. This level of self-actualisation was motivating beyond any poster campaign; "anyone" could pack up a car with essential items and drive over to Calais.

Figure 6.5 Calais Jungle Camp, France, 2016. "Main Street" where many of the population of 10,000 refugees and around 500 volunteers would meet and go to the small cafes and shops, the mosque or the Ethiopian church.
Image credit: Tess Berry-Hart.

These conditions at first resulted in a frenzy of *ad hoc* deliveries directly into the Jungle over the summer of 2015, but gradually most groups self-organised from the chaos to create effective systems. French solidarity group L'Auberge des Migrants had been operating in Calais since 2008, supporting those sleeping rough in Calais and then those who arrived in the dunes after April 2015. L'Auberge partnered with newly created British group Help Refugees to open a large warehouse on a nearby industrial estate to act as a hub for direct aid distribution. In the UK, groups such as CalAid and Calais Action opened collection points around London and other towns and then organised their delivery to the camp and the warehouse, as well as helping fund projects on the ground.

Some individuals and groups like L'Auberge focused primarily on frontline work such as distributing in camps, while others helped residents build their own shelters – groups such as Building In Calais Jungle, A Home For Winter, Side By Side and Hummingbird – while others supported existing groups or projects on the ground through funding, supplies or container and storage provision. Some volunteer groups followed NGO lines by adopting logos and marketing branded goods to supporters to raise funding, while others continued in a less formal pattern, simply bringing funding or provisions to particular camp residents to alleviate their needs. Some visited for a day as "voluntourists" to deliver aid or briefly help in a kitchen or warehouse, while others came and lived as long-term volunteers in caravans or tents, either close to the warehouses or in the camp itself – like the Women's and Children's Centre founder Liz Clegg, who lived in a caravan on-site protecting young vulnerable refugees.

Newly-arrived volunteers could help sort clothes in L'Auberge warehouse, cook in Ashram Kitchen or Kitchen in Calais, litter-pick with the Jungle Sanitation Team or teach at L'Ecole Laique du Chemin des Dunes. Volunteers with specialist skills in medicine could help in such projects as the weekend medical clinic run by Hummingbird or the medical caravan run by Refugee Support; dentists could volunteer in the Calais Dental Project run by Refugee Crisis Foundation. Many refugees also volunteered, either helping in projects such as kitchens, assisting with camp management and organisation, or by providing services such as translation or medical aid in camp – especially during the night-time hours, when there would be victims of police violence.

New concepts of aid gained understanding – for instance, the importance of phone credit and internet access for camp residents – which led to the creation of projects, such as the Phone Credit for Refugees group, and the Refugee Info Bus Wi-fi supply system. Despite frequent duplication, and a few promised schemes that came to nothing or potentially wasted funding, the longer-term projects in the main were successful and needs-based. Many lives were saved and much suffering alleviated by the fast and flexible responses of grassroots groups and individuals, particularly with regard to the safeguarding of women and unaccompanied minors in camp through volunteer-run projects like the Unofficial Women's and Children's Centre and the Baloos Youth Centre run by Refugee Youth Service (RYS).

Figure 6.6 Northern Calais, France, 2015. At the Auberge warehouse, items are sorted and stored by volunteers for daily distributions in the Jungle.
Image credit: Doug Kuntz.

Initiatives such as the RYS "tracking service" and Hummingbird Safe Space gave crucial support to minors in a situation where there were no state or NGO safeguarding systems to protect them from prostitution, sex or drug trafficking. Volunteer groups such as Jungle Canopy also helped provide caravans to house vulnerable families and establish them in a separate area of the camp.

In November 2015, Care4Calais was formed, and opened a second warehouse on the opposite side of the camp to receive and distribute supplies. In January 2016, the French association Utopia 56 was set up by French music festival and events organisers to help mobilise more citizens, mainly French, in aid of refugees in the Jungle and across France. However, legal and rights advice was something harder to achieve – there was no UK or French state-mandated legal aid provision in camp until the arrival of Terre d'Asile in spring 2016, so groups such as Calais Migrant Solidarity and No

Figure 6.7 Calais, France 2016. Volunteers sort clothing and other items at the L'Auberge des Migrants warehouse.

Image credit: Caroline Gregory.

Borders provided legal rights advice leaflets to residents from "Info Points" in the Jungle. French volunteers ran the Cabane Juridique legal shelter, while UK asylum rights groups such as Safe Passage worked with volunteers and a small number of visiting *pro bono* lawyers to identify those residents, especially unaccompanied children, with claims for asylum in the UK.

Such a broad spectrum of volunteers, ranging from independent citizens to associations and groups of many kinds, predictably did not all see eye-to-eye on issues in the camp. Often there were ideological difficulties or splits – for instance, one group choosing to wear high-visibility tabards to identify its members, while others challenged this practice, citing the hi-vis clothing as too similar to that worn by the hostile police force, and so affecting trust with residents. The issue of intimate relations between camp residents and volunteers was often under discussion, with many volunteers adopting a code of conduct to prevent creating a dynamic open to exploitation of the camp resident ("sex for aid"), while others saw creating this distinction between residents and volunteers as "othering" and anti-solidarity. Media coverage of some volunteer–resident relationships inferred that the (high proportion of female) volunteers were driven by underhand sexual motives, to the dismay of the vast majority of (mainly female-run) voluntary groups who resisted this misogynistic smear, which was often spread by online trolls who harassed volunteers by way of systematic attacks on their Facebook pages. A few UK volunteers, unable to bear the sight of minors living in dangerous and filthy conditions with their family reunion rights ignored, were convicted of offences relating to attempting to help them reach family in the UK. In doing this, they risked conviction as people smugglers or traffickers. This pushed the French courts to examine the reasons for such actions, and in at least one case they offered limited leniency in recognition of the humanitarian impulse that had driven volunteers to break the law.

Figure 6.8 Calais Jungle camp, France, 2016. The Kids Café, along with Jungle Books and the Hummingbird project, was one of the few places unaccompanied children could feel safe and get advice and friendship.

Image credit: Tess Berry-Hart.

Figure 6.9 Calais Jungle camp, France, 2016. As the date for evictions draws near, young people are denied the chance to go back to their tents to collect their few belongings.

Image credit: Tess Berry-Hart.

Despite elements of difference, duplication and ideological differences, by early 2016 an independent, functioning welfare system and mutual support system had been created by residents and volunteers in the Jungle camp, with citizen-created supply lines running to the warehouse hubs of L'Auberge and Care4Calais from all over Europe. A court action brought by Secours Catholique, Médecins du Monde and other associations had resulted in an administrative court ruling in late 2015 that the state should increase the number of water points and toilets, and improve roads, lighting and a rubbish collection service in the camp. A French emergency and disaster NGO, ACTED, was commissioned to implement these requirements, which improved conditions in camp.

Between the summer of 2015 and February 2016, new arrivals to the Jungle rose to around 5,497 (including 423 unaccompanied minors) according to the volunteer-run census conducted by Help Refugees, and the operations of the camp acquired further levels of organisation. Volunteers formed a Calais media team and facilitated visits of high-profile celebrities and politicians to visit to raise public awareness of the conditions and political situation.

Other volunteers consulted residents in building shelters, schools and safe community spaces and supported or created projects such as the Jungle Books library and café, the Dome theatre and music tent, the Legal Centre and the Welcome Caravan, which provided supplies to new arrivals. There was even a purpose-built fire truck smuggled into camp to help with the frequent fires that regularly devastated residents' tents.

Volunteers attended briefings and ACTED organised community meetings with the camp's community leaders and helped draw up codes of conduct to govern relations between volunteers and residents, conducted censuses and assessed the welfare of the camp's inhabitants. As well as providing food and community, the resident-run camp restaurants provided invaluable hospitality spaces to meet, congregate and form bases for organisation for both residents and volunteers, for instance, providing space for legal help and translation services.

By mid-2016, conservative estimates taken from warehouse logs and an enquiry email put the total number of international volunteers who had helped at or visited Calais in some capacity at well over 20,000 – as well as local French volunteers – with often as many as 300 a day in camp. And as systems became more established, many of the new international groups were able to address a long-overdue need for training and standards. It was not so much practical skills that needed to be addressed as ethical guidelines about group working, safety in camp (especially for women), responding to trauma, being aware of cultural and religious differences and navigating the complicated power relations involved in trying to supply "aid". Groups such as L'Auberge advertised best-practice rules on notice boards in their warehouse, held regular training and briefing meetings and employed a volunteer welfare co-ordinator.

Though the mayor of Calais had initially promised to "tolerate" the concentration of displaced people on the new Jungle site, the rising numbers of residents – and what was seen by the authorities as the "gentrification" of the camp by many markedly international and middle-class European volunteers – outstripped the original plan to keep residents out of sight and mind. The BBC programme "Songs of Praise" was filmed from the Jungle's beautiful Ethiopian Church of St Michael the Angel, and visits by UK politicians such as Tessa Jowell and Jeremy Corbyn had further raised the camp's profile. Consequent lockdowns and blockades of camp entry-points forbidding entry to volunteers and aid convoys carrying materials such as building works were frequent, as were confiscations and raids of goods from the refugee-run shops and restaurants in camp by CRS forces as part of a policy of control. This harassment, along with constant evictions and partial demolitions of the camp, created an unstable environment in direct opposition to the official pronouncement of "tolerance". In September 2015, the mayor had ordered the clearance of tents from an overspill camp under the bridge, and later that year evictions had taken place to clear a site destined for a container camp controlled by biometric data and also run by La Vie Active. Envisaged to house 1,500 people, this facility was still inadequate provision for the many residents who lived in tents and shelters, as well as requiring personal information in exchange for a heated cabin. A "buffer zone" strip of land was cleared by local authorities in January 2016 to stop residents camping by the motorway; volunteers helped physically move the large shelters and structures out of the danger area of destruction.

A few weeks later, in early March, the prefecture ordered the destruction of the whole southern zone of the camp and the consequent eviction of 3,455 people from their homes – this number was according to Help Refugees' census. This decision was protested by residents, in which a group of hunger-striking Iranian camp residents sewed their lips together, and four volunteers joined the hunger strike. A legal challenge brought by residents and *les associations* arguing that not enough alternative state accommodation was available failed, but did result in the judge ruling that common areas, such as churches, mosques, schools and medical centres, must remain. However, the demolition of tents and shelters, including police

Figure 6.10 Calais Jungle camp, France, 2016. A refugee burns the French
Government's eviction notice.
Image credit: Caroline Gregory.

beatings and tear-gassing of residents, forced most to relocate to the
northern zone of the camp, leaving around 8,000 people of different
nationalities pushed together in only 10 hectares of land – a situation which critics have described as a world record concentration of
population. Despite concerns raised about the lack of safeguarding
by national or regional authorities of minors in the camp, 129 children
from the camp were reported as missing after demolitions.

Over the summer of 2016, CRS raids and blockades continued
as Help Refugees' census showed the number of people in camp had
swelled again to over 10,000. French president François Hollande
then expressed an intention to remove all adults and families from the
Jungle, promising residents temporary accommodation in a network
of *centres d'accueil et d'orientation* (CAOs) while their claims were

Figure 6.11 Calais Jungle camp, France, 2016. Policing increased at the camp as mass evictions increased and fires were started. The camp was finally destroyed in October 2016.

Image credit: Caroline Gregory.

heard, but at the same time he appealed to the UK Government to accept the estimated 1,500 unaccompanied minors who had a strong case to be accepted under UK law. British prime minister Theresa May refused.

Many volunteers at first supported the "humanitarian sheltering" policy of taking residents to CAOs, but others distrusted the decision to uproot residents and provide only temporary shelter for a few months. Volunteer groups legally challenged the move but in a tribunal hearing in Lille, they lost their case, with the judge supporting governmental policy. Many camp residents, equally suspicious of the removal policy, were by now anxious to leave, and up to 2,000 set off before the final eviction, most for the "ghetto" areas of Paris and Brussels.

During the week-long eviction at the end of October 2016, the site was bulldozed, and adult residents and families were registered and transported to a number of reception centres around France, where they were told their asylum cases would be considered; 1,500 unaccompanied minors were assigned a temporary place in the repurposed container camp, yet from mid-week fires broke out, destroying many of the last tents and bringing chaos to the evictions. Shamefully, over 1,900 minors were left in or around the container area in the middle of the burning camp by the authorities at this time, in appalling and uncertain conditions with no care, adequate food, or supervision. Days before the final evictions, the UK Government had finally under pressure accepted a small number of unaccompanied minors under the Dubs Amendment (discussed further in Chapter 2 and in the UK Flashpoint), yet during demolitions one third of all the remaining unaccompanied minors tracked by Refugee Youth Service disappeared and remained unaccounted for. During the latter half of demolition week, despite media sources reporting that the camp had been successfully cleared, around 200 minors not lucky enough to have been afforded a place in the container sheltered temporarily

Figure 6.12 Calais Jungle camp, France, 2016. Many camp residents set off at night, with no planned destination, to avoid further police attacks and the final burning of the Jungle camp.

Image credit: Rowan Farrell.

in the camp's Ethiopian church and in the mosque. Over 100 others slept in the open air, safeguarded only by volunteers from groups such as Care4Calais and Help4Refugee Children. It was later established from volunteer records and from the graves in Calais' Cimetière Nord that at least 13 unaccompanied minors and two babies had died during the 18-month life of the camp. To the very end of the New Jungle experiment, governments had consistently failed the most vulnerable; as we have seen throughout the history of Calais, ordinary citizen volunteers filled the gap.

As previous events have shown, migrant camps are a symptom of larger political issues and not the cause, so that even after the complete razing of the Jungle and the relocation of most of its residents to CAOs at the end of 2016, displaced people still live in hiding in Calais woods and fields, but now without the larger shelters and support systems that the Jungle, however chaotic and dangerous at many times, had provided.

For some months after demolition the mayor enforced a local "zero tolerance" directive in Calais town, meaning that volunteers and citizens could be arrested for offering refugees food or shelter. Train stations and other points across the town were under 24-hour police surveillance. Refugees, even minors, could be held for up to four days without charge. CRS forces employed hostile tactics to clamp down on migrant presence, such as constant harassment, confiscation and destruction of belongings and tents and stopping displaced people accessing such facilities as showers and drinking water. However, a court case brought by Help Refugees and 11 other organisations in 2017 succeeded in overturning the decrees and requiring the mayor's office, prefecture and the Conseil Departemental to establish official amenities such as showers, toilets and drinking water at particular areas. CRS officers also harassed volunteers in various ways, requiring extensive ID checks during food distribution as well as making threats and employing physical and verbal violence towards them. A dossier published by four Calais volunteer groups in 2018 documented 646 incidences of police intimidation. Volunteers have also been prosecuted for filming such police violence. This was highlighted by the acquittal of a British volunteer by a French court in 2019, where a spokesman said his prosecution was "sadly emblematic of the harassment, intimidation and attacks that human rights defenders are facing at the hands of police in Calais for supporting migrants and refugees."

Slowly the population of displaced people has risen again in northern France, estimated at around 1,500–2,000 across the region in March 2020, including over 250 unaccompanied children, the youngest only 7 years old. Evictions have continued, with 1,301 having taken place from small hidden camps around Calais, and 173 from the Grande-Synthe area, including the expulsion of 700 people from a gymnasium in Dunkerque by October 2019. The constant harassment by CRS of such small camps, the unstable living conditions and the lack of will by the UK Government to process UK asylum claims in France have resulted in a boom in the smuggler market.

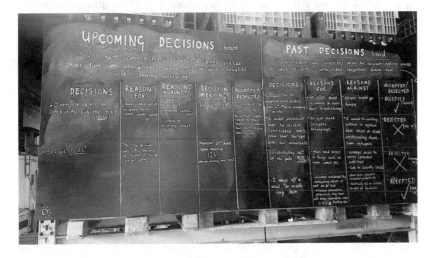

Figure 6.13 Northern Calais, France, 2018. Even after the destruction of the Jungle camp by the French authorities, L'Auberge des Migrants' warehouse continued as a focal point for the distribution of supplies and food, and as an advice centre to the many refugees still in the region.

Image credit: Charlotte Burck.

Hundreds of people have accordingly crossed or attempted to cross the English Channel in small boats, at least four dying in the attempt by late 2019. Others have died trying to enter the Channel Tunnel or while boarding vehicles. Since 2009, there have been over 200 deaths of people related to crossing the France–UK border, at least 40 of these having taken place during the life of the Jungle or in its immediate aftermath, including children with a right of reunion under the EU Dublin III Regulation (described earlier in this book) who had given up hope of legally joining relatives in the UK.

The large systems of warehouse logistics, food preparation and delivery set up by UK and French volunteer groups to assist the Jungle in 2015–2016 have diversified into warehouses and groups delivering meals and supplies in food vans to various areas where displaced people are living in itinerant fashion.

Many former Calais volunteers, shocked and radicalised by their experiences in Calais, have gone on to assist in Paris, Dunkerque and Ventimiglia on the France–Italy border, or further afield in Greece and Serbia. Others have set up new groups, joined political activist campaigns or established welcoming projects in their own countries. Several larger organisations, such as Help Refugees and Refugee Community Kitchen, have received humanitarian awards for their work, even as the hostile environment by British and French states continues against both those trapped in Calais and those who seek to aid them. The fact that 15,000 volunteers have assisted in Help Refugees projects in Calais since the Jungle's demolition belies the assertion made by governments and echoed in the mainstream media that "the public" supports their punitive policies.

It is clear that through the long history of Calais and migration, the northern French coast will always be a staging-post in the journey for those wishing to pursue legitimate asylum or human rights claims in the UK, or to simply seek better lives. Meanwhile, those of us who volunteered in its jungles and saw first-hand the violence and misery caused by both French and British policies against people trapped on the wrong side of the border experienced a seismic shift in our perceptions of the world that changed our lives forever.

Flashpoint: Dunkerque

Maddie Harris

Long before images of the tents and shelters of the Calais Jungle camp reached the news as it sheltered thousands of people from Syria, Sudan, Ethiopia, Iraq and many other countries, displaced people had settled further east along the French coast with hopes of reaching the UK from Dunkerque. Encampments near Grande-Synthe, a suburb of Dunkerque, have existed in one form or another

Figure 6.14 Dunkerque, France, 2016. One of the few shelters in Basroch camp is destroyed by fire, caused by a stove used for winter heating.

Image credit: Justin Devereux.

since 2006, though until 2015 these never exceeded more than 100 in resident numbers. But by September 2015 one camp – known as Basroch – had a population of around 300, many of whom were children, and what was once a football ground at the end of a lane just minutes from the offices and malls of Grande-Synthe town was now filled with open cooking fires and thin nylon camping tents. Local French individuals and civil society groups such as Emmaus and SALAM provided residents with clothing, tents, sleeping bags and food. As the camp grew, British volunteers began visiting the camp, initially through a Bristol-based organisation, Aid Box Community, then others came independently. During the autumn and winter of 2015, as migration to Europe swelled, the camp's population exploded to around 3,000, including many families with young children and unaccompanied minors. The population continued to be largely Iraqi-Kurdish, but others came from Iran, Kuwait and Vietnam. By now international volunteer groups from the UK, France, Belgium, Switzerland and Denmark had set up a permanent presence, aiming to drastically improve the conditions of what was to become known as the worst camp in Europe at that time – a rat-infested quagmire of knee-deep mud and human waste, with no sanitation or infrastructure. The fragile camping tents were woefully inadequate, and tent fires were frequent due to the use of gas and paraffin stoves for heating and cooking inside them.

A large central tent built by a group of independent Belgian volunteers acted as a kitchen and space for new arrivals. But the site itself was precarious – and as the weather worsened, the centre of the camp became prone to flooding. These dire conditions were made worse by restrictions introduced by the local municipality in December 2015 on what was allowed to enter – construction materials, timber or pallets, tents and often blankets, sometimes even food items, were turned away at the gates. With no processing taking place regarding asylum claims to the UK, the camp became largely controlled by a number of smuggler groups.

Violence such as shootings and stabbings was commonplace, and due to the more dangerous nature of the camp, volunteer numbers

Figure 6.15 Dunkerque, France, 2016. Police descend on Basroch camp after clashes broke out between smuggler groups, January 2016.

Image credit: Feenix Clough.

remained far lower than in Calais. In response to the situation, the international NGO Médecins sans Frontières (MSF) began to offer medical care in the camp, and conversations began with Damien Carême, the mayor of Grande-Synthe, to construct France's first humanitarian refugee camp. Conditions in Basroch were so bad that it was decided the only way to move forward was to start with a new site. The new camp would become known as La Linière, and would provide wooden shelters with heaters, communal flushing toilets and showers and community kitchens – a dramatic improvement in living conditions.

Conversations began between MSF, the residents and the volunteers to develop relations between all parties – discussing what facilities the Basroch residents wanted, and ensuring that they were confident the new camp was intended to improve living conditions and not to control the free movement of people. Many were mistrustful, having lived for months in Basroch's horrendous conditions with no evidence of action by the state – only restrictions and a heavy police presence. Volunteers set about taking people to visit the new site, attempting to ease their concerns over restriction of movement and rumours of fingerprinting upon arrival. Finally, on 6 March 2016 an estimated 3,000 people moved to La Linière, approximately 1 kilometre from Basroch.

Numbers had been predicted by the mayor and local NGOs to be lower, so many spent nights at the camp's entrance. Meanwhile Basroch burnt to the ground, the fires believed to have been started by smugglers.

Between them, MSF and the council of Grande-Synthe committed Eur. 4 million to the La Linière project. The mayor of Grande-Synthe tasked French association Utopia 56 with the running of the new camp. Utopia 56 had been working in Calais and Dunkerque for many months; the group invited long-term volunteers who had previously worked in Basroch to make up the core team, recognising the importance of established relationships and experience. Other volunteers and grassroots organisations like Refugee Community Kitchen and ABC were responsible for the construction of kitchens, a women's centre and men's clothing distribution points. Another well-established

Figure 6.16 Dunkerque, France, 2016. La Linière camp at Grande-Synthe near Dunkerque, built by Médecins Sans Frontières.
Image credit: Sue Clayton.

French organisation, L'Auberge des Migrants, provided food and material goods such as clothing, and Utopia 56 provided materials for residents to adapt their shelters. A school was constructed by the Hummingbird Project, offering education in French and English to the camp's 300 children, and there was also the option to attend local schools, negotiated by the mayor. All community spaces and items beyond fuel for the heaters inside each shelter and sanitation continued to be provided by local and international volunteer organisations and independent volunteers. Overall, living conditions were vastly improved. But with no meaningful information regarding access to asylum for the many residents with family members and links to the UK, the violence and control by smugglers continued. Throughout this time a number of police operations attempted to limit the violence that had continued since the move to the new camp. And volunteers tried to limit smuggler control by running multiple distributions accessible to all, and a robust and fair system for allocation of shelters to new arrivals. However, it was generally known that the camp remained largely controlled by smugglers, with new cartels arriving as soon as one had been removed.

By June 2016, the cost burden led Mayor Carême to pass responsibility for La Linière to the French national government, and AFEJI, a French association doing local and national work both with displaced people and French citizens, assumed management of the camp. There is no doubt that it was correct that the state should finally take responsibility for the welfare of those living within the camp, but there were concerns as to AFEJI's ability to manage the camp in the coming months as conditions began to once again deteriorate. In a communication dated 5 October 2016 sent to the company which managed security at La Linière camp, the Dunkerque sub-prefecture gave instructions that no new arrivals should be admitted to the camp, including "minors, families, pregnant women, the elderly and people in situations of difficulty". La Linière began to deteriorate, repeating the pattern seen in Basroch. Conditions worsened as numbers swelled – among those, many who had fled the Calais Jungle when it was destroyed in October 2016. Empty shelters were removed, despite there being so many new arrivals. Rats began to run free throughout the camp, and skin conditions such as scabies once again became rife as the camp became massively overcrowded and tensions grew. Violence continued, and as the camp became increasingly overcrowded, smugglers exerted more control.

Then, on 10 April 2017, a massive fire destroyed the camp. No governmental effort was made to extinguish the fire, which raged for hours; 1,500 people, including approximately 100 unaccompanied minors, fled to a nearby forest. Within days, the site of La Linière was cleared. No attempt was made to rebuild, or to investigate the reasons for the fire. The mayor requisitioned three gymnasiums to use as emergency shelters, but this was at best a short-term solution.

Since the 2017 fire, a pattern of continued displacement has emerged. The number of displaced people in the area ranges in estimate from 500 to over 1,000. On the other side of the motorway from the camp of La Linière, hundreds pitch tents in the woods surrounding a nature reserve and activity park. People wash themselves and

Figure 6.17 Dunkerque, France, 2017. An Afghan boy at La Linière camp after it was completely destroyed by fire.

Image credit: Anon.

their clothes in a lake at its centre. However, one major change is evident. Police continuously harass people there, and destroy the tents of those living in the woods, clearly to prevent any kind of fixed camp from emerging. There are regular evictions where people are instructed to board buses to one of France's many "reception centres". Others avoid the option and disappear back into the woods. Tents and belongings are destroyed by police on a daily basis and no effort is made by the state to improve living conditions in any way. During the winter of 2018 to 2019 the mayor of Grande-Synthe again opened a large gymnasium, Espace Jeunes du Moulin, in an attempt to house as many as possible and protect them from the elements. Once the gym became full, hundreds were forced to pitch camping tents outside, again provided by volunteers and grassroots groups such as Refugee Women's Centre, Emmaus and Refugee Ground Support.

The gym remained open for many months, until on 17 September 2019 the estimated 1,000 people in and outside the gym were once again evicted, and many were lost again.

The state-actioned process of constant eviction and harassment has continued for over two years now. Sanitation in the area has deteriorated even beyond the standards of Basroch. There is currently no access to a tap, no toilets and certainly no showers. Since the eviction of the Espace Jeunes du Moulin gymnasium, over 500 have returned to the woods, and local and international grassroots organisations and independent volunteers continue to provide basic shelter in the form of tents. Food is still provided by local French volunteers and by the Refugee Community Kitchen. Little has changed – and the cycle of denial, where the forced removal of displaced people is being peddled as a solution to a continual problem, perpetuates a disregard for the most basic of human rights of those who are most vulnerable.

Figure 6.18 Dunkerque, France. 2019. Gent4humanity Refugee Support's first-aid team work in a car park near the old Grande-Synthe camp site.
Image credit: Michelle Wright.

Flashpoint: Brussels

Niki Papadogiannakis

Refugees started to arrive in Belgium in the late summer of 2015, many of them Syrians who left due to the war to find safety in Europe. Many found themselves at Parc Maximilien in Brussels, a large public park that before 2015 was not well known as it sits in the north of the city, but which became the notorious temporary home for thousands of people. Situated opposite the Belgian Immigration Office, within weeks after the first arrivals the park became a small tent-city set up

Figure 6.19 Brussels, Belgium, 2015. A volunteer from SoutienBelge OverSeas does activities with young refugees.

Image credit: Niki Papadogiannakis.

by upwards of 3,000 refugees. About a 20-minute walk from the commercial centre in Brussels, this squatted space was an informal camp within the urban landscape – a very visible one to the neighbourhood and wider community, who began to mobilise once it became clear what the situation of these people were: they were refugees, mostly fleeing war in Syria or Iraq, who were not being accommodated by the government and had to resort to sleeping outside. Locals came to the park to support these individuals, children and families by giving donations of clothing, food and other basic necessities. Soon afterwards, humanitarian organisations started to set up tents alongside the temporary homes of these refugees. SB OverSeas opened the first school in a tent in the park, and began providing cultural mediation services in collaboration with Médecins du Monde, which was also providing basic needs support and psychological services. For a short while other groups like Samusocial and Oxfam also had tents providing services.

As the summer months ended and nights began to get colder, it became clear that the temporary outdoor sleeping situation in tents was no longer possible. In September 2015, the citizens' movement "Citizen's Platform for Refugee Support", or Plateforme Citoyenne, came together to not only address immediate needs in an organised way – meals, health, activities, psychological support, education – but also to organise the longer-term private housing of homeless refugees during the winter months. Individuals in the community who signalled their willingness to host an individual, family or group would connect with Plateforme Citoyenne, which was on the ground in Parc Maximilien speaking to the refugees who needed a warm place to sleep.

Initially set up as a Facebook group co-ordinating support to those sleeping rough in the park, now more than 39,000 individuals and families have welcomed a refugee in their home for the night. Since 2015, tens of thousands of Brussels citizens have hosted refugees in their homes; now, about 300 to 400 refugees per night are hosted by welcoming volunteers. Some host for just one night, but others have been

Figure 6.20 Brussels, Belgium, 2015. Volunteers erect a tent that will be the first school in Parc Maximilen.

Image credit: Niki Papadogiannakis.

engaged in regularly hosting refugees since the creation of the platform in 2015. Some are young people with roommates that have extra space on their floor, pillows and a blanket. Others are families with young children who want to show their kids the power of love and solidarity. Some are older people, with grown children, who now have an extra bedroom or two in their homes which the refugees can benefit from, but the hosts themselves also benefit from the social interaction. The volunteers host not just as a sign of solidarity and support for refugees to have a safe and dignified place to sleep, but the act of hosting itself is political: showing the government that despite its inaction to support this group in need, and while its actions have criminalized this group, citizens are ready to stand in solidarity with their struggle.

But it is clear to everyone that longer-term solutions are needed to the housing issue. There remained a lack of capacity in the government reception facilities for those seeking international protection in Belgium. In response to the crisis, Brussels authorities opened up the "Petit Chateau" accommodation centre – a former military barracks

Figure 6.21 Brussels, Belgium, 2018. Refugees wait for Belgian citizens in the hope of finding a place to sleep.

Image credit: Yoon Daix.

by the canal – as well as other specialised centres (for unaccompanied minors and for single women). While officially run by the government, groups like SB OverSeas and Médecins du Monde, with the support of local volunteers, continued working alongside them to fill the educational and psychosocial support gaps that the state support was not addressing.

From 2014 to 2015, most refugees arriving at Parc Maximilien were from Syria, and the immigration services were slow in processing the claims of those first few thousand arrivals. Since 2015, young people from Afghanistan and Pakistan also began to arrive. Protections for Syrians were guaranteed under specific protocols of the European Union; while these protected many people in need, they reinforced a system that assessed claims for protection primarily by nationality. Since Afghanistan and Pakistan were excluded from this system, many young people from these countries were staying in Brussels for weeks at a time, each day attempting to reach the UK. Since then, the group of refugees in Brussels has encompassed this mix – both of individuals navigating the asylum system in hopes of receiving refugee status, and those that have been rejected or presume they will be rejected due to their nationality, who stay only for a while as they attempt to move on elsewhere.

By summer 2017 and on into the colder months, Parc Maximilien and the nearby Gare du Nord railway station continued to be the central focus of volunteer and community support groups like Plateforme Citoyenne to welcome and support new arrivals – but with increasing opposition from the government. In an effort to prevent the park from becoming the "new Calais", police began heavily patrolling these areas and arresting many *sans-papiers* (undocumented people).

In 2017, a group of concerned Brussels-based organisations opened the Humanitarian Hub, a space where refugees can come for daily support, resources and information for people in transit. Consisting of Plateforme Citoyenne, the Belgian Red Cross, MSF, Médecins du Monde, le CIRÉ, Vluchteling Werk Vlaanderen and Oxfam Solidarité, the Hub includes a medical service, mental health support, socio-legal information and clothing distribution.

At the end of 2019, the Hub received political support in the form of written commitment by the Brussels regional government. Every day, 200 migrants are welcomed at the Hub. While this serves as a vital resource for those 200, the community and activists maintain that these services should be provisions of the government rather than citizen solidarity support. They argue that these refugees in transit are the responsibility of the government, while the government argues that its responsibility lies only with refugees asking for asylum in Belgium.

The profile of those at Gare du Nord and Parc Maximilien since 2017 is significantly different than it was in 2015. Most of the new arrivals see their future in the UK rather than in Belgium, for a variety of reasons linked to language, economic ties, diaspora groups and other networks in the UK.

In 2018, of the 17,235 *sans-papiers* estimated to be living in Belgium, 1,855 of them were unaccompanied teenagers between 14 and 17. For these young people on the move, the state has an obligation outlined in international, regional and national laws for the protection of people under 18 travelling alone. In Brussels there are four accommodation centres for this group. But at several points throughout the past three years, including at the end of 2019, the centres were all at full capacity, making it impossible to guarantee that all unaccompanied teenagers had a safe place to sleep – leaving many on the streets, or reliant on volunteers.

At the end of 2017, the political environment in Brussels for refugees again turned more hostile. The Immigration Office moved to Petit-Chateâu to deter people from camping outside in Parc Maximilien. Police began to raid the tents in the park and the informal homeless shelters. There were even proposals from the Belgian Government to conduct police raids in the homes of private citizens that were hosting refugees. It became illegal to distribute food in the park without a permit. At the end of 2018, this sentiment peaked during the upcoming elections at the regional, federal and EU level. In December 2018, Prime Minister Charles Michel signed the UN-backed Marakesh Migration Pact – designed to increase the volume of legal routes to movement – but was met by governmental opposition and led to his resignation. Brussels city saw two opposing sides demonstrate – on one, 5,500 people marched with the Flemish national right-wing party; on the other, 1,000 people marched in solidarity with migrants in Brussels and around the world.

More locally, the site of Gare du Nord became a tool for the far right to make its xenophobic argument. At the beginning of 2019, after months of seeking warmth at the Gare du Nord station, the refugees were removed by the police and regular patrols increased. Beyond security controls, there have also been violations of the right to ask for asylum; in November 2019, about 60 people were turned away from Petit-Chateâu, where people must go to make their claim. Not only were they unable to access the asylum process, but they were also denied accommodation and had to spend the night on the street.

Brussels has experienced changes in the migrants that it has received over the past five years, but despite those changes one struggle that has remained constant is the lack of sufficient housing and accommodation. This has been a constant problem, despite the efforts of citizens and humanitarian groups to close these gaps. In 2017, La Porte d'Ulysse in Haren, on the outskirts of Brussels, was created as a space with a specific purpose: to get people out of the cold. The space has enough beds to host 380 men a night and is always full. Every morning, groups of volunteers make and serve

Figure 6.22 Brussels, Belgium, January 2018. More than 2,000 people assemble in a "Human Chain" in Parc Maximilien to protect refugees against police controls. Image credit: Yoon Daix.

Figure 6.23 Brussels, Belgium, 2019. Volunteers from Plateforme Citoyenne sort food donations.

Image credit: Yoon Daix.

breakfast to those that slept there the night before. It's a vital establishment for the survival of these refugees, as almost every evening around sundown, police and police dogs sweep Gare du Nord, displacing the people who sought warmth there during the day.

Other problems facing migrants in Brussels include: the narrow asylum system in Belgium, which has created a situation where people are being denied refugee status, but are equally un-deportable and therefore stuck; young people having been sent by their families to find safety, who now are facing long and complicated family reunification procedures; and uneven integration into Belgian society, which is causing tense dynamics related to culture shock. While relative to 2015 the number of people in this precarious position has decreased, and many from that time have begun a process of finding their future in Brussels, there is still a lot of work to do.

7

The Endeavour Towards Wellbeing

Charlotte Burck, Justine Corrie and Gillian Hughes

Volunteer welfare is a key topic in this collection. Both Justine Corrie, as an independent volunteer therapist, and Charlotte Burck and Gillian Hughes, as founder members of the Refugee Resilience Collective, ran practices in Calais to support volunteer wellbeing. Here they present their complementary approaches to volunteer welfare and consider the wider lessons that may help in building a long-term sustainable refugee support movement.

Justine Corrie

I first went to Calais because, like many others in the UK, having seen the news reports I was moved to go and "do something". It was clear that in camps like the Calais Jungle there was no centralised support nor big NGOs or charities to contact, but instead loosely knit groups of people were filling up cars, vans and trucks with aid, and just turning up. I arrived in October 2015 with seven other volunteers taking an aid convoy to the UK charity Help Refugees, which was based with a long-established French group L'Auberge des Migrants at its ware-house near the Jungle. My professional work is as a psychotherapist and in developing training and workshops in sustainable activism for social change. I spent that first weekend learning about the Jungle, seeing how things worked and meeting other volunteers. I was struck by how much collective and individual effort, passion, energy and will was being harnessed in this volunteer body to support refugees and migrants within the camp. But the pressure on them was immense. An almost exclusively self-organised volunteer effort was grappling with resourcing and supporting the refugee community of thousands, with the very basics of survival requirements – food and shelter, as well as making attempts at play facilities for the children, legal advice services and medical aid. Many of the small volunteer organisations were overwhelmed, their capacity at breaking point. And the camp population was growing exponentially, from some 3,000 in that summer of 2015 to reports of over 9,000 by June 2016. Conditions in the camp fell below the UNHCR's standards for refugee camps. But the UNHCR wasn't present. The French Government had invited neither the UNHCR nor the Red Cross. The external support system, run almost entirely by volunteers, was barely able to cope. In addition, most volunteers had no prior experience of humanitarian aid. These were students, casual workers, teachers, business people, architects, parents – simply people who had seen the same images that I had, the same news reports, and had set off. Some had moved to Calais, while others with work and family commitments back home made regular visits, usually bringing aid. Most of those who lived full-time at the camp were young, in their early twenties, and it was the first experience of its kind for most of those I met. Improvisation plays a central part in "volunteer humanitarianism" (Sandri, 2017) as volunteers learn new skills and assume different roles depending on what is needed. It seemed they were able to respond well at urgent crisis points, but many struggled to deal with more complex situations that arose in the camp; trafficking, exploitation and violence were daily occurrences in the Jungle. The volunteers were rightly concerned about these issues and worried they were not doing enough to protect vulnerable people. The French police were actively hostile, attacking the camp with tear-gas and taking refugees outside the camp to beat them. Volunteers were anxious about their own safety too, but did not want to exacerbate tensions between the camp residents and the police. The lack of institutional aid was worrying not only because there was a deficit of basic services, but also because it put both refugees and volunteers at risk.

I could see that any welfare or psychological support provision from these emerging small NGOs for volunteers was minimal. There was little in place in terms of volunteer induction or debriefing – and certainly wellbeing was not covered in this. I was familiar with the dynamics of activist culture, where people would set themselves impossible goals, believing there can be no rest until all the problems are solved; where they are constantly fire-fighting; where respect is earned through relentless devotion to the cause and so a constant negating of personal wellbeing. I noticed many of the volunteers appeared to be suffering from a complex mix of guilt, shame and secondary trauma partly induced by the relentless daily witnessing of others' traumatic experiences without any filter of training or guidance. On top of this, some were also in a state of denial about their own symptoms, and if they did recognise any symptoms, they did not think they should be "allowed" to have them. Statements such as "How can I take time out and relax when people are being deported/killed/ attacked?" highlighted the emotional trauma. Taking adequate rest and time away from the camp, and eating and sleeping well, were low on the agenda for the core volunteers, whose activism had become a 24-hour preoccupation. Some volunteers lived in the camp itself in vans or tents, their immersion into this chaotic and intensely stressful environment total and complete. Taking care of personal boundaries could also be challenging in the intense atmosphere of the Jungle, where people could be tempted to push their own limits and push others to do the same.

After conversations with English full-time volunteer Liz Clegg, who had set up the impressive "Unofficial Women and Children's Centre", and with full-time volunteers from Help Refugees, an idea was born that I would buy and bring over a caravan that could be used both as an outreach centre for the many vulnerable women and children in the camp, but also as a weekend "talking space" for volunteers. The caravan would be housed within the Women's Area compound – an area of relative safety in the camp. The "caravan of calm" was fully booked in advance of its arrival and it functioned well as a confidential debrief and talking space for the long-term volunteers – both in being able to meet their immediate wellbeing needs and also to begin to create a culture where self-care was being modelled by the core

hub of the volunteer community. In gruelling conditions, freezing
temperatures and putrid viscous mud all around, the caravan of
calm was just that. This was not offered as therapy or counselling,
but as a trained ear with a professional. Listening to the experiences
of volunteers in that caravan, it became apparent that, especially
within the long-term volunteer community, unsustainable levels of
stress were driving some to breaking point. Eighteen-hour working
days; nights spent campaigning and fundraising online; the sense of
responsibility in being a humanitarian aid worker, support worker,
builder and medic all rolled into one without any basic training and
experience – it was often overwhelming. In most large NGOs, staff are
trained in stress management and encouraged to speak to counsellors
if they feel vulnerable, and a psychologist debriefs aid workers when
they return from assignments. Added to this, unlike NGO workers,
volunteers were of course unpaid so many had severe financial issues,
which made self-care choices like recreation or time off even more difficult. Over my subsequent visits throughout the winter, various spots
within the warehouse and compound were used as a therapy space –
a curtained-off area behind shelving racks of tents in the warehouse,
a temporary prefab in the building yard, a borrowed caravan space –
none entirely ideal as a "therapeutic container" and all requiring some
adaptation to support a "good enough" holding of confidentiality.
Between October 2015 and the camp's demolition in October 2016,
I made eight visits to Calais, of between three days and a week each
time. I was able to support a small number of long-term volunteers
on a regular ongoing basis – those who were aware of the impact of
the work they were engaged in, and keen to engage in a supportive
space where they could emotionally debrief. There were others who
used the space I offered as a one-off support, some self-referring and
others being recommended to take time out to meet me by their peers.
On occasion I was also asked to support in some crisis intervention
scenarios among volunteers, both mediating interpersonal conflicts
and in situations where difficult behaviours were impacting other
volunteers. Eventually, I found the warehouse environment became
too volatile and hazardous a location in which any kind of therapeutic

support felt viable. I felt that what might be needed for the volunteer seeking support was a change in environment. Many of those coming to me were so immersed in their support work that their world now encompassed only the camp, the warehouse and the small movement between. I opted to offer "walk-and-talk therapy", driving volunteers away from industrial Calais to rural hills and woodland some miles away. One volunteer who accepted this was a young woman working predominantly with supporting unaccompanied minors in the camp, who expressed her deep gratitude for being able to enjoy this time out for herself, and the space to just "be". We talked about her life outside of the refugee camp, her hopes and aspirations, her family and friends. She talked about how good it was to remember and make contact with the part of herself that existed beyond the circumstances of the refugee crisis and said it was "almost as if waking out of a relentless bad dream".

Burn-out was the most common issue faced by volunteers. Burn-out is described by Freudenberger (1974) and later by Maslach and Leiter (2005) as not just temporary fatigue but a chronic long-term condition, resulting in people once highly committed to a cause or organisation growing mentally exhausted (Schaufeli and Buunk, 2002) and, as a result, losing the idealism and the spirit that once drove them to work for social change (Pines, 1994).

Within the volunteer population of Calais, it seemed that there was less familiarity with the common signs and type of structural sources that produce burn-out among its population. Yet some structural sources were obvious: a culture and expectation to work beyond normal hours; continuous exposure to trauma without proper psychological support; and lack of clear division of responsibilities. Schaufeli and Buunk suggest five categories of burn-out symptoms (2002: 398):

I. affective manifestations, characterized by changes in mood, often related to depression and anxiety
II. cognitive manifestations, characterized by lags in attention, memory, and concentration
III. physical manifestations, characterized by health challenges such as headaches, high blood pressure, and illnesses

IV. behavioural manifestations, characterized by behavioural changes
     that impact productivity and health, ranging from increased pro-
     crastination to substance abuse
V.   motivational manifestations, characterized by diminishing drive
     and increased feelings of alienation and despondency

Among the volunteers of the Calais refugee camps all of the above signs
were abundantly clear. During the summer of 2016, UK volunteers
returning to their homes also began contacting me as many were experiencing ongoing symptoms of burn-out and secondary trauma once back
at home. Common experiences included: finding it difficult to connect
with family and friends not involved in the refugee crisis; experiencing life at home as "meaningless"; feelings of anger, guilt and shame;
nightmares; inability to sleep; and obsessively following developments
in Calais via social media.

   Throughout 2016 the volunteer movement in northern France grew
into something remarkable, with a burgeoning community and a more
organised infrastructure. But volunteer care remained a low priority –
diminished by what activism researchers have identified as a "culture of
selflessness" (Rodgers, 2010). In September 2016, I conducted a survey
in the volunteer community to discover how widespread these issues
were. It was shared via social media channels to volunteers not only in
France but throughout Europe. Within a month I received 197 replies.
In response to the question "Have you been at all concerned about
your mental health/emotional/psychological wellbeing at all while
volunteering?", 51% said "yes". Delving deeper into specific symptoms
gave cause for concern, as the chart below illustrates.

A further question on experiences after returning home also produced
disturbing results. Despite some new care initiatives in the Jungle, only
36% of respondents were aware of any support services – and of those,
many counted Facebook groups as a support service. Some services available that respondents named were via the Refugee Resilience Collective,
a voluntary team from London's Tavistock and Portman hospital who
visited regularly; myself; the SSuN (Solidarity and Support Network)

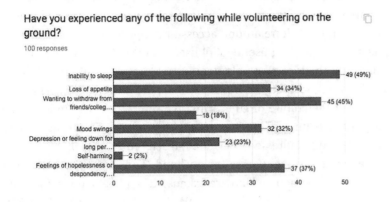

Volunteer Welfare Survey - Question 4, September 2016

Figure 7.1　Justine Corrie welfare survey question, 4 September 2016.

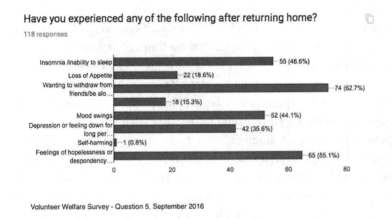

Volunteer Welfare Survey - Question 5, September 2016

Figure 7.2　Justine Corrie welfare survey question, 5 September 2016.

"buddying" service; and online counselling via the Volunteer Trauma Support Facebook group. Respondents also had varying experiences of the volunteer culture around accessing support. One said: "I flagged up self-care, and drug use/alcohol use, but I was ignored", and "In my experience, the idea that volunteers would struggle emotionally with situations was not really addressed". Others expanded on what could be considered the culture of guilt or martyrdom: "The environment is so that if you take time off you feel guilty". They talked of ways they would like to see this addressed: "A better-structured work pattern so that people aren't burning themselves out" and "I'd like to see a polite way of sending home people who are exhausted" – plus "support for long-termers to take a day off and GET AWAY FROM THE WAREHOUSE!" Among some respondents there were themes of guilt and shame around their own wellbeing needs, with beliefs that "your suffering seems so slight compared to those that you are helping" and "the refugees need it more than me". A further respondent added: "I feel like a complete fraud feeling this way".

Volunteers returning home temporarily or permanently experienced isolation, a sense of meaninglessness and difficulty settling back into ordinary life – one said "I feel so isolated and have no desire to reintegrate" – as well as guilt: "I feel guilty sometimes complaining about lack of sleep and the worry, when I know it doesn't help the residents of the camp at all and they have far greater reasons to have sleepless nights". Many volunteers experience lack of follow-up support: "I have felt pretty forgotten about, after I returned home after such a long period on the ground". Volunteers wanted debriefs, counselling and "More than just a Facebook group!" In response, in July 2016, I began planning a UK retreat for the following year with A Mindful Life, a UK charity that provides support for carers. The intention was to offer a few days respite to bring long-term volunteers together, to pause and reflect, share experiences and work with tools to support personal and organisational resilience as well as sustainable action.

Meanwhile, in October 2016 the Calais camp evictions and demolition generated a tsunami of volunteer trauma, grief and rage. It was clear that many of the volunteers were at breaking point, with little or no resources to continue their efforts, yet resolute in their determination to continue somehow. In June 2017, we held a UK retreat over two days in a woodland community centre in the New Forest. The 23 who attended included founders and affiliates in key Calais organisations, and long-term independents. Most had been active in northern France and many also in Greece and further afield volunteering, generally full-time, in aid delivery and distribution, midwifery, medical support, legal aid and in a community kitchen. Without exception, none of these individuals had been involved in any kind of humanitarian aid two years previously. Mindfulness practice and being in a natural environment helped everyone to share experiences in a supportive group, and to reflect on burn-out and resilience. Participant feedback included a sense of relief to have a space to be with the emotional response long held in, and statements like this: "Sorry for all the tears but I was holding on to them for months until I got to the woods and I was able to let them go". Along with this came a wider perspective, and with it "a greater incentive to make sure we look after ourselves and our team better".

In May–June 2018, I ran my survey for a second time to gauge, almost two years on, how the volunteer community was coping, and I received 137 responses. By now, more UK volunteers had gone to Greece, so the profile was 50% in Greece and now just 26% left in northern France. Another change was that 77% of volunteers said they were working directly with an established organisation and just 23% were independents. What was concerning was that to the question, "Have you been at all concerned about your mental health/emotional/psychological well-being at all while volunteering?", there was a leap to 69% saying "yes", and only 50% in total said that they had been offered any psychological or emotional support. A huge 57% said they were not aware of any on-the-ground wellbeing support. Given that these were mostly individuals working within organisations, it was concerning that volunteer welfare was still not being adequately attended to.

The symptoms of burn-out and trauma remained worryingly high among the volunteer sample. Asked "what changes, if any, have you experienced with regard to volunteer welfare since 2016?", responses again were concerning: "There are not enough skilled people in roles

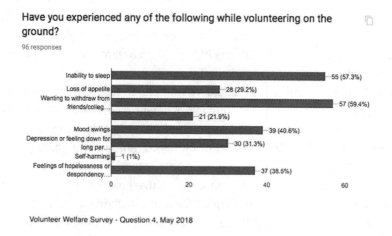

Figure 7.3 Justine Corrie welfare survey question, 4 May 2018.

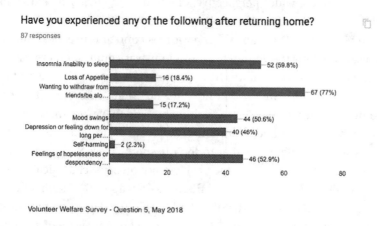

Figure 7.4 Justine Corrie welfare survey question, 5 May 2018.

to do this and the culture keeps perpetuating its own toxicity" and "Still just as lacking everywhere, few lessons learnt". This time burn-out, as a recognised symptom of the volunteer culture, was more widely named, with volunteers saying they would like to see more awareness-building to prevent it: "If people are burned-out there is no way to tell them to take a back seat". One also said "Volunteers should get information on self-care when they start, as part of any training their organisation offers. Group leaders should model this as well, taking time off as needed." There was also a greater sense of challenge within the volunteer community and the cultural norms. This was echoed by the claim that "There is a subset of volunteers who disparage the need for volunteer support, who are shaming those who need help" and "The stirring up of an atmosphere of emergency needs to end. Resenting people who know their limits and try to implement self-care must end."

In conclusion, I agree with Gillian and Charlotte's following suggestion that "support for volunteer activists in Europe needs to be built into organisational structures and whole communities". It is encouraging to hear how Gillian and Charlotte's experiences of offering therapeutic outreach support to volunteers has become more embedded within some on-the-ground organisations. I've also been heartened to see that some volunteer organisations have appointed paid volunteer welfare co-ordinators and have put some of the experience, findings and learning from the much earlier fire-fighting days of the refugee volunteer phenomenon into practice. It is vital that organisations continue to invest more in providing care and assisting in the recovery of volunteers to avoid burn-out and trauma in the future.

Charlotte Burck and Gillian Hughes

In March 2016, we (Charlotte and Gillian) first went to the Calais Jungle to explore whether we could offer anything useful to the refugees who were trying to survive there. As systemic psychotherapists (and Gillian also a clinical psychologist), with many years' experience of working in the NHS with refugees and those affected by trauma, violence and abuse, we hoped we could offer ways to support refugees in these very difficult conditions. We made contact with the Art Refuge UK team, who had been working with Médecins du Monde since September 2015 and who invited us to come into the camp with them, to see whether and what we might be able to contribute. We walked across muddy ground which until days before had been the south part of the camp, now littered with left-over belongings and discarded tarpaulins. There was a sense of unease as the demolition continued. In one of the few remaining huts, a group of Iranian men had sewn up their lips in protest against the lack of action by European governments to address the migrant crisis, holding signs saying "We are humans". We realised that any work with refugees would necessarily be focused on supporting people's abilities to survive the immediate emergency, rather than doing therapy to invite change over time. Leaving that first evening, we came across a volunteer in a highly distressed state, so distressed that it seemed unhelpful for her to remain in the camp. It was a vivid indication volunteers might also appreciate support to develop their resilience to the crisis they were witnessing, and prompted us to think about how we might include this in our work.

We formed a team, named the Refugee Resilience Collective, of ten experienced therapists working in the NHS and social care who volunteered their time and agreed that two people should go to the camp together every Friday, to offer support to refugees. We started by working with refugees and gradually took on a role of also supporting volunteers. We have described elsewhere (Burck and Hughes, 2018) how we developed this work over time. We had initially begun by offering volunteers a "pitstop" group each Friday morning at L'Auberge des Migrants, the main warehouse out of which many groups operated. Our pitstops were a space where people could discuss perturbing aspects of the work, identify and reflect on some of the small interactions which were of significance and the values which could sustain them both individually and collectively. Over time, we began to offer consultations to both individuals and teams, which we continue to do weekly to the present time.

Responses to Justine's Narrative and Surveys

Justine's narrative of her experiences of offering volunteer support chime with our own experience of the issues facing volunteers working with refugees, and the crucial importance of self-care in this context. Volunteers clearly find the work stressful and traumatic, and they push themselves to their limits – and often beyond – in their volunteering role. We were also struck by the fact that so often they do not respond to their increasing distress by making the decision to return home, and that there was something compelling which was keeping them in Calais in spite of what was clearly for many becoming more than they were able to deal with. The answer as to why people stay when they are clearly experiencing significant distress, as the survey highlighted, probably lies in several places. One is the importance of being part of a close community of people who understand the unique demands and the vast mix of emotions that volunteering provokes, and share the desire to act in the face of the crisis. As one volunteer said, "There is nothing like the feeling that you are surrounded by others who are all as angry as you!" Coupled with the concern that those back home do not share this commitment or depth of understanding, this seemed to make it difficult for many to leave Calais. However, this shared experience was clearly not enough to help with the significant distress that so many experience. There was also a paradox in this closeness, where volunteers worry about abandoning others and their shared cause when they leave, making it hard to prioritise personal wellbeing over their fellow activists.

Justine describes how there were no centralised support systems in Calais, as the volunteer force was made up of a mixture of small groups and individuals and had mainly grown organically in response to the need, and there was an absence of systematic planning for how to support volunteer welfare, or much recognition that it was necessary to prioritise this. Many groups did have informal practices like sharing experiences together in the evening, which were extremely important and could be helpful, but were sometimes experienced as too much talk about work with no break from it. This lack of attention to emotional welfare, combined with the lack of experience of volunteers, helped to perpetuate the culture we all encountered of volunteers working continuously without a break alongside feeling they were never doing enough. Volunteers often told us they could not take any time off because there weren't enough volunteers to do their work and that they felt extremely anxious because they felt so responsible: refugees needed to eat; they needed shoes; they needed sleeping bags; refugees had confided that they were cutting themselves or wanting to kill themselves. Volunteers often lay awake at night worrying, which in turn created more stress. The feeling of being indispensable worked against taking any breaks. Living in caravans with up to five others could be supportive but also meant there was no privacy to try to relax, read or write. Alongside these stresses, many volunteers talked of how difficult it was to communicate their experience to those back home, so only felt supported in a more general way, or even overtly criticised by those who took an anti-refugee position. Over the time we have been working in the Calais area, from spring 2016 to the present day, the refugees' living conditions have changed from the overcrowded Jungle camp and the utter bleakness of the Dunkerque camp (where we worked with camp residents and families), to having to sleep rough, facing daily violence and evacuations by the police. Volunteers working out of the L'Auberge des Migrants warehouse had different challenges to manage over these periods, but their levels of stress have remained quite consistently high, as is demonstrated in Justine's surveys.

Fostering Collective Care and Resilience

Justine highlights the challenges of working as a sole practitioner, mostly with individuals, whereas our practice has been more one of fostering collective support within volunteer communities – and our work of over three years in Calais and Dunkerque has taught us a great deal about this. Because of our previous experience of working with trauma and violence, we felt it was extremely important to have a team to support each other and develop ideas about this work together. We decided to go to Calais in pairs to enable us to talk about what we had witnessed and heard on the journey back. We saw it as crucial to work alongside other groups in order to try to build good connections, as systemic psychotherapy focuses on understanding people within their network of relationships and organisational systems. We put great effort into connecting with the different organisations on the ground and made attempts to bring the different groups together. For example, we initiated weekly meetings between Refugee Youth Service and Mèdicins du Monde to co-ordinate the care of unaccompanied minors, who were a particularly vulnerable group. Linking volunteers and groups to alert each other to particular individuals' vulnerabilities, to share responsibility and to make plans for support helped share the anxiety and stress.

The "pitstop" sessions we offered were open to all the organisations working out of L'Auberge (including Refugee Community Kitchen, Utopia 56, Info Bus, School Bus, Wood Yard, Women's Refugee Centre and Refugee Youth Service, among others). Like Justine, we did not frame our support as "therapy". There was a strong anti-therapy ethos among many volunteers, perhaps stemming from a bravado and sense of not wanting to be seen to need help, and we ourselves did not see therapy as appropriate in this context. Our preferred theoretical frameworks are of supporting resilience and "small acts of resistance" to the abusive context (Wade, 1997) informed by narrative approaches (Denborough, 2012) and liberation psychology (Martin-Baro, 1996; Afuape and Hughes, 2016), and we framed our offers of support as resilience-based consultations – helping volunteers survive the traumatic context in the best possible way and to identify ways to grow from it.

Consultations

We worked in the same warehouse – L'Auberge des Migrants – that Justine began in, though we never coincided. We used "out-of-ear-shot criteria" to find places to meet with individuals and teams, sometimes in an organisation's caravan, sometimes hidden behind stacks of clothing, or in the overgrown area outside, where cars were parked. We were committed from the start to try to establish a dependable presence in Calais, so that people could count on our team being there on most Fridays. The only sessions we currently (late 2019) do outside the L'Auberge warehouse now that both camps have been destroyed are those with refugees about whom volunteers are particularly concerned.

When serious concerns have arisen about a volunteer's welfare, we have discussed with the individual who it might be best to talk with in Calais or back home how to take steps to keep safe, and how we might support them. Concerns might range from a recurrence of a mental health issue to an episode of sexual harassment. We aimed to help build a culture of collective care where volunteers looked after each other as well as foregrounding their shared values. This included asking questions to invite political "conscientisation" (Freire, 1973), helping them understand their distress within the social and political conditions they were living and working within, rather than as a personal failure to cope. For example, one young English volunteer who had taken a career break from her job in the fashion business talked about her return to work after a month of volunteering. She found that when she started talking in her session about the things she had witnessed in Calais, her tears began to flow. At first, she said she felt ashamed at "obviously not being able to cope". However, through our conversation it emerged that her tears were about realising that her career in fashion was one she no longer wanted to return to. She felt angered by what refugees were being subjected to in Calais and moved by the people she had met. She realised that she wanted to commit herself to a life of more meaningful work which she felt was contributing something positive to the world. With this realisation, her tears stopped flowing and she began to talk about possibilities for how she might use her skills differently when she returned home and what the transition could look like. Together, we re-framed her tears as a sign of her commitment to a different future.

We always hold a social justice frame in our conversations with volunteers. Our approach was based on supporting the development of resilience, both individual and collective, with an emphasis on survival and growth within an extremely challenging context. We therefore often worked with groups of volunteers together, and viewed it as equally important to focus on ways of influencing the organisational cultures so that support for volunteers could be developed more widely. It was a slow process. Most of the organisations in Calais prided themselves on having no hierarchical structures – everyone was involved in decision-making – and this was impressive and fostered a very bonded activist community. However, developing and implementing guidelines for community practices was more difficult. Because working with refugees confronted all of us so acutely with our sense of privilege, this fuelled the shame and guilt aroused in volunteers and exacerbated the culture of over-work. Justine writes about a strong narrative associated with activism – the kudos attached to working hard: the harder you worked, the more committed an activist you were. Combined with the fact that there were no "job contracts" for volunteers stating when their working day started and ended, it created a perfect recipe for exhaustion. At our weekly pitstops, volunteers spoke about their difficulties in taking breaks, as well as wanting to help others at "breaking-point" to be able to take them. Discussions about never being able to do enough, and whether any of this was making a difference in any case, were important in helping volunteers make sense of their situation.

Later in 2016, we began to have conversations with some of the managers at L'Auberge des Migrants about the usefulness of inductions and reviews with volunteers, and how they might best be done. This was when Calais volunteering was at one of its busiest points, with at least 800 volunteers at any one time operating there. Help Refugees, one of the largest groups based at the L'Auberge warehouse, appointed a welfare co-ordinator who arranged for us to meet individual volunteers or teams from all the groups based there. Notices began to appear in the warehouse asking, "When did you last take a day off?" An Audre Lorde quote was posted – "Caring for myself is not self-indulgence, it is self-preservation, and that is an act of political warfare." Often our conversations involved reflecting on the shift from a more "purist" idealism which brought them to Calais, to facing some of the many complexities involved. When there were particularly upsetting incidents, teams would ask to meet us together to reflect on their experience and what they could learn from them. For instance, one group of volunteers was present when a smuggler pulled out a gun during one of the food distributions and started firing. They asked to meet to talk about their witnessing of refugees whom they knew well having been gunned down, their fear and the troubling questions raised of whether there were signs they may have missed, and whether they could have managed the situation differently.

Torn between a wish to continue immediately with distributions, or stop to see whether it would be possible to develop better safety plans, they explored with us the way this terrifying experience presented complexities not yet taken on board and how they could face those together. We helped them to think how they could take care of each other in the aftermath of this violence, and go forward with increased commitment. There did, however, continue to be differences in ethos between different organisations operating from L'Auberge des Migrants, with some taking the need for self-care on board more than others, which sometimes left the various groups concerned about each other.

We also explored, together with volunteers, ways to give feedback to each other about the need to take a break, ways to introduce breaks from work talk in their caravans and so on, to enable a culture of collective care to develop. Helping volunteers to identify moments of significance – a family with three small children for whom they managed to find wellington boots; a teenage boy who was given an Adidas sweatshirt that he was clearly delighted with; two Eritrean women who took pleasure in painting their nails with a volunteer who shared her red nail varnish – these became an important way to counteract the feelings of hopelessness and powerlessness, and questions about the effectiveness of working at this level. We suggested that volunteers give each other feedback about such interactions of significance, and what they appreciated about each other's work. What had they noticed about anything their team members had done that day which seemed to make a difference, however small? We drew on the importance of "doing hope" for each other (Weingarten, 2000) – we with the volunteers, they with each other, and they and the volunteers with the camp residents – as a way to sustain resilience. We understand resilience not so much as an individual quality, but as something created between people (Ungar, 2011), and rooted in significant moments like the ones described above. When individuals felt demoralised about the injustice being done to the refugee population, we reminded people of the strength of collectives, drawing on ancient as well as current examples and metaphors – like the ancient Indian Panchatantra story of doves trapped by a hunter in a net who became hopeless trying to escape until one suggested that they all fly up at once and they were able to lift the net together.

Making Sense of Experiences in the Social-Political Context

One of our practices is to help volunteers recognise the effect of the work and the context on themselves and on others. Thus, we had conversations to help people understand their distress as a product of the social-political context, using Freire's ideas of conscientisation – a process of developing critical awareness through reflection and action (Freire, 1973). The French and English volunteers based at L'Auberge des Migrants became ever more aware of the neglect and the cruelty of their governments, through witnessing the almost daily violence of the French police towards the refugees, as well as, at times, against themselves. Witnessing state violence in such a stark way changed perspectives, and resulted in many individuals claiming identities as activists who may not have done so before this process. Another of our practices was to situate behavioural effects of stress and burn-out (as listed in Justine's survey) as a "normal" and expected response to such traumatic circumstances. With this acknowledgement we worked with volunteers to identify some of their previous resources and interests (music, drawing, running, yoga), which they could call on to mitigate some of their distress and create times of creativity or distraction. These were spaces of remembering and being able to draw on other aspects of selves, to help manage these diffi-cult conditions. We introduced volunteers to brief (three- to five-minute) mindfulness practices which they could use whether out working or back in their caravans, to help ground them in the present and bring some small moments of calm in the midst of chaos.

Justine talks of burn-out being a common problem, and we saw how the environment invited this: the long hours, the sense of not being effective, and not having control over your work (Valent, 2002). Justine identifies what has been written on activist culture and its poten-tial for "martyrdom" and of volunteers feeling guilty about taking time off. We observed this too and note how Reynolds (2019) proposes that feeling guilty and indispensable are signs of burn-out, as, interestingly, is an opposite reaction – that of disconnection. She notes that all of us can have a tendency towards enmeshment, moving too close to people, enacting "transgressions of intimacy" (2019: 37), which involve forming unsafe "special relationships" with people (in this case the camp residents) and positioning ourselves as heroes and saviours. This leads to people feeling personally responsible for solving others' problems, and can isolate them from their colleagues and organisations. Paradoxically, this sometimes created unsafe relationships for the refugees, who have far less access to power and choice than the volunteers. To counter this, Reynolds highlights how crucial it is for us to stay connected with each other and to develop collective care.

It was also helpful to see how vicarious trauma – the negative effects on a person's wellbeing of engaging empathetically with individuals' traumatic experiences (McCann and Pearlman, 1990) – had contributed significantly to the stress that volunteers experienced. Not only the stories refugees told, but also the witnessing of police violence towards refugees, of fights over food supplies running out, of traffickers' abusiveness, of deaths on nearby roads as a result of refugees' attempts to board lorries – witnessing all this eroded people's abilities to cope. Justine describes well many of the responses among volunteers to this gruelling context in which they were working. We felt strongly that our support should not be based on an idea of an individual not coping, which is so often brought forth with labels such as post-traumatic stress disorder (PTSD), and is the reason we help people understand their distress within the sociopolitical context. There was a strong draw to this work for volunteers and ourselves – built from the sense of community, the solidarity, the meaning that the work gave to our lives, the life-changing experience that volunteering seemed to bring to so many. Drawing on narrative approaches, we therefore emphasised these aspects in our conversations with people, in order to connect them with their values and motivations and enable them to feel they have firmer ground to stand on. From this position, people are then more able to attend to the negative effects on their wellbeing of witnessing trauma and abuse.

Vicarious Resilience

Our observation that so many volunteers continue to stay committed and hopeful despite experiencing significant distress led us to the idea of vicarious resilience (Hernandez et al., 2007; Hernandez-Wolfe et al., 2015). Through witnessing the ability of refugees to survive extraordinary circumstances, volunteers draw resilience and strength. The power of standing alongside those who are going through extreme struggle, and of working together with colleagues to offer support in whatever ways possible, appeared to be an intensely sustaining and strengthening experience for volunteers. As Pearlman put it:

> Those who voluntarily engage empathically with survivors to help them restore the aftermath of psychological trauma open themselves to a deep personal transformation, which includes personal growth, a deeper connection with both individuals and human experiences, and a greater awareness of all aspects of life.
>
> (1990: 15)

We also experienced vicarious resilience in working with these passionate, dedicated volunteers through helping them identify their own resources, and found this work deeply meaningful, reinforcing the sense of purpose of our own lives. Political "conscientisation" is itself a sustaining process in framing our work as challenging injustice, and seeing the values we held in common as important in bringing together communities. Reynolds describes how vicarious trauma and burn-out can be resisted through "connection, collective care and justice-doing" (Reynolds, 2019: 36). Our support for volunteers attended closely to these three aspects. The individual volunteers whose task it was to witness and document police violence talked with us of their distress, their feelings of powerlessness and the acute shame they experienced that they were not intervening to try to stop the violence, that they were simply standing by. Thinking through with them the importance of their documenting the violence now, to provide evidence to hold the police and government to account in the future, was crucial and so was exploring how this value of future justice-doing could sustain them and their team in the present.

Guidelines – Helpful or Oppressive?

Our experience in Calais highlighted the importance of embedding collective responsibility in organisations through having clear agreements with people which work to keep everyone safe. Our own experience of work in the NHS and similar settings brought home how helpful boundaries and guidelines can be to try to ensure ethical and safe relationships with people. There were differences within the organisations on the ground at L'Auberge des Migrants about whether guidelines could be helpful or oppressive and counterproductive. When volunteers did take up roles which involved some "management" within the organisations or teams, they were often very uncomfortable and explored with us how they could enact these roles within the spirit of activist culture. These remain complex issues for individuals and the organisations as the wish to destroy barriers between "them" (refugees) and "us" (volunteers) cannot do away with the inequalities of privilege and choice. We have all been faced with seeing how the international political context and its inequalities cannot be solved through personal relationships.

Concluding Comments

Our experience has convinced us that support for volunteer activists in Europe needs to be built into organisational structures and whole communities. If we focus simply on individuals, we miss the opportunity to build on the extraordinary potential of the volunteer community to offer support, solidarity and mutual reinforcement of the values which motivate people, and sustain them in the humanitarian emergency situation in which they find themselves. So we argue that attention needs to be given towards creating healthy activist communities and building resilience through collective approaches. This requires collective acknowledgement of the emotional toll that the work can take, and understanding this as arising from the wider political context, rather than focusing on individual abilities to cope or not. There is no doubt that the impact of this work on individuals needs to be acknowledged, and support offered to people to help them find relief. However, we believe that volunteer welfare needs to go far beyond this if we are to build sustainable volunteer communities in the future. We would argue that Reynolds' (2019) three aspects of connection, collective care and justice-doing must be at the centre of any attempts to support volunteer activists across Europe.

References

Burck, C. and Hughes, G. (2018) "Challenges and Impossibilities of 'Standing Alongside' in an Intolerable Context: Learning from Refugees and Volunteers in the Calais Camp", *Clinical Child Psychology and Psychiatry*, 23(2): 223–237.

Freire, P. (1973) *Pedagogy of the Oppressed*. New York: Seabury Press.

Freudenberger, H. J. (1974) "Staff Burnout", *Journal of Social Issues*, 30: 159–165.

Hernandez, P., Gangsei, D. and Engstrom, D. (2007) "Vicarious Resilience: A New Concept in Work with Those Who Survive Trauma", *Family Process*, 46: 229–241.

Hernandez-Wolfe, P., Killian, K., Engstrom, D. and Gangsei, D. (2015) "Vicarious Resilience, Vicarious Trauma and Awareness of Equity in Trauma Work", *Journal of Humanistic Psychology*, 55(2): 153–172.

Hughes, G., Burck, C. and Roncin, L. (in press) "Therapeutic Activism: Supporting Emotional Resilience of Volunteers Working in a Refugee Camp", *Psychotherapy and Politics International*.

Maslach, C. and Leiter, M. P. (2005) "Reversing Burnout: How to Rekindle Your Passion for Your Work", *Stanford Social Innovation Review*, 3(4): 42–49.

McCann, I. L. and Pearlman, L. A. (1990) "Vicarious Traumatization: A Framework for Understanding the Psychological Effects of Working with Victims", *Journal of Traumatic Stress*, 3(1): 131–149.

Pines, A. M. (1994) "Burnout in Political Activism: An Existential Perspective", *Journal of Health and Human Resources Administration*, 16(4): 381–394.

Reynolds, V. (2019) "The Zone of Fabulousness: Resisting Vicarious Trauma with Connection, Collective Care and Justice-Doing in Ways that Centre the People We Work Alongside", *Context*, 164: 36–38.

Rodgers, K. (2010) "'Anger is Why We're All Here': Mobilizing and Managing Emotions in a Professional Activist Organization", *Social Movement Studies*, 9(3): 273–291.

Sandri, E. (2017) "Volunteer Humanitarianism: Volunteers and Humanitarian Aid in the Jungle Refugee Camp of Calais", *Journal of Ethnic and Migration Studies*. DOI:1-16.10.1080/1369183X.2017.1352467.

Schaufeli, W. B. and Buunk, P. (2002) "Burnout: An Overview of 25 Years of Research and Theorizing", in M. J. Schabracq, J. A. M. Winnubst and C. L. Cooper (eds), *The Handbook of Work and Health Psychology*, pp. 383–425. Chichester: Wiley.

Ungar, M. (2011) "The Social Ecology of Resilience: Addressing Contextual and Cultural Ambiguity of a Nascent Construct", *American Journal of Orthopsychiatry*, 81: 1–17.

Valent, P. (2002) "Diagnosis and Treatment of Helper Stresses, Traumas and Illnesses", in [editor name] (ed.), *Treating Compassion Fatigue*, pp. 17–37. New York: Brunner-Routledge.

Wade, A. (1997) "Small Acts of Living: Everyday Resistance to Violence and Other Forms of Oppression", *Contemporary Family Therapy*, 19: 23–39.

Weingarten, K. (2000) "Witnessing, Wonder, and Hope", *Family Process*, 39: 389–402.

BRINGING IT HOME

The huge response by activist volunteers to the crisis in Europe did not end when they left the Flashpoint zones across the continent. They continued to support those who reached their final destinations, and to engage with the wider issues at home, for example, around campaigns for refugee rights – as they tried to process the political and psychological implications of what they had been involved in, and consider how to build a sustainable culture of welcome for the future.

London, UK, 2016. The Refugees Welcome demonstration organised by Solidarity with Refugees heads through Central London.
Image credit: Pru Waldorf.

8

Testimonies on Welcoming and Campaigning

Sue Clayton

The Northern European countries have a chequered history of welcoming. In the UK, we can look back to actions such as our government accepting 10,000 unaccompanied child refugees in 1938–1939 from Nazi-occupied Germany, Poland, Austria and Czechoslovakia under the *Kindertransport* scheme. A less-known fact is that in 1935, grassroots petitions led to 4,000 children orphaned by Franco's troops in the Spanish Civil War being brought to Southampton, to be looked after initially by local volunteers before they were fostered around the country. It was the success of this earlier scheme that led to popular support for the *Kindertransports* – which were not initially supported by the government, though it finally yielded to public pressure. This instance may be worth bearing in mind as we think about our government today. For example, many local groups and organisations have asked central government if they can host Syrian families in their local area, and have found ways of funding this through charities and grassroots support. These offers are generally approved, but the numbers are not additional to the quota of Syrian refugees to which the government already committed, and these offers in one sense simply relieve the state of the cost. And it goes without saying that in the UK, the "hostile environment" policy, introduced by Home Secretary Theresa May in 2013, shows the government's direct opposition to welcoming. However, state hostility has been more than countered by local initiatives: as in many other European countries, the media reports of shipwrecks and the death of Alan Kurdi in the summer of 2015 caused literally thousands of UK groups and initiatives to blossom, both to welcome refugees already here and to lay the foundations to welcome more as they arrived. Many of these ran in conjunction with the sending of aid to the camps in Europe, and often also with campaigning for changes in both UK and European asylum policy.

Dan Ellis from Cambridge says:

From 2015–2018 I went to Calais 22 times. As the demands in Calais diminished I've concentrated on the care of refugees in Cambridge. I worked with the Kurdish community in La Linière (Dunkerque), and later was pleased to support the friends I'd met there when they arrived in the UK – and the Afghan boy who received the first caravan that I'd taken over, who also made it to the UK. While all this was taking place, we were receiving refugee families into Cambridge through the government scheme, and I was being Father Christmas to them, giving presents to the children, and chairing the meetings of the committee. This has now become my main concern as the demands in Calais have diminished.

So, we see a pattern of help abroad and welcoming at home being closely linked.

Ben Margolis made welcoming central to his family life. He says:

My wife and I moved to the Grange, a 10-acre smallholding in West Norfolk, to create a place of sanctuary and resilience for people who have been forced to flee to the UK. Over seven years we've welcomed hundreds of people who shared our home, which became a rich place of learning, sharing of cultures, incredible cooking and countless activities ranging from growing food, caring for animals, woodwork, art, weaving, pottery and many more. The local community supported our work, despite some being initially resistant, and we relied hugely on local volunteers. A couple of things from this experience really stand out. Without sounding trite, first was the massive impact people had on our lives. We have spent much of our lives involved in campaigning and activism in different forms and for me in particular this had led to quite serious burn-out and depression – a feeling of despair about the future but also about humanity. Sharing our home with people who had experienced in many cases the very worst of humanity and yet despite everything carried with them dignity, respect and gratitude repaired my faith in humanity. I will never be able to thank them enough.

The other is of a particular person who had fled torture in his home country. He had survived a brutal journey to the UK and received fantastic support from, among others, Room to Heal and Freedom from Torture in the UK. When he first came to the Grange he was overwhelmed. He was homeless at the time and suspicious that strangers like us were giving him a bed, but eventually was reluctant to leave. He visited many times and became more and more confident and eventually took on an important role making first-time visitors feel welcome and safe in the space. He took an opportunity to take part in some theatre projects and together this network of support – but most importantly his own strength and abilities – have transformed him. He is a remarkable human being and we feel blessed to have shared a home with him.

Ben was aware that no welcoming is simple – as for many, finally having this space to let go and unwind is likely to be the time when buried or hidden issues start to show themselves. Ben says:

A lot of the people who stayed with us have experienced significant trauma. A small number of people who came to the Grange suffered traumatic recurrences with us and we will never know if we met these challenges in the best way, although we did what we could. We recognised that, for some people, coming away to the countryside triggered traumatic memories in and of itself. Overall, as regarding faith in humanity – we feel immensely proud of the Grange. Now the project continues although in a different form and we have limited involvement. Part of the reason for this is we recognised that a life project like this would never be resilient if it relied on us, so we built in a plan for us to leave after seven years. It has informed a lot of my ongoing work with people seeking sanctuary. After this I worked full-time for City of Sanctuary and became more active in campaigning as well as helping cities, towns, boroughs and villages of sanctuary come into being.

Ahmad Al-Rashid is an ex-refugee who brings to use his skills of having volunteered in Iraq. He says:

> In early 2013, I was displaced from Syria along with thousands of others and ended up crossing the border into the Kurdistan region of Iraq. I started off volunteering by teaching English to Syrian students in camps on the Kurdish border, but then was offered a contract translating official documents into English, and later worked with UNICEF. I was there for around two years, and in my own time I volunteered interpreting for refugees as well. When I arrived in the UK, I didn't have the right to work but I wanted to do something – find out about the country and culture – and I could only do this through volunteering. I wasn't able to be politically active on the Syrian political scene because it became complicated, so I decided to focus on tangible things here. I started campaigning with UNICEF, Oxfam and the British Red Cross. I campaigned with Student Action for Refugees (STAR) because education is very important. Mostly my volunteering work has been advocacy around family reunion. Later on, I volunteered with Safe Passage doing interpretation (I travelled to Calais twice to translate for child refugees in order for their cases to be processed, and also did translation over the phone for six months). People there spend weeks, months, even years waiting to make this crossing. Just because I had one piece of a travel document at the time, I was able to make this journey in 20 minutes. My outgoing journey from Syria to the UK was 55 days; I crossed many countries, rivers, seas and continents. The hardest crossing was from Calais to the UK – it was very traumatic, challenging and tiring, and I finally ended up in the UK by hiding in the back of a lorry.

Ahmed goes on to talk about the cultural status of being a volunteer.

> There is a cultural difference here which is very important to explain: the word "volunteering" in my country and culture is seen as very problematic. People actually see volunteering in a wider sense as exploitation, because you are doing work that you are not paid for. It's a very alien concept. I like to work, and I work a lot with

different projects, courses and studying, so this took some getting used to. I want to continue working in this field because it is my life; it is my family's life; it is my people's life. I did not choose this, this was not my wish, but somehow, still, I found myself here, I was a displaced person and a refugee, but I live this now, and it is still my life. Now I have made contacts and have a platform, I would like to use it to help spread the word and disseminate the message.

The situation in Germany is important to follow. The country accepted over 800,000 refugees, mainly from Syria. While state bodies handled basic accommodation needs, activists and volunteers filled the gaps in other social, medical and cultural needs – though at the expense of their own security, as many faced right-wing backlash. **Cornelia Durkhauser** says:

I am a doctor, so I do what I can best – medical aid. I founded and ran a primary-care station inside a refugee reception centre together with some colleagues and nurses in Freital, near Dresden. Also I accompany refugees suffering from chronic diseases through their asylum procedures. And I give lectures to refugee women on topics such as contraception, pregnancy and childbirth, vaccination and disease prevention in babies, toddlers and children, hygiene and other medical topics. "My refugees", those for whom I care for months and years, are part of my family. They call me "mum", can stay in my home as long as they want, I am there for them whenever they need it for any kind of question or problem. Maybe the most significant day was a day in May 2015, when a young man without fingers on both of his hands was crying for help. He was a patient in my hospital after he made a suicide attempt. All his fingers had been cut off by his torturers in an Afghan prison. This man imploring me to help him was the first refugee I ever met. I was really shocked and promised him my support. But I had no idea how to help him. This experience sparked my entire refugee work, and of course I found a way for him as well. My biggest challenge is racism. In my area, Saxony, there is a huge problem with the neo-Nazi party named AfD (Alternative für Deutschland, "Alternative for Germany").

Many people in Saxony, Brandenburg and all of the eastern states of Germany elected AfD and are supporters of its goals. People like me who work with and for refugees face hostilities day by day. It is really dangerous to support refugees here. Neo-Nazis are attacking not only refugee homes but also supporters. They already sprayed and scratched swastikas on my car. Other supporters found swastikas on the doors of their homes, or damaged tyres. This is a sure sign that we are being watched by them and that we must face more dangerous attacks. But of course I am able to meet this challenge. I use a pseudonym in public. "Cornelia Durkhauser" isn't the real name typed in my passport. I do this to protect myself, my family and child, and also "my" refugees. What else should I do? The people I support need me. If I don't care for them, nobody else does. In 2015, when I began my work, lots of so-called "friends" said goodbye. They turned away from me and didn't want to have anything to do with me any longer because I support refugees. This was a really hard experience. But the good thing is, I've now got many more friends than before, true friends who share my point of view, true friends from all over the world who never would disappoint me.

There are many other testimonies from people who do welcoming but at a high cost to themselves. **Melanie Strickland** is a UK lawyer who has volunteered at her local migrants' support centre for many years. Her volunteer welcoming work led her to participate in a joint protest action as one of a group known as the Stansted 15 for which she faced a heavy jail sentence. (The action is described further in this book's UK Flashpoint.) She says:

I was shocked by the conditions of life for migrants in my community – mainly women and children. I was shocked to see, again and again, people in my community being at the sharp end of the hostile environment. Shortly after I started volunteering at the migrants' centre, I took part in a successful action at Stansted Airport to stop a deportation flight to Nigeria and Ghana on 28 March 2017. As a result of the action, 11 people remain in the country (including survivors of trafficking, and parents of dependent children). Doing the action at Stansted was the best thing I've done. It had a tangible impact on many people's lives and gave some people the crucial time they needed to secure good legal representation and lodge successful appeals. For some people on the flight, this meant the difference between life and death. I have since met a couple of the people meant to be on that flight and have been in contact with others by letter. They are all doing brilliant things in their communities and are strong and resilient people. It meant a lot to me to be able to make that connection with them and I hope we continue to have a connection. The action represented a long-term commitment by all the people that took part to fight for migrant justice. It wasn't a one-off action. However, for the peaceful protest that we did, we never expected to be tried and convicted under terror-related legislation! On the positive side, the campaign received a lot more attention as a result of the evidently inappropriate and vastly disproportionate charge. This ensured more media focus on the issues the action highlighted – including the injustice of the immigration system and the fact that many people who are detained and deported are survivors of trafficking or have other protection needs. The immigration system is manifestly unfair and is focused on pushing people out of the country as quickly as possible without due process. The people being pushed out are typically people from former colonial countries who are people of colour. We were able to explain some of this in the course of the trial, both in court and outside of court to the media. The trial lasted two-and-a-half months and all our lives were on hold during this time. We didn't know what would happen to us and the maximum penalty was life in prison on conviction. It's affected my relationships, work and mental health. I've had to fight to keep my job. But the most profound effect has been on my physical health. Oppression can manifest in the tissues of the body. I became very seriously ill during the trial and just after, and I am still rebuilding my life more than six months from the sentencing. At the moment I'm focused on local activism and campaigning. I'm still involved in my local migrants' centre and supporting local people. I find this most sustainable for me with my current levels of energy, but also I find it most rewarding as I can develop deep and long-term relationships with people in my community.

Another campaigner who has worked both to welcome and to mobilise for better legislation is Dublin volunteer **Caoimhe Butterly**. She tells of what drove her to become involved; I quote her entire narrative at length because I feel it represents so well a kind of process many of us went through, from initial emotional commitment, which can be accompanied by a sense of being overwhelmed and feeling powerless, to seeking and supporting broader justice and change. How Caoimhe became a volunteer through the words of others, her witnessing of the strength and resilience of those she supported and finally seeing them bring about change is a story that takes us from horror and anger to some kind of victory.

> On 3 October 2013, a ship carrying hundreds of refuge-seeking women, men and children, mainly from Eritrea and Ethiopia, sank off the coast of Lampedusa, Italy. Over 300 of those on board drowned. One of the accounts published in the aftermath was that of a local search-and-recovery diver, Renato Sollustri. He described swimming into the hold of the submerged boat and seeing the body of a young woman who seemed as if she was pregnant. He recounted taking her out of the boat – he said "We laid her on the seabed. We tied her with a rope to other bodies and then ... we rose with them from the depths of the sea". When they surfaced and lifted her body onto a waiting boat, they found that she had given birth while the boat sank, and the body of her newborn son was still attached by his umbilical cord underneath her clothes. I just could not forget this. I had spent the years prior to reading the account being active in migrant justice and refugee solidarity work in Latin America, the Middle East and back at home in Ireland. During those years I had heard many other stories of horrific, preventable, lonely deaths. The account of Sollustri, however, impacted on an even more immediate level. I had recently had a child myself, and I knew the powerful, visceral urge to protect, to keep him safe. I dreamt about the young, as-yet-unidentified woman for weeks afterwards and closely followed

the accounts of survivors, many of whom, despite initial platitudes and promises of citizenship by the government, ended up destitute and precarious, living on the streets of Italian cities, without even access to the island graves of their loved ones. I spent the following years working with medical teams, support and psycho-social projects, on land and at sea, between Lesvos and Idomeni, Lampedusa and the Balkans, Lebanon and, finally, Calais. Much of that work was done in the company of other volunteers, medics and activists from Ireland, many of us active with solidarity and anti-racism networks at home. With guidance and leadership from self-organised asylum seeker-led movements for justice, such as the Movement of Asylum Seekers in Ireland (MASI), we collectively built campaigns that challenged hierarchies of perceived worthiness, the exceptionalisation of Syrian suffering within the context of forced migration and we always tried to promote self-agency and greater autonomy for refugees.

It was on one such visit to Calais, in the final days before the demolition of the camp, that I first met Ismael. I was standing in the camp with a friend from Dublin who worked with the Refugee Youth Service, interpreting for her as she explained to a group of teenagers, from Sudan, Eritrea, Yemen and Syria, what options were available to them post-demolition. Ismael, hearing that I spoke Arabic, approached me afterwards and asked where I was from. The answer, "Irlanda", started another journey that finished with Ireland eventually becoming the place where he would continue the complex, determined steps of building a life beyond survival.

She goes on:

Ismael was from Darfur, Sudan and had already survived, in his young life, losing members of his immediate family to the sweeping violence of Janjaweed, the journey to Libya alone, much of it on foot as a 14-year-old, exploitation and abuse once there, a traumatic ship sinking near Lampedusa while crossing the sea and survival due to the presence of an NGO search-and-rescue ship. He crossed the mountains into France, like many others, and slept rough in La

Chapelle in Paris before continuing the journey to Calais with other young people from Sudan. When we met he was in poor health, tired from sleepless nights and trying to shake an upper-respiratory-tract infection – but with the calm, quiet resolve and profound dignity that so many of us who became involved in his life have come to know of him. When the demolition began – amidst the tear-gas and smoke and wrenching goodbyes – Ismael lost his phone, and with it his means of communication. I returned to Dublin, to a campaign catalysed by a solicitor friend and bolstered by the participation of volunteers from human rights organisations, trade unions, faith-based communities and solidarity groups, which we called Not On Our Watch. Through it we lobbied the political opposition and pushed through a motion in the Dáil/Irish Parliament for the relocation of up to 200 unaccompanied minors from Calais to Ireland. The motion also had a robust, agreed-upon framework around their rights, support systems, citizenship and family reunification entitlements once relocated. In the midst of this, Ismael made contact again, and the following year involved my making frequent trips to La Chapelle, where he and many other young people whose names we had submitted in Dublin were now sleeping rough. It also involved long, frustrating bureaucratic set-backs and silences and the weaving of a community of care – including a former British social worker, then a long-term resident of a village in northern France, whose offer of hospitality for three Darfurian 17-year-olds extended many months past the initially requested three weeks. Throughout the year, however, as some of the young survivors began to arrive in Ireland, the response – from communities, schools, social care worker networks, volunteers and foster families – was a source of momentary hope amidst the bleak topography of a rising right wing across Europe. When Ismael, Yahyah and Adam eventually arrived in Dublin, among the last unaccompanied minors to be relocated through the programme, they transitioned with an ease and continued resilience – emotional and psychological – that was seen in their embrace of their new city, new schools, new homes and community. It was a process that was not, is not, without pain and times of deep vulnerability, but it is a grief that has language, and a meaning-making that has been responded to with empathetic and surprisingly nuanced support by their school peers and friends. The long roads travelled by Ismael were brought home to me visibly recently, during a speaking tour we organised in Dublin for representatives of search-and-rescue crews. Speaking in the parliament alongside our friends from Médecins Sans Frontières, Open Arms, Sea-Watch and Refugee Rescue, Ismael spoke of the attempted criminalisation of sea-rescue and solidarity work, and the urgent need to provide means of safe passage for those seeking refuge. Afterwards we brought the group to meet the President of Ireland, Michael D. Higgins. Ismael told his story again, and Michael D. invited Ismael to sit next to him, grasping his hand as he told him how brave he was, and how Ireland is all the better a place for his presence here. Ismael, years on from camps and existence in an often invisible periphery, nodded and said later, "I am here so that the others who could not complete their journey, who died at sea and in the desert, can be heard – that their names and lives are remembered." It felt like a little bit of healing for him, to be properly respected and acknowledged, and know that he had made a memorial for all the others who hadn't made it.

We begin to see in stories here that "welcoming" may be the practical thing – a room, a bed, a cup of tea, help with homework – but it might also be something much more complex and negotiated: offering someone privacy, or physical or mental-health healing, or finding a way for those who have arrived here to assuage some of their grief, or gain respect and justice, as above. And we each as volunteers, as has been discussed in Chapter 7, need to find in the longer term a sustainable path that makes sense for us and for those we support. For many of us, as for Caoimhe and those quoted here, it will involve regular reprioritising, and practising a shifting set of responses that will include listening, reflecting and reporting, as well as practical help and campaigning. One testimony I am very drawn to is that of **Cecilie Thorsen**, who lives in Norway, and who recounts an extraordinary story of support, care and respect, which was all established online. She was the friend of an entire Iraqi family over the two years it took them to travel from Iraq to Germany. She says:

> It is now more than three years since I made the most extraordinary journey of my life. I was to "travel" with a friend I had not met, communicating only via my keyboard, mobile and computer, at home in my own sitting room. It was heart-stopping and challenging and was accompanied on my part by a good deal of resistance. This is perhaps not surprising, as those who were organising the trip were people smugglers who offer a journey without any predetermined departure time, information, refreshments or service. The family find themselves separated from one another on several occasions during their flight from Islamic State (ISIS). Our friendship, and the journey, both begin with a friend request on Facebook, on 28 January 2016. It comes from Osama, who is fleeing from Mosul in Iraq with his wife and four children. He wonders if I can "accompany" him and his family on their escape from Turkey to Greece. This would take the form of humanitarian support via chat. This perhaps says everything about the helpless situation in which refugees find themselves. He is only asking for my help because I went to Lesvos in October 2015, volunteering with the reception of refugees arriving by boat. The situation is absurd. There ought to have been a support system in place, able to provide information and to follow up the stream of humanity fleeing to Europe. For the most part, however, there are only volunteers and a few humanitarian organisations who are filling the gap.
>
> I promise to support them and to provide as much welfare advice as I can. I did not encourage them to come; that was always there decision. But I hope I managed to make them feel safer on the journey. Fortunately, I have contacts both among the volunteers in Greece, and in the voluntary humanitarian organisation Dråpen I Havet (Drop in the Ocean) in Norway. The family comprises a mother, father, three daughters and a newborn baby. All the children are, at this time, under the age of 7, and when Osama and I become friends on Facebook, his baby boy

is only ten days old. Our conversations for the most part concern their sea crossing, and subsequent flight through Europe. After a few days' intensive communication, I gained some insight into the Samier family's journey.

The family is from Mosul in Iraq, where they had a bakery, house, dog, car, friends and family. All this had to be left behind. There was not even time to sell anything before they had to flee. Osama's mother stayed in Mosul and his father had been killed by ISIS. They are fleeing from ISIS in Iraq with the aim of reaching Europe, but Europe has, at this point in time, little inclination to welcome refugees. When Osama contacts me the family has spent several months in Turkey. Our communication becomes more and more intense the nearer they get to Bodrum, where thousands of refugees are to be found awaiting a crossing by boat to Greece. During that period he shares his concerns about anything and every-thing: the weather conditions at sea; what they should wear for the crossing; how and what they should pack, and which boats are the safest: wooden boats with a roof or open inflatables? How can they be sure that they are buying a proper life jacket and not one that is filled with hay or sleeping pads? How do they know which of the people smugglers can be trusted, when they have no other choice? How it's best to have a foil blanket against your skin, placed inside shoes and hats and not on the outside of your clothes. That the baby must also have a foil blanket round him, and that to avoid getting ill before the onward journey everyone must change their clothes as soon as they reach dry land. What should he say to the children, who are embarking on a journey that is so unsafe? That this is dangerous and that they must behave well, or that it is a thrilling adventure that will take them to a new and exciting place? How can he ensure that they stay calm so that they don't cry or cause panic in the boat? Do people really drug their children, as many of the people smugglers recommend? Will a drugged child be spared the trauma of the boat crossing, or is that just something they say to maintain calm in the boat, so as to avoid the attention of the Turkish Coastguard who would take them back to Turkey? Can it be true that they who have never even sat in a boat before must now pilot these vessels themselves through unknown waters? What is the safest way to navigate? How do you navigate in heavy seas? What does everyone do if the boat starts to sink? What is it like to navigate towards an unfamiliar land in the dark, when they say you cannot use a light for fear of being discovered and sent back to Turkey? Which Greek island is it best to travel to? Where is the crossing shortest and the sea at its most calm?

These critical questions weighed heavily on Osama, but they were only the beginning – the family would then have a whole new life to navigate, when they reached Europe. The bigger questions kept on coming.

What should they do once they arrive in Greece? What will they find there? Which direction should they take from there? Which borders are closed within Europe? How much will it cost? How safe is it? Is ISIS active in Europe? Is it possible to travel legally through Europe? So many challenging questions for a family on the run, and equally challenging for someone such as me sitting at her computer in Norway. These questions ought to have been posed by the world's politicians; answers should have been found, and solutions put in place by now, and yet still, every day, frail boats are carrying several thousand people in fake life jackets across the sea... At the same time we are also exchanging words of hope, expectancy and a belief in the future. Osama and I are often on Facetime, and the children talk to me in Arabic. Their mother sends hugs and the baby fusses and cries in the background. I am sent photos of the baby, and of the three smiling girls who have made a peace sign on a Turkish beach where one can just glimpse the Greek island of Kos in the background.

The family is dependent on people smugglers, rumours on the grapevine and weather forecasts to be able to get onto a boat. The date they have decided for their journey is approaching, but two days before they are due to leave a storm is forecast for the day of the crossing, with waves of up to 4 metres. Osama is not used to the sea, and I flood him with words of advice not to set out on the journey with this prospect of bad weather, for many lives have been lost in these seas, despite weather warnings. After much to-ing and fro-ing, they decide to delay their crossing. On the night that they should have crossed, 14 children and 16 adults drown on the same route. Two days later the weather has settled and the sea is calm. The family of five, along with their travelling companion Mustafa, decide to make the journey. Mustafa carries two of the little girls onto the boat. Osama is holding the other daughter's hand and is helping his wife and baby as they are in the process of embarking. Suddenly the Turkish police arrive and start firing warning shots. The boat's skipper panics and leaves with the boat. The father, mother, one daughter and one son watch as their escape boat disappears with two of their daughters on board.

When Osama calls me I don't recognise his voice. He is crying and talking so fast that I can't understand what he is saying. In the background I can hear more crying, screaming and shouting voices. He is phoning as he stands and watches the boat disappear. Once again I realise how truly alone this family really is. I am sitting in Norway and there is absolutely no way I can help them in this situ-ation, and yet Osama rings me anyway. There is only one thing I can do: I stay calm and pragmatic, and promise to call anyone and everyone in the voluntary sector who might be able to help. Luckily I manage to get hold of a French volunteer from Rescue Team who is at that time on Kos. I update them about the situation and give them Mustafa's telephone number, as he has the two daughters with him. Fortunately, the family soon receive an update from Mustafa that he and the girls have landed safely on Kos after just 25 minutes in a speedboat. Rescue Team find them quickly and give them food and shelter. I contact Trude Jacobsen, who is the founder of Dråpen I Havet. I put her in direct contact with Mustafa and Osama and she pulls out all the stops and sends an experienced volunteer from Norway to Kos. They are fine.

Cecilie then details with the same care, and evidence of her support, the long further chapters – the family's incarcerations on the island, their final passage to Athens and the endless Balkan route, during which she "welcomes" them every way she can, with welfare, emotional support and friendship. And this is one story that ends well.

> On 30 December 2016, I receive photos of children at a party and smiling selfies from the adults. The family has been given the good news that they have been granted residence permits in Germany, and are now living safely in a small German town. The little girls who smiled and made a peace sign in Turkey with Kos in the background can now say "peace" and many other words in German and are happy in their new existence. As is the rest of the family.

More of Ceccilie's account, and many other testimonies, will be published in full in the online version of this book. Here, I have tried to describe not all the actions that Europeans have taken in longer-term welcoming – though many more are described in the Flashpoints that follow – but rather give an idea of the different modes of welcome, support and solidarity that are going on, stories which I hope bring depth and substance to what we mean by "welcome", and show us what a new "internationalism" might look like.

Flashpoint: The UK

Tess Berry-Hart and Sue Clayton

The "Refugees Welcome" movement that began in 2015 in response to the arrivals of over 1 million people to Europe brought the issue of welcoming and integration to the fore. Driven by empathy with the horrors that refugees flee and a growing awareness of the systems

Figure 8.1 Cornwall, UK, 2015. Local groups co-ordinate aid donations to send to Lesvos.

Image credit: Jess Coulson.

of governmental oppression that prevent them properly starting new lives in Europe, many UK citizens – whether they had volunteered abroad or not – began to fill the gaps in state support. This expanded the range of existing groups such as Migrants Rights Network and Joint Council for the Welfare of Immigrants, and established a variety of original and innovative volunteer projects helping new arrivals integrate and be part of the community, as well as helping them with their rights, status and basic survival needs.

Across Europe, well-supported "Refugees Welcome" marches in 2015 signalled a greater awareness of the issues, and consequent support. Marches in the UK were organised by the Syria Solidarity Campaign and Solidarity With Refugees – the former had been advocating with the UK Government to accept Syrian refugees since 2012. After the media focus on the large-scale refugee arrivals into Europe of summer 2015, over 100,000 people joined the September 2015 march in London. The UK Government had at that time pledged to accept 5,000 refugees from Syria, but as more mainstream support became evident, Prime Minister David Cameron increased the pledge to a promised total of 20,000 by the year 2020 in a victory for refugee rights campaign groups – and 19,353 had been resettled by the end of December 2019.

For those who arrived in the UK independently, chiefly from Iran, Iraq, Eritrea Sudan and Afghanistan, finding accommodation was very difficult. The UK Refugee Council estimated that up to 80% of recent refugees may be affected. Refugees At Home (R@H) works to find them places with hosts across the country. From its inception in 2016, R@H has arranged over 147,000 placement nights for guests.

For those experiencing hardship, ventures such as Maslow's Community Shop in Glasgow began to provide clothing and household goods to asylum seekers and people in the local community who were experiencing hardship. Legal rights group Right2Remain provides advice and toolkits to help new arrivals navigate complex settlement issues. Projects to help new arrivals settle into the community are widespread: the Church of Scotland runs a "New Scots" holiday club for volunteers to host refugee families or groups in their homes for a short holiday to offer friendship and hospitality. In Wakefield a conversation club is run by volunteers in Mill Hill Church

Figure 8.2 London, UK, 2016. The Refugees Welcome demonstration organised by Solidarity with Refugees head through Central London.
Image credit: Pru Waldorf.

for new arrivals to learn English in a friendly environment over tea and snacks. In Brighton the Global Social Club is a youth centre for young people from around the world – including refugees, asylum seekers and the local community.

In 2004, the Home Office had introduced a policy which led to asylum seekers being dispersed around the UK, often to very deprived areas where they faced few opportunities to integrate. A range of citizen-led welcoming projects began. "Cities of Sanctuary" were inaugurated in Sheffield and Swansea, and now the Sanctuary movement has over 100 groups organised not only in cities but also in towns, villages, urban boroughs and universities, as well as being affiliated to Places of Sanctuary Ireland. The UK's first designated "Home of Sanctuary" was set up in 2010 in Norfolk in "the Grange" – a home and smallholding that in partnership with groups such as Freedom From Torture and Room to Heal has given over 500 traumatised new arrivals a breathing space and the opportunity to integrate into the local community.

With the closure of the Calais Jungle at the end of 2016, many of the ex-Calais volunteers turned their attention to welcoming and

Figure 8.3 Calais, France, 2019. Volunteers from the UK's National Education Union join with supporters from Stand Up To Racism to take donations and practical support to refugees in northern France.
Image credit: Sara Tomlinson.

integrating refugees who had arrived in the UK. Projects such as Meena in Birmingham, run by the former Unofficial Women and Children's Centre from Calais, provides advice, help and support to refugee women and children, while Enthum House in Sussex, founded by former Calais volunteers, provides a safe and sustainable home for unaccompanied child asylum seekers arriving with severe trauma. Calais group Refugee Community Kitchen has frequently partnered with Streets Kitchen and other grassroots groups in the UK, giving out food to London's homeless. Some groups originally founded to collect and transfer essential aid of boots, coats and food have also expanded support to the resettlement of families, such as CEFN in North Wales. Groups such as United To Assist Refugees UK, Side By Side With Refugees, Calais Action Brighton, People In Motion and Re-Act Falkirk continue to supply both needs in northern France and further afield, as well as organising a variety of fundraising pop-up shops, fairs and benefit concerts.

It was not only basic material needs that the ex-Calais and ex-Greece volunteers addressed. In the Calais Jungle, Good Chance

Theatre had put on plays with the camp residents in the donated Dome tent and then went on to write and produce the immersive play "The Jungle", which transferred from London's Young Vic Theatre to an extended run in the West End and later to New York. Other theatre projects focused on providing arriving refugees with skillsets and allowing self-expression. Projects such as Borderline (run by theatre company PSYCHEDelight) devised shows with ex-Calais refugees. The Cardiff Cinema Club for refugee families had originally formed doing arts activities in the Calais Jungle, and expanded into welcoming and arts projects in the UK. The Citizens of the World Choir of refugees and friends in London was created by former Calais Action volunteers and music professionals, working with Action For Humanity, a House of Lords lobby group composed of volunteers which had been campaigning for refugee rights since 2015. Elsewhere, Phosphorus Theatre's "Dear Home Office" and "Pizza Shop Heroes" shows were devised and performed by asylum seeking children and young people.

Food has proved an important route to breaking down barriers and promoting integration and understanding with local communities; many refugees, especially women, have been helped to establish cooking businesses and become self-sufficient. The Lalibela Ethiopian Kitchen in Brighton is run by two Ethiopian women who cater Ethiopian food for social events in the local area. Syrian refugee entrepreneurs run a variety of pop-up restaurants, stalls and events, such as Imad's Syrian Kitchen, run by a Damascus refugee chef, and Mo's Eggs, run by a Syrian, which features on its menu "Jungle Eggs", a speciality devised in the Calais camp. Refugees can also learn and practise hostelry skills by volunteering in supper clubs such as Heart & Parcel in Manchester and cafes such as MILK in Glasgow. Another project, Refujuice, run by Bromsgrove and Redditch Welcomes Refugees, brings together refugees and local volunteers to harvest apples and create speciality bottled juices for events and catering. In Glasgow, support group Refuweegee hosts summer barbecues bringing together new arrivals and the local community, and the Syria Solidarity Campaign holds *iftar* feasts for breaking daily fasts after sundown during Ramadan, for refugees to meet local people.

Figure 8.4 Newcastle, UK, 2018. Susan Mansaray from Tees Valley of Sanctuary, and volunteer for Justice First, chairs the City of Sanctuary Annual General Meeting.

Image credit: Simone Rudolphi.

The harrowing reports from those volunteers returning from Greece and France seemed to have had a mobilising effect on the UK's more traditional and often faith-based "charity" sector, so that many who had been doing simple welcoming or donating through their churches or synagogues but who'd never planned to get directly involved were next signing up to go to Calais both before and after the Jungle was dismantled, making use of coaches booked by Student Action for Refugees (STAR) and Stand Up To Racism (SUTR).

After a London charity film screening about the abandoned Calais children, Jewish Council for Racial Equality (JCORE) members

Figure 8.5 Folkestone, UK, 2020. An Afghan boy in an English lesson run by Kent Refugee Action Network learns about International Women's Day. Image Credit: Bridget Chapman.

insisted on visiting the Jungle themselves, to understand the situation first-hand, and through Care4Calais met young Eritreans living rough after the closure of the Jungle. The Church of St John the Evangelist in Manchester, already an inter-faith space, increasingly became a hub for not just discussions and cash collections, but also for diverse groups to organise trips to Calais to deliver aid, as well as joint initiatives with their City Council to support more refugees locally. The Quakers, already supporters of refugee aid, were moved to go further – to house and support the so-called "Stansted 15" – 15 activists who, having protested the forced removal of at-risk refugees by the Home Office, faced a ten-week trial for terror-related offences (detailed further below, and in Melanie Strickland's testimony in the previous chapter).

After the highly visible "refugee crisis" of 2015–2016 and the burgeoning public response, there was a gradual shift in people's understanding of what it meant to be a volunteer. Now "volunteering" was no longer seen as simple aid-giving, but an intersectional role that may involve active citizenship, supporting human rights, protesting state aggression against both refugees and their advocates, and interrogating anew the actions that proliferated under the UK Government's "hostile environment" policy.

Along with the campaign to accept more refugees from Syria, a second major rallying call for this new movement was around the so-called Dubs Amendment, intended to allow unaccompanied children in Europe a safe and legal route to asylum in the UK, even in the absence of family members there. In 2016, Labour MP Yvette Cooper had identified the upcoming 2016 Immigration Bill as a suitable vehicle for an amendment that would require the government to settle 3,000 unaccompanied child asylum seekers in the UK from across Europe. The amendment was backed by Labour peer Alf Dubs, himself a former child refugee, and a cross-party campaign was mobilised to pressure the Conservative-led government to pass what became known as the Dubs Amendment. Grassroots groups such as Calais Action and Help Refugees helped spread the word to the general public to pressure their MPs to vote accordingly, and many volunteers created online campaigns or attended demonstrations under the slogan "Dubs Now!". Jewish faith groups like JCORE strongly supported this campaign, seeing parallels with the *Kindertransport* action of 1938–1939 which brought Jewish children to safety from Germany, Austria, Czechoslovakia and Poland on the eve of the Second World War. After being voted down in the House of Commons, the Dubs Amendment was re-drafted without the 3,000 figure and finally passed into law in May 2016 as section 67c of the 2016 Immigration Act. However, only a fraction of the children that the Amendment was originally envisaged to help entered the UK under its protection and the scheme was finally capped at 350, leaving thousands of unaccompanied children no other route than to attempt dangerous and illegal crossings. Help Refugees brought a High Court challenge, arguing that the Home Office had ignored Local Authority offers of 130 additional places in the UK and this increased the number of children able to benefit to 480. A further case, *ZS v. The Secretary of State for the Home Department* (2019), was brought in 2017 by the author of this book in 2017 on behalf of 37 of the most vulnerable children who had been in the Calais camp, supported by *pro bono* solicitors from Duncan Lewis, and Social Workers Without Borders. The Court of Appeal found that the Home Office had acted unlawfully in not providing reasons for refusal to denied applicants (for fear of later legal challenges) and had failed in its duty of candour in not making the application process clear to the young people, their advocates or the French Government. As of March 2020, four years on, the Home Office has only confirmed 220 transfers under the Dubs Amendment, although the law specified the 480 children should be brought to safety "as soon as possible."

At time of writing, the UK's Brexit negotiations with the EU have significantly impacted the future of refugee rights for unaccompanied children seeking reunion with family in the UK under the European Dublin III protocol, which will cease to apply at the end of 2020. Recent reports also indicate that another government scheme, the Vulnerable Children's scheme (which proposed in 2016 to resettle 3,000 children directly from areas of conflict) showed a 30% decrease in transfers of minors in the last months of 2019. Currently, groups are petitioning the government to grant legal protections to child refugees and families under the spirit of the late Dubs Amendment, to extend access to family reunion and to challenge the policy of preventing refugee children from having their families join them in the UK under UK immigration rules. The group Safe Passage has also been trying to secure more rapid transfers of vulnerable and sick child refugees out of the Greek camps to join family in the UK as COVID-19 threatens their safety further.

The "hostile environment" anti-immigration policies that have been promoted in the UK since 2013 have had direct effects on those who have recently arrived. Removal policies have become more draconian, and many of those already in the UK with refugee or human rights grounds for protection are detained and deported while they still have an active case. And protesters themselves are now facing more stringent measures. In March 2017, as we mentioned earlier, a group of 15 volunteers campaigned on behalf of several asylum seekers supported by the Detained Voices group – all of whom would have faced danger and persecution on return to their home countries. As the Home Office persisted with plans to remove them by

Figure 8.6 London, UK, 2019. Good Chance Theatre, which worked in the Calais camp and created the play "The Jungle", runs social sessions in the UK for local and refugee young people.

Image credit: Good Chance.

charter flight, the so-called "Stansted 15" protested their removal at the airport. The police charge of aggravated trespass was increased by the Attorney General to a terrorist charge carrying up to 25 years in jail. This was seen by the Left and by activists as state interference in a trial, designed to intimidate future forms of peaceful action. The Stansted 15 were supported not only by anti-racist, pro-refugee groups, but also by wide sections of the public. In Chelmsford where their ten-week trial was held, the 15 were housed and supported by the Quaker community, local church ministers and the Bishop of Chelmsford. They were found guilty but given non-custodial sentences – thought to be partly due to the public outcry against imprisoning them for what was a peaceful humanitarian act.

Other UK groups such as Bail for Immigration Detainees (BID) campaign for a limit on the amount of time anyone can be detained on immigration grounds. There are also volunteer groups related to other areas of civic life, such as Docs Not Cops, who fight against informing the Home Office of the immigration status of patients, and Against Borders for Children (ABC), who resisted a Home Office requirement that teachers interrogate pupils as young as four about the nationality and status of their family members – information that was then used to aggressively pursue of those with precarious status. In 2018, the incoming Home Secretary Sajid Javid announced that the hostile environment policy would be dismantled, but volunteers know very well that it continues in practice, if not in name.

We have described here just a fraction of the myriad groups that have come into being, and their connection to wider rights issues. As most of these hundreds of activist and support groups sprang up in haste, out of emergency need or in response to arbitrary government measures, what has been lacking is a wider platform where these mobilisations can take stock, debate strategies and gain a better understanding of their potential wider influence.

The first Refugee Solidarity Summit, held in Deptford, London in January and February 2020, offered a welcome first step towards this wider platform, involving over 800 grassroots activist volunteers from the UK and Europe. Key debates included moving from "crisis"

Figure 8.7 London, UK, 2020. The Women for Refugee Women choir performs at the Refugee Solidarity Summit, attended by 800 activist volunteers, at the Albany Theatre in Deptford.

Image credit: Refugee Solidarity Summit.

mode to response mode; formulating new activist policy positions and supporting those being criminalised for their work; decolonising our approach, building broader support platforms; navigating relationships with governments and NGOs; building a culture of self-care intervention and attending to trauma and burn-out; changing the media narrative; and putting care at the heart of organising and prioritising refugee and migrant participation and leadership.

For the sake of refugee rights – and indeed all human rights – it will be key in the future to foster this kind of intersectionality, understanding and co-operation between volunteer initiatives.

Flashpoint: La Chapelle, Paris

Anna-Louise Milne

The peripheral Parisian *quartier* of La Chapelle, built around a chapel, as the name suggests, has always been a way-station, between the old Basilica of Saint-Denis and the capital city of the early modern era, and between the Channel coast and gateways east, west and south as rail and road infrastructures developed. But when routes across the Channel became increasingly difficult for people seeking safe haven in the United Kingdom, La Chapelle turned into more of a dead-end – one of the many "flashpoints" where people live in administrative and existential limbo, neither able to return home nor move forward to places where they can rebuild their lives.

Since the days of the Sangatte facility – opened on the north coast of France in 1999 and closed again by French president Sarkozy in 2002 – and then throughout the 2000s up to the destruction of the Calais "Jungle" in 2016, La Chapelle has been marked as both a holding ground for those heading north and a zone of pushback for those evicted. The result has been a wave of inner-city camps – Jaurès, Éole, Flandres, Éole 2, Pajol 2, Stalingrad, Porte de la Chapelle, Porte d'Aubervilliers – some of which have seen up to several thousand people living in desperate density on the edge of streets and parks, with no sanitation and no safety. These camps have left durable marks on the material, political and lived landscape of this inner-city neighbourhood, already one of the most densely inhabited parts of the city.

One such mark was the declaration "CALAIS IS IN PARIS", painted in large white letters along a stretch of road that overlooks the Gare du Nord station's train lines. Another could be heard repeatedly

Figure 8.8 Paris, France, 2016. Refugees pushed back from Calais after the Jungle camp's closure camp in the Paris Stalingrad district.
Image credit: Brendan Woodhouse.

in descriptions of the journey north shared in local libraries, at food distributions, in the various places where refugees and asylum seekers could find a moment of peace off the streets, charge their phone, meet compatriots, learn a few useful phrases, and more: "Everyone knows La Chapelle... You arrive at Gare de Lyon... you take bus 65... and go to La Chapelle." This affirmation comes back again and again, as do the people who are pushed back to Italy and further afield by the implementation of the Dublin Regulation. In response to this situation, the local authorities under Mayor Anne Hidalgo decided to open Paris' first one-stop "humanitarian" centre for asylum seekers at Porte de La Chapelle, known locally as "La Bulle", in the most northern part of the city in November 2016. This decision was taken at the height of what Hildago chose to define as a temporary crisis, limiting the city's responsibility to a period of 18 months. The centre was built on old railway land earmarked for development. It was quickly judged desperately inadequate by a number of NGOs present as observers, denounced also as operating as a "despatch centre" (*centre de tri*) and charged with contributing to more street-level misery and violence, as well as the increase in policing and ever more brutal use of dissuasive measures, such as tear-gas and the destruction of tents and covers – as was documented by local French

Figure 8.9 Paris, France, 2017. The Stalingrad camp as it is evacuated by police, dispersing thousands across northern Paris.

Image credit: Anna-Louise Milne.

groups and the UK-based agency Refugee Rights, in co-ordination with Paris Refugee Ground Support.

This escalating violence went hand-in-hand with the authorities' extended use of crash barriers and huge blocks of stone across the neighbourhood, to prevent access to the public spaces that had seen big camp build-ups, and to public gardens. Daily queues formed, with people sleeping among the crash barriers in an effort to register with the authorities. For local people and activist volunteers, the situation was intolerable, prompting regular press releases, petitions and more disruptive practices to draw attention to the combined failure of local and national authorities to meet minimal responsibilities to ensure the protection of human rights. "La Bulle" closed in March 2018, and since then groups of people in transit or unable to access the asylum system for an increasing variety of reasons, or already ejected from it, have clung on in La Chapelle in more and more desperate conditions. Despite its previous declaration that there would be no repeat of this "humanitarian" centre, in June 2019 the city finally opened an unconditional drop-in centre, called La Halte Humanitaire, run in collaboration with the Fondation Armée du Salut and offering legal, medical and administrative aid – a recognition that La Chapelle remains a focal point for forcibly displaced people and that the situation continues to be, in the political speak of the moment, "fragile".

The reasons for people heading to La Chapelle have their roots in the longer history of migration to France too. Bordered on one side by the impoverished area of La Goutte d'Or, a focus for African, and particularly North African, migrants since the 1950s, and on the other three sides by major transport infrastructure (the ring road and A1 motorway north, the canal, the overground Metro line 2), the area is home to a number of historic support networks, including religious institutions. The NGO France Terre d'Asile has its office here, as does the community group Association for Maghrebi Workers in France (ATMF). Also here is the Saint-Bernard church, site of a major *sans-papiers* occupation in 1996–1997 which contributed to the first major wave of media and intellectual engagement with the plight of undocumented workers in Europe, including Jacques Derrida's landmark work on "hospitality". The church continues to play a key role in clothing distributions. The Saint-Bernard occupation itself drew from historic worker-priest (*prêtre ouvrier*) practices, anchoring some activist volunteer movements in the area in a long tradition of left-wing Catholicism, while other local activists chose to emphasise historical connections to the Paris Commune and the prominence of popular education clubs in that revolutionary phase, particularly as it unfolded in this largely working-class and highly industrialised part of the city.

More recently, the undocumented worker movement has developed into the *gilets noirs*, or "black jackets", spurred into this affirmation by the "yellow jacket" movement that has changed the shape of politics in France since 2018. The *gilets noirs* act both in solidarity with undocumented asylum seekers, demanding the "regularisation" of individuals, while also campaigning for better protection in low-paid labour. And Anzoumane Sissoko, an undocumented exile from Mali, is running for local election in 2020 with the Ecology Party. His campaign position is premised on the fact that he and many

Figure 8.10 Paris, France, 2018. Political posters in La Chapelle district in protest against the law restricting procedures for claiming asylum.

Image credit: Anna-Louise Milne.

others from Mali are already climate refugees and he will be fighting for better provision for migrants by the City of Paris.

Today, politicisation, both around electoral politics, and more ethically led actions flourish, and different groups often work collaboratively across Paris and its periphery. Volunteer activism ranges from a one-person-led food distribution for a small community to regular community-led distributions that feed several hundred people on a daily basis, often with only donations and unpaid labour, such as Solidarité Wilson and Utopia 56 around Porte de la Chapelle, and P'tits Déjeuners Solidaires in the lower part of La Chapelle, as well as Paris Refugee Ground Support. Composed of local people from all walks of life, students and recent immigrants who still feel very close to the vulnerability of the streets, these groups reach their support network through word-of-mouth and social media. Others, such as the Gamelle de Jaurès or the Cuisine des Migrants, grow from friendship groups. Some function primarily in French; others are more multilingual. Local churches and mosques remain key focal points too, co-ordinating clothes distributions in particular.

The activist groups present in the area intersect closely with city-wide and national groups, such as Paris d'Exil, the GISTI, and the Bureau d'Accueil et d'Accompagnement des Migrantes (BAAM), discussed in Chapter 9. Many activists in these groups have participated in protests against deportations and evacuations, while they have also spent long hours waiting with individuals in police stations or ensuring that they get a fair hearing. The relations between different groups and their hallmark activities (from frontline care to co-ordinated disruption) are porous and complex. The area has also been the object of numerous film and documentary projects, including Sylvain George's 2017 "Paris est une fête", and Hind Meddeb's 2019 "Stalingrad", both of which have been shown in national venues. The scenes described in Patrick Chamoiseau's 2018 "Frères migrants" essay are largely drawn from La Chapelle. Further materials, both artistic and intellectual, will surely emerge from the new modes of local internationalism that are currently developing through dense and wide-ranging connections between

Figure 8.11 Paris, France, 2018. Banners went up across strategic locations in Paris, here on Sacré Coeur church. This banner reads "Unconditional Welcome for All Exiled People".
Image credit: Accueil de Merde.

local businesses (from bakers and bookshops to social enterprise agencies), public services (local libraries, publicly funded theatres) and determined individuals committed to the long term of this activism.

No coincidence, then, that one such activist chose 1 May, International Workers' Day, to write a slightly longer post than normal following a stint at food distribution. He described his walk on the rounds to pick up bread and hot water past a number of key addresses – from an artists' squat to a nineteenth-century mock-Gothic church, taking in the ghostly outline of a public bench removed by the local authorities to try to chase migrants from the area and a hotel that donates left-over croissants, before saluting the group made up that day of Algerian, Chinese, French and British volunteers of very varied

Figure 8.12 Paris, France, 2015. A notice-board with community information in the unofficial camp established in the Jardins d'Éole.

Image credit: Cuervo for Alternative Libertaire.

ages – as "a rectangle of solidarity". His image captured something very important of the physical and social reality of La Chapelle. It is rectangular in shape, defined by the train tracks that have long boxed it in. And the solidarity that operates within it is also an effect of this containment and its relative isolation, up until recently, within the economic machine of the capital city.

The last bastion of industrial activity within the city walls until the late 1980s, La Chapelle has in recent years become a site of new forms of investment. The prominence of artists, students and intellectuals in volunteer activism based in this area is one reflection of groups with high social and cultural capital seeking accessible property and rental prices. "Gentrification" is another way of naming this process, and it is important to understand the dynamics in La Chapelle since 2015 as a neighbourhood "on the rise", with new businesses catering for a privileged cultural sector balanced against asylum seekers and refugees without any access to stable resources. The major new sites for the Jardins d'Éole (inaugurated in 2007) and the Halle Pajol (2013), each opening up new surface area in La Chapelle with leisure and sports resources, have been at the same time the focus for major public and private investment and sites of sprawling refugee camps. They remain key holding places for displaced people who gather there every day to meet, talk and access the community and business networks they've come to rely on.

The same convergence of city-led investment, currently in a new *Promenade urbaine* reminiscent of the New York highline, and informal gatherings of undocumented people and street-level markets and food distributions, continue to play out along the lower Boulevard de la Chapelle. Local community meetings are dominated by questions of how the long-embedded characteristics of a neigh-bourhood open to people fleeing persecution and poverty are holding up under the new interests and opportunities now being felt. The vol-unteer activism undertaken in different ways across the area both builds on past experiences of migration and welcome and seeks to invent new traditions. The writing is on the walls, all around, but the story is still in the making.

Flashpoint: Athens

Sumita Shah

When the EU–Turkey agreement came into place in March 2016, signalling the end of easier access to other European states, many asylum seekers had already left those islands where they had first landed – mainly Lesvos, Chios and Samos – and made their way to Athens. Others, having got as far as the Greek–North Macedonian border at Idomeni, had been turned back, so thousands were stranded in Athens, unable to achieve status, move forward or even turn back to where they had come from. The provision of adequate

Figure 8.13 Piraeus Port, Greece, 2016. This sign become a symbol of the Greek volunteer effort to provide aid as refugees arrived from the islands and Pireaus became their unofficial camp.

Image credit: Sumita Shah.

accommodation facilities, comprehensive information and better and faster access to asylum procedures became challenging. Greece has taken a long time to respond to the refugee influx, and even now, four to five years into the "crisis", there is still a lack of integration and services to support the refugees who remain here.

There were a number of official camps around Athens, but because of the lack of sufficient accommodation a number of refugee squats opened in 2016 and 2017, in and around the well-known anarchist area known as Exárcheia: in old disused schools, empty hotels and abandoned office buildings. The squats became self-organised, mixed-nationality communities living and working together, with families sharing rooms and cooking together, organising cleaning rotas, their kids playing in the yards and people commuting back and forth to schools. As the numbers in this area increased, so did the number

Figure 8.14 Piraeus Port, Greece, 2016. Refugees are provided with food and water by volunteers when they disembark from a ferry at Piraeus Port.
Image credit: Sumita Shah.

of grassroots projects. But, at the same time, as people played the waiting game, waiting months or years for their asylum or relocation papers, frustrations grew.

The Greek Government struggled to cope with the asylum and relocation of refugees to other countries, and as movement into other countries slowed down, the UNHCR and other larger NGOs started to house people in apartments. Cash cards to enable refugees to become a little bit more autonomous were planned, but took a long time to be implemented. As the reality dawned on many that they may never reach their ultimate destinations, symptoms of PTSD and trauma started to set in among the refugee community. In the process of concentrating on key services, government officials were too overwhelmed to put into place longer-term integration plans. Thus, independent volunteers and grassroots groups plugged this gap in services, leading to legal, medical and psychological health projects being set up as the Greek authorities struggled to cope with the increased flow of people.

Athens projects have been very much those that enable and empower refugees themselves. Volunteers set up activities: there were language classes (run by Jafra – a refugee-led organisation, and Orange House), art classes (Khora), tailoring and carpentry-type workshops (Oinofyta Community Centre), women's centres providing support specifically for women (Halycon Days, Mosaico, Orange House) and community centres providing career development and employment support (Ankaa Project). And volunteer support became more sophisticated, with many now supporting refugees in enhancing their skills and helping them to secure college and university places, get jobs or become self-employed. Soon restaurants and pop-up cafés were being set up and run by refugees. Hairdressing salons and beauty salons (Love and Serve Without Boundaries, Project Layali) were started to empower women to learn new skills and earn money. Tailors started making bags, aprons and other items. Hand-made jewellery started to be made and sold. Football (Helios Football Club) and cricket teams were formed. In the camps, too, small shops were set up, from falafel shops, barbers and hairdressers, to mobile phone shops and little corner shops selling drinks and snacks.

Figure 8.15 Athens, Greece, 2016. Refugees protest Victoria Park in Athens after borders in the north of Greece were closed in February 2016.
Image credit: Sumita Shah.

In terms of donated supplies, the Ellinikon Warehouse, run by the Pampiraiki Group (local long-term Greek volunteers who have been working since 2015), based out in the basketball court at the old Hellinikon Olympic stadium, became the main grassroots distribution hub for Athens and surrounding areas, the islands and many other parts of Greece. They received containers and pallets of aid from many countries and also received local donations of food and other basic staple food items. As the needs soared in Athens, the Warehouse began to distribute weekly food and non-food items for many informal communities. The Warehouse also became the main hub through which other warehouses around Greece and the islands sent and received aid. The Pampiraiki Group became the main logistics co-ordinator for aid distribution. Even the larger NGOs around the Athens area started to request help from the Hellinikon Warehouse.

At the same time as these positive initiatives have been going on, sadly the seamier side of the refugee environment has also thrived. Limited security and lack of any proper structures has allowed Mafia gangs to form in the camps and around the Exárcheia area. Drugs, alcohol and prostitution have become rife. People, in their desperation to earn money as well as numb the pain of their current state of limbo, have found vices that can only exist in communities forced into such desperate situations. And the closed border in the north of Greece has not, of course, stopped people from trying to make the journey. Booths where refugee families would bank their hard-earned money to help them pay for their "fare" out of Greece popped up in the squat areas. Families, tired of waiting for relocation or asylum, tried to reach other countries in whatever way was possible, buying fake passports or travelling on passports belonging to others. Young men and boys tried their luck on hazardous journeys to Italy on ferries from Patras. People desperate to earn money, to find a more stable base for their lives, took desperate and tragic risks, trying and often failing. Some succeeded, but many others failed and were returned to Athens.

Moving forward to early 2020, people are still stuck in Greece and many refugees' lives are in limbo as they wait for asylum interviews. Millions of euros have been donated through the worldwide grassroots movement and thousands of tonnes of aid have been transported across from the USA, the UK and from other parts of Europe. Over time, the grassroots groups have grown, developed, adapted and reacted quickly to provide aid and support to refugees. Many overseas groups have collaborated to co-ordinate aid.

But measures for facilitating refugees' medium- and long-term stays in the country are still pending, more than three years later. This year, the Greek Government made a decision to stop both accommodation and cash cards for those who had received international protection status. Its rationale was that people should now become independent and fend for themselves. This has led to much controversy around how families will manage without money or jobs, with

Figure 8.16 Athens, Greece, 2017. Street art in Metaxourgeio district: "Healing Hands", which became the symbol of the Athens Volunteers Information and Co-ordination Group.

Image: Sumita Shah.

the unemployment rates still remaining high in Greece. Promises of integration structures have been slow to be implemented. The International Organization for Migration (IOM) has only recently put some integration workshops into place, but information is sparse. Regarding accommodation, Greece still lags behind providing safe and decent living conditions for the entire asylum seeker and refugee population. The conditions at many sites (camps and private accommodation) are less than inadequate, even to host people for a few days, let alone for months and years.

While the Greek state has made attempts to address the significant gaps, with some support from the EU, it is questionable whether these current efforts together with the pledged additional EU support are enough to meet the ever-emerging needs in the medium and long term. Each winter for the last few years, there has been a lack of preparation. The year 2020 will be no different, with more refugees arriving by boat – and, while there are plans to process them, it is extremely slow, with overall numbers remaining high in Greece.

In 2019, Greece elected a new government, led by the established right-wing New Democracy party, which takes a heavily nationalist approach to migration. Its policies will certainly make life harder for refugees. Four years after the first squats were opened, during the summer of 2019, the new government emptied squat after squat, and evictions have come without specific strategic plans for the residents.

Belongings have been trashed and discarded and people have been put into makeshift camps (large communal tents) far away from Athens, with no access to any services. Schooling, jobs and medical/psychosocial projects have been interrupted without a thought about the impact on the people that were receiving these services. Where previously the government appeared to support the integration of refugees, by its recent acts it has overturned the integration that had been so painstakingly put in place.

People who had lost their homes in their countries were yet again losing their homes in Athens, however small and make-shift they had been. The kids who were in Greek schools were suddenly uprooted once again. Volunteers who had since 2016 been providing

Figure 8.17 Piraeus Port, Greece, 2019. Refugee families are evicted by police from squats in Exárcheia district.

Image credit: Marios Lolos.

activities and support to many families were torn away from refugees, leaving many bereft and lacking in the stability and security that is so important for their wellbeing. Time will tell how this further trauma will affect the lives of those left homeless again.

As of September 2019, the number of arrivals had increased again to just under 42,000. This was because Turkey had decided to now ignore the 2016 EU–Turkey agreement on the basis, it stated, that the EU had not held up its end of the bargain. There are currently 88,750 refugees and migrants in Greece (25,250 on the islands and 63,500 on the mainland; of these, 4,393 are unaccompanied minors). Of these, around 14,000 (6,500 families) have received cash assistance to date.

Athens is in turmoil. The aftermath of the evictions has left volunteers and families reeling. The numbers on the streets are once again high and rising. There is a desperate need for food and basic non-food items, as well as accommodation and more help with integration. But many grassroots organisations have now moved on or packed up their operations. Many long-term volunteers and locals who have worked at the heart of the crisis are burnt out. And the numbers of new volunteers have slowed down – intensified, of course, by the COVID-19 pandemic since March 2020. The current government's policies and future plans are unknown, which has left everyone unsettled. The future for refugees in Greece remains uncertain and even more at risk.

Going forward, we need to think about the longevity of existing projects. While there are emergency needs to support new people coming into Athens, we also need to think about how to help refugees to continue to integrate. We need more than anything to continue to empower and enable, upskill and give them the tools to become independent and self-sufficient.

9

A New Politics of Solidarity?

Anna-Louise Milne

What does it mean to describe the uprising of solidarity that spread across Europe in 2015, producing a surge in refugee-directed initiatives, as "political"? In her Introduction to this book, Sue Clayton coins the term "activist volunteer" as a response to the ways in which the initiatives described and discussed here signal a "new kind of social intervention". In this chapter I explore this claim in relation to some historical precedents, and open it towards other contemporary experiences – for instance, of resistance to racism and police violence, as well as of environmental activism. Also crucial to this chapter will be the question of what it means to be a "new internationalist". To what extent did people spring into action out of a sense of solidarity with other humans, only to find themselves mired in struggles with predominantly *national* implications? How do the transnational politics of solidarity intersect with European legislation? What sort of connections are at play between the internationalist perspectives of people seeking safe haven in Europe, particularly in their determination to break with colonial legacies, and those of European citizens? And what new forms of action and dissent developed, which understand themselves to be not so much "for" refugees, as much more significantly to be radically "with" refugees in equal exposure to the challenges and possibilities for shared life on this planet?

Whether they started from a charitable or humanitarian impulse, or out of a demand that fundamental human rights be respected, or with an acute sense of the legacy of oppression and stigmatisation from European wars or from colonial and postcolonial struggle – or indeed a combination of all this and more – the work and experiences charted here are fundamentally reshaping the grounds of political action today. While nation-states and transnational bodies such as the European Union, largely amplified by mainstream media, insist on a politics of borders and quotas – supporting the idea that the right to seek asylum has to be considered a marginal phenomenon, operative only *in extremis* – the perspectives opened up here place solidarity across borders, and between cultures, right in the centre of the political agenda. In looking at a few central scenes (Athens, Paris, Rome, Brussels, Calais), connected by more dispersed or isolated locations (Lampedusa, La Roya/Ventimiglia, Lesvos, Malta, the Croatian border with Serbia), I will consider how "welcome" has become politicised both in the face of rising repression, by sharp disillusion with parliamentary politics among many activist volunteers, and by contact with migrating peoples whose own political cultures and horizons have enabled new desires and new finalities, which are today transforming activism in Europe and beyond.

The time-frame of this book stretches broadly from Mayor of Palermo Leoluca Orlando's landmark decision in March 2015 to found the Charter of Palermo (Orlando, 2015), which enshrines the right to human mobility, through the summer of 2019, when national Italian politics regrouped under extreme right-wing leader Matteo Salvini and responses to both arriving migrants and those attempting to save them at sea because punitive and harsh. Between these dates and reaching back, forwards and outwards to other forms of protest, we will look at how activist volunteers have adapted as initial experiences of emergency gave way to long-haul commitments. We will see how creative strategies of opposition are establishing a continental frame for activism, at the same time as the transnational project of the European Union is under pressure from rising nationalist movements and the impact of austerity politics. And we will also ask how the "new internationalists" intersect with deeply embedded structures of radical politics, conditioned in some countries by decades of struggle on behalf of migrant workers. In so doing, this chapter aims to explore what we might mean by a new politics of solidarity, in order to understand what sort of future and what sort of "we" these politics are engaged in building.

"We Are All Children of Immigrants"

In April 2018, leading a street demonstration against the bill presented by President Emmanuel Macron's government to strengthen France's legal arsenal for "combatting" the so-called migrant crisis, the BAAM organisation was joined by students and members of the French railway workers' union as they danced noisily through central Paris. LGBTI flags and signs denouncing "Dublin"[1] waved over the demonstrators as people chanted the lyrics to Amel Bent's song "Ma Philosophie": "*Toujours le poing levé*" (Always fist held high). "This is the 'social project' for the future", declared one of the BAAM activists, co-opting and redirecting Macron's term of a *projet social* from a lorry above the crowd. "It's happening here, in the street, in the fight for social rights, for migrant rights, for LGBTI rights ... and not in the Senate, not in the National Assembly." Though the issue at stake that day was the increasingly repressive legislation governing mobility and border control, the demand that rose up in a common voice was for a new conception of society, one opposed to ever greater police powers and restrictive conceptions of "worthy" or "chosen" immigrants; one open to fluid gender politics and new forms of community. The political platform was both modest and massive: a local group of refugee-oriented volunteers taking time out of their daily activities and, at the same time, a radical recasting of political alliances. So what is the BAAM?

BAAM stands for Bureau d'Accueil et d'Accompagnement des Migrantes (Office for the Welcome and Accompaniment of Migrants), but there is nothing "official" about it. Launched in November 2015 after the evacuation by police of one of the main squats in Paris, located in the disused Jean Quarré high school and occupied by over 900 asylum seekers from Afghanistan, Iran, Sudan, Eritrea, Ethiopia and elsewhere, it has grown into one of many such landmarks of local activism and support in Northern Europe. The squat was initially opened by migrants themselves.[2] Its visibility in a central Parisian district and its relative stability made it a focal point for people across the city and further afield to get involved. Like many central-city mobilisations, it drew intellectuals and professionals: lawyers, students, teachers, social workers and journalists. Yet it was located in an area of the city marked by a long history of immigration and industry, so there were also many poor people, jobseekers, pensioners, as well as many who had themselves negotiated the asylum system in Europe. This diverse medley of volunteers joined forces – sometimes living on the site until it was evacuated and they had to seek other provisional premises – to help provide language classes, legal advice and orientation, to accompany people to hospitals, to point them towards places to find food and shelter and also to help them find work. In this sense, the work of BAAM was initially "humanitarian", but it was always also "political". It brought together highly politicised global citizens with their next-door neighbours regularly on the brunt of racialised discrimination; it established connections between French professionals and migrants who were also, though often differently, highly skilled and politicised. It is explicit in the expression of its political demands, through manifestos as well as street demonstrations, and it also functions mainly by donations and uses informal spaces (including outdoors) for its activities. So it has remained resolutely independent of major NGOs, though it locates some of its classes in public libraries and so depends, if indirectly, on municipal services. The BAAM is just one example among many, and each context generates its own specificities. But what it tells us is that there is no easy answer to who is political today (McNevin, 2007; Elias and Moraru, 2015).

Many observers have criticised the traditional humanitarian sector, fearing that it may limit the capacities for self-determination of people whose presence in Europe is very often the result of an uncompromising bid to take control of their conditions of life (Agier, 2011; Fassin, 2011; Holzer and Warren, 2015; Malkki 2015). BAAM grew out of a refugee-centred mobilisation and its politics are anchored in efforts to enable people without any access to mainstream forms of political representation to continue to fight in their own names. The second part of this chapter will focus in particular on what it has meant within the volunteer activist movement to enable this sort of "unauthorised" or "non-citizen" agency to emerge, on how "peer-to-peer" volunteerism within refugee communities is finding its place in the landscape and how together these new configurations are conditioning the places and forms of activism in European states.

First, however, we will counter the tendency to consider activism as simply an attribute of particular individuals or organisations by considering more broadly the types of actions taken and how, for instance, a support network such as BAAM, and others like it across Europe, potentially develop recognisably political forms of activism. These include occupations, demonstrations, solidarity with established political organisations, including parties and unions, and even strikes. These forms of opposition are underpinned by a range of rights that are integral to the liberal democratic tradition: the right to freedom of expression, to freedom of movement, to freedom of association. For many Europeans such rights are the unquestionable horizon of life. And yet increasing numbers of activists have found themselves obliged to reaffirm and defend these rights, through the courts in some emblematic cases. Whether carried out in knowledge of the risk of criminalisation or not, actions that go from ensuring basic assistance to people forced into the streets, to accepting "irregular" people into homes, to helping people through Alpine passes, preventing planes from taking off or bringing a rescue ship into port (Fekete, 2018) have gradually extended what it means to do politics today into new scenes that are both domestic and private, such as inviting someone to sleep on the sofa, and affirmative use of public spaces. This fast-changing reality, which has been the subject of much recent media attention and the object of a major study by Amnesty International published in March 2020 (Amnesty International, 2020), shows how the frame for activist volunteerism does not only prompt people to embrace more politicised or oppositional positions in their own politics, whether through their vote or in engagement in radical organisations; but also "humanitarian" activities are also being constructed as political by the ways they are being policed and punished. In other words, the convergence of activism and humanitarianism is today, in part, the result of reciprocal radicalisation of individual citizens and state institutions. And this is happening in a context where the constraining of ever larger numbers of people, both in Europe and at its frontiers in North Africa and Turkey, is generating competing uses and interpretations of law, from the Palermo Charter mentioned above to maritime law, from the Universal Declarations of Human Rights to varying national codifications of rights. Meanwhile, unprecedented experiences of shared life – in camps, squares, parks, squats and back gardens across Europe – are also contributing to the complex landscape within which we have to plot the politics of solidarity today. Together these factors underpin the claim that this is a "new internationalism", yet it remains essential to understand how these forms of radicalism and dissidence relate to and draw from earlier models of "unlawful" activities and new solidarities they built, including, to name but some, the French Resistance and solidarity during the Second World War with persecuted Jewish people, and the Black Panthers and their conception of Pan-Africanism.

Occupations and "Visible" Alternatives

In August 2019, as is noted in our Athens Flashpoint, heavily armed Greek police marched into the self-governing community of Exárcheia in central Athens, targeting squats that have been home to autonomous groups of migrants and volunteers since the autumn of 2015, when at the height of the crisis in the Mediterranean steadily increasing numbers of asylum seekers found themselves sleeping in their hundreds on the streets of the city. As the police filed past the mosaics of protest graffiti and community posters, the inhabitants of this traditional student area were gathered around their street-based "Resistance Breakfast," showing a combination of determination to hold their ground and a commitment to feeding those in need. The decision to break the network of squats and anarchist groups that has grown over the years to make Exárcheia a hub of radical thinking and alternative living follows the election of a new Greek government in July 2019 committed to restoring "law and order". By the time the police left on 26 August, four major squats – Spirou Trikoupi 17, Transito, Rosa de Fon and Gare – had been evicted, but the oldest and most symbolic squat among those initiated with and by migrants, Notara 26, was exempted in what was perhaps a reflection of the solidity of its organisation and protection. How does this recent history of Exárcheia fit within the broader sequence of "the hospitality crisis" and the rise of increasingly authoritarian governments across Europe?

Surrounded by university buildings, including the Polytechnic School that was the bastion of opposition to the military regime of the early 1970s (Le Blanc, 2017), this district of Athens has always been a space of resistance, cosmopolitan encounter and countercultural living, but the recent concentration of anti-authoritarian action and its engagement with people seeking safe haven and a future in Europe draws its radicalism from events in December 2008, when the country was reeling from the effects of financial crisis. Then, during a night of riots in Exárcheia, 15-year-old Alexis Grigoropoulos died under police fire. The outpourings of anger spread across the country were channelled into many anarchist and oppositional formations, which were to lay the groundwork for the following victory of the democratic-socialist Syriza movement. One such group was Alpha Kappa, which helped create the Micropolis model of free social centres built around solidarity and participatory economies, the development of small enterprises, the pooling of care and support through education, childcare and cooking. These experiments in new forms of sustainability, with their strong anchoring in ecological thinking, were a forerunner of actions that gained new urgency as refugees found themselves stranded in Greece, particularly after the EU–Turkey agreement in March 2016. It was against this background of EU policy, which confirmed the prevailing high-handed and technocratic approach adopted by European states and institutions, that people from groups such as Alpha Kappa contributed significantly to the opening of squats for refugees, including Notara 26, and later the City Plaza Hotel outside Exárcheia, which survived from April 2016 until May 2017, when the hotel's owner presented the local authorities with a massive bill for usage of the building in an attempt to force their hand by treating the population of East Africans, Syrians, Afghanis and others along with local activist volunteers living in the "hotel" as regular paying guests.

Though the political inflection of these squats varies, what they share and shared is a determination to offer an autonomous alternative to the centres and camps funded by the UNHCR in particular, through unauthorised occupation of empty city-centre premises. But they are also inseparable from the rich tradition of anarchist struggle recently revitalised as activists fight the effects of the financial crisis and the endemic corruption of Greek political institutions. And this historic underpinning has had important effects on the way these autonomous spaces later evolved, particularly in the commitment to direct democracy and collective decision-making, as this chapter will go on to discuss (Brugère and Le Blanc, 2017). In turn, the challenges generated by the situation of those who found refuge in these alternative spaces are reshaping the landscape of political opposition in Greece, bringing a discourse of international solidarity to the fore in the demands for a new politics.

The internationalist character of these occupations functions at many levels. Within these sites interactions take place across major language differences. Residents communicate in combinations not only of Greek, English, Pashto, Arabic and Farsi, but also French, Spanish and Italian. Food has to be negotiated across a huge range of preferences and prepared collectively with limited resources. Rosters and responsibilities have to be shared out despite radically different individual and group priorities. These occupied spaces are also key hubs on a transcontinental map of solidarity, both for people pursuing their attempt to obtain asylum elsewhere in Europe and for activist volunteers concerned to channel their efforts towards places of greatest need. So when the Notara 26 squat was the target of a racist fire-bombs and Molotov cocktails in August 2016, resulting in the destruction of all of its supplies, 24 vans set off from across Europe, uniting in a convoy of solidarity from France, Spain, Belgium and Switzerland. Most of the squats with refugee residents also include European residents from countries further north, and the walls of Exárcheia are papered with expressions of resistance and anti-authoritarianism in English, Arabic, French, Pashto as well as, of course, Greek, while a banner over the door at Notara 26 merely announces "REFUGEES WELCOME" and "HOME", re-enforcing the strength of movements of occupation and their role in wider forms of opposition. One of the most frequent slogans heard in demonstrations against the repression in Athens is "Solidarity is the weapon of the people", as can be heard and seen in Yann Youlountas's 2018 "L'Amour et la révolution", made in support of self-governing spaces in Athens, which features scenes in Notara 26. "Solidarity does not only bring help and support. It also allows us to see the society we want", declares one of the cartels. For these activist volunteers, their politics are inseparable from their capacity to offer care.

The same observation can be made of similar forms of unauthorised occupation in other cities across Europe. Rome's Baobab Experience, a huge camp installation that was established in an abandoned lot near the Tiburtina station in 2015, is another well-documented example of a combined volunteer-refugee-led mobilisation, where the effort has been to produce a collaborative environment of care and counsel, as well as to meet the immediate needs of food and shelter (Paynter, 2018). Baobab Experience extended its work from a "humanitarian" response towards initiatives to change the discourse in Italy, to explore interconnected factors evident in the failure of European institutions to provide for the rise in asylum seekers entering Europe. And its primary strength was its visibility as a point of resistance to the growing extremist tendencies within Italian politics. Baobab's momentum was crushed by Salvini's rise to power as Minister for the Interior when he ordered its destruction and the eviction of those living there into the streets in November 2018.

For the people who ran the Jean Quarré squat in Paris, Notara 26 in Athens and Baobab in Rome, high visibility is a key part of their politics. By taking over strategic locations in partially abandoned areas or "unremarkable" areas in major capital cities, they are able to align the cause of refugees and asylum seekers with efforts to make urban deprivation visible and to signify to public authorities that a different approach to social inclusion is possible (Vandervoort, 2019). The location of these squats, or alternative communities, in major cultural and intellectual capitals enables them to draw on the organisation and experience of what are often university-based politics, while the plight of refugees and asylum seekers galvanises university-led opposition to broader neoliberal policies, including the increasing financialisation of education (rising fees for international students) and research, as well as increasingly restrictive visa protocols.

Another crucial example of this sort of alliance between high social capital and those most deprived of economic, social and legal security is Parc Maximilien in Brussels, where, as discussed in the Brussels Flashpoint, the Plateforme Citoyenne de Soutien aux Réfugiés launched a different approach to occupation, by using the relative centrality of a rundown square to serve as a point of contact for a network of beds that could be provided in individual homes. Although the square was only a point of access to dispersed and "invisible" solutions for shelter, it shared the same strategy of attracting media attention in such a way that materialised the very claim it was making, i.e., that new social relations are possible. This was akin to how "Occupy Wall Street" had demonstrated that a new power ratio could take hold right within the heart of global capital. And the more the Belgian Government sought to downplay the presence of the asylum seekers, the more these visible alternatives became powerful, generating ever greater numbers of volunteers and yet more public attention.

Yet we should be wary of insisting too much on the centrality of these urban sites, for in many ways what is most significant about the ways in which these autonomous communities and occupations are transforming political opposition across Europe lies in the sheer number of initiatives of this sort, and their variations in scale and duration, in modes of interaction and negotiation, as John Borman's chapter in this volume (Chapter 2) shows. What unites these actions, though, is the key relation to a particular area or *zone à defendre*, which anchors a discourse of solidarity in acts of inaugurating and sustaining new territories based on openness and hospitality, yet which is also self-contained and resistant (Subra, 2017; Barbe, 2016).

Strikes, Campaigns, and the "Value" of Volunteer Labour

The unofficial nature of the spaces and squats so far discussed makes it impossible to record with any certainty the numbers of people who have found refuge and solidarity for longer or shorter periods in these sorts of informal environments. In the middle of 2017, the Athens authorities recognised that there were probably 2,500 to 3,000 asylum seekers living in squats across the city, while the waiting list for a space at City Plaza Hotel ran to 4,000 names; Notara 26 would later claim that over 6,000 people had lived there for some period of time (Chrysopoulos, 2017). But if local authorities in all contexts across Europe attempt to minimise the phenomenon, many commentators know, and this book clearly documents, that the informal or civil-society sector has filled a glaring gap in both NGO and governmental provision (Mayblin and James, 2019; Brugère and Le Blanc, 2017). The key role borne by these organisations whose work is by definition uncounted and unrewarded, at least in monetary form, explains why some have used the threat and actual implementation of strike action to draw attention to what they denounce as the irresponsibility of national governments. Clearly the context of volunteerism, where for many their commitment was prompted by the sense of absolute necessity, means that this traditional mode of resistance by withdrawing labour power is only a marginal occurrence, but still a very significant one if we are to look at solidarity, and particularly transnational solidarity, through a political lens. It also reflects the way in which some of the initiatives, that began in a surge of compassion and sense of urgency, have now become part of a new landscape in which street breakfasts, camps, clothes distributions and outdoor language classes have become "normal". Several years on from the outpouring of volunteer action, distributions and donations that marked the summer of 2015 in the UK in particular, the crisis is still ongoing, and the volunteer organisations have moved in different ways towards more stable configurations. Recourse to the weapon of strike action reflects the often highly punitive conditions under which volunteers work (Blanchard and Rodier, 2016) and, in tandem with the "burn-out" phenomenon discussed here by Corrie, Burck and Hughes in Chapter 7, it reveals a number of key facets of what we mean by the politics of refugee volunteerism. For some volunteers, there was a sense that they were doing work that they expected to be done by the state or other organsations, whereas others saw the possibilities for instituting new forms of self-rule, new modes of shared life, including the negotiation of different divisions of labour with more attention on care for the community, and different conceptions of value less oriented towards efficiency. But perhaps more importantly still, in practice, these two horizons often blur, particularly in highly charged and complex environments such as the "campification" of northern France, which arguably stretches from the city of Paris in straggling forms up to the coast and Calais, Dunkerque, Grande-Synthe... Here it is not unusual to find groups wrestling with the competing sense of outrage at the manifest failure of the authorities, while also celebrating the perspectives and joys opened up by pitching in, by doing better, by celebrating the fact that grassroots ingenuity and determination can be much more enabling than institutional services. These experiences and the dilemmas that they imply – rudimentarily expressed as a "choice" between campaigning, nationally and locally, or sorting and supporting – have generated an incredible laboratory in political experimentation. They have been fundamental to my own practice of the politics of solidarity, and what follows here draws directly on both observation of, and participation in, the new terrains of "internationalism" in Europe today, shaped as they are, by changing ideas of citizenship and citizen action.

Withdrawing labour is a classic form of collective action, relying on solidarity among those exposed to unfair practice or injustice. What conditions have to prevail in order to achieve this sort of solidarity, and how does it relate to the expressions of solidarity with destitute refugees? A broad swathe of the main volunteer organisations active in Paris put the commonality of their cause to the test in April 2019 by calling for a one-day strike on all "informal" food distributions in the capital. Although still unauthorised and so constantly at risk of criminal proceedings being brought against them, the 15 citizen groups who joined the strike, including international, national and local groups (Solidarité Migrants Wilson, P'tits Déjeuners Solidaires, Utopia 56, Emmaüs France, Médecins du Monde), provide a vast amount of frontline support in the French capital for victims of the asylum process in Europe. They estimate that each week more than 15,000 meals are provided, and that over 1,500 people receive a cover or a tent in which to sleep every week on the strength of donations and unpaid labour, while 600 people are housed by local people on a voluntary basis, which still leaves anywhere up to 1,600 people on the streets in and around the city because of the inadequacies in processing claims for asylum. The director of the major NGO France Terre d'Asile, mandated by the French Government to function as a first port of call for asylum seekers, expressed his support for the strike, saying that if the capacity to manage the pressure on the system is not rethought, the whole chain of engagement will continue to run behind the needs, until everyone is exhausted (Birchem, 2019). This strike echoes earlier action expressed in Calais back in the early summer of 2015, prior to the major mobilisation from the UK, when the Calais Ouverture et Humanité collective publicly withdrew its support and organisation. More recently, in May 2019 and again in the Calais area, Jean-Pierre Boutoille, known as the *curé des migrants* or "priest of the migrants", called for a suspending of volunteer activity in order to provoke the authorities into responsible action. And in a context I will return to further on, it is also worth noting here that Utopia 56 and Doctors Without Borders took the decision to pull out of the work they were mandated to do on behalf of the Paris municipal authorities less than a year after the creation of the "one-stop" Humanitarian Centre at La Chapelle in Paris. They were protesting against the conditions inflicted by this very centre, in particular through desperate management of the queue system, on people hoping to claim asylum in the French capital.

In all these cases, the target of the action has been the national government or the local authorities, situating this activism firmly within the classic political arena of welfare provision and rights within a nation-state. This context explains some of the difficulties and differences that characterised the initial arrival of large numbers of British volunteer organisations in Calais in 2015. Reviewing the impact of the British presence one year on, the local *député* or MP for the Calais area, Yann Capet, pointed in particular to what he perceived as the absence of any political understanding among the scores of people who had upped and taken the ferry to the French coast. "Why are they not campaigning with the British Government who is equally responsible for this situation?" he asked, revealing his own ignorance of British politics (Laurent, 2016).

Evidently he was not taking account of the broad and significant mobil-isation in the UK in a year when the campaign led particularly by Lord Alf Dubs, and a number of UK groups such as Safe Passage and Calais Action, capitalised on increasing national awareness of the plight of unaccompanied minors stuck in Calais with a claim to travel to the UK. Tens of thousands of people marched to Downing Street under banners reading "Refugees Welcome Here" in the autumn of 2016 when Capet was interviewed, and many of these people had already taken to the streets a year earlier, in September 2015, when the group Solidarity with Refugees spearheaded what would become a massive demonstration, channelling the major shift in consciousness prompted by the photo of Alan Kurdi. With over 100,000 demonstrators, this march was the biggest expression of collective solidarity with refugees that the UK had ever seen. Prior to that, and as these pioneer organisations acknowledged, the frame of action had been much more grassroots, and their small gains were hard-won. The Syria Solidarity Campaign is a case in point. It had been active since 2012, joining forces with the broader organisa-tion Citizens UK to lobby local councils to get them to agree to house 50 refugees. As described in the UK Flashpoint, by the end of 2015, they had extracted a pledge from Prime Minister David Cameron to welcome a total of 20,000 Syrian refugees. Capet's comments are, then, more a reflection of the relatively insular or national quality of mainstream media reporting, on both sides of the Channel. This insularity and its essentially "monolingual" character, which establishes the tone of the national "conversation" on immigration, is in sharp contrast with the complexity of experience among activist volunteers often working in multilingual environments and adapting to different cultural practices, both within and between groups of displaced people and the different European organisations.

Yet drawing a neat distinction between "mobile" people and "fixated" national media spheres would also be inaccurate. For, as this chapter argues, many of the citizen-led, self-rule organisations are deeply embedded within national and local political dynamics, unwilling to disconnect their actions from the frame of their own national and local authority politics, where they may well have been active in other, non-refugee campaigns (Cantet, 2016). The effects of this intersection between the local, the national and the transnational were particularly complex in Calais, where the initial experiences of cohabitation between British and French groups were not always easy.

L'Auberge des Migrants in particular, present in Calais since 2008 when the informal camps started to spread along the coast and into the sand dunes after the Red Cross Sangatte Centre was closed partly at British request, was critical of what it perceived as disorganisation, with the sudden arrival of large numbers of people and the initially somewhat chaotic distribution of donations, pointing to what from its perspective looked to be a cavalier attitude on the part of groups with little experience of the complexity of the situations at play, and less concern for the evolving ecology of the settlement that would become known across the world as "the Jungle". This was a problem of solidarity in the eyes of the local activists, who feared a "drive-and-drop" model of engagement that risked running counter to a longer-term political response to the situation. In contrast, many UK activist volunteers were appalled by their impression of public indifference to the suffering in and around Calais. To some extent these differences still endure today and raise the question of what it would mean for this mass mobilisation across Europe to evolve towards the more structured form of a truly internationalist "movement".

And the contrast is striking between the evolution in and around Calais and how things evolved between British and French volunteers in nearby Grande-Synthe, a suburb of Dunkerque, where the local mayor and authorities, and least in 2015–2016, took a more progressive approach and worked more directly with both local French and international volunteer groups. Here we see how different political leanings at a local level can have a hugely significant impact on the way an internationalist situation plays out.

It is also important to observe that even within the UK "charity sector" operating in and around Calais, significantly different approaches emerged as the situation evolved. Care4Calais, for example, has preserved a primarily British profile and sought to build connections with UK organisations such as the historic formation of Stand Up to Racism, and newer networks such as the very active Student Action for

Refugees (STAR) organisation, with whom Care4Calais co-ordinates mass volunteer visits to Calais several times a year. Care4Calais also extended its operations to developing a supply chain towards Syria, while on the home front it has been among the most prominent voices denouncing the massive funding by the British Government of security at the UK border in Calais, drawing attention to British complicity in the nightly tear-gassing of "Jungle" residents including children, the firing of rubber bullets and the regular imprisonment of undocumented migrants. In contrast, Help Refugees, initially viewed as an outsider organisation by the locally based L'Auberge des Migrants, has now built a partnership with that organisation, contributing significantly to swelling the collective budget. It flags up its engagement in research as well as day-to-day work, describes itself as adopting a field-work-first approach to aid, establishing local networks and working with local partners.

These Calais examples show some of the difficulties not only in describing the mobilisation in 2015 as a collective political movement, but also in assessing in what ways action can be described as meaningful. When volunteers sprang into action in the face of what they saw happening in Calais, the time-scale in which they acted was quite radically at odds with those local volunteers who had been present since the early 2000s, and different again from that of the refugees themselves, who, as priest Jean-Pierre Boutoille points out, have often spent years in forced displacement in Africa and the Middle East before they reach Europe. Throughout all these examples, we see clearly the inevitable tension between volunteers seeking to meet immediate mass-survival needs such as food, drinking water and basic shelter, and the project of laying the groundwork for a new politics of solidarity. Many of the testimonies in this book speak to the frustration felt by those committed to short-term emergency aid when they also clearly grasp the need to engage with the political ramifications and implications of the "crisis".

In and Out of the Public Eye

Resistance to a discourse of "crisis" with its short-term, quick-fix implications explains a lot of what has prompted many refugee and undocumented-worker-led movements to insist on building a sustainable autonomous movement which would not be reliant on charitable appeals and traditional "disaster aid". In many instances, groups of refugee-led action remain fluid and invisible, or, when they are visible, tend to be only local and mobilised around specific demands for equal pay, access to healthcare or accommodation (Nyers, 2015). There are exceptions, perhaps most notably the International Committee of Refugees initiated in the UK in 2015 and now based in Germany. This is one way in which the "long-haul" realities of global migration have redirected and absorbed the "uprising" of solidarity at its height in 2015–2016. In most instances, though, it has resulted in relatively local initiatives, where the project of building a politics of solidarity outside traditional forms of representation has been described as "kinetic politics" (Cantat, 2016, 2018). The focus for these movements is generally more on internal communication and less on high-visibility websites. The other way is through alliance with intermediary bodies and most notably city authorities, whose position enables them to stand in opposition to national governments yet offer a stabilising platform, as well as recognition and resources for citizen activism. We will consider both of these horizons in the following discussion, which will start with the longer history of undocumented struggle in Europe and extend towards the more scattered and often isolated situations of political experimentation that are developing.

Undocumented Citizenship, from the *Sans-Papier* Movement to Refugee Support Work

There was perhaps no more charged distinction at play in the fraught events of 2015–2016 than that of the asylum seeker versus the undocumented or irregular migrant. The *sans-papiers* ("no papers") movement, launched in the mid-1990s in France, had long decided that there was nothing to be gained in that debate and the only possible course of action was to reject the distinction by drawing its own terms. These terms had to bring attention to the fact that the people in question had all the attributes of citizens – jobs, qualifications, families, tax returns, responsibilities – and what they lacked were the papers that would allow them to circulate freely and potentially, in the longer term, to vote. They came into view after the large numbers of Vietnamese and later Albanian refugees had found safe haven in France in particular, and before the major population movements from the Middle East and Africa of the first two decades of the twenty-first century. They were not claiming to have fled war, though many had lived under repressive regimes. They were in France, and had been for numerous years in many cases, for mixed reasons: some push factors, some pull factors. The legal framework prevailing on them had changed gradually through a series of reforms, reducing their rights and sometimes compromising their continued existence in the country where they had built a life, founded a family. The *sans-papiers* were campaigning for *régularisation*, and they still are. In 1996, they occupied the Saint Bernard church in Paris, drawing substantial media attention until they were evicted and some were put in detention. The occupation was the moment of self-declaration as an autonomous political movement. In 2008, they led another high-profile occupation, this time against the general workers' union that had represented some of them. This second occupation was important for the way it focused solidarities. Though the CGT union had supported the claims to papers for some of its *sans-papiers* members, it refused to extend its support to isolated and often non-salaried workers, particularly women who earn their living doing "informal" labour like cleaning. In opposition to this discrimination, the *sans-papiers* occupied the union headquarters near the Place de la République. This choice was highly strategic and bears out what many commentators observe as the parting of ways between new forms of political protest and traditional representative mechanisms, such as unions. The actual location, much closer to the centre of the city than the Saint Bernard church, was also significant. Place de la République would later to be the site of the massive homage to the victims of the *Charlie Hebdo* attacks after the Kouachi brothers broke into the offices of the satirical newspaper in January 2015 in the name of an Islamist terrorist group and killed 12 members of the editorial team, seriously injuring 11 more in the process. The following year, the radical street occupation known as Nuit Debout that grew out of opposition to new French labour legislation also centred its actions on this square, prompting some efforts to create visibility for migrant camps in and around this period of revolt. While not achieving anything of the scale and visibility of the several-thousand-strong camps on the northern fringes of the city since 2015, these gatherings were still significant in this very visible and symbolic urban intersection.

This layering of political significance within one site, from "migrant politics" to solidarity with a historic national newspaper (anchored on the Left though strongly criticised today for its incendiary representations of religious symbols) is important for, like in Exárcheia, it reveals how actions of refugee solidarity in spaces of long and dense political culture, such as Paris and Athens, draw from their antecedents while also transforming the landscape. Around the Place de la République during the *sans-papiers* occupation, the walls were papered with large prints of photographs taken of two people holding one passport between them. The pairings blurred any easy categories, playing also with strategies of "making visible". They were the result of spontaneous requests from individuals who presented themselves to be photographed with people in the occupation, inserting themselves into a story that was and wasn't theirs. Since that time the *sans-papiers* collective, known as CPS75, has continued to fight for rights to residency permits, while also bringing its long experience to bear in support of more recent groups mobilised in the name of newer generations of undocumented people. A number of the groups active today in Paris have direct connections with CSP75, and other organisations created to assist migrant workers recruited in the 1960s by French and European businesses now offer key legal support for people caught in the inequities of the ever more complex and punitive asylum system. A similar account could be given of the connections between the Plateforme Citoyenne du Soutien aux Réfugiés (BXL-Refugees) in Brussels, mentioned earlier, and the Belgium *sans-papiers* collective, founded in 2009 after a series of failed efforts at regularisation, which has been particularly active in fighting the efforts in Belgium to pass a law allowing the police to enter individual homes to arrest "irregular" migrants. In Malta, Lampedusa and in Palermo, too, as is noted in the respective Flashpoint sections, there have been parallel initiatives where citizens and migrants have worked in association to seek "regular" housing and employment status for refugees, seeing their cause as the same and not allowing themselves to be divided by "us and them" rhetoric.

This longer history helps us to understand the significance of autonomous organisation, and also its longer time-frame relative to actions prompted by a sense of urgency. We find a similar emphasis and time-frame in the work of Lesvos Solidarity in the Pipka camp at Mytilene, which has been active in an affirmatively self-organised and autonomous way since 2011, directing its actions towards the sustainable perspectives for refugees and asylum seekers. The Mosaik Support Center, which is today the focus of Lesvos Solidarity's work, is based on principles of empowerment and places the decision-making of migrant peoples at the heart of its processes, rather than "what Europeans believe is best", to quote the group directly. In the context of increasingly repressive action on the part of the Greek authorities, and the desperate conditions in the government camp at Moria, the work of the Mosaik Center is all about the longer process of negotiating daily life together between languages and cultures. For Mariam, the Afghani community leader, and Diego, who represents Congolese people in Mytilene, what is at stake is finding ways to articulate a "we" that allows them a voice.

Back in Paris and with a group such as the BAAM, we find another version of this re-positioning of politics within the slow transformation of communities of expression and practice, in an example that also allows us to understand what this process can draw from prior forms of politicisation of undocumented people. "Adam" (not his real name) from Sudan spent months in 2016–2017 in a street camp near the Saint Bernard church, mentioned previously as the rallying point for the *sans-papiers*, surviving in permanent expectation of imminent deportation back to Italy under the Dublin Regulation (Adam, 2017; see note 1). There is a longstanding connection between the BAAM and the Association for Maghrebi Workers (ATMF), which was founded in 1982 when the French Government finally repealed a 1940 law that forbade immigrants (then mainly Jewish refugees) from organising under "association" status. Adam learnt of the ATMF's work and decided to volunteer as a translator from Arabic to English to help in the legal advice sessions it offers to new arrivals needing advice on their status. In so doing, Adam is both signifying a new era of transnational solidarity and his own place within that era as a "new internationalist", while he is also engaging in a continuum that runs through postcolonial politics in France and into today's "migrant crisis".

Attention to the necessity of translation is one of the most significant characteristics of movements led by those most directly exposed to repressive and violent border politics. Regular assemblies during which collective decisions are lengthily debated and simultaneously translated are a feature of the squats and camps in Exárcheia as they are elsewhere. These practices are increasingly structuring academic work too, evident in the effort to ensure simultaneous translation during conferences and more generally to "decolonise multilingualism" (Phipps, 2019). Similar practices are also at the heart of the Silent University, an international education platform initiated by the Dutch-based Turkish artist Ahmet Ögüt to foster "transversal pedagogies" and obtain the recognition for refugees and asylum seekers with academic qualifications so that they can continue to do their work and research in Europe, in some cases despite death threats against them. The Silent University has developed radical practices of opposition in its development of "decolonial universities" in Sweden, Germany and Jordan after its beginnings in a collaboration in the UK with the Delfina Foundation and the Tate Museum. Though not at all premised on volunteer contributions, the Silent University, with its ambitious educational programme, has necessitated long and persistent negotiations with local participants, as well as the fostering of a strong internal community.[3] The emphasis on long-term commitment and full "buy-in" to its principles and demands, as opposed to top-down direction or opportunistic gains, is fundamental to its approach. The internationalism of these facets of the mobilisation, built outside legal limitations and through fully participatory processes, is a protracted, highly complex, often contentious affair, frequently anchored in the idea that "we live together, we fight together". What we can hear in this expression is forging new forms of political subjectivity in the joint objective of caring for people's needs and building new forms of participatory organisation. It is in part this dynamic that makes the politics of solidarity and the situation of activist volunteers so importantly complex: neither political nor humanitarian professionals nor stateless refugees, many activists have found their own relation to state protection as European citizens is much less assured than they might have assumed. Confronted with the reality or risk of disqualification and criminalisation, their self-perception as members of a functional political order has been stretched. And in their battles to affirm that Europe's capacity to protect must extend beyond the preservation of their own wellbeing and livelihood, they have found themselves putting the latter at stake. In so doing, they point up how the politics of solidarity is defining the fundamental challenges "we" – as a "we" that takes nothing for granted – all face today.

Local Communities, Global Cities and the Courts

The examples discussed here have tended to focus on major cities and on sites located within time-hallowed districts of these cities marked by histories of immigration and/or resistance to power. Accounts from these communities often invoke the significance of being in the centre. Proximity to shops, schools and services helps refugees negotiate a new environment while allowing them to blend into the diversity of a major urban area. But the practices of embedded solidarity and attention to the complex ecology of a community are equally characteristic of remote locations, and it is in these contexts that the most significant tension between humanitarian action and political endeavour is currently evident. The La Roya Citoyenne movement, discussed in the Ventimiglia Flashpoint, is a case in point, as is the situation of Cédric Herrou, Pierre Mumber, Pierre Alain Manoni and the group known as the "Briançon 7", who have all been charged with illegally helping people cross the

Italian–French frontier in a context in which a long history of autonomous solidarity anchored in the movement of workers between Italy and France, as well as Alpine traditions of offering refuge, have clashed with the hardening realities of border control.

It is in border regions that the changing framework of legislative provision and actual policing practices can be most clearly seen. This is evidently the case along external borders such as the one between Greece and Turkey, which has been the focus for a new phase in European intolerance and the use of repressive force as I write, in March 2020. And the border between Croatia and Serbia, which, as discussed in the Balkan Route Flashpoint, has seen some of the most grievous "pushbacks" and violations of human rights. Local associations in Croatia, including Are You Syrious? and the Center for Peace Studies (CMS) have come under direct attack from the country's Minister of the Interior, with attempts to defame and delegitimise the groups' actions as forms of assistance to "smugglers". Amnesty International reports frequent harassment and intimidation of staff and volunteers, and the Center for Peace Studies has lost all financial support for its work in integration activities carried out for over 15 years. The compounded effect detailed by Amnesty International has been one of "chilling" public opinion and undermining the credibility of these organisations (Amnesty International, 2020).

The particular significance of the French–Italian border in the context of this discussion is that it is internal to the European Union, making the issues emerging around a few emblematic sites and situations internal to the political community of Europe, both in the interpretation of European directives and in cultures of policing. In fact, this national frontier only exists once more today as a border with provision for "random and mobile" police controls because of exceptional anti-terrorist measures introduced in the wake of the 2015 attacks on Paris. Though obliged to re-evaluate these measures every six months in the face of "persistent terrorist threat", the French Government has enforced them uninterruptedly since 2015. The result has been to criminalise and intimidate a number of local-community actions and to make this border one of the most significant scenes for the politics of solidarity today. Here, we can see perhaps most clearly how a culture of welcome and the humanitarian duty to preserve life in conditions of extreme danger and physical deprivation has become the testing ground for the preservation of fundamental rights to freedom of opinion and association.

The key concept here is a French legal phrasing, "activist gain" or *contrepartie milintante,* invoked by the public prosecutor in the Hautes-Alpes town of Gap as part of an accusation that assisting someone in crossing the frontier is punishable under the laws against smuggling because it is carried out for motives other than "exclusively humanitarian" ends, i.e., for "political" gains, if not for directly monetary gains. Though subsequently judged to be of no judicial significance by the highest French appeals court, the Cour de Cassation, the idea of an "activist gain" has also been expressed within parliamentary debate in France. In both these cases, we see a tendency to collapse the distinction between actions of solidarity and anti-authoritarian politics. In this context, the victims of ever more aggressive enforcement of border regulations are not only asylum seekers and undocumented people, but also those who wish to speak out about police practices, for example. Anti-police slogans and posts on social media were cited in the hearings against the "Briançon 7", a group of Swiss, Italian and French supporters of migrant and refugee rights to claim asylum in Europe, in an attempt to use laws against people trafficking to curtail freedom of expression and assembly. So the authorities have succeeded in drawing attention to these relatively remote and inaccessible valleys, where the organisation Tous Migrants – All Migrants – now runs regular "solidarity walks" (*maraudes solidaires*) and other activist demonstrations.

The cases of Sarah Mardini and Séan Binder, discussed by John Borton in Chapter 2, are also significant in this respect, both for the way they have been intimidated and criminalised for their rescue activities at sea, but also for the "internationalist" trajectories that they reveal. Sarah Mardini is a young Syrian woman who was granted refugee status in Germany before moving to Lesvos to contribute to humanitarian efforts with the NGO Emergency Response Centre International (ERCI). Séan Binder is a German national who lives in Ireland, who also joined the same ERCI rescue endeavour. While both have found their lives thrown upside-down by their prosecution for conducting sea-rescues off the coast of Lesvos, the difficulties for Sarah Mardini are compounded by the further suggestion that she used her status as a Syrian refugee to advance a political argument.

The risk of criminalisation is obviously the most detrimental to those whose rights are already under suspicion. Such is the case for three young men, two only 16 years old, from the Ivory Coast and Guinea, accused by the Maltese authorities of having illegally hijacked a boat in order to prevent it from being returned to Libya – against their claims that they took command of the ship with the authorisation of its captain in order to ensure the safety of the people on board. In addition to the high penalties invoked for these young people, the "El Hiblu 1" case is also significant for the use the accusation has made of anti-terrorist legislation, a legal "opportunity" that has more purchase when the accused originate from countries with large Muslim communities. In this, as in the reinforced border regime through the Alps, the questions of refugee and migrant rights, as well as the way in which peer-to-peer solidarity is perceived, are it seems becoming inseparable from the way in which national security is invoked, enabling special state prerogatives, against a broad background of racism and xenophobia.

Back in the city environment, some urban local authorities have challenged these state-led attempts to associate humanitarian behaviours with other political "crimes". The is notable in Paris, where the mayor Anne Hildago has at least waved the "refugees welcome" flag in opposition to national government (though she has not delivered the practical facilities in Paris that are still very much needed). For local activist volunteer groups, such as Utopia 56, which initially agreed to support the city's humanitarian camp in November 2016, distrust in the city's will to address these desperate situations led it in 2019 to install a highly visible camp for women and children in a public park. This overt use of the camp to persuade the mayor to make a more thorough-going commitment is another example of "independent" humanitarian groups increasingly demanding to be part of the local and national political discourse.

Other cities have managed to embrace the actions of volunteer solidarity more successfully and in turn amplify citizen resistance to the persecution and grievous neglect of refugees, whether on land or at sea. Perhaps the most prominent example of this is the City of Sanctuary movement, which has been widely acknowledged particularly in the UK as exemplifying hospitality and empowerment of asylum seekers. Many cities have distinguished themselves in this way since Sheffield became the first City of Sanctuary in 2007, but perhaps none more than Glasgow, which quickly became the city to house the largest number of asylum seekers in the UK after a national dispersal policy was introduced in 2000. The focus of a large range of arts-based and social outreach initiatives has been to provide hope for a "desired future", particularly during the long waiting periods when asylum claims are processed. To this end the Glasgow City Council has also developed substantial provision of internship possibilities and networks to enable refugees and their children to gain language skills, experience and confidence, with a view to enabling them to integrate more easily (Darling, 2010; Bagelman, 2013). A lot of these initiatives depend on citizen engagement to run effectively, but many involved are acutely aware that they offer little interface with the protracted legal battles and uncertainties that are also part of everyday reality. A more dissident model of city-versus-national government has emerged in the commune of Riace, in the southern Italian province of Calabria – detailed in the Sicily Flashpoint in this book. Italy has led the way with a number of dissident mayors against the positions taken by Salvini, along with Spanish "Tourists go home; refugees welcome" message that has been affirmed by the city of Barcelona. The Dunkerque suburb of Grande-Synthe, on the Channel coast, has also positioned itself in opposition to national and regional policy by working with non-aligned solidarity groups, and this has added momentum to the creation of the Migrations Alliance, bringing together local authorities and civil-sector organisations. The Alliance is significant for its inclusion of the Mayor of Sao Paulo and the explicit intention to draw on the dynamic launched by the 8th World Social Forum on Migrations in Mexico in 2018 and the 8th Africities event in Morocco, also in 2018. This new development, broadening the scope of this chapter towards non-European horizons in conclusion, reflects the growing ambition and scale of the new activist volunteer movements that have been the subject of this chapter. From often quite improvised and reactive beginnings we can see new patterns of political practice emerging. These practices often speak in many tongues and try out as many forms of participation as possible, thereby bringing into the political arena aspects of life that are traditionally assumed to be "merely" domestic, such as questions of who cooks and what food is served, or who gets to speak in an assembly and in what language, and meanwhile who is caring for the children... They draw their disruptive and innovative qualities from the fact that they often operate outside the legal framework, turned towards new horizons and unexpected joys, sometimes in overt contempt of law, sometimes in canny negotiation with local or national authorities. The notion that draws these different forms of contemporary radicalism together is solidarity, the watchword of a new international citizenship such as philosopher Michel Foucault defined in 1981, during a press conference on the plight of the Vietnamese boat people.

> There exists an international citizenship which as such has its rights and duties, and which is obliged to stand up against all forms of abuse of power, no matter who commits them, no matter who are their victims. After all, we are all governed, and, by that fact, joined in solidarity.
>
> (Foucault, 1994: 707–708)

It may not yet be clear what the most effective forms of this citizenship are, but the premises for its development are more and more manifest.

References

Adam (2017) "Yesterday I Didn't Speak a Word of French, Today I Am Translating Into That Language", *Z, revue itinérante d'enquête et de critique sociale*, 11: 28–30.

Agier, M. (2011) *Managing the Undesirables: Refugee Camps and Humanitarian Government*. Cambridge: Polity.

Amnesty International (2020) "Punishing Compassion. Solidarity on Trial in Fortress Europe", March. www.amnesty.eu/wp-content/uploads/2020/03/Punishing-compassion_Final-3-March.pdf.

Bagelman, J. (2013) "A Politics of Ease?", *Alternatives: Global, Local, Political*, 38(1): 49–62.

Barbe, Fr. (2016) "La 'zone à défendre' de Notre-Dame-des-Landes ou l'habiter comme politique", *Norois*, 238, 239: 109–130.

Blanchard, E. and Rodier, Cl. (2016) " 'Crise migratoire': ce que cachent les mots", *Plein droit*, 111(4): 3–6.

Birchem, N. (2019) "A Paris, des associations en grève pour dénoncer la situation des migrants", *La Croix*, 9 April. www.france-terre-asile.org/accueil/ftda-actu/a-paris-des-associations-en-greve-pour-denoncer-la-situation-des-migrants.

Brugère, F. and Le Blanc, G. (2017) *La fin de l'hospitalité, L'Europe terre d'asile?* Paris: Flammarion.

Cantat, C. (2016) "Rethinking Mobilities: Solidarity and Migrant Struggles Beyond Narratives of Crisis", *Intersections: East European Journal of Society and Politics*, 2(special issue): 11–32.

Cantat, C. (2018) "The Politics of Refugee Solidarity in Greece: Bordered Identities and Political Mobilization", Migsol Working Papers Series, 1. Center for Policy Studies.

Chrysopoulos, P. (2017) "Number of Refugees Living in Athens Squats on the Rise", *Greek Reporter*, 11 May. https://greece.greekreporter.com/2017/05/11/number-of-refugees-living-in-athens-squats-on-the-rise/.

Darling, J. (2010) "A City of Sanctuary: The Relational Re-Imagining of Sheffield's Asylum Politics", *Transactions of the Institute of British Geographers I*, New Series, 35(1): 125–140.

Elias, A. J. and Moraru, Ch. (2015) *The Planetary Turn: Relationality and Geoaesthetics in the Twenty-First Century*. Evanston, IL: Northwestern University Press.

Fassin, D. (2011) *Humanitarian Reason: A Moral History of the Present*. Berkeley, CA: University of California Press.

Fekete, L. (2018) "Migrants, Borders and the Criminalisation of Solidarity in the EU", *Race & Class*, 59(4): 65–83.

Foucault, M. (1994) *Dits et ecrits IV*. Paris: Gallimard.

Holzer E. and Warren K. (2015) "Humanitarian Spectacles from Below: A Study of Social Connections in Unsettled Contexts", *Ethnography*, 16(4): 482–502.

Laurent, A. (2016) "Quand les Anglais migrent vers Calais", *L'Express*

Le Blanc, N. (2017) "Santé! Et que la police se tienne loin de nous!", *Mouvements*, 92: 145–156.

Malkki, L. (2015) *The Need to Help: The Domestic Arts of International Humanitarianism*. Durham, NC: Duke University Press.

Mayblin, L. and James, P. (2019) "Asylum and Refugee Support in the UK: Civil Society Filling the Gaps?", *Journal of Ethnic and Migration Studies*, 45: 375–394.

McNevin, A. (2007) "Irregular Migrants, Neoliberal Geographies and Spatial Frontiers of 'The Political' ", *Review of International Studies*, 33(4): 655–674.

Nyers, P. (2015) "Migrant Citizenships and Autonomous Mobilities", *Migration, Mobility & Displacement*, 1(1): 23–39.

Orlando, L. (2015) "International Human Mobility Charter of Palermo 2015", 13–15 March. www.iom.int/sites/default/files/our_work/ICP/IDM/2015_CMC/Session-IIIb/Orlando/PDF-CARTA-DI-PALERMO-Statement.pdf.

Paynter, E. (2018) "The Liminal Lives of Europe's Transit Migrants", *Contexts*, 17(2): 40–45.

Phipps, A. (2019) *Decolonising Multilingualism: Struggles to Decreate*. Bristol: Multilingual Matters.

Subra, Ph. (2017) "De Notre-Dame-des-Landes à Bure, la folle décennie des 'zones à défendre' (2008–2017)", *Hérodote*, 165: 11–30.

Vandervoordt, R. (2019) "Subversive Humanitarianism: Rethinking Refugee Solidarity through Grass-Roots Initiatives", *Refugee Survey Quarterly*, 38(3): 245–265.

Youlountas, Y. (2018) "L'Amour et le révolution" (film, Greek/French, prod. Berceau d'un autre monde).

Notes

1 "Dublin" is the colloquial term used across Europe to refer to the Dublin Regulation as described in Chapter 2. In particular it dictates that a person must seek asylum in the first country of entry, which enables EU states to transfer asylum seekers back to the first state in which their arrival in Europe was recorded, through fingerprinting – often in Southern Europe.

2 This chapter is not concerned with delineating the distinctions between "migrants", "asylum seekers", "refugees", *sans-papiers*; it is interested in situations which encompass these shifting and selective differentiations.

3 One of the primary principles of the Silent University is full salaried pay even for academics living in illegality due to forced displacement. This commitment distinguishes it significantly from most of the organisations discussed here, but is nonetheless indicative of efforts to shift action away from the framework imposed by European differentiations between legality and illegality and towards new forms of alliance.

Flashpoint: Returns to Lesvos, 2019–20

Elle Wilkins and Sue Clayton

We began this book by looking at the arrival of higher numbers of asylum seekers to the Greek islands in 2015, and how this increased local peoples' involvement, and triggering an international response that was to send tides of support eventually across the whole of Europe. We saw how patterns and practices around rescue, care and encouraging self-determination for the new arrivals began to define this new wave of grassroots volunteer activism. At that point, no one – neither asylum seekers, volunteers, nor local communities and government – could have foreseen that with the closure of borders to the north of Greece, and the enactment of the pernicious EU–Turkey deal of 2016, people who in the main saw these small islands as a momentary stopping-point on their long migrant journey would find themselves, four or five years later, still incarcerated there, with no apparent means of moving forward through Europe or even, in extreme necessity, back to where they had come from. **Elle Wilkins**, a legal volunteer, worked on Lesvos in 2019. Her account below describes the terrible conditions for those still trapped on the islands at that time – and highlights the dire consequences of Europe having failed to address the ongoing humanitarian crisis, which has now descended into national and border squabbles, blaming and shaming, the criminalising of migrants and the treatment of them, first and foremost, as a "security risk", and the politically motivated denouncing of grassroots aid and support. Elle's account is below.

Figure 9.1 Lesvos, Greece, 2019. The entrance to the "official" Moria refugee camp. Thousands more live destitute on the land behind it.
Image credit: Elle Wilkins.

"In July 2019, I worked on the island of Lesvos, Greece, volunteering with a legal charity. I am trained as a caseworker in public law, and my role was to prepare asylum claimants for their interview with the Greek authorities. This is a vital part of the process for those claiming asylum in Greece, as their claim is decided following a sometimes hours-long interview assessing their credibility and consistency. Claimants received no formal preparation for this interview; the gaps were filled by overworked European lawyers volunteering their time with charities operating on the island. Supporting evidence may be submitted, but most claimants are unable to produce documents corroborating their story, and it is not unusual for claims to be decided on the interview alone.

Lesvos is one of the main arrival points in Europe for people fleeing conflict, persecution and extreme hardship. The International Organisation for Migration (IOM) reported 1.13 million new arrivals from January 2015 to June 2019. During 2015, headlines were dominated by tragic mass drownings in the Aegean, and these tragedies continue to occur. The EU–Turkey deal, however, greatly reduced the number of new arrivals. The impact of the deal was stark: practically overnight, reception facilities and temporary camps on the Greek islands were transformed into detention centres. From 20 March 2016, new arrivals were held on the islands on which they arrived while their asylum claims were processed – sometimes for a year or more. Conditions, already poor, deteriorated further.

The majority of the 8,000 refugees on Lesvos live in Moria camp, a former military base surrounded by razor wire; originally built for 2,000, it is now accommodating more than twice as many people. Although residents are not formally detained, the camp is situated miles away from amenities. Inside the camp, refugees live in tightly packed shipping containers or large tents housing hundreds of people in bunk beds. More than 2,000 occupants overflow the main camp into the surrounding olive grove, where they live in UNCHR tents, or else makeshift huts constructed from tarpaulins and scrap wood. The women in the camp avoid using the toilets at night due to the high risk of sexual assault. There is no formal system for supporting vulnerable people, because there are just too many of them; some simply go missing from their assigned bunk and leave no trace. There are piles of rubbish everywhere because there are no disposal facilities. The electricity is unreliable, supplied only a few hours a day. Running water is supplied only at wash stations – and cooking facilities are not provided at all. Those who are unable to afford the bus into town to buy food must wait for hours in line to receive meals.

Around the camp there are notices about the warning signs of hypothermia, and what people should do to prevent it. Despite these warnings, in early January 2019 a young Cameroonian man was found dead in his tent during sub-zero temperatures, and I saw no solution for preventing more of these deaths, given the inadequate housing and medical provision. Healthcare for those who need it is limited. People must produce evidence of their appointment to police officers outside the health clinic, or else wait outside in the hope that a member of staff passing by will spot them and invite them inside. Otherwise, they queue by the tents occupied by NGOs just outside the camp and hope that they can be seen there instead. Many of these clinics are staffed by volunteers, and there are not enough. Needless to say, a few health clinics in tents and shipping containers simply cannot provide for the complex needs of over 5,000 people, many of whom are suffering from serious mental health problems and the lasting impact of torture or other violence.

When I was preparing claimants for their interview, many of them told me about their experiences of torture, imprisonment, sexual violence and forced marriage. Some presented with psychotic symptoms. Others were glazed, unable to hold a conversation. One woman pushed bits of broken metal into her hand as we spoke. Despite what these people had been through, none of the claimants I spoke to were receiving any kind of psychiatric help.

I was surprised by the number of children in Moria – it seemed as though half the camp were children, their mothers queuing up outside makeshift NGO offices in the camp each morning to register their children for school. Many children endure the same conditions as the adults. Although the Greek authorities made efforts to house

Figure 9.2 Lesvos, Greece, 2019. Moria refugee camp. Those living in the camp queue early to get food. For the thousands beyond the camp, nothing is officially provided.

Image credit: Elle Wilkins.

families in nearby towns, I saw months-old babies carried around the camp, even in the freezing cold. There was no safeguarding, and no space left in the children's areas of the camp. Many were therefore staying alone in the main camp or in the olive grove, with little adult intervention. There were no provisions for childcare when their parents were attending legal or medical appointments, so children were left to run around unsupervised. One day, I helped the police search for a young girl who had gone missing a few days before; I don't know if they found her. Occasionally I would mind the children while my colleagues prepared their parents for interview. They were quiet, withdrawn and generally terrified of men. It is worth noting that there are no child psychiatrists on Lesvos.

The EU–Turkey deal has done nothing to stop people putting their lives at risk to travel to Europe to seek protection. Instead, people must wait on the island, sometimes for years, in squalid conditions, to have their claims processed. The minimum conditions enshrined in EU asylum law are just not being met. The claimants I prepared endured sexual assault, police brutality and torture before they even reached the island; when they arrived, they were met with inhumane living conditions, limited access to healthcare services, exposure to violence and a lack of real protection.

The European Court of Human Rights (ECHR) has recognised that the conditions for asylum seekers in Greece breach their Article 3 rights under the European Convention on Human Rights, as the conditions amount to inhuman and degrading treatment; and the asylum process is chronically understaffed and under-resourced. Many claimants have their interview stopped if the interviewing officer considers the individual may be vulnerable; they may require a psychiatric assessment to determine whether they suffer from a mental illness, as this informs the type of asylum process that applies to them. But arranging and conducting this assessment can take up to two years. In my experience, lack of staff meant that claimants due to be assessed by a social worker (due to vulnerabilities such as age, illness etc.) had their claims delayed indefinitely – yet in practice this was the majority of claimants. In March 2019, when I was there, the contracts for the social workers at Moria were due to end, with no new employees to take their place.

Following a grant of asylum, the conditions are not much better. Greek law provides that beneficiaries of international protection should enjoy the same rights as Greek citizens and receive any necessary social assistance, according to the same terms applicable

Figure 9.3 Lesvos, Greece, 2018. A small cemetery of refugees near Skala Sykounta, hidden and inaccessible.
Image credit: Nils-Uwe Kettner.

to Greek citizens. However, the Federal Constitutional Court ruled on 31 July 2018 that it cannot be generally assumed that recognised beneficiaries of international protection who have since sought refuge elsewhere in Europe can be returned to Greece, due to the lack of access to provisions such as shelter, healthcare and financial assistance. [As well as confirming the lack of facilities in Greece, this judgment also impacted those who had moved forward from Greece to North Macedonia or beyond, as thousands did only to find borders closed – and now, as above, they were given no chance to return south to Greece either.] A 2018 report by Pro Asyl, "Deportation into a Dead End: The Situation of Recognised Refugees in Greece", states:

> The current living conditions of beneficiaries of international protection in Greece are alarming, as beneficiaries do not only suffer from the lack of integration prospects into Greek society, but they

are often faced with inadequate living conditions and humanitarian standards.

In early February 2019, the Greek Ministry of Migration Policy announced the gradual termination of accommodation to beneficiaries of international protection living in refugee camps in mainland Greece. The first group of beneficiaries required to leave were those recognised before the end of July 2017, and the deadline for their exit was 31 March 2019, though it was unclear where they were supposed to go. Refugees also face near-insurmountable administrative and bureaucratic barriers preventing access to benefits in Greece; the procedures make no provision to accommodate their lack of documents, such as family status documents, birth certificates or diplomas. Those who have nowhere to go can theoretically be accommodated in existing shelters for the homeless on the mainland, but these shelters have only a limited number of places. In practice, it is almost impossible to find a place there. As a result, even recognised refugees still have no secure and effective access to shelter, food, the labour market and healthcare, including mental healthcare. International protection status

Figure 9.4 Lesvos, Greece, 2016. A slogan from 2016 that survived until the fire of 2020 on the wall of Moria camp.

Image credit: Marianne Robertsen.

in Greece does not guarantee a dignified life for beneficiaries of protection and is no more than protection "on paper".

EU initiatives are being phased out, leaving asylum claimants and refugees unable to meet their basic living needs. Recognised refugees now lose access to camps, UNHCR accommodation and cash only six months after they receive refugee status or subsidiary protection. This results in already-traumatised individuals enduring further hardship. Despite international condemnation, conditions remain inhuman and degrading.

The "crisis" is not over; even if they can reach it, Greece is not safe for refugees.

December 2019: Since I wrote the above in July 2019, Greece's newly elected centre-right government has proposed a number of changes to the way it handles refugees, who are still arriving on the islands in their thousands. "Welcome in Greece are only those we choose", Prime Minister Kyriakos Mitsotakis announced to the Greek Parliament in November 2019. "Those who are not welcome will be returned. We will permanently shut the door to illegal human traffickers, to those who want to enter even though they are not entitled to asylum." In an attempt to ease overcrowding in the camps on Lesvos, Chios and Samos, the government has announced that it will be replacing the existing camps with "closed facilities", similar to detention centres, and relocating some 20,000 refugees to the mainland. The country's civil protection minister, Michalis Chrysohoidis, has promised to accelerate applications, cut the number of refugees granted status and return more people to Turkey under the terms of the EU–Turkey deal. These announcements were made against the backdrop of severe overcrowding owing to the Greek policy of "containing" those who arrive on the islands, and an overburdened asylum system that sees refugees wait an average of 215 days to receive a decision on their claim. Médecins Sans Frontières chief Christos Christou spoke to reporters in Athens in November 2019 following a visit to the islands of Chios and Lesvos, saying that those in the camps are living "in utter chaos and without any dignity", and the organisation released a further report calling the situation on the islands "a policy-made humanitarian crisis". In October 2019, a nine-month-old baby died in Moria after suffering from severe dehydration, and there have been a number of accidental fires resulting in the deaths of inhabitants.

But the government's decision to overhaul the way those arriving on the islands are received will not solve the crisis; Efi Latsoudi from RSA (Refugee Support Aegean) speaking to the *New Humanitarian* in November 2019 said that transfers to the mainland won't be able to solve the problem: "there simply aren't enough reception spaces to accommodate all of the people who need to be moved, and the ones that do exist are often in remote areas, lack facilities, and will also be hit by harsh winter weather". The Greek Government's choice to adopt a political, rather than a humanitarian, response to the crisis will only cause further harm to those who have risked their lives to reach the relative safety of Europe; it is just another example of how we across Europe are failing those most in need of protection."

The unlawful overcrowding of the Moria camp continued into 2020, when from March of that year, the onset of the COVID-19 virus brought more restrictions to movement in and around the camp, and less chance for those with a case to move on to mainland Europe to be transferred. With the onset of the virus more and more responsibility fell to local ad international grassroots groups as NGOs pulled back on their operations. On the night of 8th September 2020, a massive fire broke out that engulfed the entire camp and surroundings, and 13,000 refugees became instantly homeless. While the case of the fire is under investigation, the organisation Human Rights Watch (2020) points out that after some tested positive for COVID, all Moria inmates continued to be incarcerated for four to five months after restrictions were lifted for the rest of the Greek population. They also report that right-wing vigilante groups have moved into the area and made it impossible for people to find a safe place of shelter near Moria town since the fire destroyed their tents and possessions. As of September 2020, we wait to see if Greece will continue its plans for a new permanent and prison-like detention centre on Lesvos.

10

Postscript: September 2020

Sue Clayton

We began this history, this series of Flashpoints and testimonies, by looking at the situation on the Greek islands in 2015, and then have followed the story of our new arrivals as they tried to make their way across Europe to find a place to settle and build a future. Above, with the account of a legal worker who recently visited Lesvos, we came back to where we began. The overall picture has not been good. The hasty, ugly and – many would argue in human rights terms – unlawful arrangements that the EU made with Turkey and Libya, coupled with the sudden and drastic closure of many national borders in Central and Eastern Europe, have led to tens of thousands of people in permanent limbo at borders where there is no place for them, and centres that were designed for a few nights' stay, overcrowded and filthy, are now their permanent homes. The war of attrition continues between the Southern and Northern European states; Merkel's proposed quotas failed to take effect; right-wing nationalist movements caused borders to be closed; the media and our governments are anxious that we European citizens believe the "problem" has gone away. So I offer this final report as a kind of epitaph to a Europe that we thought we knew, a Europe we thought was fairer and more democratic than this, and as a call to action for all those who believe the crisis is over, or who think that they are free to forget what was done in our name in the terrible years of 2015–2020, when Europe decided it could not increase its population by less than half-a-percent to help assuage a global crisis. When it tear-gassed children in the name of "security". When, despite the shocking phenomenon of the death of Alan Kurdi, it continued to allow 35,000 people to drown in our seas, many within sight of land and safety.

On 27 February 2020, the controversial EU–Turkey deal came under pressure as Turkish president Recep Tayyip Erdoğan announced that Turkey was opening its border with Greece to allow refugees to move forward to Europe, saying Turkey could no longer cope with the numbers of refugees fleeing Idlib province in Syria, and accusing Europe of failing to meet its obligations under the deal. Thousands in Turkey began to move forward to Greece. In response, Greek prime minister Kyriakos Mitsotakis announced that Greece would increase the level of deterrence at the country's borders to "the maximum" and would stop accepting new asylum applications for a month. EU ministers held an emergency meeting in Zagreb in early March, where they criticised Turkey's "use of migratory pressure for political purposes" and admonished "Don't go to the border. The border is not open" (Brzozowski, 2020). As Turkey allowed asylum seekers to leave their shores, the EU border agency Frontex launched an intervention at Greece's sea border in the Aegean. According to Médecins Sans Frontières' 4 March emergency statement, titled "EU Must Address Migration Emergency as Greek Islands Reach Breaking Point", one child died and 47 asylum seekers were rescued after their boat capsized off the coast of Lesvos; video footage released by the Turkish Government appears to show Greek Coastguard agents shooting into the water near the asylum seekers (MSF, 2020).

Meanwhile Greek plans to build large permanent detention facilities on the islands, announced in December 2019 (and discussed in the previous section of this book), had already stalled by March 2020. The plans were opposed by NGOs and volunteer organisations, who feared they may effectively become permanent prisons. They were also opposed by many local people who felt the islands were bearing disproportionate responsibility in the crisis – and tensions have been further fuelled by the appearance on the islands of extreme-right-wing groups from other European countries, such as the German neo-fascist Identitäre Bewegung (Identitarian Movement). A local journal, *Ekathimerini*, reflected on how:

> The situation in the past month, after the arrival of the riot police, has been tense. "The people are tired and this has buoyed the far-right"

says [local resident] Valiamos. "I don't think that the locals, even those who are opposed to the migrants, would refuse to help if a boat got into trouble right in front of them. They're just saying things they haven't really thought about. Maybe it's desperation. Maybe it's that no one's paying attention to us, the feeling that we're being used."

(Ekathimerini, 2020)

The tragic irony is that Lesvos only five years earlier was nominated for a Nobel Peace Prize for local peoples' exemplary response to the new arrivals. Further, returning to the first testimony quoted in this book, many Greeks had remembered themselves or their parents having sought refuge in Syria during the Second Word War. But they now bear the brunt of an issue that it seems the whole of Europe cannot or will not solve without militarisation and racialisation.

With no clear strategy, and escalating political differences, the situation in Lesvos, Samos, Chios, Leros and Kos grows ever more chaotic. Under the EU–Turkey deal, asylum seekers must remain on the Greek islands until their asylum requests are completed, but there was in April 2020 a backlog of over 90,000 applications. More than 42,000 people are now crammed into camps designed to accommodate 5,400 (Reliefweb, 2020). Volunteer Pru Waldorf reports from colleagues on the islands.

Conditions for volunteers and grassroots projects have become almost impossible to sustain and the climate has grown increasingly stressful and hostile. In many areas of Lesvos, police instructed project co-ordinators that they had to cease all refugee support activities "for their own safety". In early March 2020, they began to evacuate the island of volunteer groups, including large and well-resourced organisations like MSF: such were the fears for the safety of the responders there, due to the attacks against staff and property. Some activists criticised this move by the police, saying that the Greek state was simply seeking to remove all witnesses from the site of a mass human rights violation, rather than tackling the perpetrators of the violence against refugees grassroots operatives and NGOs. On 7 March 2020, there was a serious fire at the One

Happy Family school building and it was entirely destroyed. This was a beautiful community-run project, one of the few that enabled children detained on Lesvos to access their basic right to education – something that isn't given to them in Moria camp. In Chios the main volunteer warehouse was burnt to the ground, and on Samos a vehicle belonging to a nurse from the Greek refugee support organisation Arsis was deliberately set alight in the night. On Samos, the only official facility is built to house 750 and currently holds 7,000. There is a large "jungle area" around the official camp where over 5,000 live in terrible conditions with no access to services. There is no shelter provision, people wait three to six hours for food and then don't always receive anything at all.

On 2 March 2020, the UNHCR issued an emergency statement demanding that EU member states:

- urgently reduce the crowding and risks by ensuring additional reception places on the mainland for at least 20,000 people and move them there as quickly as possible
- review the EU's common rules on asylum, saying that the EU must help Greece manage its border with Turkey, and ensure the right of asylum for those who need it (UNHCR 2020)

Meanwhile, Action for Education has launched a petition demanding the EU effect an immediate decongestion of the Aegean islands – as of April 2020 it has been endorsed by nearly 100,000 individuals and 156 activist and humanitarian groups, including prominent organisations like Help Refugees, Safe Passage, Cities of Sanctuary, Are you Syrious?, Calais Action, No Name Kitchen and Refugee Aid Europe. It states:

This ongoing political stalemate between the EU, Greece and Turkey must be resolved. This game, played by the powerful, is putting innocent human lives at risk. It must stop now. Added to this already volatile mix is rising panic over the coronavirus. With healthcare severely lacking in the "Hotspot" camps, NGOs fear that an outbreak would have disastrous consequences ... Greece has been left alone to deal with this crisis – and the island communities more than anyone. Today, Europe must act to correct five years of negligent policy-making. It must own up to its chronic shunning of this international burden and recognise that good policy can fix this man-made catastrophe. As the humanitarian situation worsens beyond anyone's reckoning, it is your responsibility, as EU leaders, to ensure decisive and coordinated action to protect human life.

(Action for Education, 2020)

The effects of the COVID-19 pandemic were soon felt in Spring 2020, as many legally sanctioned family reunions between relatives in different European states have had to be halted. As of April 2020, major UK volunteer suppliers of food and aid such as Help Refugees, JCORE and Care4Calais have launched emergency appeals, reporting drastically reduced deliveries of essential supplies and fewer volunteers on the ground. Local urban meal distributions in cities such as Paris and Brussels have been severely curtailed, leaving homeless refugees vulnerable and exposed.

From Greece, Sumitah Shah reported.

> The COVID-19 situation has resulted in a total shutdown of Greece. The government has put stringent restrictions into place, especially for refugees and migrants. On 1 June 2020, for approximately 11,000 refugees, accommodation and cash provision supplied by Emergency Support to Integration and Accommodation (ESTIA) has been taken away.

From Malta, Maria Pisani adds:

COVID-19 has not only exposed and intensified the structural violence and human rights violations experienced by asylum seekers and refugees on a daily basis, but was also used to justify further human rights violations that also resulted in unnecessary loss of life. This included, but was not limited to, forging secret deals with the Libyan Coastguard, the ongoing criminalisation of search-and-rescue NGOs, abandonment at sea, engaging private vessels to conduct illegal "pushbacks", port closures and the use of private vessels usually for tourist excursions to detain asylum seekers for weeks on end, outside Maltese territorial waters.

Elsewhere there are signs that asylum seekers will lose important rights and liberties during the pandemic – *The Guardian* newspaper reports that authorities in Bosnia and Herzegovina have ordered the transfer of thousands of asylum seekers to a remote tent camp in Lipa, a village about 25 kilometres from the border with Croatia, since the virus outbreak. They add that according to sources, residents will not be able to leave the camp, which will be under surveillance by the police. The Border Violence Monitoring Network, an alliance of independent volunteer groups, is quoted as responding:

> The move by authorities to set up a further tent camp in Lipa shows a cyclical regression in the treatment of people-on-the-move in western Bosnia-Herzegovina. With the onset of Covid-19, the internal dispersion of people to a remote tent settlement marks a further stage in the suppression of living conditions and restriction on movement.
>
> (Tondo, 2020)

No wonder the Network is concerned – between 2016 and April 2020, it has documented over 140 serious abuses of police and army power along the Balkan route where asylum seekers have been tortured, abused and subject to unlawful "pushbacks".

The criminalising of volunteers, both local and international, is also becoming more fully documented. As early as 2017, the UK's Institute of Race Relations (IRR) detailed 45 volunteer individuals or groups in Europe who had faced prison, fines or both, for everything from simply feeding a hungry person, to transporting them to medical facilities, to conducting rescues at sea in the absence of an effective state rescue force. In its report "Humanitarianism: the Unacceptable Face of Solidarity", it argues that EU member states are using laws aimed at traffickers and smugglers to criminalise those acting out of humanitarian motives. They conclude: "The rhetoric of EU politicians and its border force, Frontex, may be fuelling far-right extremism, and we urge the European Commission to reassert support for humanitarian values" (Institute of Race Relations, 2017). Since the report was produced, incidences of state attacks on humanitarians have increased. This book details elsewhere (see UK Flashpoint) the case of disproportionate charges brought against the Stansted 15, where the submission of evidence of their well-documented concern for the safety of those being returned on a deportation flight was not allowed as defence grounds by the court. In France, Cedric Herrou, an olive grower from the La Roya border region, was fined and handed a four-month suspended sentence for helping some 200 migrants illegally cross the border from Italy, but the judgment was overturned in December 2018 by France's highest appeals court, which ruled that people cannot be prosecuted for helping migrants in distress, citing France's emblem principle of solidarity or fraternity. However, the "Briançon 7" case, discussed in Chapter 9 of this book, had a different result, with the volunteers found guilty even though they were protecting vulnerable migrants – people travelling unguided in Alpine temperatures of –10°C – from attacks by far-right groups from outside the region (Nordstrom, 2018).

Independent rescue ships continue be forced into a cat-and-mouse game with authorities. As of April 2020, the case of Sarah Mardini and Séan Binder, volunteers on an Emergency Response Centre International (ERCI) rescue mission that brought a migrant boat to safety on Lesvos in 2018 (discussed in Chapters 2 and 9 of this book), is still outstanding, and is now supported by an Amnesty International campaign, in which Amnesty urges the Greek Government to not only drop the charges against them but also to "Publicly acknowledge the legitimacy of humanitarian work which supports refugee and migrant rights" (Amnesty International, 2020).

The rescue vessel *Sea-Watch 3* was detained for six months following the June 2019 arrest of its captain, Carola Rackete, for docking the ship at Lampedusa with 53 rescued asylum seekers. Rackete was arrested, then freed, then subjected to further investigation by Italian authorities for possible criminal activities in relation to undocumented migration. If convicted, she would have faced up to 15 years in prison. In January 2020, the Italian Supreme Court of Cassation finally ruled that Rackete should never have been arrested. After her release the council of the City of Paris announced that Rackete and co-captain Pia Klempt would be given the Grand Vermeil Medal, the city's highest honour, for saving lives at sea. Both refused it. Klempt wrote:

> You want to award me a medal because our crews 'work to rescue migrants from difficult conditions on a daily basis'. At the same time your police steal blankets from people you force to live on the streets while you suppress protests and criminalise people who defend the rights of migrants and asylum seekers.
>
> (Crellin, 2019)

Sea-Watch also had to fight an appeal in the Italian civil court against the illegal seizure of the ship. In the words of Johannes Bayer, Head of Mission on board *Sea-Watch 3*:

> Hundreds of people have drowned while the *Sea-Watch 3* was unfairly held in port by Italian authorities. But now, we are finally able to set sail for our next rescue mission. We will never stop assisting people in distress in the Mediterranean, even despite the political games played all around us and the obstacles thrown at us.
>
> (Sea-Watch, 2019)

The number of independent rescue vessels has grown in the last two years, despite the threats they face of being denied docking and their crews being arrested for assisting migrants. The *Poseidon*, a boat recently purchased by the Alliance United4Rescue and Sea-Watch in January 2020, had to be acquired by covert bidding process. The Sea-Watch website proudly announced "The hashtag of the alliance #WirSchickenEinSchiff [We send a ship] is to become reality this spring and the *Poseidon* will soon be saving lives in the Mediterranean". Tragically, the sea-rescues, like aid at camps and borders, are also being hit by coronavirus restrictions. Arturo Centore, a regular Sea-Watch volunteer, sent this bleak update in April 2020.

> Ship *Alan Kurdi* from the NGO Sea Eye. They want to start a mission soon despite the general trend of other NGOs' decisions but it is not easy. On standby off the coast of Malta.

Ship *Mare Liberum* in Lesvos, in port. Getting ready for operations but on standby due to Greece/Turkey crisis, and now the Covid-19 crisis.

Ship *Mare Jonio* from Mediterranea NGO, standby and operations suspended. Moored in Licata, Sicily.

Ship *Open Arms*: standby and operations suspended, moored in Spain.

Ship *Life Line*: operations suspended, moored in Malta.

Ship *Juventa* from Jugend Rettet: still confiscated, in port in Sicily.

Ship *Louise Michel* from Solidarity at Sea: due to start the first mission but all on standby/suspended, ship is in a "secret" location in France.

Ship *Ocean Viking* from Médecins Sans Frontières: operations suspended, ship in Marseille.

The work of the independent rescue ships is already extremely challenging: to buy and prepare these ships to make them compliant and fit for rescue, the constant battle to have them recognised under state flags, the direct attacks from Frontex and the Libyan Coastguard vessels, the dangerous rescue process itself and the dire prospect of then not being allowed to dock at any port, or face jail for doing so. Now on top of this, the sea-rescues, as well as people working on land, must factor in the COVID-19 pandemic and protect the safety of refugees and volunteers alike. But they will not give up and will find a way to balance safety with rescue, as they always must.

Now the charred ruin of Moria camp in Lesvos has become, like the Alan Kurdi image five years before it, a potent symbol of everything that is wrong with Europe's policy. Journalist Iannis-Orestis Papadimitriou writing for Novaramedia (2020), described it as "...the most visible symbol of the hard-line stance European countries have taken on migrants since 2016, where Europe's ideals – solidarity, human rights, a haven for victims of war and violence – dissolve in a tangle of bureaucracy, indifference and lack of political will – or more simply, some variation of hell". The volunteer groups are already fighting back, not only with fundraising and emergency care, but in political and governmental arenas to demand new policies and enlightened change. I hope this book provides them with more ammunition for this struggle.

In the current pandemic, many countries each week at a specified time collectively applauded emergency workers and others who are currently supporting our society. Let us also for once applaud the invisible grassroots army described in this book, that has done so much and remains a beacon of commitment and hope in challenging times. Whatever the activist volunteers collectively can or cannot achieve to turn the tide of closed borders and xenophobia in the coming months and years; to re-set the compass towards fair and legal humanitarian values; to explore and embody new forms of action and solidarity – whatever we can or cannot achieve, at least we did not turn our faces away, but looked straight at the ugliness and pain, and continued to walk forward.

I will end with the optimistic words of **Mahmoud Ri**, himself a victim of the war in Syria, who became a volunteer in Lesvos and Athens.

> During my time as a volunteer, one of the greatest experiences was to see how people from different countries, backgrounds and cultures were able to communicate despite the language barrier, by sharing the same hope and the belief that together we can manage any situation. My aim will always be to help those in need. I always aspire to bigger projects to help more people and provide them with the resources they need to help themselves. I think the key to supporting refugees is to help them back onto their own feet. It is most important to believe in them and their ideas. Their experiences and knowledge is crucial to building a support system for them. The only difference between you and us is merely the passport you are holding.

References

Action for Education (2020) "Europe Must Act Now for the Immediate Decongestion of the Aegean Islands", Change.org, 2 March. www.change.org/p/as-covid-19-spreads-europe-must-act-now-for-the-immediate-decongestion-of-the-aegean-islands?signed=true.

Amnesty International (2020) "Demand the Charges against Sarah and Seán are Dropped". www.amnesty.org/en/get-involved/take-action/w4r-2019-greece-sean-binder-and-sarah-mardini/.

Brzozowski, A. (2020) "EU Foreign Ministers Promise More Humanitarian Aid to Syria", Euractiv, 6 March. www.euractiv.com/section/global-europe/news/eu-foreign-ministers-promise-more-humanitarian-aid-to-syria/.

Crellin, F. (2019) "Captain of Migrant Rescue Vessel Refuses Honour from Paris", Euronews, 9 December. www.euronews.com/2019/08/21/captain-of-migrant-rescue-vessel-refuses-honour-from-paris.

Ekathimerini (2020) "Uncertainty and Division on an Aegean Island", 13 March. www.ekathimerini.com/250589/interactive/ekathimerini/special-report/uncertainty-and-division-on-an-aegean-island.

Human Rights Watch (2020) "Greece's Moria Camp Fire: What's Next?" 12 Sept 2020. www.hrw.org/news/2020/09/12/greeces-moria-camp-fire-whats-next

Institute of Race Relations (2017) "EU Member States, in Criminalising Humanitarians, are Feeding Europe's Far Right", 11 November. www.irr.org.uk/news/eu-member-states-in-criminalising-humanitarians-are-feeding-europes-far-right/.

Médicins Sans Frontières (MSF) (2020) "EU Must Address Migration Emergency as Greek Islands Reach Breaking Point", 4 March. www.msf.org/eu-must-address-migration-emergency-greek-islands.

Nordstrom, L. (2018) " 'The Alps Have Always Protected People', Says Frenchman Convicted of Helping Migrants", France24, 6 December. www.france24.com/en/20181216-france-alps-migrants-mountains-activists-convicted-winter-deaths-far-right-protests-refugee.

Papadimitriou. Y.O. (2020) "The Road to Moria: how Greece's Refugee Disaster Became Business as Usual Novaramedia", 12 September 2020. https://novaramedia.com/2020/09/12/the-road-to-moria-how-greeces-refugee-disaster-became-business-as-usual/.

Tondo, L. (2020) "Bosnia Crams Thousands of Migrants into Tent Camp to 'Halt Covid-19 Spread' ", *The Guardian*, 27 March. www.theguardian.com/global-development/2020/mar/27/bosnia-crams-thousands-of-migrants-into-tent-camp-to-halt-covid-19-spread.

Reliefweb (2020) "Greece Aegean Islands Weekly Snapshot: 24 February–1 March 2020", 3 March. https://reliefweb.int/report/greece/greece-aegean-islands-weekly-snapshot-24-february-01-march-2020.

Sea-Watch (2019) "Sea-Watch Starts First Rescue Mission under German Flag after Six Months of Blockade", 30 December. https://sea-watch.org/en/sea-watch-starts-rescue-mission-after-six-months-of-blockade/.

UNHCR (2020) "UNHCR Statement on the Situation at the Turkey–EU Border", 2 March. www.unhcr.org/news/press/2020/3/5e5d08ad4/unhcr-statement-situation-turkey-eu-border.html.

Dedication

Anna Campbell was a British feminist and activist from Lewes in Sussex who went on to live in Bristol. Always an activist, she volunteered in the Calais Jungle in its early days with Bristol colleagues, where she was a fervent campaigner against the use of CRS (French riot police) violence against camp residents, especially children.

In 2017, appalled by General Assad's attacks on the Kurds in Syria, she volunteered with the Kurdish Women's Protection Units there. She was the first British woman to die fighting for the Kurdish forces in Rojava, northern Syria.

In response to her death, her friends and protesters from the Bristol Kurdish Solidarity Network (BKSN) blocked the offices of BAE Systems in Bristol, who activists accuse of having supplied Turkey with weapons which have been used against civilians in northern Syria.

Her death, and my witnessing of the severe stress illnesses of several friends and colleagues working as long-term volunteers in Europe, were what motivated me to begin this book.

The collection is dedicated to her memory, and to all volunteers, and our new arrivals, in solidarity.

Glossary of Proper Names

Brexit   Common term for the UK's departure from the EU.

CRS   Compagnies Républicaines de Sécurité, the armed reserve of the French National Police.

Dublin Regulation   An EU regulation that determines which member state is responsible for responding to applications for asylum from those already within the European Union. Its basic principle is that applications should be made in the first port of entry. In theory, it allows minors to proceed to have their asylum case heard in any EU state where they have close family members.

Dubs Amendment   Section 67 of the UK Immigration Act 2016, named after its proposer, Lord Alf Dubs, which required the government to make arrangements "as soon as possible" to relocate and support a specified number of unaccompanied refugee children from Europe.

EASO   European Asylum Support Office.

ECCHR   European Centre for Constitutional and Human Rights.

ECHR   European Convention on Human Rights.

ECRE   European Council on Refugees and Exiles

ERCI   Emergency Response Centre International.

ESTIA   Emergency Support to Integration and Accommodation – a UNHCR-sponsored scheme in Greece to provide additional accommodation for asylum seekers.

EU   European Union – an economic and political organisation of 27 member states in Europe.

EU–Turkey deal   A 2016 statement of co-operation between the EU and the Turkish Government to control the crossing of asylum seekers from Turkey to the Greek islands. It provided that anyone arriving irregularly to the Greek islands could be returned to Turkey. In exchange, EU member states would pay Eur. 6 billion to Turkey, and accept one Syrian refugee from Turkey for every Syrian returned from the islands.

Eur.   Currency used by many of the European Union countries (the Euro).

Frontex   The name of the European Border and Coast Guard Agency – an EU agency based in Warsaw, Poland, which supervises border control of the European Schengen area in co-ordination with the border authorities and coastguards of member states.

GLAN   Global Legal Action Network

Home Office   The UK ministry of interior affairs.

Hotspot policy   Developed by the European Commission to assist EU member states at key locations – Hotspots – near external EU borders where large numbers of asylum seekers gathered. Hotspots were provided with operational support to aid registration, identification, fingerprinting and debriefing of asylum seekers, and to activate return operations.

IMO   International Maritime Organisation.

INGO   International non-governmental organisation.

IOM   International Organisation for Migration.

IRR   Institute of Race Relations.

Italy–Libya deal   The 2017 agreement between Italy and Libya under which the Libyan Coastguard stops migrant boats at sea and sends their passengers back to the North African country. The deal was widely criticised as returnees are likely to face torture and abuse.

JCORE   Jewish Council for Racial Equality.

MASI   Movement of Asylum Seekers in Ireland.

MSF   Médecins Sans Frontières.

NGO   Non-governmental organisation.

Operation Mare Nostrum   A naval and air operation established in the Mediterranean by the Italian Government in 2013 to tackle the increasing numbers of boat arrivals and the many shipwrecks off the island of Lampedusa. During its operation at least 150,000 migrants arrived safely to Europe. Italy was unable to bear the continued cost of the mission and it was superseded in 2014 by Frontex's Operation Triton.

Operation Triton A maritime border security operation in the Mediterranean established in 2014 by Frontex, the EU's border security agency, to replace Operation Mare Nostrum. It involved voluntary contributions from 15 other European nations, both EU member states and non-members. It has been widely criticised for prioritising security issues over carrying out rescues, with the IOM reporting that deaths at sea rose ninefold compared with during Operation Mare Nostrum.

PTSD Post-traumatic stress disorder – a type of anxiety disorder triggered by traumatic events in a person's life such as the real or threatened risk of death, severe injury or assault.

Pushback A set of state measures where refugees and migrants are forced back over a border – generally immediately after they have crossed it – without consideration of their individual circumstances and without any possibility to apply for asylum. According to the ECCHR, pushbacks violate, among other laws, the prohibition on collective expulsions stipulated in the European Convention on Human Rights.

SAR Search and rescue – the search for and provision of aid to people who are in distress or imminent danger.

Schengen area An area of free movement between 26 European countries, mostly but not exclusively EU member states, that have abolished passport and border control at their borders.

SRR Search-and-Rescue Region.

Stansted 15 A group of 15 UK activists who in 2017 staged a peaceful protest at Stansted Airport to draw attention to the forced removal of refugees whose cases had not been fully heard. The case became notorious after their charge was raised from a minor infraction to one carrying a 25-year jail sentence.

UASC Unaccompanied asylum seeking child or children.

UNHCR United Nations High Commissioner for Refugees.

UNICEF United Nations International Children's Emergency Fund.

Vicarious trauma Anxiety disorder caused by repeated exposure to the trauma of others.

Visegrád Group A cultural and political alliance between the Czech Republic, Hungary, Poland and Slovakia.

Appendix: Full List of Testimony Contributors

Thanks to everyone who sent in their testimonies. Each one of them has informed the observations, arguments and commentary, and added to the significance of this collection. In the print version of this book, many are quoted at length. In the subsequent online version, all will be presented more fully than space allows here. Thank you.

Abdulaziz Almashi
Ahmad Al-Rashid
Ahmad Hanifa
Aidan Pettitt
Alex Holmes
Ali Reid
Amber Bauer
Angela Prusa
Angelo Lo Maglio
Anne-Marie Brennan
Annie Gavrilescu
Anonymous
Anton Zhyzhyn
Ariel Ricker
Arturo Centore
Asif Rahimi
Barbara Held
Bartolomeo Maggiore
Becky Dell
Benoit Alavoine
Ben Margolis
Benedict O'Boyle

Boomer Callaghan
Brendan Woodhouse
Caoimhe Butterly
Caroline Cottet
Catarina Oliveira de Paulo
Catherine Bailey
Catherine Peyron
Cecilie Thorsen
Christina Hansen
Claire Earl
Claire Millot
Clare Struthers
Claudine Brancart
Cornelia Durkhauser
Cornelia Tiez
Dan Dowling
Dan Ellis
Danica Jurisic
Darla Eno
David Rey
Dillon Savala
Dirty Girls of Lesvos

Dylan Longman
Elaine Lawson
Eleni Melirrytou
Emanuele Cardella
Eve Machado
Francesco Tripoli
Francois Flennert
Gaelle Gormley
Giacomo Sferlazzo
Glenys Newton
Heather Clarke
Herts Welcomes Refugees
Heulwen Dickinson
Holly Kal-Weiss
Ian Shaw
India Nunan
Isabel Rey Sastre
Ingrid Kragh Swang
Isis Aurora
Jack Sapoch
Janie Mac
Jay Bignose Green
Jean-Francois Marguerin
Jean-Noel Fessy
Jess Coulson
Jess Egan
Joost Poppe Jan Rentema
Katharina Wuropulos
Katina Avanti
Kay Pinto
Kesha Niya
Kester Ratcliff
Kristina Quintano
Laila Ben Abbou
Latifa
Laurence De Donder
Laurent Picheron
Leah-Rose Thomas
Libby Freeman
Lira Marko

Liz Davis
Lorena Fornasir
Luke Hodgkin
Maddie Harris
Mahmoud Ri
Majida Alaskary
Marcia Corrao
Maria McCloskey
Maria Pisani
Marianne Robertsen
Mark Seymour
Marta Lodola
Marta Pezzati
Martin Lahme
Martin Tipping
Mauro Chiarabba
Megan Newmark
Meghan McIver
Mehdi Kassou
Melanie Strickland
Merel Graeve
Merlin Koetz
Michael D'Arata
Michelle Wright
Mirko Orlando
Muriel Fallon
Nadine Algeier
Negia Milian
Nidzara Ahmetasevic
Nils-Uwe Kettner
Paul Hutchings
Pepi Lourantou
Peter Rendell
Phil Kerton
Phoenix
Phosphoros Theatre
Pitsmoor To Calais
Polly Martin
Pru Waldorf
"Puffi To The Rescue" Volunteers

Rachel Mantell
Rando Wagner
Rawad Ajameah
Rebeca Ferrin Castro
Renke Pieter Meuwese
Riaz Ahmad
Robin Adlem
Rojo Red
Ros Ereira
Ruhi Loren Akhtar
Saef Haroun
Safia Laouail
Saleh Harifue
Sally Kinkaid
Sam Styan
Sandra Uselli
Sara Nathan
Sara Roberts
Sarah Berry

Sarah Fenby-Dixon
Sarah Story
Shaffira Gayatri
Shakir
Sheilagh Guthrie
Shernaz Dinshaw
Simon de Bruxelles
Simona Bonardi
Sophie Besse
Sue "Gladys" Partridge
Sumita Shah
Suzanne Harrington
Sylvie Vicente
Tamsin Gatewood
Tess Berry-Hart
Viv Dale
Welcome Cinema Kids
Yanick Bonichon
Zora O'Neill

We would also like to thank Pru Waldorf and WeAreOne collective for providing the interview with Katina Avanti.

BENDS

Bends are knots that are used to join
two ropes together.

ASHLEY'S BEND

THIS USEFUL KNOT works well in a wide variety of materials, even bungee cords. Because it will accept pulling in any of the four directions of its ends, it can be used to form the center of a four-way tie-down. Credited to Clifford Ashley, this knot is very dependable and can be untied even after heavy loading.

HOW TO TIE:

Form a loop at the end of one rope, preparing to tie it into an Overhand Knot (see page 96).

Take the end of the second rope and feed it up through the first loop, making its own loop to be tied into an Overhand Knot.

Complete the two Overhand Knots, taking care to feed the working ends through each other's loop as well as their own.

Pull all ends to tighten.

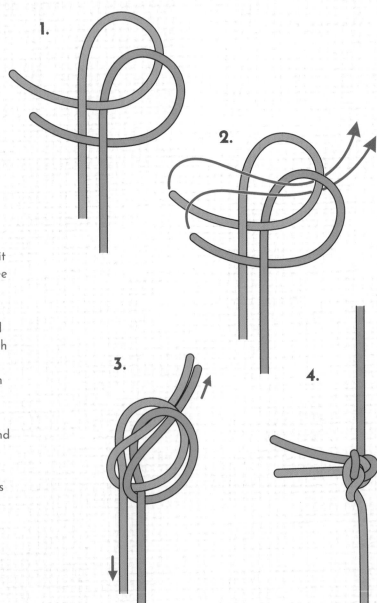

1.

2.

3.

4.

CARRICK BEND

THE CARRICK BEND is an excellent knot to join two ropes, particularly large-diameter ropes and hawsers. It draws up tight under a load and, although it may lose its symmetrical shape, remains secure. The tag ends may be seized to the standing lines for added security.

HOW TO TIE:

Form an underhand loop with the larger rope and lay the loop on top of and across the working end of the second rope.

Remember the sequence: over, under, over, under, over. Pass the working end of the second rope around the first loop and itself following the sequence.

The ends come out of opposite sides of the knot. The knot loses its beautiful symmetry when tightened.

The ends should be seized to the standing parts if the ropes are large.

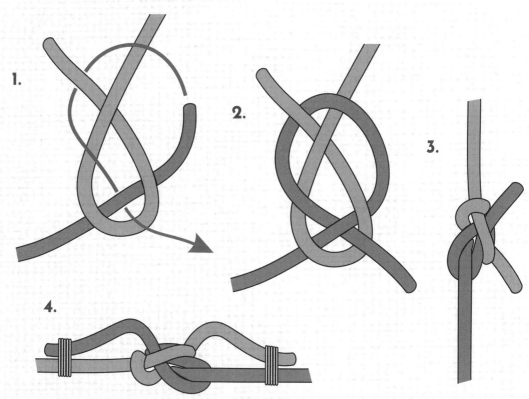

1.

2.

3.

4.

FISHERMAN'S KNOT

THE FISHERMAN'S KNOT is used to quickly tie two ropes of equal diameter together. The knot weakens the ropes with which it is tied and should not be trusted in critical applications, particularly when using slippery synthetic rope.

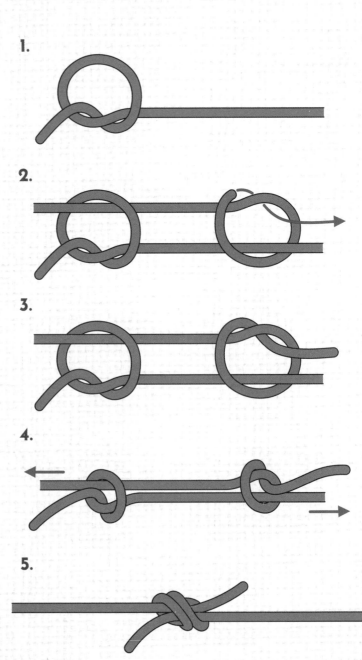

1.

2.

3.

4.

5.

HOW TO TIE:

Tie a loose Overhand Knot (see page 96) with the working end of one rope around the other rope.

Repeat with the working end of the second rope around the first rope and tighten both knots.

Pull the standing parts of both ropes in opposite directions to seat the two knots together.

DOUBLE FISHERMAN'S KNOT

THIS KNOT securely ties two ropes together or can be used to fasten the ends of a rope or cord to make a closed loop or sling. Rarely used in fishing, the Double Fisherman's Knot is essentially two knots that slide together when tightened to form the finished knot. Mountain climbers also use just one side of the knot to tie a backup knot with the working end of the primary knot. When tied in short lengths of rope, this knot can secure rope "grab handles" to kayaks and canoes.

BENDS

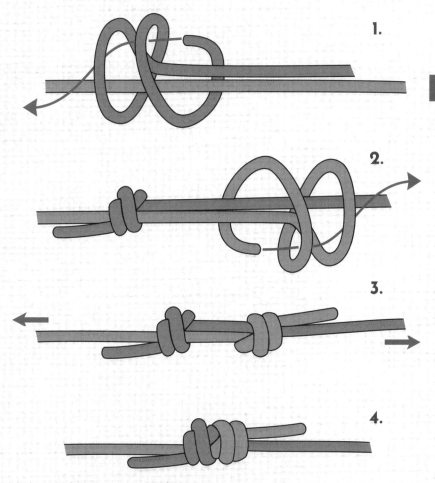

1.

2.

3.

4.

HOW TO TIE:

Lay the ends of two lines parallel to each other.

Coil the free end of one rope twice around the second rope, working it back over itself and the other rope, and pass it back through the inside of the coils.

Repeat with second rope in the opposite direction. Pull the working ends to tighten the knots, and then pull the standing lines to slide the knots together.

FLEMISH BEND

ALSO CALLED THE FIGURE EIGHT BEND, it is one of the strongest, safest, and simplest ways to join two ropes. It is also is relatively easy to undo in modern synthetic ropes and can be readily checked. For utmost security, the working ends can be tied into backup knots.

BENDS

1.

2.

HOW TO TIE:

Form the first rope into a loosely tied figure-eight shape.

3.

Following the working end of the first rope where it exits the knot, feed the working end of the second rope around the knot, parallel at all times with the first so that it exits alongside the standing part of the first rope.

4.

Tighten the knot a bit at a time by alternately pulling on the working ends and standing lines, making sure it is symmetrical and neat.

5.

HARNESS BEND

ALSO KNOWN AS A PARCEL BEND, the Harness Bend is useful for tying two lines together when the line has to remain under tension. The name is thought to come from saddling a horse with the knot, tightening as the horse exhales to take up the slack.

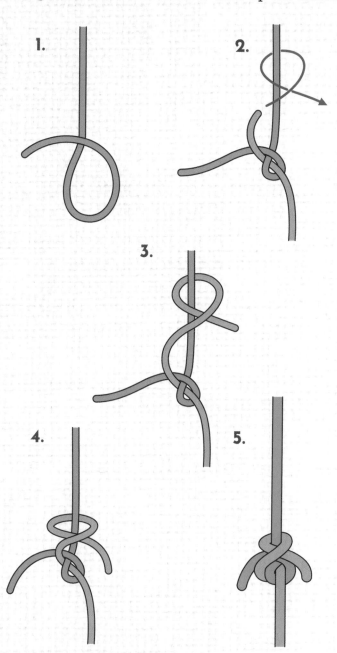

1.

2.

3.

4.

5.

HOW TO TIE:

Make an overhand loop with the rope being held under tension.

Feed the working end of the second rope through the loop and over the working end of the first rope. Pinch the loop down, maintaining tension on that line.

Tie a Half Hitch (see page 54) with the second line around the standing part of the first line, and tighten it down onto the first loop.

RACKING BEND

SERVING a somewhat similar purpose as a single or double Sheet Bend (see page 17), but more secure, the Racking Bend is used for joining ropes of different diameter. The term *racking* refers to the weaving that binds the two sides of the bight of the larger rope together. The thinner line may then be used to throw a thick line such as a hawser from ship to shore or ship to ship.

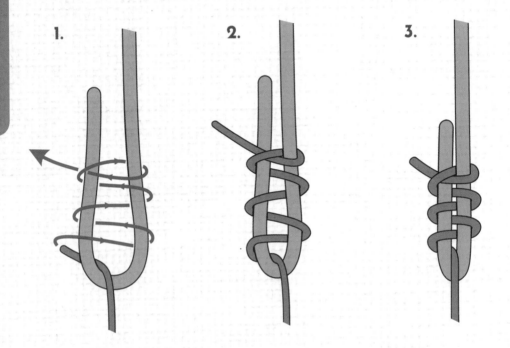

1.   2.   3.

HOW TO TIE:

Form a bight at the end of the heavy rope. Pass the thinner line into the bight and begin weaving the line in a figure-eight fashion around and through the loop, working from the bottom up.

Make at least four complete turns around the bight. It helps to pull each one tight as it is completed.

Finish the knot with a Half Hitch (see page 54) or two around both parts of the heavy rope.

BENDS

SHEET BEND

THE SHEET BEND is useful even when rope sizes and materials differ greatly. Suitable for most non-critical applications, it is important that the tag ends of both ropes of this bend be on the same side of the finished knot. For more security, use the doubled version (called the Double Sheet Bend), which is the same as the single version but with an extra coil around the standing loop. The Sheet Bend also goes by the name of Weaver's Knot when employed in yarn or twine. It is commonly used for joining threads that have parted in a loom or as a permanent knot tied in small material.

BENDS

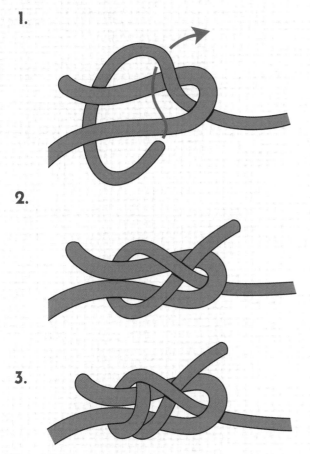

1.

2.

3.

Double Sheet Bend

HOW TO TIE:

Form a bight in the end of one rope. Pass the free end of the rope to be joined through the bight, around both parts of the first rope and back under itself.

Pull all four ends to tighten.

(Optional) Two wraps around both parts of the first rope make a Double Sheet Bend.

SLIPPED SHEET BEND

THE SLIPPED VERSION OF THE SHEET BEND (see page 17) allows you to quickly untie the two ropes, even when the ropes are under a load, by pulling on the working end. This can be a very useful feature, but at the same time, for this reason, **never use this knot in critical applications!**

1.

HOW TO TIE:

Form a bight in the end of one rope. Pass the free end of the rope to be joined through the bight, around both parts of the first rope and back under itself.

Before tightening the knot, slip the working end back under the standing part right next to where it exited the knot and pull the standing ends of both ropes to tighten.

2.

3.

4.

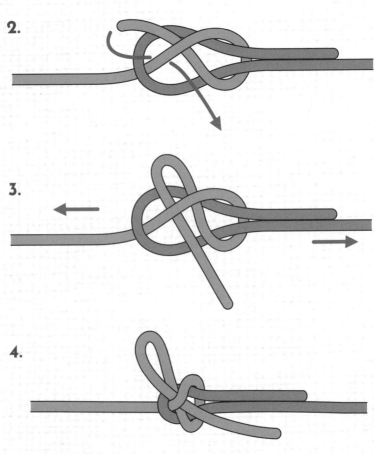

Pull to release.

TUCKED SHEET BEND

ALSO KNOWN AS THE ONE-WAY SHEET BEND, this
knot can be useful when joining ropes that might be hauled over an
object or edge. With this method of tying, the working ends point
the same way as the rope being hauled and are thus less likely to
snag on an obstruction.

1.

2.

HOW TO TIE:

Form a bight in the
end of one rope. Pass
the free end of the
rope to be joined
through the bight,
around both parts
of the first rope and
back under itself. Do
not tighten.

3.

Next, pass the
working end back
over the standing
part and then
through the loop
formed by the first
part of the Sheet
Bend.

4.

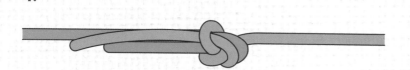

Pull all ends tight.

WATER KNOT

ALSO KNOWN AS THE RING BEND, the Water Knot is the best knot to use when tying knots in webbing. It can be used to make slings and grab handles. Climbers most commonly use the Water Knot for tying webbing into closed loops or slings. Make sure that the tails exit from different sides of the knot and that they are at least three inches long to be inspected for any slippage of the knot.

BENDS

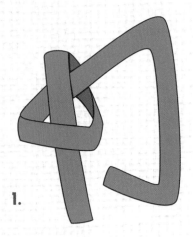

1.

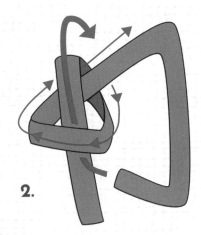

2.

HOW TO TIE:

Tie a loose, open Overhand Knot (see page 96) in one end of the webbing strap.

Feed the other end of the strap into the exit point of the first Overhand Knot and follow in the reverse direction the exact path of the first Overhand Knot. Pull tight.

Make sure the free ends are a couple inches long to visually inspect for slippage during use.

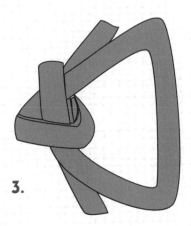

3.

ZEPPELIN BEND

THE ZEPPELIN BEND, also known as the Rosendahl Bend, is an easy knot to tie, very secure, and jam proof. The Zeppelin Bend gets its name from its association with the great lighter-than-air ships, or dirigibles, of the 1920s, which were commonly called "zeppelins," in honor of Count Ferdinand von Zeppelin, an early pioneer and advocate of the behemoths. Of immense size and filled with hydrogen or helium, zeppelins had a huge lifting capacity, which also meant the knots used to tie them to the ground had to be completely secure and take massive strain yet remain easy to untie when wanted. The knot commonly used that fulfilled all of these requirements was the Zeppelin Bend.

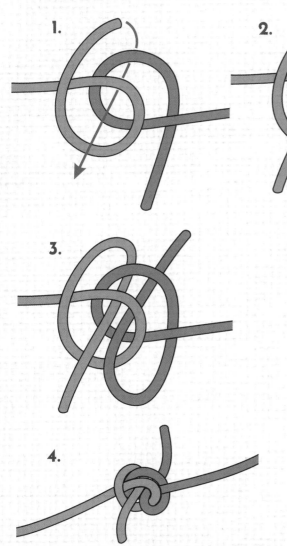

1.

2.

3.

4.

HOW TO TIE:

An easy way to start the Zeppelin Bend is to form a "6" with one rope with the working end over (an "overhand loop") and form a "9" with the other rope with the working line under (an "underhand loop"). Then lay the 6 partially over the 9.

Take the working end of the 6 and pass it through the opening of the 9 and the 6.

Repeat with the end of the 9 in the opposite direction—through the opening of the 6 and through the opening of the 9.

Pull ends tight.

LOOP KNOTS

These knots are for making a loop with a rope, and there are many different types of loops you can choose from. Loops can be tied at the end of a rope or in the middle, or even tied to result in multiple loops. There are fixed or locked loops, and there are sliding loops. Loops can be tied around an object such as a bar, ring, or post (thus serving the function of another type of knot called a "hitch") or tied first and then thrown over an object, or used in other ways.

A fixed loop does not slide and holds its shape, such as the ever-useful and popular Bowline. A sliding loop, such as the Running Bowline, makes a loop that is adjustable in size. When you need a fixed loop in the middle of a line, the Alpine Butterfly will best serve that purpose.

Note: Never play literal "hangman" with any sliding loop or noose knot. They can kill.

Loop knots enable any piece of rope to gain a multitude of useful functions. Indeed, loop knots are probably the most advantageous type of knot that can be tied.

ALPINE BUTTERFLY KNOT

THE ALPINE BUTTERFLY KNOT, also known simply as the Butterfly Knot due to the form it takes while tying, forms a secure loop in the middle of a rope. It will accommodate a load in any of three directions independently or together. Mountain climbers use the Alpine Butterfly for tying in the middle climber when traveling three to a rope. Also useful for making non-slip loops in the middle of a rope to attach carabiners to provide points of attachment for other lines, the Alpine Butterfly is essential in canoe rescue work. The knot can also be used to isolate a damaged section of a rope.

1.

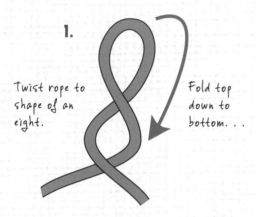

Twist rope to shape of an eight.

Fold top down to bottom. . .

2.

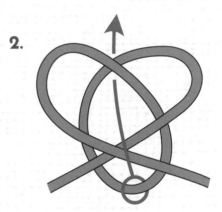

. . . then up and out through the lower opening in the eight.

HOW TO TIE:

Make a loop in the rope and twist it one full rotation into an eight shape.

Fold the top of the eight down around the bottom of the eight, creating the butterfly shape.

Now pull up and out through the center opening and pull tight.

3.

BOWLINE

ONE OF THE MOST USEFUL KNOTS you can know is the Bowline. The Bowline forms a secure loop that will not jam and is easy to tie and untie. The Bowline is most commonly used for forming a fixed loop, large or small, at the end of a line. Tried and tested over centuries, this knot is reliable, strong, and stable. Even after severe tension is applied, it is easy to untie. However, because it does untie so easily, it should not be trusted in a life or death situation, such as mountain climbing.

HOW TO TIE:

Lay the rope across your left hand with the free end hanging down. Form a small loop or "eye" in the line in your hand.

Bring the free end up to and pass through the eye from the underside. Or, by the popular mnemonic for the Bowline, the rabbit comes out of the hole.

Wrap the line around the standing line and back down through the loop. Or, go around the tree and back down the hole.

Tighten the knot by pulling on the free end while holding the standing line.

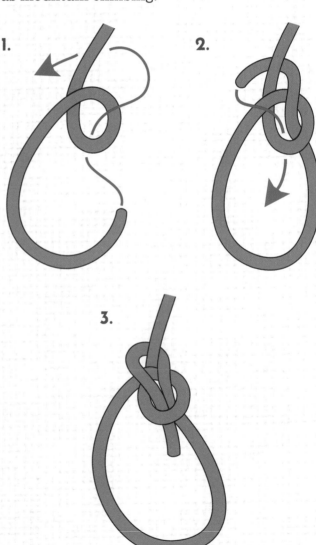

1.

2.

3.

BOWLINE ON A BIGHT

THIS KNOT FORMS A BOWLINE or a secure loop in the middle of a line. It is also useful to provide two loops in the end of a line or when you want a non-slip loop but a free end is not handy. This knot can be used as a sling, seat, or bosun's chair in an emergency rescue situation. The two loops can be worked to different sizes if needed.

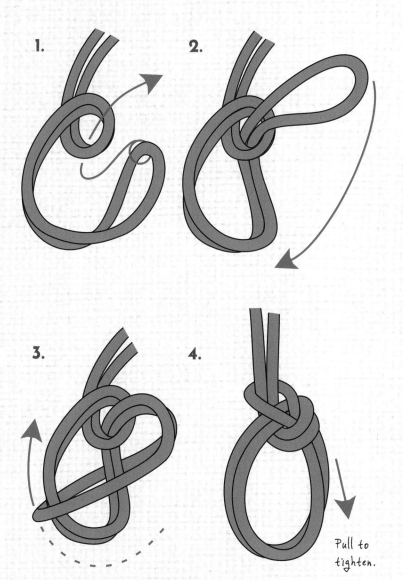

1.

2.

3.

4.

Pull to
tighten.

HOW TO TIE:

Double a section of line and form a loop or "eye" in the double line.

Pass the free end up through the eye, forming a double loop below the eye.

Spread open the free end and bring it down to the bottom of the double loop.

Pass over the double loop and continue up to the top of the eye.

Seat the knot by pulling on the double loop while holding the standing lines.

DOUBLE BOWLINE

THE DOUBLE BOWLINE is also known as the Round-Turn Bowline and often mistaken for the very similar Water Bowline. It is basically a classic Bowline Knot with two overhand loops. The added strength and robustness of the Double Bowline makes it well suited for rough activities and heavy-duty rigging.

The title of this knot can be misleading, as it does not result in a Bowline with two loops, such as a Spanish Bowline (see page 37). Clifford Ashley says of this knot, "It holds the Bowline together in such a way as to lessen the danger of it capsizing, which is liable to occur when a single Bowline is carelessly drawn up."

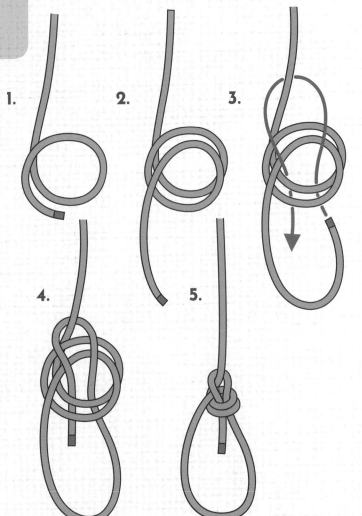

1.

2.

3.

4.

5.

Lay the rope across your left hand with the free end hanging down. Form a small loop in the line in your hand.

Repeat to form a second small loop on top of the first.

Bring the free end up to and pass through both small loops from the underside.

Wrap the line around the standing line and back down through the two loops.

Tighten the knot by pulling on free end while holding standing line.

FARMER'S LOOP

THE FARMER'S LOOP is very useful when you want to make a loop in a rope away from an end of the rope. The loop can serve as a handhold or place to attach tools and other objects. You can also tie Farmer's Loops to take up slack in a line or isolate a bad section of a rope. It is easy to untie and is tied in the bight—that is, without the ends. It is similar in that way to the Alpine Butterfly (see page 23).

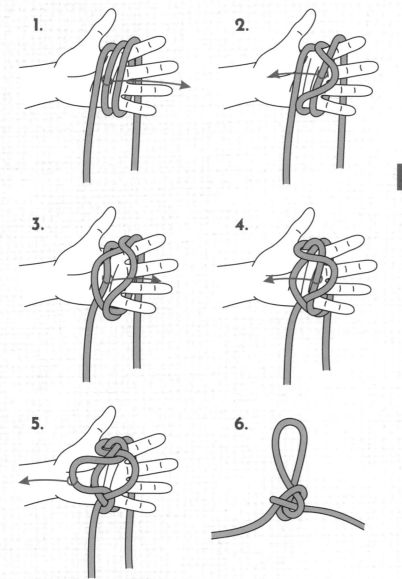

1.
2.
3.
4.
5.
6.

HOW TO TIE:

Start by wrapping the rope around your palm three times, letting the ends hang.

Next, lift the middle loop over the right loop (which becomes the middle).

In the same manner, pull the new middle loop over the left loop.

Again, middle over right.

Now middle over left, and pull out a little further to make the final loop of desired size.

FIGURE EIGHT FOLLOW THROUGH

THE FIGURE EIGHT FOLLOW THROUGH, sometimes called the Figure Eight Loop, is one of the strongest knots. It forms a secure, non-slip loop at the end of a rope, and this is the most widely used tie-in knot by mountain climbers. The reason is that it is strong, secure, and easy to visually inspect. Climbers often further secure it by tying a backup knot with the working end.

The knot can also be tied with a doubled line at the end of a rope (follow step 1, but don't come back through the bottom loop). The doubled line version is faster, but it cannot be used if tying into a fixed object, so it is good to learn to tie this knot with the follow-through steps. A single Figure Eight also makes a good stopper knot at the end of a rope (see step 1 with the single line, but don't come back up through the bottom loop–just tighten the knot). Consider using a Backup Knot (see page 87) tied with the working end for extra security.

HOW TO TIE:

Tie a single figure eight in the rope two feet from its end. Pass the free end through any tie-in point if desired.

Retrace the original eight with the free end, leaving a loop at the bottom of the desired size.

Pull all four strands of rope to cinch down the knot.

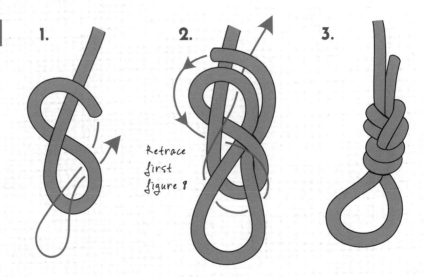

1.

2. Retrace first figure 8

3.

This knot can also be tied by tying a Figure Eight knot with doubled line at the end of a rope (Fig. 1. with doubled line and don't come back through bottom loop.) It is faster but cannot be used if tying onto a fixed object. A single Figure Eight also makes a good "Stopped Knot" at the end of a rope.

HONDA KNOT

THE HONDA KNOT is what all cowboys use to form their lasso or lariat. The Honda Knot creates the most nearly-perfect circle of any knot. Its round shape, especially when tied in stiff rope, helps it slide freely along the rope it is tied around, which is what makes it good for a lariat.

	L O O P K N O T S

HOW TO TIE:

Tie a loose Overhand Knot (see page 96) near the end of a rope.

Now tie a tight Overhand Knot at the very end of the rope for a stopper and pass the end back through one side of the Overhand Knot.

Tighten down the loose Overhand Knot and pull the stopper knot up tight. That is the circular Honda Knot.

Now feed the main line through the Honda to form a lasso of any size.

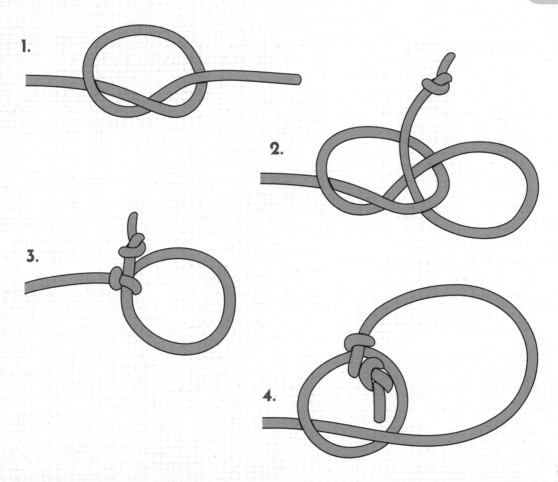

1.

2.

3.

4.

OVERHAND LOOP KNOT

THE OVERHAND LOOP KNOT provides a quick and easy method of forming a fixed loop at the end of a line or anywhere in a rope by forming a bight at the desired location. The knot jams tight and is difficult to untie after it has been pulled tight.

1.

2.

HOW TO TIE:

Double the end of a rope or form a bight anywhere on a line. Tie an Overhand Knot (see page 96) with the doubled rope of the loop that was formed.

Adjust the loop before tightening to make it as small or large as desired.

3.

4.

PORTUGUESE BOWLINE

THIS KNOT forms a Bowline with two adjustable loops. It is best to adjust the loops to fit the task at hand before tightening the knot. However, even after tightening, rope can be pulled from one loop to the other.

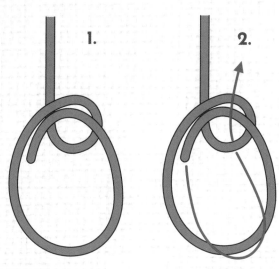

HOW TO TIE:

Cross the working end of the rope over the standing part to form a small overhand loop. Pinch and hold the lines together.

Now make a large loop of the desired size and cross its working end over the small loop. Pinch and hold in place.

Moving in the same direction, bring the working end around to make the second loop, but this time feed the working end up through the small loop from behind.

Pass the working end around the backside of the standing line and back down into the small loop.

Pull the standing line and the working end to tighten the knot.

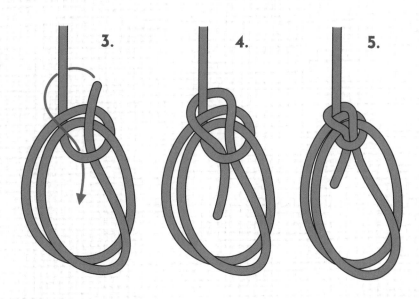

RUNNING BOWLINE

THE RUNNING BOWLINE produces a noose or sliding loop. It is made with a Bowline tied around its own standing line. This can be useful for retrieving objects by throwing the open loop around them, and the loop will tighten down on the object as the standing line is pulled tight. The knot does not bind against the standing line and can be easily undone.

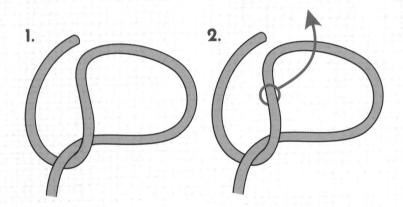

HOW TO TIE:

Double the end of a rope and wrap the tag end over and then under the standing line and up to the side of the new loop created.

Make a small loop on the topside of the original loop by twisting the line over itself.

Feed the tag end through the small loop.

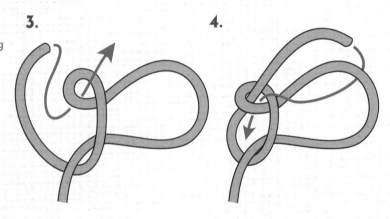

Wrap the tag end once around the topside of the large loop and back down through the small loop.

Pull tag end tight, creating fixed loop that the main line can slip through.

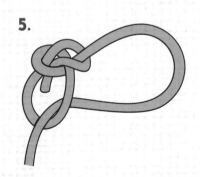

SCAFFOLD KNOT

THE SCAFFOLD KNOT makes a sturdy loop that slides like a noose to fit snugly around a bar, rail, or other object. It may be protected against wear due to chafing by inserting a lining called a thimble, creating what sailors refer to as a "hard eye." Thimbles come in a range of sizes and are obtainable from boat and yacht chandlers. The Scaffold Knot is similar to what is called the Poacher's Knot, but it has an extra turn. It is sometimes called a Triple Overhand Noose, whereas the Poacher's is sometimes called a Double, or Two-Turn, Scaffold. Another simple sliding noose can be made with the Slip Knot (see page 34).

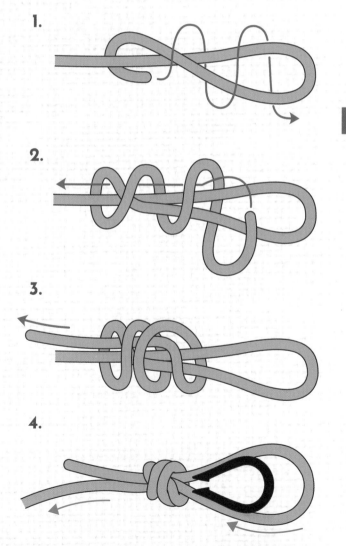

1.

2.

3.

4.

(see page 34)

HOW TO TIE:

Form a loop at the end of the rope and wrap the working end around both the standing line and the working end. Note that if you are securing the loop to an object such as a post, do so at the beginning of tying the knot by forming the loop around the object.

Work back toward the loop, making three loose wraps around both lines. After the third turn, feed the working end back through the openings of the wraps, running parallel to the standing line.

Pull the knot tight by the working end. If you are making a hard eye with a thimble, insert the thimble and tighten the loop down onto it by pulling on the standing line.

SLIP KNOT

THIS VERSION of a slip knot is very quick and easy to tie. It is technically a "slip noose" and is made using the fisherman's Uni Knot (see page 112) with just two or three turns. The Scaffold Knot (see page 33) is another slip knot that makes a noose (hence its name), and it's a good alternate to this simple slip knot.

HOW TO TIE:

Make a loop at the end of a line by doubling the line back onto itself.

Run the working end back toward the loop and lay it over the doubled lines.

Make two or three turns around the doubled lines and through the new loop created with the working end.

Hold the loop and pull the working end to tighten the knot.

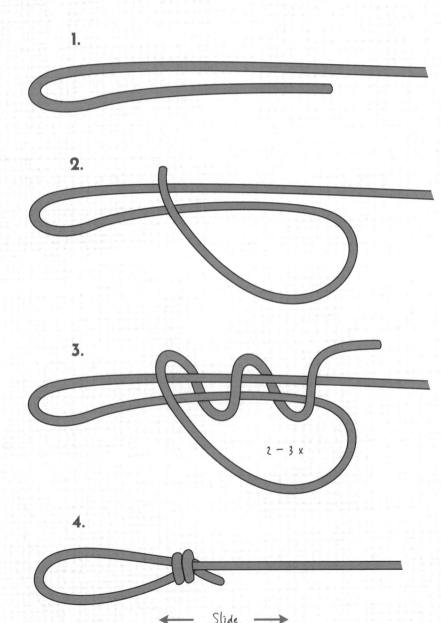

1.

2.

3.

2 – 3 x

4.

← Slide →

SLIPPED OVERHAND KNOT

THE SLIPPED OVERHAND KNOT forms a simple slip knot or "draw-loop" that tightens under a load on the working end. The knot is easily undone by pulling on the working end when the loop is empty. Note that if you pull a bight of the long standing line through the loop (instead of a bight of the working end), you have the **Overhand Noose** or Simple Noose, useful as a starter knot for tying up parcels and to form the mid-rope loop of a Trucker's Hitch (see page 72).

1.

2.

3.

4.

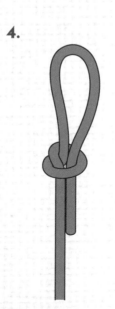

HOW TO TIE:

Form a crossed loop in the line.

Pass a bight of line from the working end up through the loop.

Pull on the standing line while holding the loop to tighten.

Adjust the loop size with the working end.

SLIPPERY EIGHT LOOP

THE SLIPPERY EIGHT LOOP is attributed to Dave Poston, and he named it the HFP Slippery Eight in honor of his father, who originally introduced him to knots. It has surprising security—though not for critical applications such as person support—for an adjustable loop.

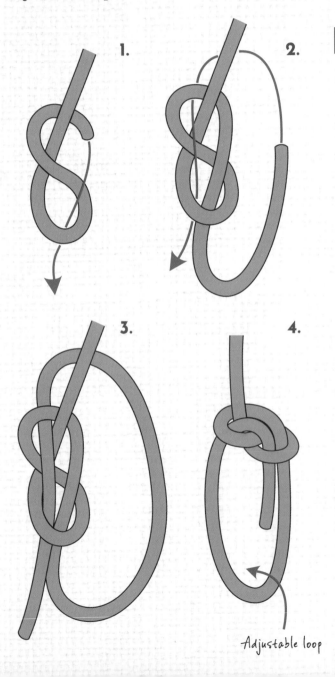

1.

2.

3.

4.

Adjustable loop

HOW TO TIE:

Begin by tying a figure eight at the end of a rope with enough extra line to make a loop of the desired size.

Leave the eight loose and bring the working end back to the top of the knot.

Pass behind the standing line and feed the end through the eight as illustrated, up and out through the top loop and down into the lower loop of the eight.

Pull the knot tight.

To adjust the loop, just bring the working end up to make a straight line through the knot. Pull the loop side to make the loop larger or the working end to make it smaller. Set the working end back to its 90-degree angle from the knot to secure the loop.

SPANISH BOWLINE

THE SPANISH BOWLINE is a double loop knot, which can be useful for light rescue work. However, care should be taken that the load on the loops is equal to avoid slipping because the loops are directly connected to each other. To avoid having the loops slip, the knot must be drawn up very tight. Also note that the loops can be adjusted to different sizes before the knot is fully tightened down.

1.

2.

3.

4.

HOW TO TIE:

Make a loop in the end of a rope and tuck the loop under the parallel lines. Make a twist in each of the two sides of the loop, twisting in toward the center with the outer part of the loops.

Now take the left loop and insert it in through the right loop, moving first under then over the ropes it is crossing.

Grasp the new small lower loop by each side and pull those sides through the loops above.

Once you have the ropes part way through, pull the two vertical ropes to help tighten down the knot.

5.

6.

Adjust the loops and pull everything to be very tight.

YOSEMITE BOWLINE

A YOSEMITE BOWLINE can be a very secure loop knot when tied correctly. It is a version of the Bowline (see page 24) with the free end wrapped around one leg of the loop and tucked back through the knot, commonly known as a "Yosemite finish."

In addition to potentially being more secure than a standard bowline, the Yosemite variant is also easier to untie after a load. Some climbers prefer the advantages it offers over other knots and use the Yosemite Bowline as an alternative tie-in to the Figure Eight Follow Through (see page 28). They also use the Yosemite to secure heavy loads such as haul bags. But the Yosemite Finish requires very careful diligence in getting the knot right. If tied incorrectly, it is a disaster waiting to happen, and all its benefits are lost.

The downside to the Yosemite Bowline is that it is more difficult to visually inspect than the Figure Eight. It was a Yosemite Bowline that was believed to have been used by Lynn Hill in France, and failed, due most likely to being improperly tied or tightened, causing her to careen 70 feet to the base of the climb.

To gain the benefits of the Yosemite Finish, it must be tied carefully and correctly. Whether its benefits are worth the risk of tying incorrectly is debated among climbers. Be sure to practice the Yosemite Bowline and in particular the tightening of the knot many times before trusting it with your life.

HOW TO TIE:

First, tie a regular Bowline (see page 24) with a little longer working end.

Now wrap the tag end around the front of the loop and follow exactly the path of the standing line up through the top eye, finishing on the right side of the standing line as you look at the knot from the front.

The tightening of this knot must be done exactly right to set it in the right order! To do that, take the standing part and the bottom of the loop and pull tight. This tightens the original Bowline, which must be done first. Then tug on the working end to tighten the Yosemite Finish.

If you were to tighten the knot with the working end first, you would actually loosen the original bowline, and the knot is something completely different and is not a secure knot at all!

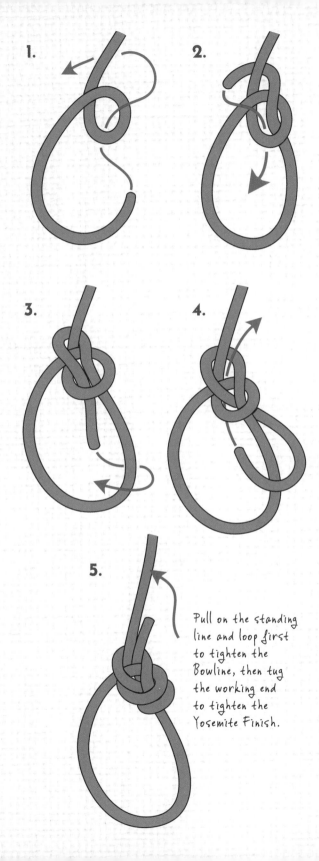

1.

2.

3.

4.

5.

Pull on the standing line and loop first to tighten the Bowline, then tug the working end to tighten the Yosemite Finish.

3

HITCHES

Hitches are knots used to tie a rope to an object or even to another rope. Hitches are essential knots for climbers, arborists, sailors, and anyone needing to tie a rope to something!

ANCHOR BEND

THE ANCHOR BEND or Anchor Hitch is the knot generally used to fasten a line to an anchor. The free end should be secured with seizing to the standing line for a permanent, secure knot. One side of a Double Fisherman's Knot (see page 13) can be used as a backup knot to secure the Anchor Bend.

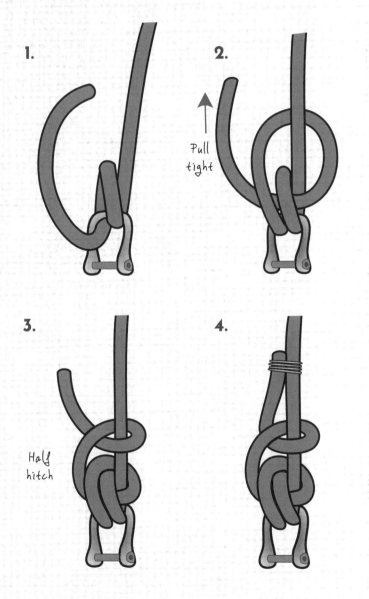

1.

Pull tight

2.

3.

Half hitch

4.

HOW TO TIE:

Make two turns around the shackle, leaving turns open.

Pass the free end behind the standing line and feed the free end through the two turns and pull tight.

Now tie a Half Hitch (see page 54) around the standing line and pull tight.

Seize the free end or tie the knot with a long tag end and tie a backup knot such as one half of a Double Fisherman's (see page 13) with the tag end around the standing line.

41

AUTOBLOCK KNOT

THE AUTOBLOCK KNOT is a quick and easy-to-tie friction hitch commonly used to back up rappels. The autoblock is often made using either a factory-made or temporary loop which grips in either direction and can slide freely over the rope during a controlled descent. If a sudden drop occurs, the knot will jam in the rappel device, which will stop the descent. Always use an autoblock knot on the rope as a safety backup when rappelling.

HOW TO TIE:

Wrap your Autoblock Hitch cord four or five times around the rappel ropes. Use a thin cord such as 5mm or 6mm static cordage. Use up most of the cord on the wraps. The more wraps that you use, the more friction generated.

Then clip both ends of the cord into the locking carabiner on your harness leg loop. Lock the carabiner so the cord can't come undone. Finally, arrange all the wraps so they're neat and not crossed.

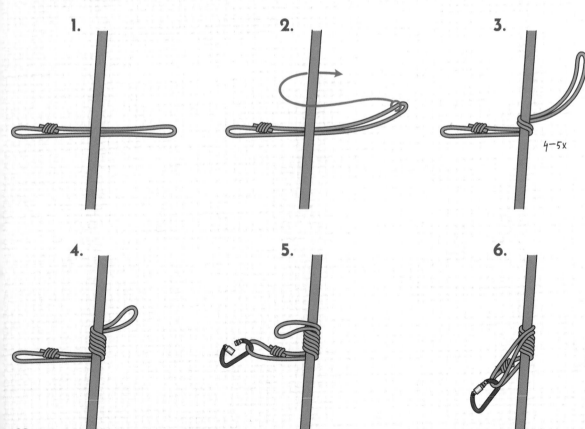

1.

2.

3.

4—5x

4.

5.

6.

BACHMANN KNOT

THE BACHMANN KNOT is a popular friction hitch with climbers and arborists. It can be tied with either a factory-made or temporary strop (rope or webbing made into a large loop) or loop that is no more than half the diameter of the vertical rope.

The Bachmann Knot requires the use of a round, cross-section carabiner for friction. Grabbing hold of the carabiner while unweighting the load on the hitch will release the friction and allow the hitch to slide freely and thus to be moved up or down appropriately. To remove the Bachmann hitch, just unclip the top loop, hold onto the carabiner, and pull the cord free. Use a locking carabiner for the Bachmann, because you'll be grabbing it to move the hitch. When using a self-constructed strop or loop made with a Double Fisherman's Knot (see page 13), make sure not to wrap the section of your loop with the knot in the wrapping, which can decrease the knot's effectiveness.

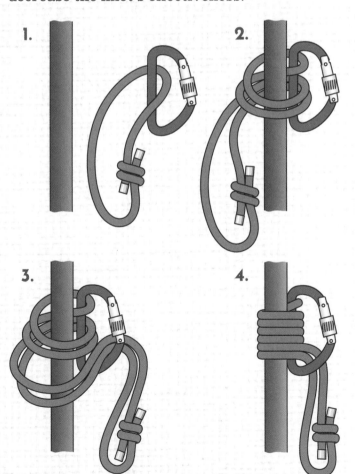

1.

2.

3.

4.

HOW TO TIE:

Construct a loop of rope (not more than $1/2$ the diameter of the vertical rope) or use a pre-made strop. Clip the loop into the carabiner.

Hold the carabiner against the vertical rope and wrap the loop around the rope, passing through the carabiner.

Repeat, wrapping around the vertical rope and through the carabiner again. An additional wrap can be made if there is room in the carabiner.

Apply load to the end of the loop to bind the knot in place with friction.

BARREL HITCH

THE BARREL HITCH is used to lift a barrel in its upright position effectively. The other method of hoisting a barrel (with closed ends) is the Barrel Sling (see page 45), which does so with the barrel on its side. The Barrel Hitch can be used to hoist a container that has liquid in it with the top open. Be sure that the rope that encircles the barrel (or other container) is not only above the center of gravity so that it doesn't tip but also far enough below the top lip so that it doesn't slip off.

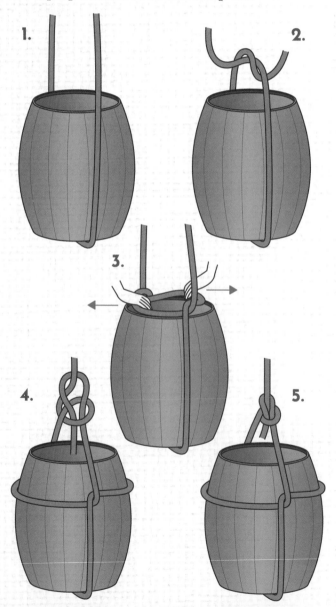

1.

2.

3.

4.

5.

HOW TO TIE:

Stand the barrel on the lifting rope.

Tie the ends of the rope together by passing one end over and then around the other across the top of the barrel. This creates what is called a Half Knot.

Spread the Half Knot until it opens wide enough to slip over the sides of the barrel. Adjust the ropes to embrace the top third of the barrel.

Tie a Bowline Knot (see page 24) with the ends of the rope to join together and lift.

BARREL SLING

THE BARREL SLING is used as a method of hoisting a sealed barrel or a drum on its side using a strop (rope or webbing made into a large loop). Make sure the strop is splayed out toward the ends of the barrel before hoisting.

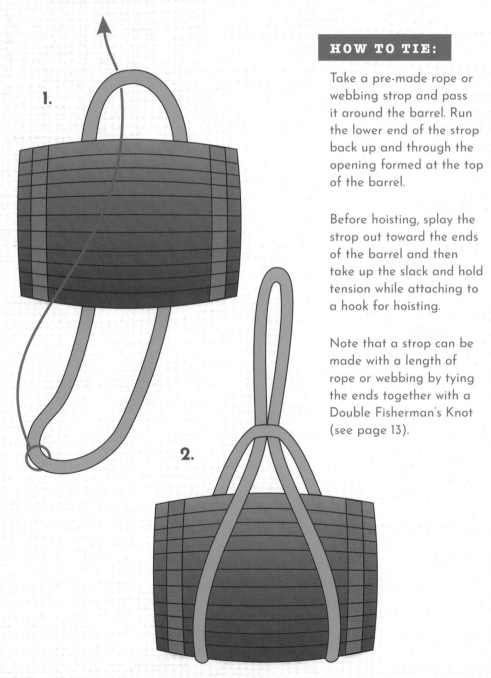

HOW TO TIE:

Take a pre-made rope or webbing strop and pass it around the barrel. Run the lower end of the strop back up and through the opening formed at the top of the barrel.

Before hoisting, splay the strop out toward the ends of the barrel and then take up the slack and hold tension while attaching to a hook for hoisting.

Note that a strop can be made with a length of rope or webbing by tying the ends together with a Double Fisherman's Knot (see page 13).

BLAKE'S HITCH

BLAKE'S HITCH is a friction knot popular with arborists for ascending and descending on ropes. The name derives from Jason Blake, who is credited with describing the knot to other arborists in 1994. This hitch has the advantage that it can be tied with the end of a rope instead of requiring a loop. A stopper knot such as the Figure Eight (see page 28) is recommended to be tied with the tag end after the knot is drawn up.

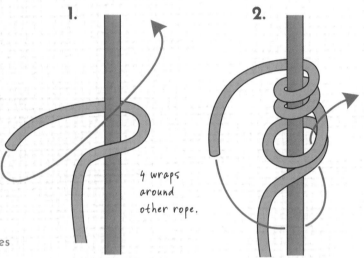

1.

2.

4 wraps around other rope.

HOW TO TIE:

Wrap the line four times around the other rope, working from bottom to top. Leave room in the second wrap to accommodate the working end of the rope.

Run the working end down to and over the standing line, behind the static rope, and out through the second wrap.

Tighten knot.

Finish with a stopper knot (like a Figure Eight) at the end of the line.

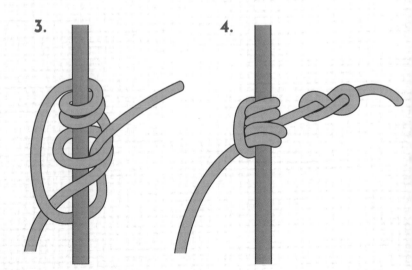

3.

4.

BUNTLINE HITCH

USE THE BUNTLINE HITCH to fasten items such as snaps and rings to rope or cord. It forms a small, neat, and very reliable knot. Simple and effective, the buntline hitch dates to the Age of Sail when it was used to secure buntline to the foot of the sails on square-rigged ships. The fact that the Buntline Hitch was the preferred knot speaks to its security and reliability.

Once set, repeated jerking tends to tighten it further rather than loosen it. It has gained in popularity in recent years due to its performance in slippery modern synthetic lines.

HOW TO TIE:

Pass the end of a line through the object being attached to the rope. Bring the free end up and cross over and then back under the standing line.

Bring the free end to the front of the knot, and you will now finish by tying a Half Hitch (see page 54) around the standing line.

Pull the knot tight and slide down onto the attached object.

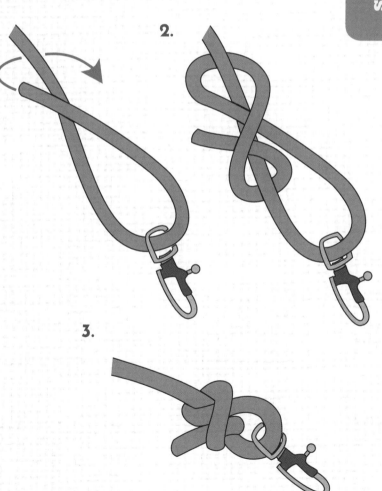

1.

2.

3.

CAT'S PAW

THIS IS THE BEST KNOT for attaching a sling to a hook for lifting loads.

1.

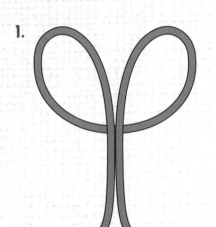

2.

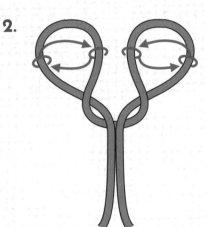

3.

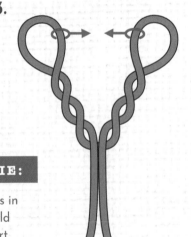

4.

HOW TO TIE:

Form two loops in a sling and hold them well apart.

Twist both for three full turns.

Bring together and slip them over a cargo hook.

CLEAT HITCH

THE CLEAT HITCH is a quick and easy method of tying a rope to a cleat on a dock or boat that is also easy to untie. Learn the Cleat Hitch especially if you own a boat. It is amazing how many boat owners do not know this easy and essential boating knot. Even if you don't own a boat, you will impress everyone if you tie this knot when handed a rope at the dock!

HOW TO TIE:

Take a turn around the base of the cleat, and then bring the line over the top of the cleat.

Wrap the line back under the arm of the cleat opposite the first turn, then back over the top of the cleat.

Wrap under the first arm a second time and then back over the top of the cleat. You have now made a figure eight pattern over and around the cleat. Now form an underhand loop and slip that loop over the arm of the cleat, which pins the free end under the last wrap.

Pull the free end tight and you have the neat, tidy, and secure Cleat Hitch.

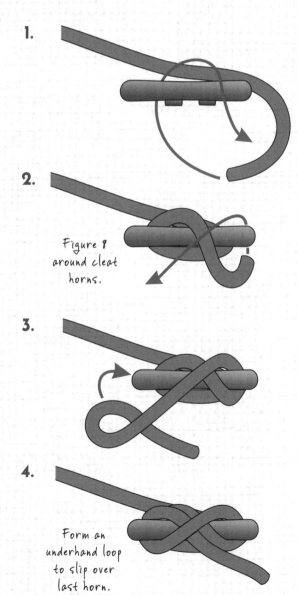

1.

2. Figure 8 around cleat horns.

3.

4. Form an underhand loop to slip over last horn.

CLOVE HITCH

THE CLOVE HITCH is a simple, all-purpose hitch that is easy to tie and untie. However, as a hitch it should be used with caution because it can slip or come undone if the object it is tied to rotates or if constant pressure is not maintained on the line.

A TOP-
20 KNOT
CARD

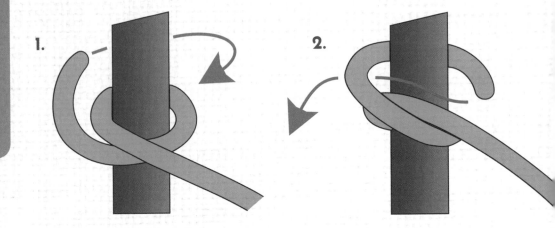

1.

2.

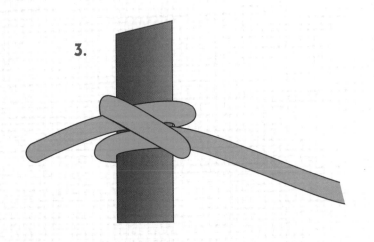

3.

HOW TO TIE:

Wrap the free end of a rope around a post.

Cross the rope over itself and around the post again.

Slip the working end under last wrap. Pull tight.

COW HITCH

THE COW HITCH is tied using the end of a rope and is also called the Lark's Head or Lanyard Hitch. It is used to secure a rope to a post or other object including another rope. It is similar to a Clove Hitch (see page 50) except that the second Half Hitch is in the opposite direction. It is about as reliable as a Clove Hitch, which is to say it should not be trusted in critical applications. When tied with a closed loop, such as when attaching luggage tags with a loop of cord, the same knot is called a Girth Hitch (see page 53).

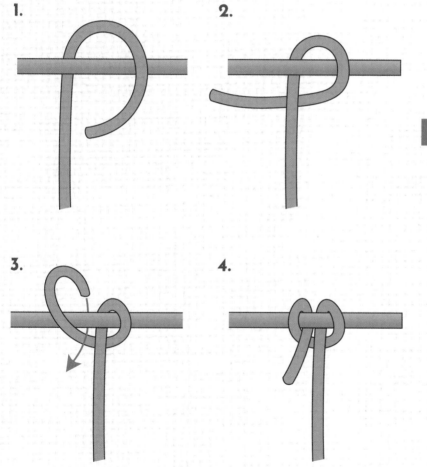

1.

2.

3.

4.

HOW TO TIE:

Wrap the end of the rope around the object from behind.

Cross the working end behind the standing line.

Wrap the working end around the object in the opposite direction as the first wrap (or Half Hitch) and feed through opening created by the second wrap.

Pull both ends to tighten the knot.

DISTEL HITCH

THE DISTEL HITCH is a very responsive friction knot, also
called a slide and grip knot, and popular with arborists. It tends not
to jam or slip when set and dressed correctly. The Distel will only
grip in one direction. If using a friction cord or lanyard without
pre-made loops on the ends, you can make your own and secure
them with one side of a Double Fisherman's Knot (see page 13)
around the cord.

HOW TO TIE:

Make four wraps
around main static
rope with a friction
cord with loops on the
ends.

After the fourth wrap,
bring the wrapping
tail down and make an
additional wrap at the
bottom of the other
wraps in the same
direction while tying a
Half Hitch (see page
54) by tucking the
tail under itself in the
front of the knot.

Join loops in front and
clip together with a
carabiner.

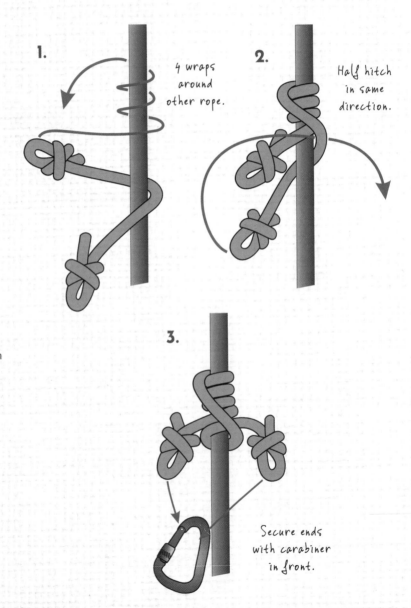

1.

4 wraps
around
other rope.

2.

Half hitch
in same
direction.

3.

Secure ends
with carabiner
in front.

GIRTH HITCH

THE GIRTH HITCH is a knot commonly tied to attach a sling or loop of webbing (although rope can also be used) to a harness, carabiner, rope or other fixed point. It is also the knot commonly used to attach luggage tags with a loop of cord. Other names for this knot are the Strap Knot and Ring Hitch. It is similar in structure to the Cow Hitch (see page 51) which is tied using the end of a rope as opposed to a closed loop.

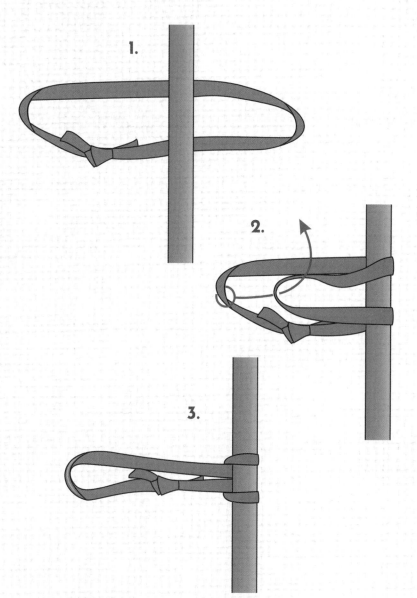

1.

2.

3.

Place the sling behind the object to which it is to be attached.

Wrap the right side loop over the object and feed the left side loop through the right side loop. Note: You may also feed the right side loop through the left side loop. Either loop can be fed through the other loop.

Pull the remaining loop away from object to tighten.

HALF HITCH

ALTHOUGH THE HALF HITCH is a knot in its own right, it is rarely used alone as it is unsafe by itself. The first Half Hitch is usually followed by a second. When tying the second half hitch, pass the rope the same way around as the first which then creates a Clove Hitch around the standing end. Two Half Hitches can be used to tie a rope to a tree, boat, or any object. It is often used in a supporting role, for example, to increase the security of a primary knot.

HITCHES

HOW TO TIE:

Pass the end of a rope around the object and tie an Overhand Knot (see page 96).

For the two Half Hitches, repeat with a second Overhand Knot in the same direction. If you were to reverse the direction of the second Half Hitch, it would simply result in a Cow Hitch around the standing end and be of similar stability.

Single Half Hitch

Two Half Hitches

HALYARD HITCH

THE HALYARD HITCH forms a very compact knot, which makes it a good choice for tying on a halyard, a shackle, or even a small ring. Once tightened down or put under load, the Halyard Hitch is nearly impossible to untie and will likely require being cut off if needed. A similar and effective knot is the Buntline Hitch (see page 47).

HOW TO TIE:

Pass the end of a rope through the shackle and make a turn around the standing line.

Make a second turn around the standing line below the first turn.

Bring the working end of the rope back up to the top of the knot and feed the end down through the two loops just created.

Pull the working end to tighten the knot, and then pull the standing line to seat the knot against the shackle.

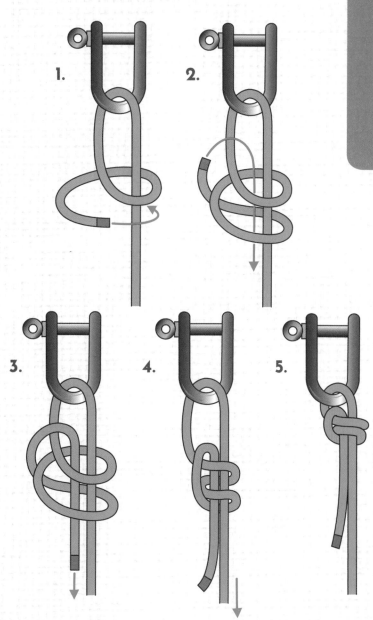

1.

2.

3.

4.

5.

HIGHWAYMAN'S HITCH

SIMILAR TO THE MOORING HITCH (see page 62), the Highwayman's Hitch can be used as a temporary mooring knot for a small boat or to tether an animal. The standing part of the rope takes the load while the working end is tied, but the knot can slip free with a tug on the working end. The Highwayman's Hitch is not a safe knot for any type of human load as it can be released or slip accidentally!

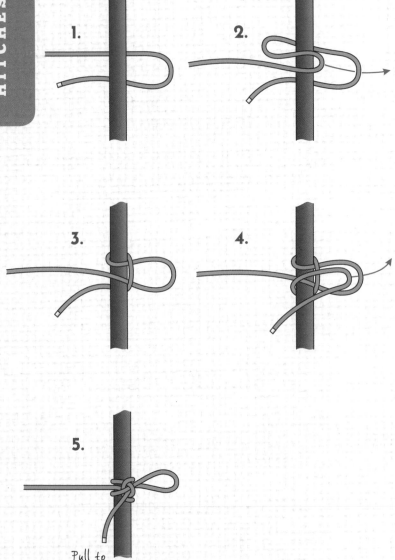

1.

2.

3.

4.

5.

Pull to release

HOW TO TIE:

Double the line to make the first bight in the rope, and place the bight behind a post or rail.

Make a second bight in the standing line and pass that bight through the first bight. Give a little pull on the working end to tighten down on the second bight and hold it in place.

Take the working line (which should be longer than it appears in the accompanying illustration) and make a third bight.

Pass the third bight through second and pull on the standing line to tighten the knot.

ICICLE HITCH

THE ICICLE HITCH is a good knot for connecting to a post when either hoisting the post vertically or dragging it in a direction parallel to the post. This hitch will hold its place even when holding a substantial load on a smooth surface and even grip a tapered post, hence its name.

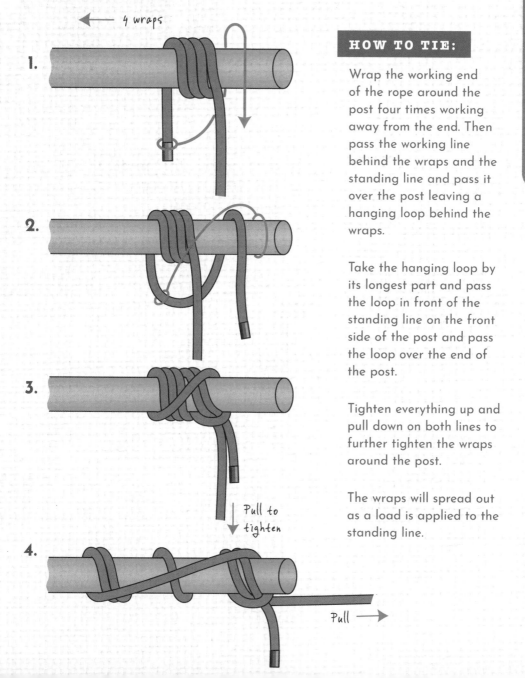

4 wraps

1.

2.

3.

Pull to tighten

4.

Pull

HOW TO TIE:

Wrap the working end of the rope around the post four times working away from the end. Then pass the working line behind the wraps and the standing line and pass it over the post leaving a hanging loop behind the wraps.

Take the hanging loop by its longest part and pass the loop in front of the standing line on the front side of the post and pass the loop over the end of the post.

Tighten everything up and pull down on both lines to further tighten the wraps around the post.

The wraps will spread out as a load is applied to the standing line.

KLEMHEIST

THE KLEMHEIST KNOT is tied by making a loop of cordage with line or rope that is no more than half the diameter of the main, static rope. Often referred to as a "Prusik Loop," it is made by joining the ends of a line with a Double Fisherman's Knot (see page 13). The resulting friction knot loop can then be tied into a Klemheist Knot and will slide up the rope but grips when subjected to a load. With no load applied, it can also slide down a line by gripping the knot itself.

HOW TO TIE:

Place a loop consisting of cordage no more than half the diameter of the main line behind the static line.

Make a wrap around the static line with the loop on the right.

Repeat two more times, working from bottom to top.

Feed the left hand loop through the loop on the right.

Pull the left-hand loop back over to the left side of the static line and pull down hard to set the knot.

Grasp the entire knot and slide up the static line. Load and grip the knot to the static line with weight on the loop.

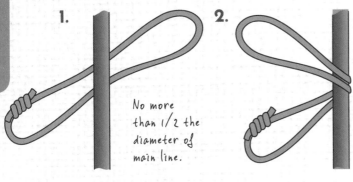

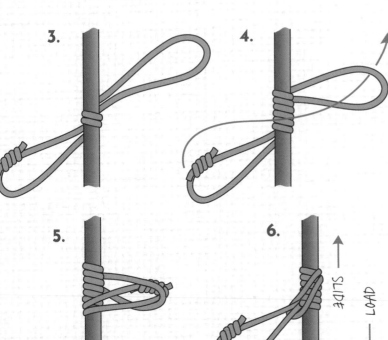

58

KNUTE HITCH

THE KNUTE HITCH is a knot used to attach a lanyard of paracord or other small-diameter cordage to an object such as a knife, marlinspike (a tool used in marine rope work), or other tool. Rigger Brion Toss is credited with naming the hitch after his favorite marlinspike of the same name, although the hitch is likely much older.

The lanyard line should be just small enough to fit doubled through the lanyard hole in the tool.

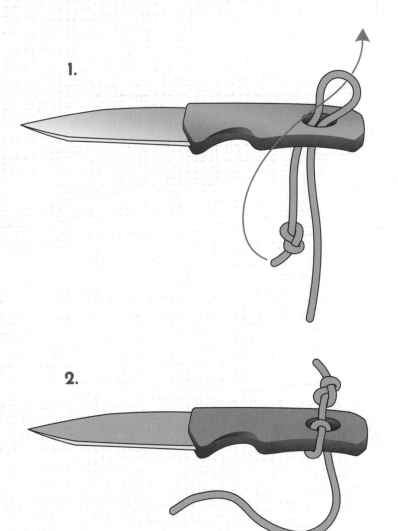

1.

2.

Tie a Figure Eight (see page 28) or another stopper knot in the end of the lanyard. Form a bight and pass the bight through the hole in the tool.

Pass the stopper knot through the bight and tighten the bight down by pulling on the standing line.

MIDSHIPMAN'S HITCH

THE MIDSHIPMAN'S HITCH is an excellent knot to create an adjustable loop at the end of a rope. The knot can be slid up and down the standing line to increase or decrease the size of the loop (and thus increase or decrease the length and/or tightness of the standing line with the loop around a fixed object such as a tree or tent stake). But when a load is applied, the knot holds securely.

The Midshipman's Hitch is similar to the Tautline Hitch (see page 69) but has one important difference and benefit. When tying the Midshipman's, the second wrap forms an intermediate awning hitch, which temporarily locks the knot and takes any strain on the rope while tying the final Half Hitch (see page 54). The completed Midshipman's Hitch is also more secure than the Tautline.

This knot is relatively easy to tie or untie under a load.

HOW TO TIE:

Pass the working end of a rope around an object such as a post or cleat.

Pass the working end around the standing line, creating the first Half Hitch.

Pass it around again, working back away from the object and tucked up tight to the first turn.

Pull tight. This forms an awning hitch that can take a load while the next step is tied.

Now make a Half Hitch in the same direction outside of the loop and around the standing line.

Pull the knot tight. The Midshipman's Hitch can now be slid on the standing line when there is no load and will hold tight when a load is applied.

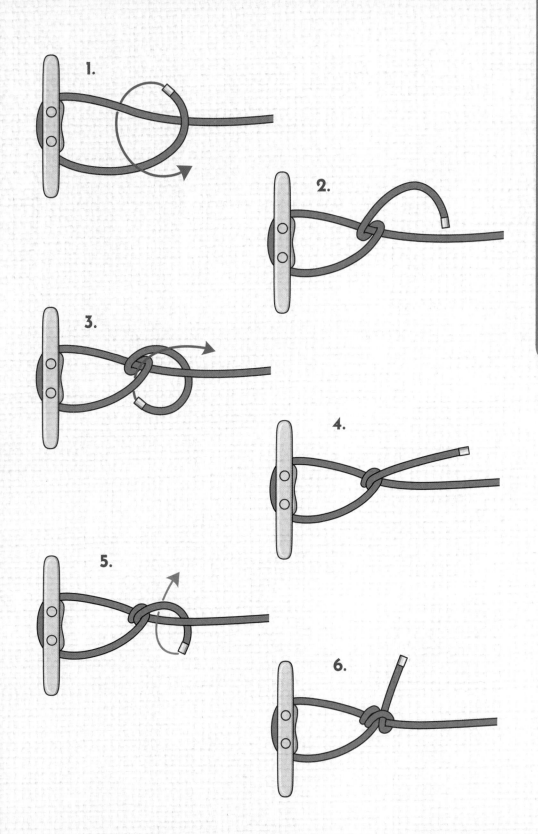

MOORING HITCH

THE MOORING HITCH is a good temporary knot that holds fast under a load yet can be released quickly with a tug on the free end. It can be tied up tight to an object or anywhere along the length of the rope, so you can reach and release it without getting off your horse or out of your boat.

The Slipped Buntline (see page 68) is another good quick-release knot.

A TOP-
20 KNOT
CARD

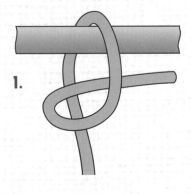

1.

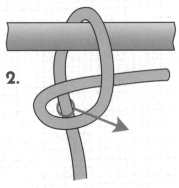

2.

HOW TO TIE:

Make a turn around a post and then form a loop with the working end exiting the loop on the inside (leave longer working end than illustrated).

Grasp the standing line and pull a section through your loop.

Take a section of the working end (but not the very end) and pull partway through the new loop.

Tighten the knot by pulling down on the standing line. Release the knot by pulling the working end.

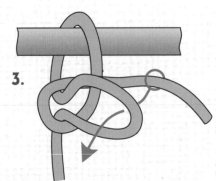

3.

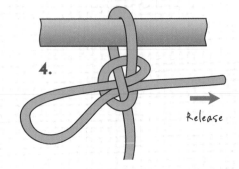

4.

Release

MUNTER HITCH

THE MUNTER HITCH provides a method for belaying and rappelling without a belay or rappel device or can be used on an anchor to lower or belay another. As such it is an important knot for climbers to know. It works best in large pear-shaped carabiners and should only be used with a locking carabiner. When belaying a leader with the Munter Hitch, be sure that the strand of rope carrying the load is next to the spine of the carabiner to obtain the maximum strength of the carabiner. There must always be at least one brakehand firmly in place on the brake strand of the rope to manage the friction provided by the hitch. Find a brake hand position that keeps the rope clear of the gate mechanism. This knot can cause kinks or twists in the rope. Practice this knot and be sure to set this knot up correctly, because someone's life is on the other end of the rope!

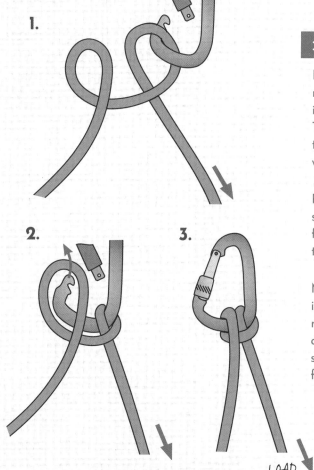

1.

2.

3.

LOAD

HOW TO TIE:

Make an overhand loop in the rope and slip a locking carabiner into the loop from the front. Tighten down the loop by holding the standing line and pulling the working end across standing line.

Form a second overhand loop and slip this loop into the carabiner from the backside of the loop. Pull tight and lock the carabiner.

Make sure the standing line, which is the strand carrying the load, is next to the spine of the carabiner and keep a firm hand on the brake strand of the rope to manage the friction provided by the hitch.

PILE HITCH KNOT

THE PILE HITCH KNOT is a simple knot that is used to attach a rope to a post or other object. When the end of the post is available, the knot can be tied with a loop in the rope without access to the end of the rope (as illustrated here).

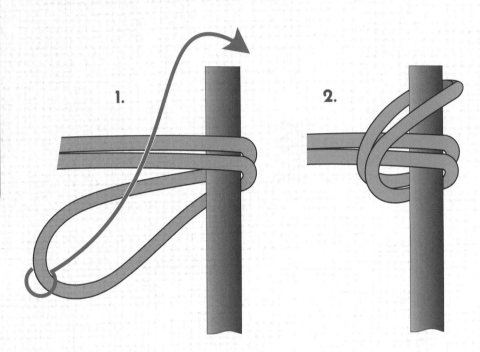

1.

2.

HOW TO TIE:

Double the end of a line into a loop and wrap around the post or object from front to back.

Cross over the standing lines and slide the open end of loop over the top of the post.

Pull tight.

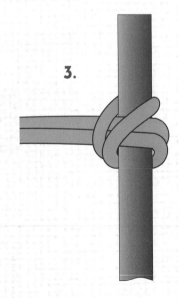

3.

PRUSIK HITCH

USE THE PRUSIK HITCH to secure a loop to a
tight line. It slides when not weighted along a tight
rope but jams solidly upon loading. Mountaineers
use this knot to form footholds to help them climb a
vertical rope. The loop needs to be made in rope or
cord that is at most half the diameter of the main
line. It is often referred to as a Prusik Loop.

HITCHES

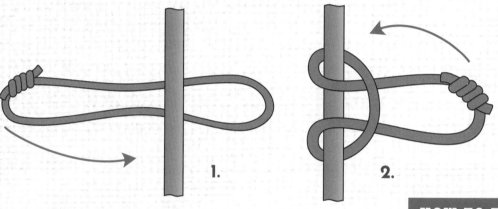

1.

2.

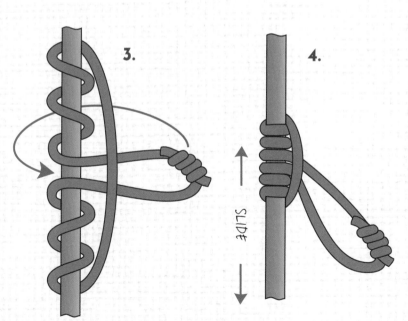

3.

4.

SLIDE

HOW TO TIE:

Make a sling of cordage
(no more than half the
diameter of the main
rope).

Tie a loose and open
Girth Hitch (see page
53) around the main
rope.

Pass the loop of the
sling back through the
center of the Girth Hitch
three or four more times.

Dress the knot so it is
nice and even, then load
with weight to make
sure it is set correctly.

ROLLING HITCH

THE ROLLING HITCH KNOT is a very secure and easy-to-tie method of fastening a rope to a post or another rope. The knot holds firmly in the direction of the standing line, which is pulled against the first two turns. The Rolling Hitch is similar to the Clove Hitch (see page 50) except that it is used when there is a lengthwise pull.

HITCHES

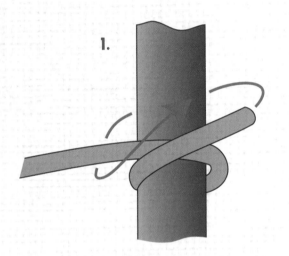

1.

HOW TO TIE:

Wrap the end of a line around an object and cross over the standing part. Repeat, crossing over the standing line a second time.

Wrap a third time around the object but wrap above the standing line so as to not cross over it.

Pass the free end under the last wrap and pull tight.

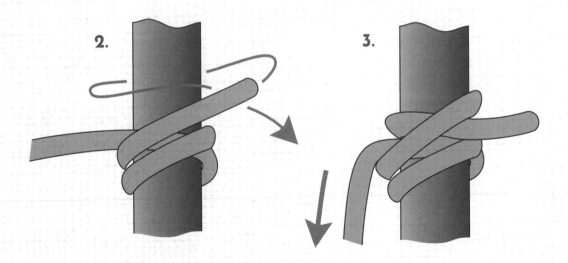

2.

3.

SCHWABISCH HITCH

THE SCHWABISCH (pronounced "sway-bish") Hitch holds securely. This arborist friction hitch was first documented by seven-time International Tree Climbing Champion Bernd Strasser of Germany. The cord that is used to wrap around the main static line is often referred to as a "spliced_eye or split-tail friction cord." This can be factory made with sewn or spliced loops at each end or hand tied with a pair of loops made with one side of a Double Fisherman's Knot at the ends. The Schwabisch slides and releases relatively easily after bearing a load, and it grips reliably upon loading.

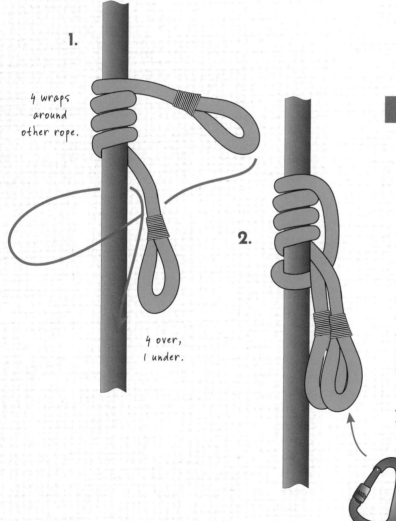

1.

4 wraps around other rope.

2.

4 over, 1 under.

HOW TO TIE:

Make four wraps around the main static rope with a hand-tied or sewn spliced-eye split-tail friction cord.

After the fourth wrap, bring the wrapping end down and make an additional wrap at bottom of other wraps in opposite direction while tying a Half Hitch (see page 54) around the other rope. This results in both tails exiting the knot together.

Join eyes in front and clip together with a carabiner.

SLIPPED BUNTLINE

THE SLIPPED BUNTLINE is a quick-release knot, similar to the Mooring Hitch (see page 62). It will hold fast under a load, yet it comes undone quickly with a firm pull on the free end.

(see page 62)

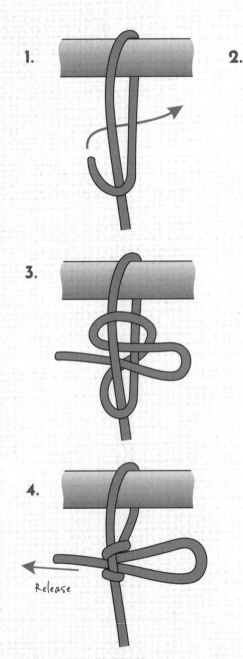

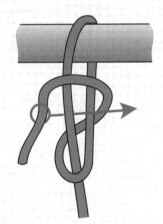

HOW TO TIE:

Wrap the working end around the object and run the end behind the loop just created.

Bring working end back to the front of the knot and grasp in the middle of working line.

Feed the bight just formed between the front and back lines of the original loop.

Carefully tighten the knot. To release the knot, pull on the tag end.

HITCHES

TAUTLINE HITCH

THIS KNOT CAN BE SLIPPED to tighten or loosen a line and then holds fast under a load. The Tautline Hitch is useful for lines that may need adjustment and is similar to the Rolling Hitch (see page 66) tied on the standing part of a tight line after it has been secured around an object. Campers like to use this knot to secure tent guy lines because the hitch slides freely yet jams under a load, making adjustments to the line easy.

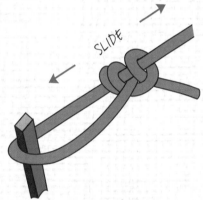

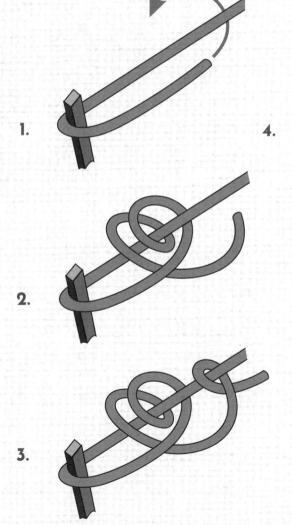

1.

2.

3.

4.

HOW TO TIE:

Make a turn around a post or other object several feet from the free end.

Wrap the free end twice around the standing line, working back toward the post.

Make one additional wrap around the standing line on the outside of the wraps just made.

Tighten the knot by pulling on the working end and slide it on the standing line to adjust tension.

69

TAUTLINE HITCH TO ROPE

THE TAUTLINE HITCH is often used as an adjustable knot to tighten or loosen a line when it is wrapped around an object and then tied to its own standing line. An alternative use for the Tautline is to tie it to another rope or object where it can then be moved up or down that rope or object. This illustration specifically shows how to tie the Tautline to an object.

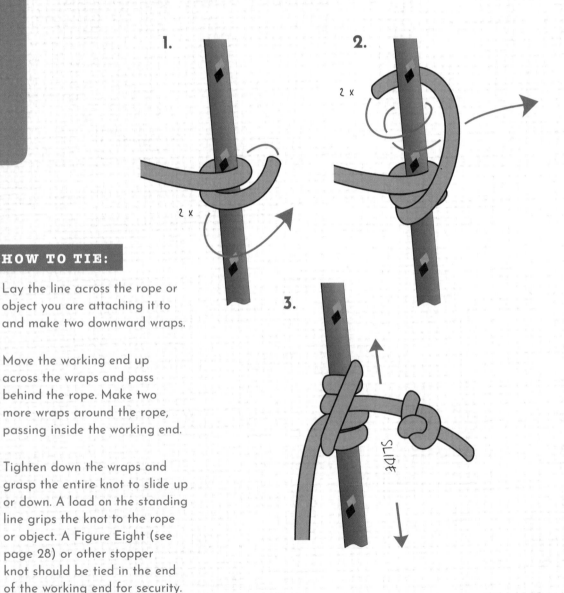

HOW TO TIE:

Lay the line across the rope or object you are attaching it to and make two downward wraps.

Move the working end up across the wraps and pass behind the rope. Make two more wraps around the rope, passing inside the working end.

Tighten down the wraps and grasp the entire knot to slide up or down. A load on the standing line grips the knot to the rope or object. A Figure Eight (see page 28) or other stopper knot should be tied in the end of the working end for security.

TIMBER HITCH

USE THE TIMBER HITCH for securing a rope around a post or any cylindrical object. It does not jam or slip, no matter how heavy the load, and is easy to tie and untie.

1.

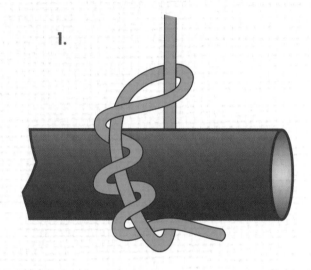

2.

← PULL

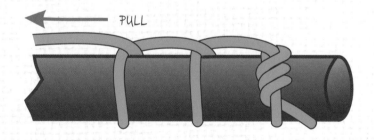

HOW TO TIE:

Pass the working end of a rope around the object and take a turn around the standing line. Tuck the working end back around itself three times.

Add one or two Half Hitches (see page 54) a distance away from the knot near the hauling end for hoisting and to keep the load from twisting.

TRUCKER'S HITCH

USE THE TRUCKER'S HITCH to cinch down a load. This combination of knots allows a line to be pulled very tight. Probably the most useful hitch there is, the Trucker's Hitch allows a line to be pulled as tight as a guitar string and secured. It is used by truckers to secure heavy loads in place and works equally well tying canoes and other objects to the tops of cars. Once the line is pulled to the desired tension using the pulley effect of the loop in the middle of the line, the knot is secured with a couple Half Hitches (see page 54) around one or both lines.

HITCHES

HOW TO TIE:

Tie one end of the rope to a fixed object such as a cleat or car bumper. About midway on the rope, tie a slippery Half Hitch to form a loop in the middle of the line. Be sure the loop part is formed with the free end of the rope or it will tighten down on itself under pressure.

Wrap the standing line around an object like a bar or cleat opposite the tie-in point and feed the free end through the loop.

Using the loop as a pulley, pull down with the free end as tight as you can and secure the knot with two Half Hitches around one or both lines.

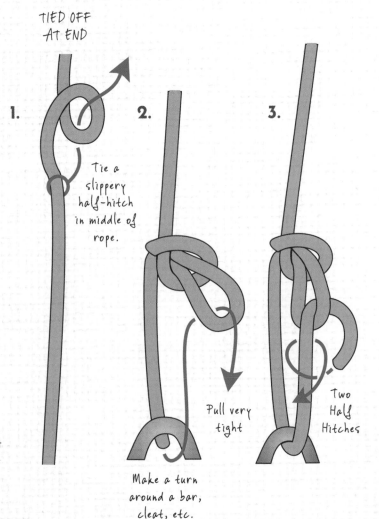

TIED OFF AT END

1.

Tie a slippery half-hitch in middle of rope.

2.

Pull very tight

Make a turn around a bar, cleat, etc.

3.

Two Half Hitches

TUMBLE HITCH

THE TUMBLE HITCH is an excellent quick-release knot that holds a load until released by a pull on the free end. We have a few quick release hitches in this book: the Mooring Hitch (see page 62) and the Highwayman's Hitch (see page 56). Of the three options, the Tumble Hitch is considered by many to be the most secure. However, with any knot that has an untying mechanism for convenience, caution must be exercised. It can be accidentally pulled or snagged and is not compatible with critical applications. When tying the Tumble Hitch, notice and remember that the standing part remains passive during tying.

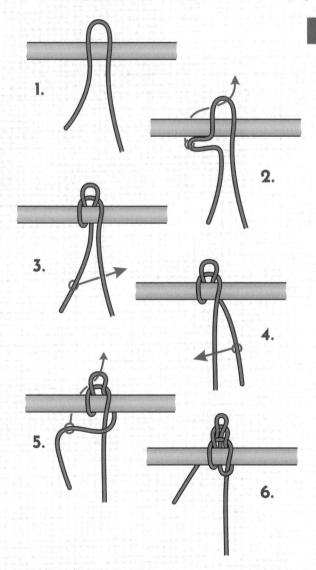

1.

2.

3.

4.

5.

6.

HOW TO TIE:

Form a bight in the rope in front of the bar or post to which you are attaching the rope.

Now form a bight in the working end and run that bight behind the bar. Pass it through the loop created by the first bight formed. A slight tug on the standing line can help to hold the second loop in place.

Pass the working end behind the standing line.

Pass the working end in front of the standing line.

Form another bight in the working end, run behind bar, and pass up and through the second loop.

Tighten the knot by applying a load to the standing line while adjusting the knot down onto the final pass of the working end. Release the knot with a pull to the working end.

VALDOTAIN TRESSE

THE VALDOTAIN TRESSE or VT Knot is a friction knot used to ascend and descend on ropes, making it popular with arborists. The cord used to wrap around the static line is commonly known as a spliced-eye split-tail friction cord. These cords have permanently sewn or spliced loops at each end. In absence of this specialty cord, a cord with a pair of hand-tied loops secured with one side of a Double Fisherman's Knot (see page 13) can be used.

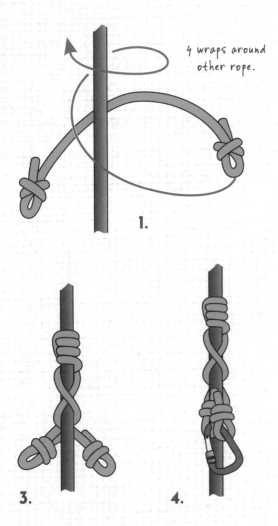

4 wraps around other rope.

1.

2.

3.

4.

HOW TO TIE:

Make four wraps around the main static rope with a hand tied or spliced-eye split-tail friction cord.

After the fourth wrap, bring the tails down even with each other.

Cross the lines in front and then again in back of static line for a total of six wraps for the knot.

Join eyes in the front and clip together with a carabiner.

4

BINDING KNOTS

Binding knots are used to secure, wrap, or grip objects and usually are made with both ends of the same line.

BETTER BOW KNOT

SIMILAR TO THE REGULAR SHOELACES KNOT, use this version to tie your shoelaces and never worry about having it come undone. Untying with a simple tug on a free end, it is great for kids' shoes.

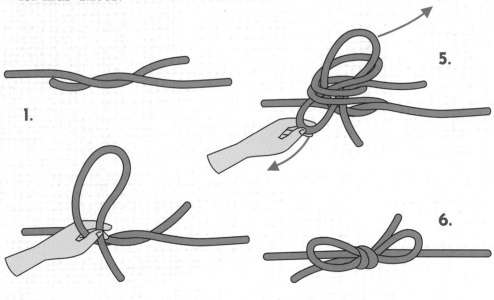

1.

5.

6.

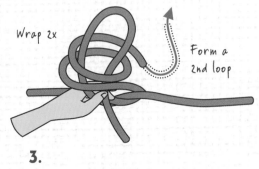

2.

Wrap 2x

Form a 2nd loop

3.

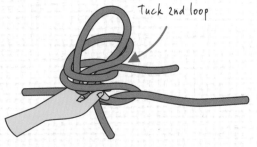

Tuck 2nd loop

4.

HOW TO TIE:

Begin as if tying the standard shoelace knot with an Overhand Knot (see page 96).

Make a loop on one side.

Now wrap two times around the loop with the other shoelace. Be sure to wrap both these turns around the end of your thumb or finger.

Form a second loop at the end of the line you made the wraps with and push it through the space made by your thumb or finger while making the wraps.

Pull both loops in opposite directions.

Tighten and adjust loops.

BUTCHER'S KNOT

THE BUTCHER'S KNOT is used when tying up roasts and other meat for cooking or pickling/marinating. It can also be used as the first loop around a package. A twine material works best, and roasts are generally tied at one-inch intervals with this knot.

HOW TO TIE:

Pass the twine or cord around the roast.

Tie an Overhand Knot (see page 96) with the working end around the standing line and pull tight.

Tie a Half Hitch (see page 54) around the tag end of the first knot with the standing line. An easy method to do this is to form a loop around your fingers and slide that loop onto the tag end.

Pull both ends to tighten and trim the long end.

Repeat at one-inch intervals down the length of the roast.

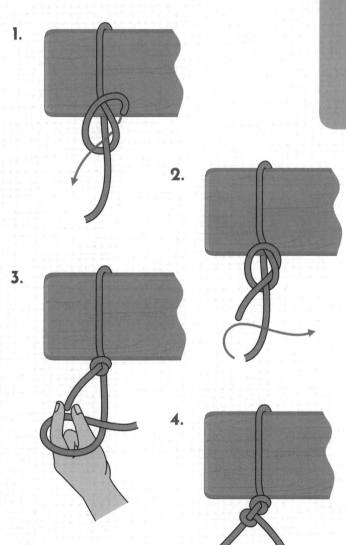

1.

2.

3.

4.

CONSTRICTOR KNOT

THE CONSTRICTOR KNOT is a useful knot to tie up loose materials or the ends of bags. Simple to tie, it grips itself and will not work loose. This knot is useful for securing the end of a sack, or bundles of items or even as a temporary seizing on a rope's end. The knot stays tied so well that it is often impossible to untie.

A TOP-20 KNOT CARD

HOW TO TIE:

Starting in front of the object(s), make one wrap from right to left around the object(s) to be bound and cross the working end over in the front.

Wrap around the back of the object again.

Bring working end to front of knot and feed it back under the two wraps, making sure you first cross over the standing line.

Pull both ends to tighten up the knot.

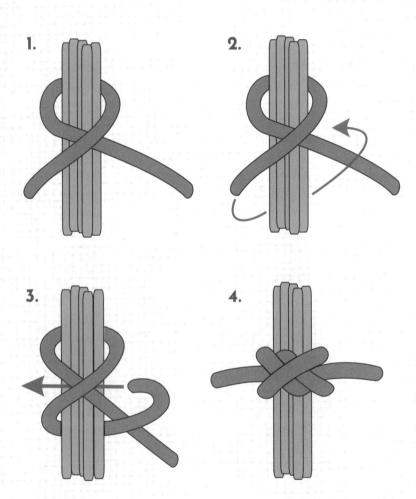

1.

2.

3.

4.

MARLINE HITCHING

MARLINE HITCHING is used to secure long bundles, such as a roll of carpet. The advantage of using the Marline Hitch is that, because it uses a series of Overhand Knots (see page 96), when force is applied, they tend to tighten down and hold the surrounding knots in place.

HOW TO TIE:

Tie a sliding noose such as a Running Bowline (see page 32) around the end of the bundle. When pulled tight, it will cinch down to secure that end of the load.

Run the rope a short way down the bundle and wrap it around. Feed the working end of the rope under the wrap just made, effectively tying an Overhand Knot.

Repeat as many times as needed, spaced evenly along the length of the bundle. When you come to the end of the installation, tie a securing knot such as a Constrictor Knot (see page 78).

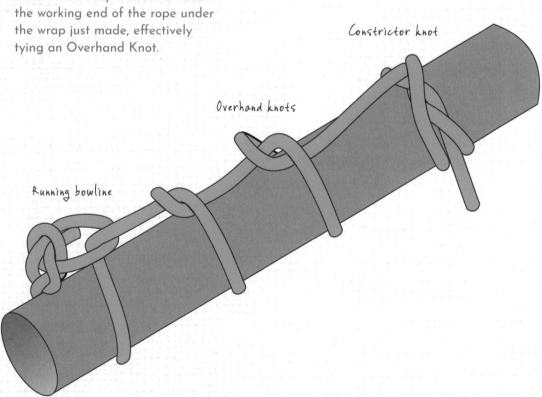

Constrictor knot

Overhand knots

Running bowline

SLEDGE KNOT

THE SLEDGE KNOT is the ultimate construction knot for securing items such as poles and logs together. Once tied, it will hold everything together very firmly. You can even use it to make a raft from poles!

It's easy to tie, stays absolutely secure, and is an excellent choice for binding things together. The ratcheting action allows you to make it far tighter than most other knots. The only downside is that it can be made so tight that you can't untie it, and it usually must be cut to unbind the items.

The Sledge Knot is an excellent knot to add to your knowledge base.

1.   **2.**

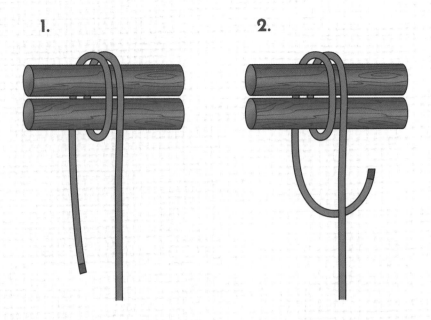

3.

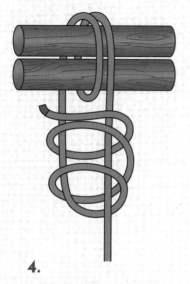

HOW TO TIE:

Wrap working end of rope twice around the items to be lashed together.

Pass the working end behind the standing line.

Wrap the working end around the standing line and itself three times, working from the bottom of the knot up toward the top of the knot.

After passing the working end over the front of both ropes for the third time, wrap behind only the left side rope and feed the working end down through the topmost loop formed. Next, pass the end *over* the next two parts of lower loop and *behind* the bottom part of the lower loop.

Tighten the knot by pulling first on the working end to tighten up the loops. Now pull on the standing line to move the knot up to your anchor point, just like any slip knot, and continue pulling and working the knot tighter and tighter.

4.

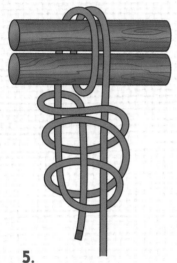

5.

BINDING KNOTS

SQUARE KNOT

THE SQUARE KNOT, or Reef Knot, is quick and easy to tie; it is a good knot for securing non-critical items with the ends of the same rope. This knot was used for centuries by sailors for reefing sails, hence the alternate name Reef Knot, and tying things aboard a ship.

It is important that this knot not be used to join two separate ropes. It is unsafe and can come apart. Be sure to form the Square Knot and avoid tying the similar but inferior Granny Knot by making sure that both parts of the rope, the standing line and the working end, exit the knot together. With the Granny Knot, the working ends and standing lines are on opposite sides of the loop they exit.

HOW TO TIE:

Tie two Overhand Knots (see page 96). First pass the right end over the left end and twist once around.

Then repeat the process moving left to right passing the left end over the right and twist to complete the knot.

Make sure both parts of the rope exit the knot together!

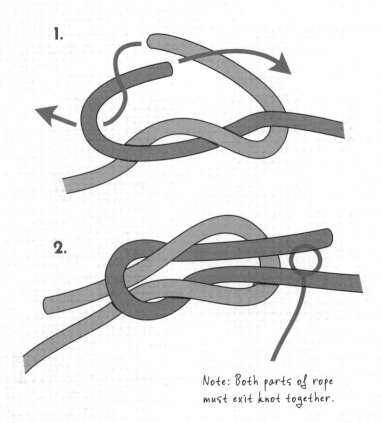

1.

2.

Note: Both parts of rope must exit knot together.

BINDING KNOTS

82

TRANSOM KNOT

THE TRANSOM KNOT is a lashing knot and is similar to the Constrictor Knot (see page 78). It is used to fix together crossed pieces of rigid material at right angles and has a wide range of camping and outdoor uses—for example, to fasten tent poles together. If used as a permanent knot, the ends may be trimmed off for neatness. To reinforce, a second Transom Knot can be made on the opposite side and at a right angle to the first.

1.
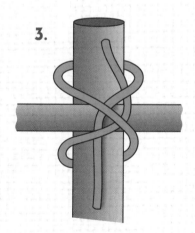

2.
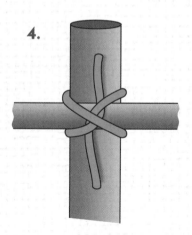

3.
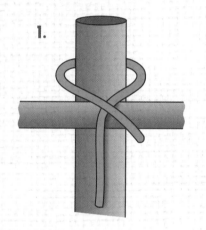

4.
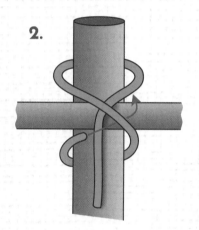

HOW TO TIE:

Pass the working end behind the upright spar and back across the standing line.

Now pass the working end below the horizontal spar and behind the upright spar.

Working back toward the top, pass over standing line and tuck the working end under both turns.

Pull both the working end and the standing line to tighten the knot. Trim the ends if desired.

5

SPECIAL PURPOSE KNOTS

In this section are some rope knots that don't quite fall into the other categories or need a category of their own. Many of these knots are super useful to know for various purposes. For example, whipping knots control the strands or fibers at the end of a rope, stopper knots add bulk to the end of a rope to keep a rope from slipping through an opening or to aid in throwing the rope, and coils are methods of taming a length of rope for storage or transport.

ALPINE COIL

THE ALPINE COIL is a method used by climbers for carrying a rope, such that the rope remains attached to harnesses and ready for use. It is also known as the Mountaineer's Coil.

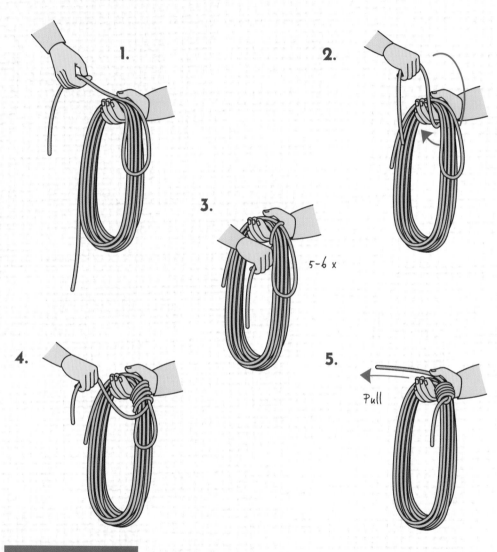

HOW TO TIE:

Bring both ends to the top of the newly made coil and form a bight in one of the ends.

Wrap the working end of the other rope around the strands of the coil and the bight five or six times, working forward as shown.

Tuck the working end of the rope being wrapped around through the bight first formed.

Pull the standing end of the bight to capture the working end tight.

85

ASHLEY'S STOPPER KNOT

A TOP-20 KNOT CARD

A STOPPER KNOT is tied at the end of a rope to prevent the end from unraveling, slipping through another knot, or passing back through a hole, block, or device. This version, Ashley's Stopper Knot, also known as the Oysterman's Stopper, is a knot developed by Clifford Ashley around 1910. It makes a well-balanced trefoil-faced stopper at the end of the rope, giving greater resistance to pulling through an opening than other common stoppers. Essentially, the knot is a common Overhand Knot (see page 96) but with the end of the rope passing through the eye of the loop, which closes up on it.

HOW TO TIE:

Form a small loop at the end of a line by running working end over standing line.

Tie an Overhand Knot (see page 96) around both sides of the loop at its base.

Pull Overhand Knot tight and feed working end through the loop from below.

Pull working end all the way through and slide knot down tight.

Pull both ends tight.

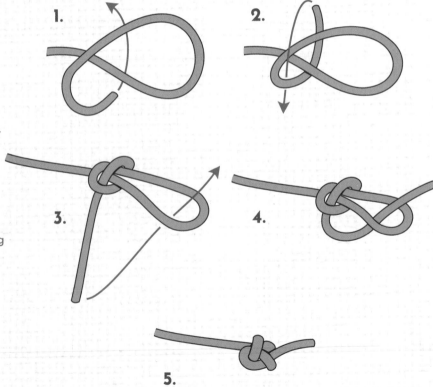

1.

2.

3.

4.

5.

BACKUP KNOT

CLIMBERS OFTEN ADD A BACKUP KNOT to their primary knot for additional security. The purpose of the backup knot is to avoid the primary knot from untying itself. This version is simply one side of a Double Fisherman's Knot (see page 13) tied with a long working end (fifteen to eighteen inches) of the primary knot.

Primary knot

1.

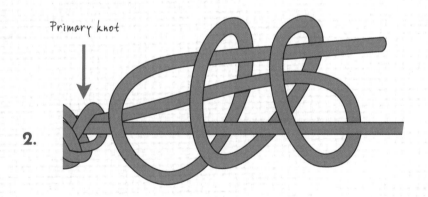

Primary knot

2.

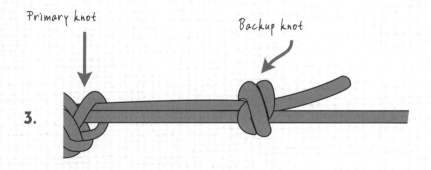

Primary knot

Backup knot

3.

HOW TO TIE:

Wrap the free end twice around the standing rope and the working part of the free end, moving back toward the primary knot.

Feed the free end back through the loops just made.

Pull the free end to tighten the Backup Knot down onto the standing line.

COMMON WHIPPING

THE COMMON WHIPPING is a knot tied at the end of a rope to keep it from unraveling. The benefit of the Common Whipping Knot over other whipping knots is that it is quite easy to tie and no tools are required. However, the knot is more appropriate for temporary use or on decorative ropes as it is known to slip off the rope easily. It is best used on a natural fiber rope and tied with natural twine, both of which afford the maximum friction for the knot to hold its position at the end of the rope. When dealing with synthetic ropes, it is best to wrap the ends with tape and then heat the ends to melting point to fuse the strands. Also see French Whipping (page 91).

HOW TO TIE:

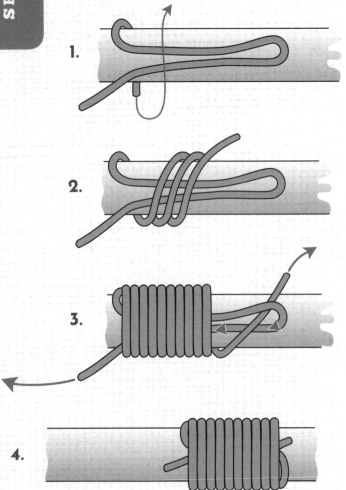

1.

2.

3.

4.

Lay the twine along the rope and make a bight back along the rope. Note that the rope should be whipped a short distance (one and a half times the diameter) from its end.

Begin wrapping the twine around the rope and bight of twine securely. Wrap until the whipping is one-and-a-half times wider than the rope is thick.

Run the working end of the twine through the bight. Carefully pull on the standing end of the twine until the bight and working end are pulled under the whipping. (Note: It is normally necessary to maintain tension on the working end to prevent the bight from being dragged completely through; otherwise the whipping will fall apart.)

Cut the twine flush with the edges of the whipping to give the rope end a finished look.

DOUBLE OVERHAND KNOT

THE DOUBLE OVERHAND KNOT is easy to tie and makes a fairly bulky knot and a good stopper knot at the end of a rope. Other good choices for the task of stopper knot are the Figure Eight (see page 28) and Ashley's Stopper (see page 86).

1.

HOW TO TIE:

Tie an Overhand Knot (see page 96) at the end of a rope, but do not tighten the knot down.

Pass the end of the line through the loop created by the first Overhand Knot.

Tighten the knot down while sliding it into place at the end of the line. Be sure to leave some tail sticking out from the end of the knot.

2.

3.

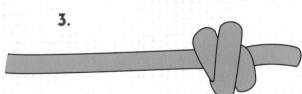

FIREMAN'S COIL

THE FIREMAN'S COIL is a knot for keeping coiled rope under control. There are several good knots for coiling a rope, but one benefit of the Fireman's Coil is that it can be released by a simple pull of the rope end. Many folks are stymied when coiling a rope and needing to finish it off with a knot to keep it under control. The Fireman's Coil is one of the easiest methods to accomplish this task. The completed knot also creates a rope hook for hanging. Other good coil knots include the Alpine Coil (see page 85) and the Sailor's Coil (see page 97).

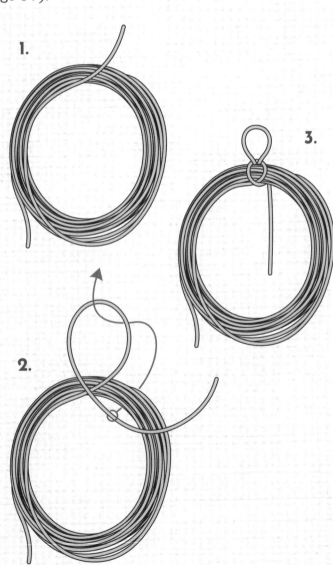

HOW TO TIE:

Make a coil with your rope by looping it in circles. Use one hand to make the circles and the other to hold them in place.

Take the working end of the rope (the end after the last coil is made) and make a loop mid-rope at the top of the coils. Take hold of the working end just below the loop, bring it to the back side of the coil, and run it up through the loop. That essentially makes a loop going through a loop.

Tighten down the first loop onto the second loop. This loop can be used for a hanging hook. Pull on the end of the rope to release.

FRENCH WHIPPING

FRENCH WHIPPING is very similar to Common Whipping (see page 88), but it differs in that each wrap around the rope is done with a Half Hitch (see page 54) instead of simply wrapping around the rope. This results in both a more secure whipping and an attractive spiral design of the Half Hitch knots within the whipping. The French Whipping should be constructed to be between one and one-and-a-half times the diameter of the rope being whipped.

HOW TO TIE:

Near the end of the rope, tie a simple Overhand Knot (see page 96), leaving a short standing end and a long working end. Lay the short standing end on top of the rope and begin making Half Hitches over it and around the rope end being whipped.

Continue this same process of tying Half Hitches around the rope and burying the standing end in the new wraps.

Once you have wrapped past the tag and approximately one to one-and-a-half times the diameter of the rope being whipped, you will now secure the knot by making two loose wraps around the rope and inserting the working end through both loops. You can repeat this a second time if desired.

Pull the working end very tight and trim close to the wraps.

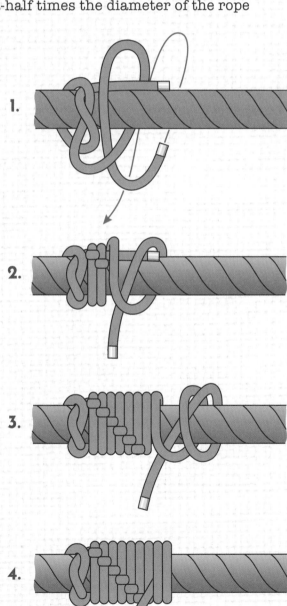

1.

2.

3.

4.

HANDCUFF KNOT

THE HANDCUFF KNOT produces two adjustable loops in opposing directions, which can be tightened down around a person's hands or feet. However, to be even remotely secure, the working ends should be secured with one or more Overhand (see page 96) or Square Knots (see page 82). The Handcuff Knot can also be used to hobble a horse to limit its ability to move.

1.
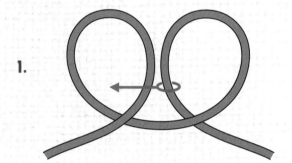

4.

2.
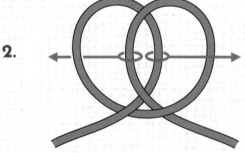

HOW TO TIE:

Form two loops, overlaying the second loop partway on top of the first as in the formation of a clove hitch.

Pull each loop through the other loop and tighten the knot.

Then pass the loops over the limbs to be secured and pull the working ends to tighten the loops to the desired size.

Finish with one or more Overhand Knots (see page 96) or a Square Knot (see page 82).

3.

HEAVING LINE KNOT

THE HEAVING LINE KNOT adds bulk and weight to the end of a rope, making it easier to throw the line. The number of turns is optional.

HOW TO TIE:

Make a two bights next to each other in opposite directions at the end of a rope. Make the bights approximately the desired size of the finished knot. Leave plenty of rope for the working end to make the wraps needed next.

Pass the working end through the top bight and wrap around both strands of that bight only.

Continue making wraps, but now encircle all three strands, working down the ropes.

Pass the working end through the opening of the bottom bight to finish the knot.

Tighten the knot by first pulling up on the top loop then pulling down on the standing line.

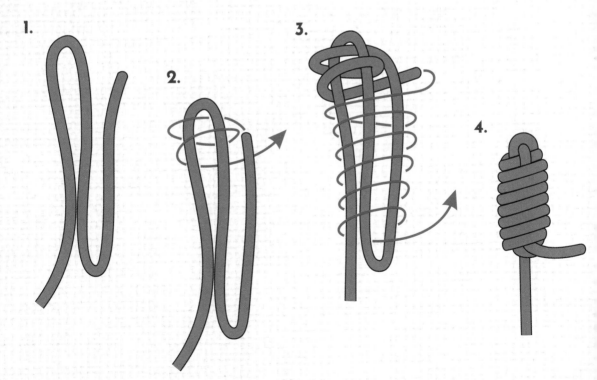

1.

2.

3.

4.

MONKEY'S FIST

THE ORIGIN OF THE MONKEY'S FIST knot is similar to the Heaving Line Knot (see page 93) used on sail ships of yesteryear. However, the knot is now more popular as a decorative knot and can be found in sizes small to large: from key-chains to door stopper weights. The size of the knot is dependent on the thickness of the rope in which it is tied and the number of turns made. Often a spherical object such as a golf ball, marble, or tennis ball is used in the center of the knot to help attain a more perfect round shape and give the knot weight when used for decoration. (If objects are placed inside, do not use the Monkey's Fist for throwing. It is already more than heavy enough with the coiled rope for throwing purposes.) Both ends of the rope can be tucked inside the knot upon completion, or they can both be left long and tied together. This knot may take several attempts through trial and error to get a nice, perfectly round and tight-fitting knot!

HOW TO TIE:

Take your rope, and with the long working end, make three wraps around the fingers of your hand.

While holding the first set of turns in place, make three more turns, passing outside the middle of the first three turns. Finish this step by passing the working end around one side of the first set of turns. This sets up the working end for the next step, which passes the end through the inside of the previous wraps.

Now make three turns around the set of wraps made in the previous step, passing through the inside of the knot. Double check that you have made the same number of turns for each step.

At this point, a round object can be inserted in the center of the wraps, or the standing end of the rope can be tucked inside either with or without a stopper knot at the end as well. Working slowly (and patiently), begin tightening by working on each wrap, starting near the buried stopper knot and finishing with the other end of the rope. Do not pull too hard on the first few wraps. You will need to work your way through the knot more than once. The use of a small screwdriver or awl can help on the last tightening session through the knot.

1.

2

3

4

OVERHAND KNOT

THE OVERHAND KNOT is a foundation knot (forming the basis of other knots) and is probably the easiest and first knot most people learn to tie. When tied by itself at the end of a rope, cord, or even sewing thread, it makes a simple stopper knot, or it can prevent the end from unraveling. When tied with two ends of one rope or cord around an object, such as when tying up parcels or tying shoelaces together, it is called the Half Knot. When it is tied with one end of a rope passed around an object and then secured to its own standing part, it is called a Half Hitch (see page 54). Three different names for what is fundamentally the same knot but used in different applications.

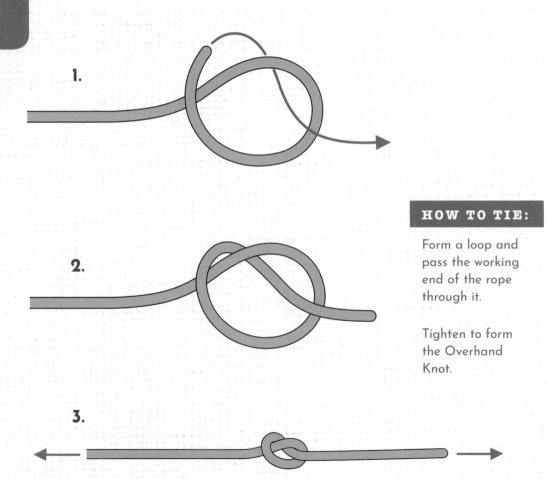

1.

2.

3.

HOW TO TIE:

Form a loop and pass the working end of the rope through it.

Tighten to form the Overhand Knot.

SAILOR'S COIL

THE SAILOR'S COIL is used for storing rope at sea. It is a secure knot that will stand considerable handling without unraveling because of the two Half Hitches (see page 54) on either side of each other around the coiled rope. You can tie it with a long end and use that for hanging it up, if desired. Other good coil knots include the Fireman's Coil (see page 90) and the Alpine Coil (see page 85). It is a good idea to learn one or two coil knots and commit them to memory, because there are always times that a rope needs to be neatly coiled for storage or transit.

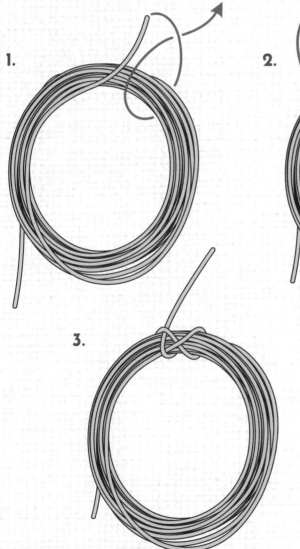

1.

2.

3.

HOW TO TIE:

Coil the rope by making consecutive circles of the rope of equal size, gathering them up with one hand while using the other hand to make the circles.

Make a single Half Hitch around a section of the coil. Then make a second Half Hitch to the left of the first hitch.

Pull end tight.

SHEEPSHANK

THE SHEEPSHANK is included here as it has been in virtually every knotting work since the 1600s, but in reality it is seldom used and should be avoided. It is most commonly used to shorten a rope, but it is not a stable knot and can fall apart quickly with the interruption of tension on the knot, especially in synthetic ropes. A damaged section of rope can be isolated using the Sheepshank, but tension must be maintained on the knot. The Alpine Butterfly Knot (see page 23) can be made to substitute the rope-isolation and rope-shortening duties quite well and is a knot that can be trusted.

HOW TO TIE:

Fold the rope to isolate the damaged section or to attain the new length desired. Form Half Hitches (see page 54) in both sides of the standing line (A and B).

Pass bight A1 through Half Hitch A and tighten. Repeat with bight B1 through Half Hitch B and tighten.

Pull free ends of rope in opposite directions to apply load. Maintain tension on knot, and never trust this knot with critical applications!

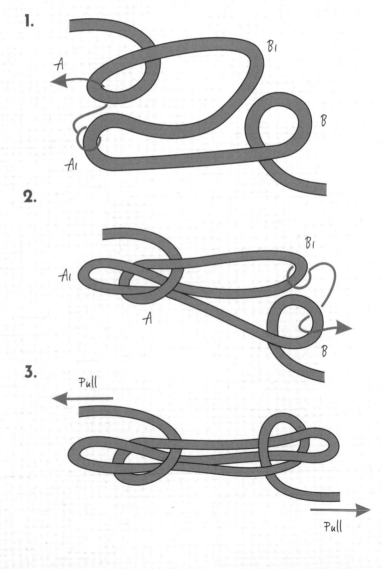

STEVEDORE STOPPER KNOT

THE STEVEDORE KNOT likely gets its name from its use as a stopper knot by a stevedore (a person employed at a dock to load and unload cargo from ships). To raise and lower cargo, they used large block and tackle, and these required a rather large stopper knot to prevent the rope from running completely through the block. The Stevedore Stopper Knot is an excellent stopper knot, is quite bulky, and is one of four stopper knots in this book, if you include the Figure Eight (see page 28) tied at the end of a rope (the least desirable of the four). Pick one and learn it well as the use for a stopper knot at the end of a rope comes in handy quite often. Other stopper knots are Ashley's Stopper (see page 86) and the Double Overhand Knot (see page 89).

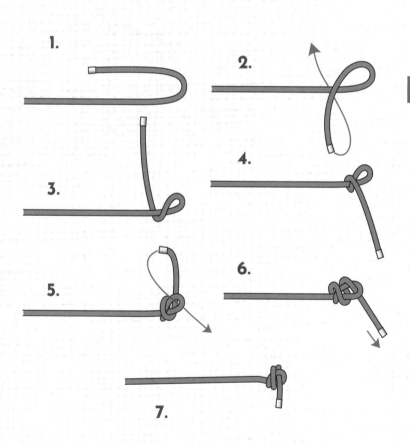

1.

2.

3.

4.

5.

6.

7.

HOW TO TIE:

Form a bight in the end of the rope.

Pass the working end over the standing line and continue around, making one complete turn around the standing line.

Repeat two or three times, making complete turns around the standing line, working back toward the end of the rope.

Pass the end down through the original bight and tighten down the turns.

Pull on both ends to tighten the stopper knot.

WEST COUNTRY WHIPPING

WEST COUNTRY WHIPPING secures the end of a rope fairly well from unraveling. It is extremely easy to tie as it simply involves tying alternating Overhand Knots (see page 96) to the front and back of a rope. It can be tied either working toward the end of the rope or away from the end. The ends of the final Square Knot (see page 82) can be tucked back under the whipping with a sharp implement.

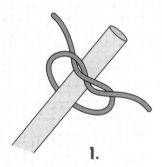

1.

2.

HOW TO TIE:

Pass the whipping twine around the rope a short distance from the end.

Form an Overhand Knot and pull very tight.

Repeat the process behind the rope opposite the first knot.

Continue until the length of the whipping is about one to one-and-a-half times the diameter of the rope.

Finish with one or more Square Knots.

3.

4.

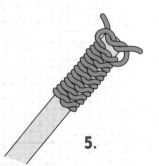

5.

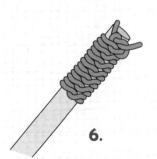

6.

FISHING KNOTS

Here is a selection of knots used for fishing. As with rope knots, they fall into several categories—Terminal Connections are like hitches, in that you tie your line to an object such as a hook, swivel, or lure. Line-to-Line Knots are like bends; you use them to tie two lines together. Loop Knots are used to create a loop in your line.

6

TERMINAL CONNECTION KNOTS

Use these knots to tie your fishing line
to a hook, swivel, lure, or fly.

ARBOR KNOT

USE THE SIMPLE ARBOR KNOT to tie your fishing line to the spool of any type of fishing reel—fly reel, spinning reel, or bait-casting reel. The goal here really isn't that a knot is going to hold if a fish has taken all the line down to the end your reel spool but to have something strong enough to hold if you lose a rod and reel overboard and have to pull it up by the line. Another knot that can be used to tie a line to a reel is the Uni Knot (see page 112), but with just a couple of wraps instead of the five or six used to tie on a hook.

1.

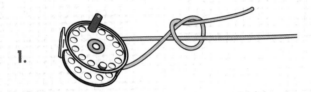

HOW TO TIE:

Wrap your line around the arbor of the spool with the tag end of the line. Then tie a simple Overhand Knot (see page 96) around the standing part with the tag end.

2.

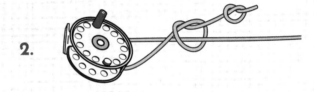

Tie a second Overhand Knot in the tag end just an inch or two from the first Overhand Knot. Tighten both knots.

3.

Pull the standing part of the line to slide the first Overhand Knot down to the spool and the second Overhand Knot to jam against the first. Trim tag end close.

4.

5.

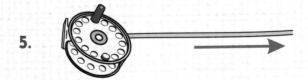

DAVY KNOT

THE DAVY KNOT is attributed to Davy Wotton, a British fly fishing pro. The positive aspects of this knot are in speed, size, and strength—all great attributes for a fishing knot. Once learned, the Davy Knot can be tied very quickly, which gets you back to fishing in a minimal amount of time. It is also a very compact knot, making it an appropriate knot for small flies, and various tests rate it between 85 to 100 percent (with 90% probably a safe assumption) of line strength. The Davy Knot should be in every fly fisher's arsenal of knots!

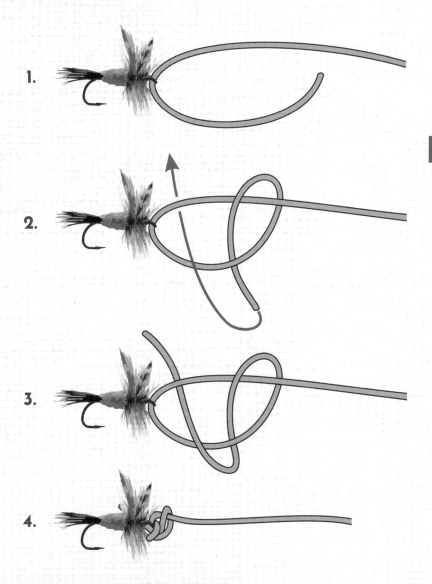

1.

2.

3.

4.

HOW TO TIE:

Thread 3 to 4 inches of leader (or tippet) through the hook eye.

Loosely form a simple Overhand Knot (see page 96) ahead of the hook.

Bring the tag end back through the loop, making sure to pass between the Overhand Knot and the hook itself.

Tighten the knot by pulling first on the tag end to draw up the knot and then on the main line to set the knot.

DROP SHOT RIG

DROP SHOTTING is a popular bass fishing technique, but it was actually invented by saltwater fishermen. The technique was introduced to the bass fishing world by pro bass fishermen on the West Coast, where it proved successful in the highly pressured lakes of the West. It is considered a finesse technique. The idea is to suspend a bait off the bottom at a level that will put the bait in front of the fish and/or keep the bait up and out of the gunk at the bottom. The weight drops vertically to the bottom, and the bait needs to be lightly shaken to attract attention. For this type of knot and fishing technique, light line and spinning equipment are preferred.

HOW TO TIE:

Begin by tying a Palomar Knot (see page 110) with a long tag end. Double 12 to 30 inches of line (depending on how high you want the bait off the bottom) and pass the end of the loop through the eye of the hook.

Tie a loose Overhand Knot (see page 96) with the hook hanging from the bottom of the loop formed.

While holding the Overhand Knot between thumb and forefinger, pass the end of loop over the hook. Slide the loop to above the eye of the hook.

Pull on both standing line and tag end to tighten down the knot onto the eye of the hook. Now feed the tag end back through the hook eye from above.

Attach a small weight to the end of the line at the desired distance from hook and trim tag. Attach bait to the hook.

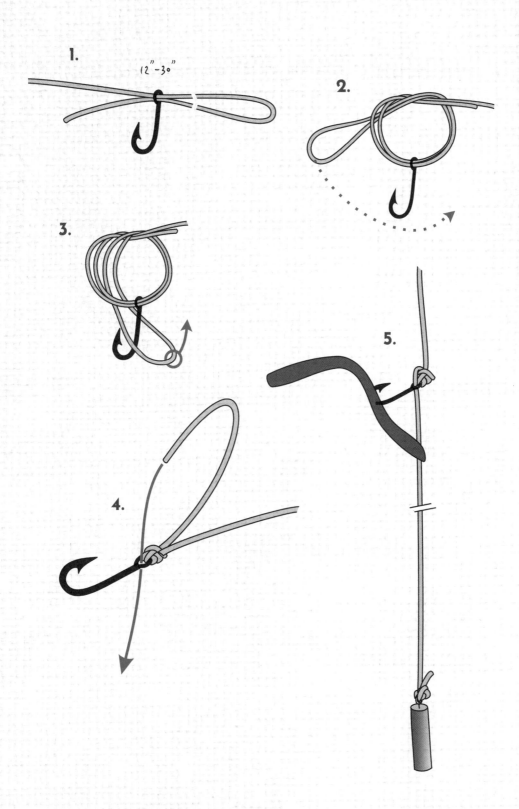

1.

12"-30"

2.

3.

5.

4.

IMPROVED CLINCH KNOT

THE IMPROVED CLINCH is a time-tested and a very popular choice for tying terminal tackle to monofilament line. It is quick and easy to tie and reliable. It can be difficult to tie in lines testing greater than 25 pounds breaking strength and is not recommended for braided line. Use the Palomar Knot (see page 110) for braided lines.

1.

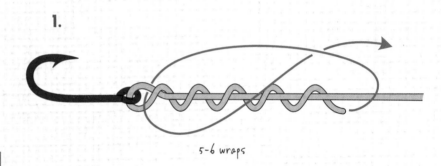

5-6 wraps

HOW TO TIE:

Thread the end of the line through the eye of the hook. Double back, making five or more turns around the standing line.

2.

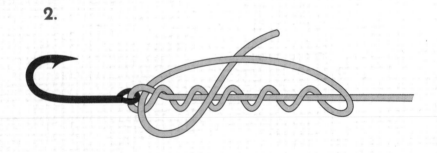

Bring the end of the line back through the first loop formed behind the eye and then through the big loop.

3.

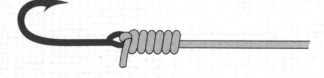

Wet the knot and pull on the tag end to tighten down the coils. Slide tight against the eye and clip the tag end close.

NON-SLIP MONO LOOP

THE NON-SLIP MONO LOOP is also known as the "Kreh Loop," as it has been popularized by fishing legend Lefty Kreh. As its name suggests, it forms a non-slip loop at the end of a fishing line. It is included here, in the Terminal Connection chapter, because it is commonly used to attach a fly or lure to the fishing line. Using a loop connection can give the fly or lure a more fluid and natural action in the water.

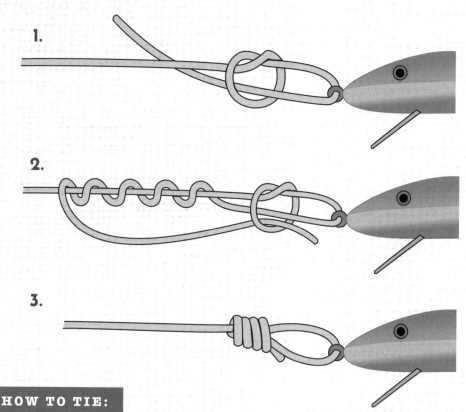

1.

2.

3.

HOW TO TIE:

Make an Overhand Knot (see page 96) in the line about 10 inches from the end. Pass the tag end through the eye of the lure or fly and back through the loop of the Overhand Knot on the same side of the loop as it had exited.

Wrap the tag end around the standing part five or six times. Bring the tag end back through Overhand Knot, entering from the same side it exited from before.

Moisten the knot, then pull slowly on the tag end to cinch the wraps loosely together. Then pull the loop and the standing line in opposite directions to seat the knot. Trim tag end.

PALOMAR KNOT

THE PALOMAR KNOT comes close to performing at 100% of line strength when tied properly. Be sure that when the hook or lure is passed through the loop that all parts of the knot cinch up together. Many depictions of this knot elsewhere make it look like the loop part of the knot goes up against the bottom of the eye of the hook or lure. The knot can fail if tied in that manner. **This is also the best knot to use with braided fishing line.**

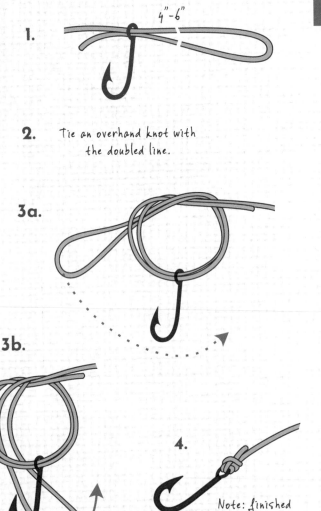

1.

4"–6"

2. Tie an overhand knot with the doubled line.

3a.

3b.

4.

Note: finished knot is on hook eye, not hook shank.

HOW TO TIE:

Double 6 inches of line and pass the end of the loop through the eye of the hook. Alternately, for small hook eyes, pass the end of the line through the hook eye once, then double back and pass the end of the line through the hook eye again from the opposite direction, leaving about 6 inches of doubled line outside the hook eye.

Tie a loose Overhand Knot (see page 96) **with the hook hanging from bottom**.

Holding the Overhand Knot between thumb and forefinger, pass the loop of line over the hook. Slide the loop above the eye of the hook.

Moisten the line and pull on both the standing line and tag end to tighten the knot onto the eye. Clip the tag end close.

SNELL KNOT

THE SNELL KNOT provides a reliable straight-line pull when setting the hook. There are several ways to tie this knot, and we have found this version to be the easiest and best way. The Snell Knot is a good knot for all fishermen to have in their arsenal of go-to knots.

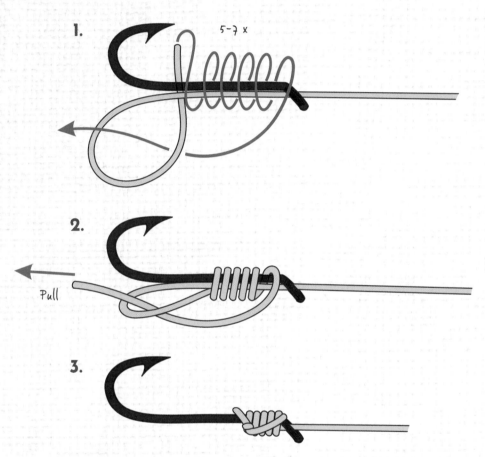

HOW TO TIE:

Run tag end through hook eye toward point of hook, form a small loop, and bring tag end behind hook shank. You will want about four inches of tag to work with.

Begin wrapping the tag end around the hook shank and the line, working from the point to the eye. Make six to seven wraps and then feed tag out through loop, from underside to topside.

While holding wraps in place, pull the tag end to tighten. Make sure wraps are nice and neat on the hook shank and pull both ends very tight. Clip tag end.

111

UNI KNOT

ALSO KNOWN AS THE GRINNER KNOT, the Uni Knot is a good and reliable knot for monofilament to terminal tackle connections. Some anglers find it easier to tie than the Improved Clinch (see page 108) and equally dependable.

1.

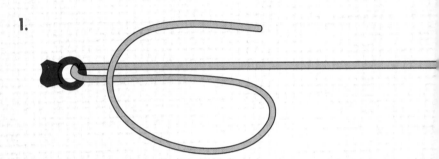

HOW TO TIE:

Run line through the eye of the hook and double back parallel to the standing line. Make a loop by laying the tag end over the doubled line.

Make five or six turns with the tag end around the double line and through the loop.

Moisten the lines and pull the tag end to tighten the turns.

Slide knot down to the eye or leave a small loop if desired. Trim tag end.

2. Hold here

Pull

5–6 x

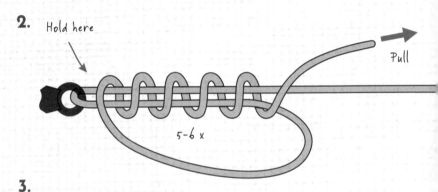

3.

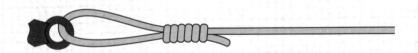

4.

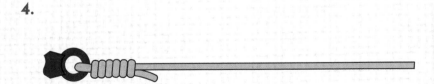

LINE-TO-LINE KNOTS

Use these knots to tie two fishing lines together, such as a leader or tippet to the main line.

ALBRIGHT SPECIAL KNOT

THE ALBRIGHT KNOT is one of the most reliable knots for joining lines of greatly unequal diameters or different materials, such as monofilament to braided line. Many experienced fly fishermen prefer the Albright to attach their fly line to leader material, some even going so far as to cut off a factory-welded loop to use the Albright! It certainly is the go-to choice knot for tying dacron backing to fly line for most fly fishermen. It is easy to tie and should be in every angler's knot arsenal.

HOW TO TIE:

Make a loop in the heavier line and run about 10 inches of the lighter line through the loop.

1.

Hold the three lines between your thumb and index finger. Wrap the light line back over itself and both strands of the loop as shown.

2.

Hold here

Make ten tightly wrapped turns. Feed the tag end back through the loop from behind and exit the loop on the same side as it entered.

3.

10 wraps

Hold both ends of the heavy line and slide the wraps to the end of the loop. Pull the light line to tighten and clip the tag end close to the knot, then trim the heavy line, also close to the knot.

4.

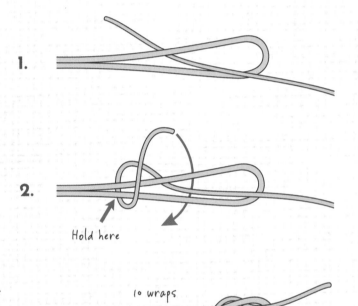

BLOOD KNOT

USED FOR JOINING TWO LINES TOGETHER, the Blood Knot is a tried and true fishing knot and a favorite of fly fishermen. The strength of the knot is increased by making at least five and up to seven wraps on each side of the knot. It works best with lines of approximately equal diameter.

1.

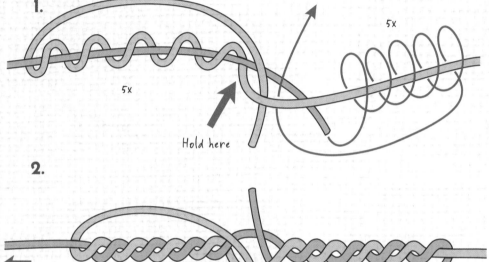

5x

5x

Hold here

2.

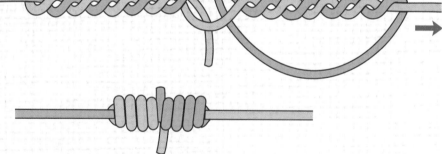

3.

HOW TO TIE:

Overlap the ends of the lines to be joined. Twist one around the other, making five turns. Bring the tag end back between the two lines where they meet.

Repeat with the other end, wrapping in the opposite direction for the same number of turns. Bring this line's tag end back to the loop formed in the middle and pass it through in the opposite direction of the other line.

Moisten the knot and slowly pull the lines in opposite directions. The turns will wrap and gather. Clip the ends close to the knot.

DOUBLE UNI KNOT

THIS KNOT IS USED BY ANGLERS in both salt and fresh water for joining lines of similar or different strengths. It works well, and some find it easier to tie than the Blood Knot (see page 115). When tying in braided line to monofilament, make eight turns with the slippery braided line and five or more turns with the monofilament.

HOW TO TIE:

Overlap the ends of the lines to be joined. Take the end of the line from the left, double back, and make three to five wraps around both lines and through the loop that was formed underneath. Pull the tag end to tighten.

Repeat with the end of the line from the right, making the same number of wraps (unless tying with braided line, in which case you should make eight wraps).

You have now tied two Uni Knots. Moisten the knot and pull the standing lines in the opposite direction to slide the two knots together.

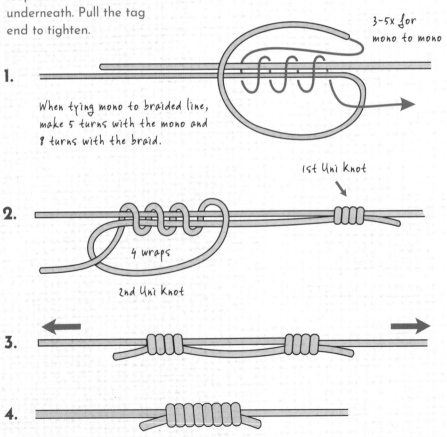

3-5x for mono to mono

1.

When tying mono to braided line, make 5 turns with the mono and 8 turns with the braid.

1st Uni Knot

2.

4 wraps

2nd Uni Knot

3.

4.

NAIL KNOT

THE NAIL KNOT is a time-tested and popular knot to join fly line to leader. The use of a small, hollow tube (like a coffee stirrer stick) instead of a nail is effective.

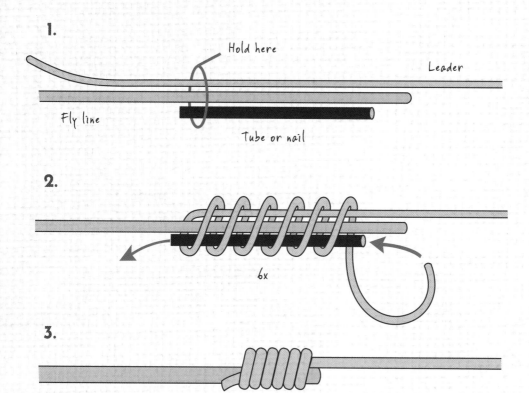

1.

Hold here

Leader

Fly line

Tube or nail

2.

6x

3.

HOW TO TIE:

Lay a nail or hollow tube against the end of a fly line. Set the butt section end of a leader against the line and tube. Leave an extra 10-12 inches of its tag end to tie the knot.

Make six to eight wraps close together with the leader, working left to right, back around the leader, line, and tube or nail. Pass the tag end through the tube or the space made by the nail and remove the tube or nail.

Pull the tag end to tighten the coils. Then pull the tag end and leader to seat the knot firmly onto the fly line.

Trim the tag end and fly line close to the knot.

NEEDLE KNOT

THE NEEDLE KNOT is a method for connecting leader to fly line when not using a loop-to-loop connection. It is more streamlined and reliable than tying a Nail Knot (see page 113) to the fly line. Many instructions for this knot say to insert the butt end of the leader into the hole at the end of the fly line. However, it is easier to insert the thin end of the leader into the exit hole of the needle and pull the leader out the end, leaving the correct amount of butt end to tie the knot with.

HOW TO TIE:

Use a needle that is slightly wider than the butt end of the leader. Push the needle incrementally into the center of the fly line through its end to a depth of about 1/8 of an inch.

Push the needle all the way out the side of the fly line and remove.

Quickly feed the small end of the leader into the hole just created in the side so that it exits out the end of the fly line.

Pull the whole leader through, leaving about 8 inches of leader outside the hole to tie the knot with.

Lay a large needle, nail, or toothpick on the fly line and wrap the leader five times around the fly line, the nail, and itself, working toward the end of the fly line.

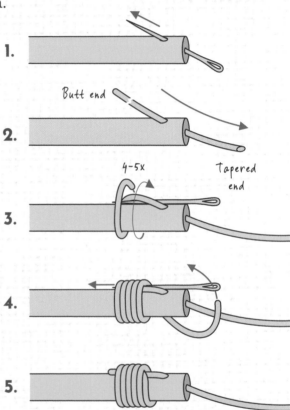

1.

2. Butt end

4-5x   Tapered end

3.

4.

5.

Use the needle or the space provided by the nail to insert the end of the leader back under the wraps in the opposite direction of the wraps, remove the needle or nail, and pull tight.

Get all of the slack out of the lines and work the wraps down to the exit hole.

Pull very tight and cut the tag end close.

SURGEON'S KNOT

THIS KNOT ranks as one of the best and easiest-to-tie knots for joining lines of equal or unequal diameters. It can also be used to join lines of different materials. It is simply two Overhand Knots (see page 96) with the entire leader pulled through the knot each time. When properly tied, the Surgeon's Knot approaches 100 percent line strength. It must be tightened by pulling on all four strands to properly seat the knot.

To tie the Triple Surgeon's Knot, proceed to do a total of three wraps (hence the name) of the loop through the Overhand Knot. There is some measure of added security with the Triple Surgeon's, but the knot does get a bit bulky.

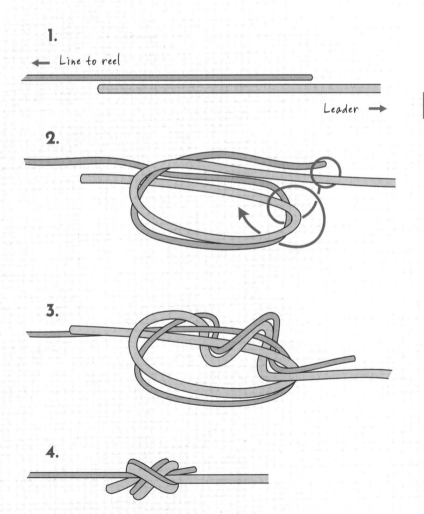

1.

← Line to reel

Leader →

2.

3.

4.

HOW TO TIE:

Lay the line and leader on top of one another, overlapping each other by several inches.

Form a simple loop with both lines. Pass both the tag end and the entire leader through the loop two times.

(Optional) Pass both tag end and leader through the loop an additional time to tie the Triple Surgeon's Knot.

Moisten knot and pull all four ends tight.

8

LOOP
KNOTS

Use these knots to make a loop at the end
of your line or, in the case of the Dropper
Loop, anywhere on your line.

DROPPER LOOP

USING A DROPPER LOOP is a method of attaching additional flies, baits, or jigs to a single fishing line. If the loop is tied particularly large, one side of the loop can be cut where it exits the knot, leaving a single strand line upon which baits can be tied directly.

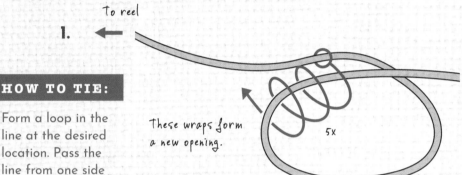

1. To reel

These wraps form a new opening.

5x

HOW TO TIE:

Form a loop in the line at the desired location. Pass the line from one side of the loop through and around that side of the loop. Make five or more wraps and keep the newly formed loop open.

Push the bottom of original loop up through the new opening and hold with your teeth. Wet the knot with saliva and pull both ends in opposite directions.

Pull the ends of the line evenly until coils tighten and the loop stands out from the line.

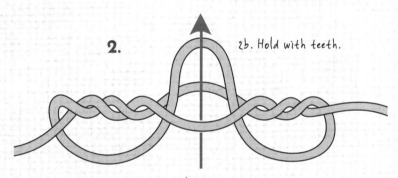

2.

2b. Hold with teeth.

2a. Feed bottom of loop through new opening.

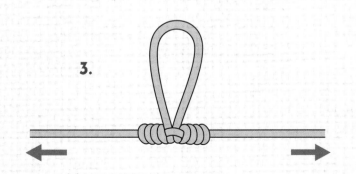

3.

PERFECTION LOOP

STRONG AND EFFECTIVE, THE PERFECTION LOOP is a favorite for tying a loop at the end of a line. Besides being strong and reliable, it can be crafted to make a very small loop if desired.

LOOP KNOTS

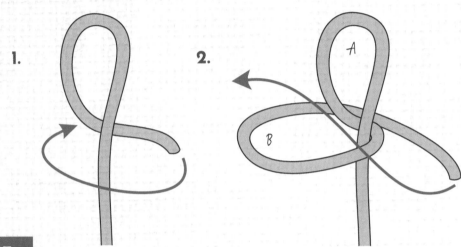

HOW TO TIE:

Form a loop (A) at the end of the line by passing the tag end behind the standing line.

Take a turn around the standing line, forming a second loop (B). Hold in place, and take another turn around the line, this time crossing on the topside of the second loop (B).

Hold the tag end in place and pass loop B through loop A.

Pull loop B up until the knot jams tight. Trim the tag end.

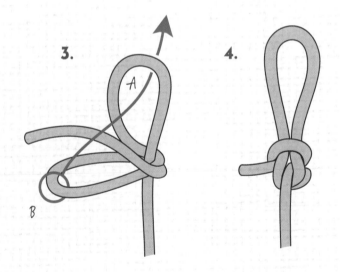

SURGEON'S END LOOP

THE POPULARITY OF THE SURGEON'S END LOOP lies in its simplicity as well as its strength. Tie two Overhand Knots (see page 96) with doubled line and you're done! This creates a strong, trustworthy loop at the end of your line. This can be used to attach store-bought, pre-made Snell leaders to your line by interlocking the two loops. To do this, just insert the leader's factory loop through the Surgeon's End Loop and then pass the leader's hook and rest of the leader through its own loop and pull tight.

To tie the Triple Surgeon's End Loop, just add another pass through the first Overhand Knot. This makes the knot a little more secure.

LOOP KNOTS

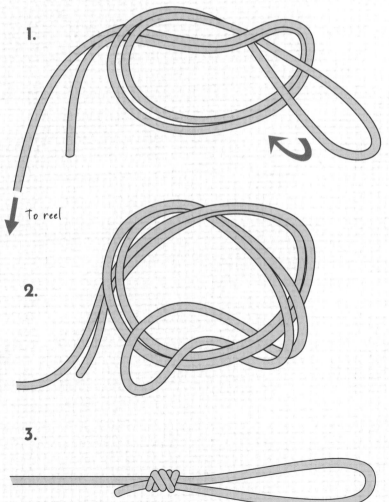

1.

To reel

2.

3.

Double the end of the line and tie a loose Overhand Knot with the doubled line.

Pass the end of the loop through the knot again.

(Optional) For the Triple Surgeon's End Loop, pass the end of the loop through the knot again.

Hold the standing line and tag end and pull the loop to tighten the knot. Clip the tag end close to the knot.

GLOSSARY

AWNING HITCH: A temporary hitch used when adjusting lines which locks the rope under a load.

BACKUP KNOT: Because all knots have the potential to untie, a backup knot is often tied as an additional knot to secure the primary knot. It is tied with the working end and it can be as simple as a Half Hitch (see page 54), but in critical applications, one side of the Double Fisherman's (see page 13) is preferred.

BIGHT: Any part of a rope between the ends. "Bight" also is used to refer to a curved section of a rope within a knot being tied.

BUTT END: The thick end of a factory-made leader.

EYE: A permanent loop at the end of a length of rope, made by method of splicing, seizing, or knotting.

FRICTION HITCH: A knot used to attach one rope to another in a way that is easily adjusted (sliding), then holds tight under load. These knots are commonly used in climbing and by arborists.

LEADER: A length of line attached to the end of your main fishing line or fly line to which flies, lures, or bait rigs are tied. Fly fishing leaders are factory made in various lengths such as nine feet and taper from heavy to thin to help with the casting of flies by fly fishermen. Other leaders may be used to make the fishing line harder for a fish to see or bite through than the main line.

LOOP: A bight becomes a loop when the two ropes cross. If the working end is crossed over the standing line, it is an overhand loop. It is an underhand loop if the working end runs under the standing part.

PRUSIK LOOP: A loop of cord that is constructed by tying the ends of a cord together with a Double Fisherman's Knot (see page 13). The Prusik Loop is used by climbers and arborists in many friction knots such as the Klemheist, Distel, and Prusik Hitch.

PURCHASE POINT: The point of attachment on a rope or object.

ROUND TURN: Two passes of a rope around an object to completely encircle it.

RUNNING LINE: The the long, thin part of a fly line that connects to the backing line at the reel. Also used as the term for the long end of a rope going away from a knot.

SEIZE: to secure two parallel parts of a rope together with small diameter cord or twine.

STANDING END: The end not being used in the tying of the knot. The rope part that is not being used is called the standing part or standing line.

STOPPER KNOT: A knot in the end of a rope that is used to prevent fraying or to prevent the end passing through a hole or tackle.

TAG END: The term used by fishermen for the working end of the line during the tying of a knot.

TURN: One pass of the rope around or through an object such as a post, ring, or another rope.

WHIP: The act of tightly wrapping twine or small-diameter cord around the end of a rope to prevent it from fraying.

WORKING END: The active end being used to tie the knot. The rope part that is being used to the tie the knot is called the working part or working line.

INDEX